PREFACE

The aim of this book is to introduce students and the general reader to the major beliefs, perspectives, and traditions which are contained within the dominant religions of Western culture, Judaism and Christianity. It is the outgrowth of the author's many years of teaching a course in introduction to Western religion and is intended to serve as a text for such a course.

Given the fact that there are currently in print a plethora of textbooks designed for introductory courses in religion, the question naturally arises as to what justification, if any, may be given for adding to this list. In light of my own teaching experience and research in the field of religion, I would offer the following considerations as providing a justification:

1. Most, if not all, of the recently published texts contain what George Lindbeck calls "generic religious studies."[1] That is, they approach religion as a generic reality which is to be investigated from phenomenological, sociological, psychological, and philosophical perspectives. Such "religious studies," as characterized by a student, engage in a "nebulous 'idea of the Holy' approach," and thus generally fail to provide the student with a knowledge of the scriptures, history, and theology of particular traditions. By contrast, what Lindbeck calls "particularistic religious studies" concentrate on the description and explanation of specific religions such as Hinduism, Buddhism, Judaism, Christianity, or Islam. In my judgment this approach is to be preferred. I do not mean to say that generic studies are of no value, have no place in a curriculum, or should be abandoned by scholars in the field of religion. Rather I simply mean that "particularistic studies" should have priority and provide the foundation for the curriculum. Generic studies might well be pursued in seminars with advanced students who already have a foundation in particularistic studies. It seems to me, in light of my teaching experience, that a familiarity with the scriptures, history, and theology of particular traditions--a

---

[1] George Lindbeck, "Theological Education in North America Today," Bulletin: The Council on the Study of Religion (Vol. 8, No. 4, October 1977), pp. 85-89.

knowledge of particular contents--along with some
knowledge of sociological, psychological, phenomenological, and philosophical methodologies, is a necessary condition for the effective pursuit of generic
studies.

2. Obviously an introductory text or course
cannot present a complete description and explanation
of all the great religions of the world. It cannot
do this even with respect to one of the great religious traditions. Yet it can deal with the broad
outlines of development, the basic concepts, perspectives, and theologies which have found expression in
the scriptures, institutions, creeds, and major theologians contained within the history of the particular
tradition. Since one must start somewhere, it seems
to me appropriate for an introductory study of religion to investigate the dominant tradition informing
Western culture, namely, the Judeo-Christian tradition.

Such an approach, I think, may be justified by
the following considerations:

First, there is, in spite of the multiplicity of
religious institutions and programs in our country,
a widespread ignorance concerning Judaism and Christianity. While numerous surveys have shown this to
be the case, anyone who teaches in the field is pain-
fully aware of this fact from firsthand experience.
Further, this ignorance is characteristic not simply
of those who are unaffiliated but also of those who
claim to be loyal adherents. Session after session I
encounter students who claim to be adherents and yet
who lack even an elementary knowledge of the scriptures, traditions, and theologies of Judaism and Christianity. Even worse, perhaps, is the fact that many
who think they have some knowledge of these religions
do not because they are misinformed. Thus the claims
they make are contrary to actual facts, historical or
otherwise.

Secondly, since the ethos of any culture is so
much influenced by the religious tradition of the
culture, it follows that a necessary condition for a
full understanding of the culture is an underderstand-
ing of the religious tradition of that culture. Surely
also a necessary condition for functioning intelligently
in a culture is an understanding of that culture. Even
though there may be other reasons why religious studies
should provide students with the opportunity of becoming

JUDAISM AND CHRISTIANITY

Origins, Developments, and Recent Trends

Robert H. Ayers
University of Georgia

UNIVERSITY
PRESS OF
AMERICA

LANHAM • NEW YORK • LONDON

Library of Congress Cataloging in Publication Data

Ayers, Robert H. (Robert Hyman), 1918—
    Judaism and Christianity.

    Includes bibliographical references and index.
    1. Church history. 2. Judaism—History. 3. Bible—
Criticism, interpretation, etc. I. Title.
BR145.2.A93 1983   270   83-3548
ISBN 0-8191-3156-3
ISBN 0-8191-3157-1 (pbk.)

In gratitude for her constant

encouragement and invaluable help

TO

Mary Frances Ayers

ACKNOWLEDGEMENTS

Appreciation is expressed to the following authors, publishers and organizations for permission to reprint selections from copyrighted material:

Abingdon Press, Roland H. Bainton, Here I Stand, 1978.

America Press, Walter M. Abbott, S.J. (ed.), The Documents of Vatican II, 1966.

Baker Book House, Clyde L. Manschreck (ed.), A History of Christianity, copyright 1964 by Clyde L. Manschreck, reprinted by Baker Book House, 1981.

Bantam Books, Inc., Adin Steinsaltz, The Essential Talmud, 1976.

Bethany Press, J. Philip Hyatt, The Heritage of Biblical Faith, 1964.

Doubleday and Co., Inc., E. E. Y. Hales, Pope John and His Revolution, 1965.

Fortress Press, Martin Luther, Three Treatises, 1960.

John H. Leith, Creeds of the Churches, originally published by Aldine Publishing Co., 1963; republished by John Knox Press, 1973. Quotations from "The Creed of the Council of Trent" are from The Church Teaches, published by B. Herder and Co., and used by permission.

B. Davie Napier, The Song of the Vineyard, copyright 1962 by B. Davie Napier, published by Harper and Brothers, 1962; revision published by Fortress Press, 1981.

National Council of the Churches of Christ in the U.S.A., The Revised Standard Version of the Bible, 1946, 1952 c 1971, 1973.

Oxford University Press, Samuel Sandmel, Judaism and Christian Beginnings, 1978; Henry Bettenson (ed.), Documents of the Christian Church, Second Edition, 1963.

CONTENTS

familiar with the major religious traditions of Western culture, the fundamental and crucial need for persons to understand Western culture in order to operate intelligently within it is reason enough to concentrate an introductory study of religion on the Judeo-Christian tradition. While genuine education is more than simply transmission, it certainly includes transmission, especially of the great heritage of the past. Given the fact that introductory courses are often service courses and the majority of students will not pursue further studies in the discipline, it seems appropriate to provide them with an opportunity for acquiring an enlarged understanding of the Judeo-Christian tradition.

Thirdly, I have observed that generally it is easier for persons to understand other religious traditions if they genuinely understand the one which informs their own culture. Since in contemporary times our world has become a relatively small "neighborhood," we need to understand cultures and religions different from our own so as to function intelligently as world citizens. Thus a study of other great religions is most helpful. However, experience has convinced me that such study is most fruitful if approached with a background of knowledge and understanding of one's own tradition. Since, as I said above, we must begin somewhere, it seems to me that it is the best procedure to concentrate our study on the Judeo-Christian tradition. Hopefully, with this background at least some students may then proceed to investigate other religions and to arrive at a genuine understanding of these religions.

It is impossible in this small volume to do justice to all the perspectives and developments in the long history of Judaism and Christianity. Of necessity I have had to be selective and such selectivity will inevitably betray my own interests. However, I have made a conscious attempt to discuss topics which are generally held to be of primary significance. While many of these topics are relevant for my own personal theology and thus are of great consequence for me personally, I have attempted to discuss them as objectively and impartially as I possibly can.

Given the selectivity of this volume, it should, of course, be used in conjunction with others, especially primary sources. The serious reader who is concerned to expand his or her knowledge beyond the material presented in this book will find many references to other works not only in the footnotes but also in the "Suggestions For Further Reading" provided at the end of each chapter.

Obviously, a book of this kind is dependent to a large extent on the creative work of numerous scholars. Many of them to whom I am especially indebted are cited in the footnotes. Others to whom I owe special thanks include the following: (1) Colleagues, Professor George E. Howard for his constant encouragement, and Professor Anthony Nemetz for sharing valuable insights with me out of his vast knowledge of medieval thinkers; (2) Graduate Assistants, Mark Todd, Annette Cook, and David Williams for their sustained interest and helpful suggestions, especially Annette Cook for her competent work in proofreading and in preparing the index for this book; (3) Secretaries, Beverly Chandler and Phyllis Smith for their efficiency and patience in transforming my handwritten copy into a typed manuscript; and (4) Mrs. Mary Ricks for her competence and skill in preparing the final draft of my manuscript for the University Press of America.

Robert H. Ayers

University of Georgia

PART I

INTRODUCTION

CHAPTER I

THE STUDY OF RELIGION AND
THE JUDEO-CHRISTIAN TRADITION

In this chapter the discussion is centered
primarily on the following topics: (1) the nature
and method of an academic study of religion, (2) a
working definition for the term "religion," (3) certain basic characteristics which must be included in
any adequate description of the Judeo-Christian
tradition, and (4) a brief preview of the major themes
discussed in the remaining parts and chapters of this
book.

I.   The Nature and Method of an Academic Study of
     Religion

Unlike many other disciplines in higher education--
disciplines such as chemistry, literature, psychology,
or history--there is a considerable amount of confusion,
at least among students and the public in general,
concerning the nature and function of an academic study
of religion. In part this confusion seems to arise
from the vagueness which infects the common or popular
use of such expressions as "religion," "religious,"
"religious education," and "religious studies," and in
part from the fact that the study of religion need not
use any one particular or special methodology as in
psychology or chemistry, but in fact may employ
several.

The vagueness in the common usage of such terms as
"religious" and "religion" appears to pose the most
serious obstacle to gaining clarity of understanding
with respect to the nature of an academic study of
religion. Often these two terms are used as though
they had an identical meaning, and such usage leads to
the serious misunderstanding that the study of religion
is an exercise in piety or devotional discipline. However difficult it may be to define descriptively, the
term "religion" is a noun designating a certain domain
of human experience or a certain complex of phenomena

1

such as systems of certain beliefs and activities which
have appeared in the history of mankind.

On the other hand, the term "religious" is an adjective and means to feel or manifest religion; to be
pious, devout, or godly; to have thorough and genuine
fidelity; to belong to a religious order.[1] Obviously,
the existence of religion is a necessary condition for
being religious, but it is not a sufficient condition.
The latter involves personal commitment to some particular religion or combination of religions with the
former being generally the case. In a pluralistic and
relatively free society religious education simply
cannot be pursued in public, tax-supported schools.
Further, it may be questioned as to whether or not
religious "education" is educational in the strict
sense of the term, namely, a free, disciplined, sustained, and critical inquiry of a particular domain or
domains of human experience. Religious "education"
may, and sometimes does, destroy education in this
sense, but it does not follow from this that it is
necessarily anti-educational. Sometimes religious
faith itself motivates some people to seek open encounter and dialogue with those of different persua-
sions, and surely such encounter and dialogue are
essential ingredients of a genuine educational process.
But be that as it may, even if we assume that being
religious is necessarily antithetical to education, it
does not follow from this that religion is anti-educational. The domain of human experience designated by
this term is as proper a subject of scholarly inquiry
as any other domain of human experience. It is an
appropriate and necessary academic discipline which may
be studied in as free, disciplined, sustained, and
critical a way as any other academic discipline.

Further support for this claim may be found in the
following considerations:

First, religion is a fact. As Robert Michaelson
has put it:

> It [religion] is a fact which the
> community of learning cannot responsi-
> bly ignore. To be sure, one can debate
> whether religion is phenomenon or
> epiphenomenon; whether religious behav-
> ior is normal behavior or an abberation;
> whether religion is sui generis or

merely the function of something else more fundamental. These are important debates which are of significance to the study of religion and will be invariably raised in connection with such study. But to deny the fact of religion by ignoring it is to engage in a kind of irresponsibility which does not befit the proud heritage of the community of learning.[2]

Secondly, religion is universal and exceptionally rich in variety. Some cultures of very diverse characteristics have been dominated by very diverse religions, and there seems to be no culture which has not been influenced to some degree by some religion. The study of religion can be the key which unlocks some doors into the meanings of cultures and which provides us with a more profound understanding of man in general. Surely it is impossible to understand Indian culture and its particular view of nature unless one has some understanding of Hindu Pantheism, law of Karma (one gets precisely what he deserves), and doctrine of ahimsa (non-injury to any living thing). Similarly one can understand the Western view of nature better if he is aware of the Judeo-Christian view of the creation-- that is, that God created the world of nature for the use of man rather than as a power to dominate man. It might well be argued that this view was one of the causal conditions that led to the development of Western technology.

Thirdly, as a fact religion is a domain of experience available to public scrutiny. This means that it can be studied and taught impartially and objectively. Objectivity involves appropriateness to the domain being studied. Much of the confusion about the appropriateness of religion as an academic discipline arises from the mistaken notion that to understand an interior act of faith one must experience the faith from within, and thus the religion course is an exercise in "religious" education. Nothing could be further from the truth, for what is appropriate for study is precisely that which can be made intelligible and can be communicated across the line of faith. It is what can be understood imaginatively by the non-believer, and this is a great deal if one pays close attention to that discourse which arises from internal perspectives. It

3

is not always the case that the believer understands his religion better than the non-believer.

An academic study of religion excludes that which Claude Welch calls the "confessional principle,"[3] the idea that only a confessing believer in a religion can teach that religion. Rather, as in any other academic discipline, all that is required is that the teacher have some degree of competence in his field, a commitment to education, an honesty and openness to facts, and a sense of the importance of the kinds of questions involved in his discipline. Surely no one thinks of requiring a political scientist to become a Democrat before he can teach his students about the Democratic Party, or an anthropologist to become a witchdoctor before he can teach about witchcraft. It is just as absurd to think that a religion professor must be a confessor before he can teach any particular religion. There can be understanding without commitment, and the responsibility of the religion teacher is not to convert his students but to help them to arrive at a greater understanding of the subject.

Fourthly, as an academic discipline religion is more an area for investigation, a complex of phenomena to be studied, than it is a set methodology. Its study requires the use of many methodologies--historical, linguistic, sociological, psychological, literary, and philosophical. To be sure, certain aspects of the phenomena can be and often are studied in the separate disciplines whose methodologies were just mentioned. Yet if this area of inquiry is to be studied adequately, they must be brought together in one program of study. It is the combined application of the diverse methodologies that enables one to better understand the field of religion than when considered in separate disciplines. Thus, a sound program for the study of religion should involve both a coordinated curriculum of courses in religion and a core of qualified scholars trained in the appropriate methodologies and engaged in studies of various kinds. At least two general ways of approach should be involved. The first is what Michaelson calls the horizontal,[4] which is the study of certain basic and recurring phenomena and patterns or types. The second Michaelson calls the vertical,[5] which is the study of the historical religions in their development including, of course, their contemporary self-understanding. All the methods mentioned above are appropriate for full investigation in terms of these two

approaches. The approach employed in this study is, of
course, the "vertical" and our investigation of the
trends, perspectives, and theologies of the Judeo-
Christian tradition will utilize many methods in the
attempt to gain as full an understanding as possible of
this tradition.

In conclusion, it may be said that if religion is a
fact, is universal, is open to public scrutiny, and is a
complex of phenomena subject to investigation by several
methods, then as such a domain of human experience it is
an appropriate academic discipline yielding knowledge
and understanding to those who approach it in terms of
free, disciplined, sustained, and critical inquiry. As
an academic discipline, it is an essential ingredient
for any genuine education.

II. What is "Religion"?

The claim was made in Section I that "religion" is
a noun designating a certain domain of human experience
or complex of phenomena. While this is true enough, it
alone does not provide us with an adequate designation
for the term "religion" such that we can distinguish
with some degree of clarity that which is to be labeled
by this term from that which is not to be so labeled.
Thus, it is important that we seek for at least a working definition for "religion." Since a multitude of
definitions have been suggested in various dictionaries
and by scholars in the field of religion, it is probably a practical impossibility to offer one which would
be universally accepted in all respects. However, the
need for as much clarity as possible in our discourse
requires that we seek to formulate an adequate, descriptive, working definition.

A. Some Preliminary Considerations

In the attempt to arrive at a descriptive definition, it may prove helpful to consider briefly certain
elementary distinctions in semantics. This modern term
"semantics" designates the scientific study of signs
and symbols (words constitute the largest class of
signs and symbols) and what they designate or mean. Semantics involves an analysis of the nature and function
of language in general in contrast to learning a particular language. While this term "semantics" is of relatively recent origin, language analysis has a very
ancient history. The uniquely human characteristics of

5

using language has intrigued many thinkers from ancient times to the present.

Since so many of the difficulties which arise in human relationships are rooted in the failure to adequately and clearly communicate our meanings, semantical considerations are of practical importance in any field of endeavor. Surely some attention to language analysis is an essential ingredient of the educational process, for education necessarily entails a relatively high degree of clarity in communication between teachers and students. Throughout the course of this study, semantical considerations will receive attention from time to time. But a few such considerations are introduced here in order that we may arrive at some clarity with respect to the meaning of the word "religion" and the signification it will have when this term is used in the course of this study. Given our limited purpose, the discussion which follows has a limitation in scope and involves only a very few elementary semantical distinctions in the absence of which there is apt to be serious confusion about word meanings and functions.

1. It is important to recognize that most of the words used in any language have both designation and denotation. Logicians often use the terms "intension" and "extension" to indicate this distinction. The designation or intension of a word refers simply to the characteristics a thing or group of things must have in order for the word to apply (the word "thing" is used here in a very broad sense and not limited to physical objects). The meaning of the word "chair" consists of precisely those characteristics which enable us to distinguish this class of objects from those things which are excluded from this class. The denotation of a word, on the other hand, is the sum total of all the particular things included in the class. Thus the word "dog" denotes Lassie, Spot, Rover, and all other particular animals to which the word is applicable.

With respect to designation and denotation, it is important to note the following:

(a) A word may have a designation, but no denotation. That is, the word may label an empty class. For example, the word "centaur" has a designation, namely, a monster with a man's head, trunk, and arms and a horse's body and legs. It can be used meaningfully. However,

6

it has no denotation since, unlike cows, tables, horses, etc., there are no such things in the world. True, we can have centaur images and draw centaur pictures, both of which have denotations as well as designations, but "centaur images" and "centaur pictures" have different designations or meanings than "centaur." The latter has no denotation.

(b) There are some words which have denotation, but no designation, namely, proper names. A proper name arbitrarily denotes the bearer of the name. Whatever may have been its origin, it does not now have a definitional meaning, or designation, as do the words contained in a dictionary. Occasionally a proper name, due to events associated with the name, may have a designation attributed to it. "Watergate" is an example of a proper name which now, in common usage, has a designation as well as a denotation. Generally, however, proper names simply denote.

(c) If two words have identical designations ("sister" and "female sibling," for example), they have precisely the same denotation. However, two words may have precisely the same denotation and yet have different designations or meanings. An example of this would be the words, "morning star" and "evening star," or "President of the United States" and "father of the Reagan children."

(d) Although in actual discourse we may often use denotation in the attempt to indicate the meanings of the words we use, it is preferable to seek for designations since in some cases certain words have no denotation, in other cases two words may denote the same thing while having different meanings, and in all cases knowledge of the designation will enable us to determine whether a particular thing we want to talk about is to be included in a particular class or not.

2. The distinction between designation and denotation is important because it enables us to make another distinction, namely, the distinction between the meaning

of <u>words</u> and the meaning of <u>things</u> labeled by the words. Actual things have "meanings" in terms of cause, effect, purpose, explanation, importance, and sign. Thus, we might respond to the question, "What is the meaning of that ringing bell?" by talking about the purpose or cause or explanation of the thing labeled by the words "ringing bell." Only if the questioner were a very small child would we bother to talk about the meanings of the words "ringing" and "bell." On the other hand, word-meanings have to do with the functions which words perform in a language--with the formal and/or informal rules for their use. We know what a word means when we know in what circumstances it can be used to apply to something <u>and</u> in what circumstances it is not applicable. Just as we must know the designation of a word before we can know its denotation, so also we must know the word-meaning before we can even raise the question of the thing-meaning. As expressed by many philosophers, this is simply to say that the question of meaning (with respect to words, sentences, entire discourse) is <u>logically</u> prior to the question of the truth or falsity of the claims asserted in the discourse. Questions such as "What is the meaning of X?" or "What is X?" may simply serve to produce confusion in discourse if there is a failure to indicate whether one is concerned with a word-meaning or a thing-meaning. In the field of religion, for example, there are many facts about the phenomena designated by the term "religion" which are relevant to the meaning of these things (particular religions) in terms of cause, effect, purpose, explanation, and so on, but which are not relevant with respect to the meaning of the word "religion."

3. Another issue related to the distinction between designation and denotation is the question as to whether or not a proposed designation or definition of a word provides an adequate scope for the generally accepted denotation of this word. That is, the definition of a word should specify those characteristics which exclude from the denotation those phenomena which are not called by this word and which include those that are. Sometimes the proposed definition of a word is too broad such that it includes phenomena in its denotation which are not called by this word. For example, if one defines "religion" simply as that to which one is ultimately committed, such a definition makes the range of the denotation much too broad. Human beings are ultimately committed to a variety of things

8

which in common usage are not called religion. Even though this characteristic may be one defining characteristic of "religion," other characteristics must be added in order to exclude from the denotation those phenomena which are not labeled by the term "religion." On the other hand, sometimes the proposed definition is too narrow such that it excludes from the denotation phenomena which are called by this word. For example, if one defines "religion" as a belief binding the spiritual nature of persons to a personal supernatural being, then Theravada Buddhism and early Taoism must be excluded from the scope of the denotation. Yet in common usage both are called religions. Consequently, the definition must be broadened. The concept of a supernatural being must be eliminated as a defining characteristic. In its place the concept of an object or objects of devotion might be substituted as a defining characteristic. Such an object or objects of devotion may be either a personal supernatural deity or deities, or some ultimate impersonal force or forces. In this case also other defining characteristics must be added to the one just mentioned in order to insure that the denotation includes only those phenomena commonly called "religions."

4. In the section above, the terms "designation" and "definition" have been used synonymously. Both have to do with word-meaning--with the circumstances in which a word is applicable and those in which it is not, with the rules of use, and with the characteristics which particular things must have in order to be named by particular words. Concern with word-meanings or definitions naturally entails the giving of attention to the distinction between <u>defining</u> and <u>accompanying</u> characteristics. A defining characteristic is a characteristic without which this thing would not be named by the word. Thus, to state a defining characteristic is to state something about the <u>meaning of the word</u>. On the other hand, an accompanying characteristic is a characteristic which may or may not be present in the thing named by the word. That is, it may sometimes be present and sometimes absent. Occasionally it may be always present, or universally accompanying (at least as far as our experience goes). Yet it is not to be taken as defining (example: the black of the class Blackbirds). To state an accompanying characteristic is to state a <u>fact</u> about the <u>thing</u> named by the word rather than to state something about the meaning of the word.

B. Defining Characteristics of "Religion"

Given the distinctions made above, it may now be possible for us to gain some clarity with respect to the meaning of the word "religion." That is, our task now is that of seeking to specify those characteristics which are always and everywhere present in those phenomena we name "religions" and which, if one or more is absent, we would not so label the phenomena. If successful, this will provide us with the defining characteristics of religion. Thus, whenever we are required to make a decision as to whether or not we will label a particular phenomenon with the term "religion," we will seek to ascertain whether or not this phenomenon possesses all of the defining characteristics. In light of my own study in the field of religion, I would suggest that the characteristics described below may well be taken as defining in that the stating of each appears to be saying something about the word-meaning of "religion." The order in which these characteristics are discussed does not imply an order of importance, for they are of equal importance.

1. As far as I am able to judge, all the phenomena we name "religions" have an object or objects of devotion understood to be ultimate in the order of reality and to elicit ultimate concern from adherents. The object(s) of devotion is taken to be, in the words of Rudolph Otto, the "_mysterium_ _tremendum_" which is both awesome and fascinating.[6]

Two things are entailed in the description of this defining characteristic. First, it does not exclude from the scope of the denotation _various_ _forms_ of theism such as monotheism, polytheism, and pantheism. That is, the object(s) of devotion may be one, and only one, God who has created all that is _ex_ _nihilo_ (out of nothing), or many Gods, or a pantheistic deity which is the inner essence of each and everything that exists in the universe such that God does not transcend what is, but rather _is_ everything that exists. Secondly, object(s) of devotion as a defining characteristic does not exclude from the realm of denotation non-theistic religions such as Theravada Buddhism and early Taoism. Object(s) of devotion can denote that impersonal source (_Tao_) of the active power in all existent things as in Taoism or the Noble Eightfold path with its attendant _dhamma_ (rules of conduct) which is the path to nirvana in Theravada Buddhism. Yet at the same time, the

10

expression "object(s) of devotion" can denote the various forms of theism. Thus, while theistic concepts are not defining for the word-meaning of "religion," such concepts are an important class of accompanying characteristics in that a relatively large number of religions do in fact have some type of theistic orientation.

2. Another characteristic which seems to be defining is rites or ceremonies through which the adherents of religions seek to establish some sort of relationship with the object(s) of devotion. Even though there is considerable variation with respect to the nature and function of rites, it seems to be the case that some kinds of rites are always present in the phenomena we name "religions."

3. If we are careful to refrain from associating only Jewish and Christian connotations with the expression such that we take it in too narrow a sense, we may designate a third defining characteristic as a promise of salvation. The English word "salvation" is derived from the Latin salvus, which means "unharmed," "healthy," "sound," or "whole." Thus salvation has to do with the "wholeness" or "fulfillment" of human life, and all religions claim to provide such a condition for their adherents. Of course there is a wide variation in the views among particular religions concerning the nature and means of salvation. Questions concerning whether salvation occurs only in this life or only in a life after death or in both, whether salvation is totally self-achieved or totally the work of the object(s) of devotion or a matter of divine-human cooperation, receive different answers in different religions. Yet, however great the difference may be in the particular understandings of the nature and means of salvation, all religions do contain this feature of salvation or the fulfillment of human life.

4. A fourth feature which is always present in those phenomena we label "religions" is a mythology or collection of myths. Even though the number and contents of the myths vary greatly between religions, no religion seems to be totally lacking in some sort of myths. Care must be taken at this point to indicate as clearly as possible what is meant by the term "myth" in this context. The definition proposed here is simply this: <u>"myth" is a value-charged story expressing to some degree the life orientation of a group and/or individual</u>. The two defining characteristics involved

11

in this definition, namely (a) "a value-charged story," and (b) "expressing to some degree the life orientation of a group and/or individual," provide the word "myth" with a designation or intension which is adequate for its denotation or extension. The word so defined does not exclude from its area of denotation those things which traditionally have been labeled myths, nor does it include too much. Rather it emphasizes a feature, namely life orientation, which for the most part has been overlooked until recent times--a feature which broadens somewhat the scope of the word's designation and denotation.

The definition of "myth" proposed above has been formulated in light of certain contemporary studies.[7] Twentieth-century studies have denied that myth is a purely intellectual phenomenon arising out of curiosity; so the words "life orientation" have been used, implying thereby that myth involves the whole person in his understanding of life's direction and purpose. Twentieth-century studies have denied that myth is primarily concerned with explanation; so the word "expression" has been used, implying that this involves one in participating in that which is believed to be one's life orientation. Twentieth-century studies have denied that myths necessarily posses unreality or are false; so the words "value-charged story" have been used, thereby leaving open the question of reality or unreality, truth or falsity, but indicating that, for those who believe them, myths express the most profound meanings of life. These considerations, then, are the justification for the definition of "myth" as a value-charged story expressing to some degree the life orientation of a group and/or individual. This seems to be a rather common-sense definition and that, as defined, myth or a mythology (a collection of myths) is a defining characteristic of "religion."

C. A Proposed Working Definition of "Religion"

If it is the case that the characteristics discussed in Section B above are in fact defining, then the following statement may be useful as a summary or a brief definition of "religion."

> Religion is that attitude or active
> relationship and the actions growing
> out of that attitude or active re-
> lationship toward the object or objects

12

of devotion which a group of persons takes to be of ultimate concern and reality and in light of which the persons in the group establish their existence.

Is this proposed definition of adequate scope such that it does not exclude from the denotation phenomena which are commonly named "religions"? If the sum total of the defining characteristics as described provides a designation adequate for the denotation, then this proposed definition is adequate in this regard provided it contains or entails these characteristics. The following brief analysis indicates that this is the case.

First, the definition explicitly mentions the first defining characteristic discussed, namely, an object or objects of devotion understood to be of ultimate concern and reality. Secondly, the second and fourth defining characteristics--rites or ceremonies and myths--are entailed in the phrase "the actions growing out of that attitude or active relationship." Obviously rites involve actions on the part of a group of persons. Since myths and rites are closely associated in that both entail participation, and since the creation, communication, and ritual reciting of myths are activities, then this defining characteristic is also entailed in this phrase. Thirdly, the defining characteristic of "a promise of salvation" is entailed in the phrase "in light of which the persons in the group establish their existence." In light of this analysis, then, our proposed definition contains all the defining characteristics and can guide us in distinguishing those phenomena which are to be named "religions" from those which are not to be so named. Further, this definition has the advantage of being descriptive rather than prescriptive. Since it is based on actual characteristics which are always present and never absent in the phenomena we name "religions," it prevents the formulation of a definition in terms of what one personally might wish religion to be or think it ought to be. In the entire discussion of both the defining characteristics and the definition, an effort has been made to formulate a reportive definition instead of a stipulative one in which is prescribed for the word-meaning of "religion" one's own personal religious convictions.

Given this definition of "religion," it is evident that Judaism and Christianity are included in the

13

denotation of this word. In the history and current manifestations of both are to be found the defining characteristics specified for the designation of "religion." However, it does not follow from the fact that Judaism and Christianity contain the four defining characteristics that they are essentially the same as the other religions of the world, nor for that matter, even though Judaism is considered the "parent" religion of Christianity, that these two can be reduced to one. Even though all the religions of the world demonstrate the four defining characteristics, they cannot be reduced to one common denominator. To be sure, there are some similarities since all the religions of the world are challenged by many of the same questions and problems which naturally arise out of human existence--problems such as finitude, estrangement, unmerited suffering. Yet the responses to these problems are very varied.[8] The definition of "religion" guides us in our use of this word, but does not provide us with factual information about the perspectives, belief-systems, creeds, and practices in particular religions. To gain knowledge in these areas, the critical tools of historical and analytical investigation must be employed.

        In the section which follows we will attempt to specify certain basic characteristics which Judaism and Christianity have in common, and which are of fundamental importance in the perspective of the Judeo-Christian tradition.

III.   Some Basic Characteristics or Perspectives of
       the Judeo-Christian Tradition

        Three things need to be said by way of introduction to this discussion. First, it is quite brief and simply a kind of "preview of coming attractions." All the characteristics mentioned will receive fuller elaboration in the course of this study. Secondly, in the discussion of these characteristics, they will sometimes be contrasted with characteristics in other religions. Such contrasts do not imply value judgments, that the characteristics in the Judeo-Christian tradition are _better_ than those in other religions. Rather our purpose is to be descriptive, and the contrasts are drawn simply as an aid to _understanding_ what is involved in these basic characteristics of the Judeo-Christian tradition. Thirdly, since the words "Judaism" and "Christianity" function as proper names, we

14

will not call these characteristics defining. However, they do seem to be essential, even if not
exhaustive, for an adequate definite description of
the Judeo-Christian tradition. A complete definite
description of either Judaism or Christianity would
necessarily mention certain features which distinguish
the one from the other, but our description here will
concentrate only on certain features which they have
in common. The following six characteristics are of
fundamental importance in the Judeo-Christian tradition.

1. Judaism and Christianity agree in their insistence on an ethical monotheism. God is viewed as a
totally good, personal, supernatural being who created
ex nihilo (out of nothing). That is, there was God and
nothing else. Then God engaged in a creative activity,
and there was God and something else. Obviously this
view is opposed to polytheism (the belief in many gods).
Also it is different from pantheism (the belief that
the sum total of the inner essences of everything is
God). In the Judeo-Christian view God is not thought
to be identical with the sum total of everything that
actually exists, but rather he is understood to be a
personal, supernatural being who transcends that which
he has made. Further, it follows from the view of God
creating ex nihilo that everything as created is good.
Of course human beings may spoil God's creation, but
it is originally and essentially good. In the words of
Genesis 1:31,

> "And God saw everything that he had made
> and behold it was very good" (R.S.V.).

This view also stands in contrast with certain
views found in Greek philosophy. In the Platonic view
there is an eternal prime stuff or undifferentiated
matter. The creative activity of the "demiurge" (the
intermediary maker of the World) consists of the imposition of forms on the already existing undifferentiated
matter. While there could be no world of actual objects without the forms imposed on matter, matter is
resistant to the imposition of forms. So in the actual
world the representations of the forms in matter are
always imperfect. Indeed, it would appear that for
Plato matter is the source of evil, for in his dialogue
the Phaedo (66) he has Socrates say that the body (composed of matter, of course) is the source of endless
troubles and evils and infects the soul with its evils.
By contrast in the Judeo-Christian view it is the one

personal God who has created _everything_ _ex_ _nihilo_ and, because of this, everything in the created order is originally and essentially good.

2. Given this monotheism and this view of creation, it follows that the realm of physical nature possesses a relative autonomy or separateness. Unlike the pantheistic view in which everything is God, in the Judeo-Christian view physical nature exists in its own right, at least to a degree. Thus, in Genesis 1:28 (R.S.V.), the writer can say,

> "And God said to them (male and female),
> 'Be fruitful and multiply and fill the
> earth and subdue it.'"

(In the _Jerusalem_ _Bible_ the Hebrew word is rendered as "conquer" instead of "subdue"). That is, physical nature is a reality which human beings can use and, at least to some degree, modify and shape. While the Psalmist declares,

> "The heavens are telling the glory of God
> and the firmament proclaims his handiwork"
> (Psalms 19:1, [R.S.V.]),

this does not imply that the heavens and firmament are God. It means only that he has created them and that they demonstrate signs of his creative power and design. As we shall see, in the Judeo-Christian view God discloses himself, or at least his will, primarily in historical events. Yet, since he is Creator, the works of nature also witness to him, at least to some extent and in a secondary way.

The relation between an artist and his art product may provide a helpful analogy for understanding the Judeo-Christian view of the relation between God and nature. The art product reflects not only the style of the artist who is its creator, but also may reflect other aspects of his personality and of his perspectives concerning the world and human life. Sometimes this may be so obvious that we say that we see the artist in his painting, but obviously we do not mean this in any literal sense. No matter what the painting may reflect about its creator, it has a certain existence of its own once it is created. It may be bought and shown by an art gallery, and for those viewing it, it may suggest certain things never intended by its creator. It may be

16

bought by some collector who, considering himself to be a painter, modifies to some extent what the original artist had painted, even though certain features of the original artist's style remain such that the painting may be still recognized as originally his work. This is similar to the Judeo-Christian view of the relation between God and nature. Nature, although created by God and reflecting his handiwork, nevertheless has a certain relative autonomy--a certain existence of its own. It can be used and modified by human beings. This is not thought to be an impious activity for, unlike the pantheistic view, the objects and processes of nature are not considered to be _identical_ with God in their inner essences.

3. Not only physical nature, but also human beings are viewed in the Judeo-Christian tradition as having a relative autonomy. As applied to human beings, this autonomy is understood as some kind and degree of freedom. In the history of the tradition, there have been differences among various groups as to the precise nature and degree of human freedom, but even those who have held strictly to divine foreordination have nevertheless admitted that human beings have some sort of freedom. Many theologians in the tradition have taken the statement in Genesis 1:27, "So God created man in his own image" (R.S.V.) to mean that God granted human beings at least some portion of one of his own attributes, namely freedom. It is of the same kind, even though limited, because human beings, unlike God, are limited, finite, and contingent creatures. The _imago_ _dei_ (divine image) has often been regarded to be the faculty of rational decision-making which God implanted in human beings.

4. This view of human freedom makes possible another characteristic perspective, namely a distinctive view of sin as willful rebellion against God rather than as ignorance or failure. By way of contrast, a rather dominant view in Hinduism is that human beings are led astray by attachment to appearances. That is, the major problem of human life is that persons tend to be content to remain attached to, or immersed in, the world of sense experience. Such a world is called the veils of _Maya_ (ignorance or illusion) which prevents one from understanding and realizing the genuine nature of the self and of the ultimate.[9] Only through escaping from the veils of _Maya_ by means of a rigorous personal discipline can one achieve the absorption of the self

17

in the ultimate, Brahman. In the Judeo-Christian tradition, however, the major problem of human life is
sin which is understood to be the willful rebellion of
human beings against the Creator--the willful pretensions of the self which disrupt community, the community
of God and persons, and of persons with persons.

Due to sin, human history becomes a scene of estrangement, of the competition of ego with ego, of
group with group, in various power struggles for the
perceived vested interests of persons and groups,
instead of that fellowship of perfect freedom and
faithfulness which God had intended in creating human
life. Since any genuine human community necessarily
entails the free decision of persons to participate in
the community, even God himself must run the risks of
granting freedom to human beings if there is to be any
possibility of genuine community. Not even God can
create free beings and then guarantee that they will
always be loving and accepting of him and others and
will always do the right thing. If he did so guarantee,
then they would not be free. Therefore God, in creating human beings for community, created them as free
beings, and since they are free, they may decide to
rebel or to sin against him and others. So human history becomes the scene of estrangement instead of
community. Yet God has not left mankind alone but,
taking the initiative, acts in various ways in history
to lure human beings into community. Such a view provides the basis for yet another Judeo-Christian perspective or characteristic which is discussed below.

5. In the Judeo-Christian tradition, God's self-
disclosure, or at least the disclosure of his will, is
to be found primarily in the events of history. What
is meant by this claim may become clearer in light of
the following considerations.

(a) First, it is important to understand what is
meant by the term "history" in this claim. It
is not history in the sense of a critical,
scientific reconstruction of the past--of the
activity engaged in by those scholars who are
labeled historians. While history in this
sense has an important, and perhaps even
essential, relevance for the Judeo-Christian
tradition, "history" as understood in this
tradition transcends the critical and objective "history" of a history department in a

university. Rather it is history in the sense of the past (or at least certain crucial past events) impinging upon the present, giving meaning and significance to the present. Even though no longer _actual_, past events are not _unreal_ as far as the present is concerned but, so to speak, "live on" in the present. This view is certainly central to the Biblical perspective and is strikingly illustrated in Deuteronomy 5:2-3. This book in the Pentateuch or Torah was written approximately six centuries after Israel's acceptance of the Covenant at Sinai or Horeb (Horeb is another name for Sinai) and yet the writer says,

> "The LORD our God made a convenant with us in Horeb. Not with our fathers did the LORD make this covenant, but _with_ _us_, _who_ _are_ _all_ _of_ _us_ _here_ _alive_ _this_ _day_."[10] (R.S.V.)

This perspective on history is so fundamental to the Judeo-Christian tradition that any attempt to understand this tradition must fail without clarification of this point. I hope, therefore, that the following hypothetical example or analogy may help us to become aware of the full dimensions of the Judeo-Christian view on history.

Let us suppose that in a certain spot in the woods behind my house there is what appears to be a rather small hill. Although I have often walked by it, I have assumed that it was simply a natural feature of the topography of the region. One day, however, I notice protruding from the side of the "hill" what appears to be the tip of what may be an interestingly shaped stone. I manage to dislodge it and discover that it is an Indian arrowhead. Having an amateur's interest in archaeology, I secure my wife's garden trowel and carefully dislodging some more of the dirt from the side of the "hill," find more arrowheads and a piece or two of broken pottery. It now occurs to me that what I had previously thought to be a hill might instead be a mound built up from the remains of several Indian villages which throughout several generations had occupied that spot. Thereupon I contact a colleague in the Archaeology Department, who, assisted by some of his graduate students, engages in a scientific archaeological dig at this spot. Not only do their findings verify what I had suspected to be the case, but also in the last strata of the mound (dated about 1800 A.D.) they discover some rusted musket barrels and some musket balls. These, along with some other objects, provide ample evidence for the conclusion that the village of this last strata had been destroyed by white settlers in this region.

At this point, for me at least, what has been learned from this scientific enterprise transcends merely an interesting reconstruction of the past. It begins to take on meaning for my present existence. I remember that my ancestors were among those who drove the Cherokees off their lands. Indeed, this fact is still symbolized each year at the Commencement exercises at the University of Georgia when the Sheriff of Clarke County, dressed in a black morning coat, red sash around his waist, and saber buckled to his waist, walks at the head of the Commencement processional. According to the traditional story, the presence of the Sheriff was required at the early commencement exercises in the late seventeen hundreds in order to protect faculty and students from the Indians. Whatever the truth about this legend, it is a fact that these Native Americans were driven into the mountains of North Georgia and of North Carolina and later were forced to go west into what is now Oklahoma. In the process of this forced migration, thousands died. It is easy for such thoughts to remind one also of the general mistreatment of Native Americans by white settlers throughout the course of American history, and of the fact that current policy and practice with respect to Native Americans is often lacking in fairness and equity. Thus history as a scientific discipline which discloses what actually occurred in the past may provide that knowledge on the basis of which "history" in the sense of the past as meaningful and significant for the present may be experienced.

While history in the first sense--as a scientific, critical, process of inquiry--is, for the most part, a modern phenomenon, history in the second sense is quite ancient, predating even the advent of a written language. Even though history as a critical process of inquiry has been accepted and used by many in the Judeo-Christian tradition, especially in modern and contemporary times, history in the second sense has always been fundamental in the tradition. For both those who experienced them and for those who transmitted narratives concerning them, the happenings of history were not perceived as <u>bare</u> <u>happenings</u>. They were regarded as <u>events</u> which had meaning for their own existence and for their understanding of God's will for mankind and his entire creation. Obviously, history in this latter sense transcends history as a critical process of inquiry, but there is no necessary incompatibility between the two. History as a critical process of inquiry can render an important service to contemporary adherents of the Judeo-Christian tradition in that it enables them to acquire an enlarged knowledge of the actual life situations out of which the major perspectives and tenets of the tradition arose such that the history of the tradition may in a meaningful way become their <u>own</u> <u>history</u>.

(b) What is meant by saying that a certain historical tradition may become one's own history may become clearer in terms of contrasting different answers to the question, "Who am I?". The typical answer to this question in Hinduism is that I (my real self) am essentially the same as Brahman and this concept is expressed in the famous Hindu saying, "Thou art That."[11] The meaning of this saying is illustrated in the following delightful story.

A student greatly concerned with what or who he was, upon agreeing to do whatever was commanded, was able to persuade a famous <u>guru</u> (teacher) to become his teacher. The first thing

21

which the guru did was to lock the student in a small room with nothing to eat. The next morning he returned and, shouting the student's name, asked "Now do you know what you are?". The student replied that he was hungry. The guru went away, returned the next morning, asked the same question, and received the same reply from the student.

Upon returning on the third morning, the guru opened the door and gave the student food and said, "Now we know what you are: You are hungry." But the student, having eaten, responded, "Oh no, guru, I am not hungry. I am filled and satisfied." To this the guru replied, "Isn't it strange what a bowl of rice can do? Within a few minutes your identity has been changed from being hungry to being filled and satisfied. You are a fool. You were not hungry and you are not now satisfied. You are the eternal atman (self) within. But for some reason that must be examined closely you persist in identifying yourself with all the transitory moods that you feel and see but which are not your true being."[12]

The adherent of the Judeo-Christian tradition, by contrast, could respond to the question of personal identity by saying I am a Jew or I am a Christian by virtue of the fact that I identify with a certain history or heritage. The history of this tradition is my history. Even though I may not agree with all the specific theological arguments, claims or counter-claims which have appeared in the history of the tradition, the crucial events and the great heroes of the heritage are as much a "living" part of my past as my own immediate ancestors. I identify with this tradition, for in my memory are the stories of the great events and heroes of the faith. Whatever other features may be found in my own personal sense of who I am, this memory provides a most fundamental and essential ingredient. Indeed, it provides the clues not only to the meaning of my own personal existence but also of all existence.

(c) Since for the Judeo-Christian tradition God

22

discloses his will in history, it follows that he is viewed as a dynamic, active God rather than as a static absolute, an unmoved mover. He acts in history to persuade human beings to accept community with him, with other human beings, and with all creation.

An analogy based on the understanding of "politics" and "politician" in the writings of the Greek philosopher Aristotle may help us understand this Judeo-Christian view of God acting in history. The use of this analogy does not mean that Aristotle knew anything about ancient Judaism nor that he had a similar view of God (he most certainly did not, for he viewed God as the unmoved mover). Rather, it is simply that his definition of "politics" may be used as an analogous description of the Judeo-Christian view of God's acting in history.

In his Ethics and Politics Aristotle is concerned with what he regards as a single practical "science" with two parts. Ethics and politics deal respectively with the interrelated subjects of human behavior and human associations. In the Ethics Aristotle discusses the "science" of moral virtue or that which is essential for moral education. In the Politics he deals with the ideal form of human association, the Koinonia (community), which is the precondition for and expression of the fulfillment of human life. The term polis, which was used to designate the actual Greek city state, is used by Aristotle in the Politics to designate also that ideal form of human association, the Koinonia. "Politics," then, is the "science" of what makes for Koinonia in human associations and as such is the science of the highest good. As Aristotle himself put it:

> But, if all communities aim at some good, the state or political community, which is the highest of all, and which embraces all the rest, aims at a good in a greater degree than any other, and at the highest good.13

23

Given this definition of "politics," the task of the "politician" is that of striving to create those conditions which will make possible the actualization of the ideal form of human association, the Koinonia. In the Judeo-Christian tradition this is precisely what God is seeking for by means of his acts in history. In the Aristotelian sense of the term, then, he may be called the supremely good, all wise, and all loving "politician."

6. We have said above that in the Judeo-Christian tradition the past is seen as impinging on the present, giving meaning and significance to the present. This, however, is not to ignore the future, for it is seen also to have meaning and significance for the present.

We must be careful not to assume that this perspective entails a cyclic view of time. Unlike some religions of Asia, the Judeo-Christian tradition views time as linear rather than cyclic. History does not repeat itself either on a large scale or on a personal level as in transmigration or reincarnation perspectives. Rather time runs on, so to speak, in a straight line. But historical existence as we know it is not unending. There is this age and the age to come. There is an eschaton.

As generally expressed today among theologians, the Judeo-Christian view is "eschatological." The term "eschatology," which has been in use only since the nineteenth century, was derived from the Greek term, eschaton (the last thing) and logos (science, theory, or view of) and designates a theory or view of the end of an age. Here "end" means both "goal" and "last" such that the end time (the eschaton) is both the abolition of the old age and also the realization of the divine purpose or goal for history. This goal is the universal consummation of the kingdom of God (i.e., the reign of God). Thus the Judeo-Christian tradition looks to the future with hope for a better day.

It may be said that the Judeo-Christian tradition incorporates the Janus principle. The Roman God Janus, from which was derived the name January, the first month of the year, was the patron of beginnings and endings. He had two faces, one of them looking backwards and the other forwards. To say that the Judeo-Christian tradition incorporates the Janus principle

24

is simply to say that it looks both to the past and to the future, finding meaning and significance in both for present existence. It is precisely because of the view of God acting in history in the past that the Judeo-Christian tradition holds to the view that he will continue to act in history with the purpose of universally actualizing his kingdom.

To summarize this section concerning basic characteristics of the Judeo-Christian tradition, an adequate definite description of this tradition would certainly include: (1) An ethical monotheism, (2) a view of physical nature as having a relative autonomy, (3) a view of human nature as possessing a relative autonomy (freedom), (4) a view of sin as willful rebellion against God, (5) the view of God as active in history, and (6) the view of time as linear with an end-time understood as both the abolition of the old age and the actualization of the kingdom of God. As this study progresses, these characteristics will be exemplified time and again, both in the Bible and in Jewish and Christian theologies. We will, of course, give attention not only to these common characteristics but also to other characteristics which distinguish Judaism from Christianity.

IV. Preview of Major Themes in Subsequent Chapters

In the chapters which follow an attempt is made to describe more fully the major trends and perspectives which arose in Judaism and Christianity. Since in both religions the Bible plays an important role, Part II deals with the biblical period. Chapter II of this part describes the agreements and disagreements between and among Jews, Catholics, and Protestants concerning the precise extent and authority of Scripture, and delineates the method employed by biblical scholars in the study of Scripture. Chapter III indicates some of the results of the scientific, historical study of the Old Testament and in light of these results describes briefly major Old Testament themes. Chapter IV deals with the New Testament in a similar way, with special attention given to the teachings of Jesus and the thought of the Apostle Paul. Chapter V describes those causal conditions which resulted in the emergence of Rabbinic Judaism during the biblical period, and discusses the typical modes of thought and characteristic perspectives of the rabbis.

Chapters VI and VII of Part III deal with the expansion of Christianity into the Western World, the problems encountered, the major theologies and practices which arose, and the emergence of the Catholic Church.

Part IV indicates some of the basic causal conditions for the rise of Protestantism in Christendom, and Chapter VIII of this part summarizes the major perspectives of the Reformers, Luther and Calvin.

Part V describes briefly the nature of the challenge which arose in the modern period to the traditional views and practices within the Judeo-Christian tradition, and the three typical kinds of response to this challenge, namely the "right-wing" response (uncompromising and unchanging), the "left-wing" response (liberal, modernist or radical), and the moderate response. Chapters IX, X, and XI describe these three types of response in modern Judaism, Catholicism and Protestantism respectively.

Of necessity, the discussion in this book omits many interesting and important developments. Yet a conscious and serious effort has been made to discuss in as unbiased, objective and thorough manner as possible those trends and perspectives which generally are regarded as essential for an understanding of the Judeo-Christian tradition.

NOTES

Chapter I

1 The American College Dictionary (New York: Random House, 1960).

2 Robert Michaelson, "The Scholarly Study of Religion in College and University," (New Haven, Connecticut: Society for Religion in Higher Education, 400 Prospect Street, 1965), p. 7.

3 Claude Welch, "The Function of the Study of Religion," Karl Hartzell and Harrison Sasscer (eds.), The Study of Religion on the Campus Today, (Washington: Association of American Colleges, 1967), p. 11.

4 Michaelson, op. cit., p. 29.

5 Ibid.

6 Rudolph Otto, The Idea of the Holy, (London: Oxford University Press, 1926), pp. 1-41.

7 Mircea Eliade, Myths, Dreams and Mysteries, (New York: Harper and Brothers, 1960); The Myth of the Eternal Return, (New York: Pantheon Books, 1954); G. van der Leeuw, Religion in Essence and Manifestation, (London: George Allen and Unwin, 1938); Willem F. Zuurdeeg, An Analytical Philosophy of Religion, (New York: Abingdon Press, 1958). In Chapter V Professor Zuurdeeg summarized the findings of two Dutch scholars, W. B. Kristensen and K. A. H. Hedding. All of these scholars have emphasized what might be called the "participating" feature of myth.

8 W. S. Taylor, "Encounter," The Meaning of Life in Five Great Religions, R. C. Chalmers and John A. Irving (eds.), (Philadelphia: The Westminster Press, 1965), pp. 1-22.

9 John B. Noss, Man's Religions, Fifth edition, (Macmillan Company, 1974), pp. 99, 197, 199f.

10 Italics are mine.

11 Noss, op. cit., pp. 99-100.

12 The source of this story is Frederic Spiegelberg, Living Religions of the World, (Englewood Cliff, New Jersey: Prentice-Hall, Inc., 1956), p. 151.

[13] _Politics_ I.1. 1252.5., cf. Richard McKeon, _Introduction to Aristotle_, Second edition, (University of Chicago Press, 1973), p. 595. Also see pp. 332-659.

SUGGESTIONS FOR FURTHER READING

Alston, W. P., Philosophy of Language, Prentice-Hall, 1964.

Anderson, Robert T. and Peter B. Fisher, An Introduction to Christianity, Harper and Row, 1966.

Ayers, Robert H., "'Myth' In Theological Discourse," Anglican Theological Review, Vol. XLVIII, No. 2, April, 1966.

Ayers, Robert H., "Is Religion Anti-Educational," Philosophy of Education, Philosophy of Education Society, 1969.

Berthold, Fred., et al., Basic Sources of the Judeo-Christian Tradition, Prentice-Hall, 1962.

Black, Max (ed.), The Importance of Language, Prentice-Hall, 1962.

Blackstone, William T., The Problem of Religious Knowledge, Prentice-Hall, 1963.

Burtt, E. A., Man Seeks The Divine, Second Edition, Harper and Row, 1964.

Burtt, E. A., Types of Religious Philosophy, Harper and Row, 1939.

Chalmers, R. C. and J. H. Irving, The Meaning of Life In Five Great Religions, The Westminster Press, 1965.

Edwards, Rem B., Reason and Religion, Harcourt and Brace, 1972.

Harshbarger, Luther H. and John A. Mourant, Judaism and Christianity: Perspectives and Traditions, Allyn and Bacon, Inc., 1968.

Hick, John, Philosophy of Religion, Prentice-Hall, 1963.

Hutchinson, John A., Paths of Faith, Second Edition, McGraw-Hill, Inc., 1975.

King, Winston L., Introduction to Religion, Harper and Row, 1968.

Kitagawa, Joseph M., Religions of the East, The Westminster Press, 1960.

Lohse, Bernhard, A Short History of Christian Doctrine, Fortress Press, 1966.

Miller, Ed L., God and Reason, The Macmillan Co., 1972.

Niebuhr, H. Richard, The Responsible Self, Harper and Row, 1963.

Niebuhr, Reinhold, Faith and History, Charles Scribner's Sons, 1949.

Niebuhr, Reinhold, The Self and the Dramas of History, Charles Scribner's Sons, 1955.

Roth, Cecil, A Short History of the Jewish People, Hebrew Publishing Co.

Sandmel, Samuel, Judaism and Christian Beginnings, Oxford University Press, 1978.

Smart, Ninian, The Religious Experience of Mankind, Charles Scribner's Sons, 1969.

Steinberg, Milton, Basic Judaism, Harcourt, Brace and Co., 1947.

Zuurdeeg, Willem F., An Analytical Philosophy of Religion, Abingdon Press, 1958.

PART II

THE BIBLICAL PERIOD

CHAPTER II

INTRODUCTION: THE EXTENT, AUTHORITY,
AND EXEGESIS OF THE BIBLE

In order to gain an understanding of any religion,
it is necessary to investigate the sacred scriptures
of that religion. It is generally the case that the
sacred scriptures of a religion provide what might be
called the source of sources for the beliefs, theologies, and practices of that religion. Thus, the
attempt to understand the Judeo-Christian tradition
requires us to seek for a basic general understanding
of the Bible. No matter how many and varied are the
perspectives which have arisen in this tradition, they
have, or at least are thought to have, some relevance
to this source of sources, the Bible.

While there is general agreement among groups
within the Judeo-Christian tradition that the Bible (or
at least very large portions of it) functions as the
source of sources, there is disagreement as to the precise extent of Scripture and as to the precise nature
of its authority.

A. Jews, Catholics, and Protestants disagree as
to the actual scope of the Biblical canon. The term
"canon" designates a list of the books of the Bible
officially accepted as genuine or authoritative Scripture. The Jewish Canon of Scripture does not contain
the twenty-seven books of the Christian New Testament.
Yet there is a further disagreement. Even though the
Jewish canon of Scripture, the Tanak,[1] and the Protestant Old Testament are identical in content (only the
numbering of the books is different--24 in the Tanak
and 39 in the Protestant Old Testament), the Catholic
canon of the Old Testament contains additional material.
There are seven additional separate books plus additions to some of the other books. Thus the Catholic
canon of the Old Testament is more extensive than the
Jewish Tanak and the Protestant Old Testament. This
additional material constitutes most of what Protestants now generally call the "Apocrypha," a term which

31

literally means "books that were hidden away."[2] The Apocrypha is occasionally printed in some Protestant Bibles in a special section between the Old and New Testaments and sometimes is printed in a separate volume. However, neither Jews nor Protestants regard it as sacred scripture.

The reason for this discrepancy between the Catholic canon of the Old Testament and the Jewish and Protestant is due to the following historical events. In the third and second centuries B.C. there was a relatively large community of Greek-speaking Jews living in Egypt. Since the books of the Tanak (most of which had been written by this time) were written in Hebrew and many of these Jews could not read Hebrew, it was felt that these books should be translated into Greek. According to the legend, seventy scholars prepared a translation called the Septuagint, from the Greek word for seventy. But, since as yet there was no official canon of the Tanak, the Septuagint eventually contained not only Greek translations of the Hebrew originals of the Tanak, but also some writings originally composed in Greek and for which, of course, there were no Hebrew originals. One criterion used by a group of rabbis who formulated the official canon of the Tanak at the Council of Jamnia in about one hundred A.D. was that there must be Hebrew originals. Since none was found for the material contained in the so-called "Apocrypha," these works were excluded from the official list of canonical books.[3]

Given the fact that the version of the Old Testament used by the early Christian church was generally the Septuagint, the writings of the Apocrypha were retained as a part of its canon. However, in the sixteenth century A.D. Martin Luther, in preparing a German translation of the Bible, accepted as canonical Old Testament only that material accepted by the rabbis at the Council of Jamnia. He placed the works of the Apocrypha in a section between the Old and New Testaments and held that while they were profitable for instruction, they were not essential for salvation. In the nineteenth and twentieth centuries many publishers of Protestant Bibles simply omitted the Apocrypha from their editions.[4]

So it is that Protestants and Jews agree as to the extent of the Old Testament canon but disagree with the Catholics who add the works of the Apocrypha (except the Prayer of Manasseh and I and II Esdras). On the other hand, Protestants and Catholics agree in accepting the twenty-seven books of the New Testament as canonical Scripture and in this respect disagree with the Jews who do not.

B. Not only is there disagreement as to the extent of Holy Scripture, but also there is disagreement as to the precise nature of the authority of that which is accepted as Scripture. Unlike the disagreement concerning the extent of Scripture which is a disagreement between Jews, Catholics, and Protestants, the disagreement as to the precise nature of Scriptural authority is, for the most part, a disagreement among various sub-groups within Judaism, Catholicism, and Protestantism.

Orthodox Jews tend to believe that the Tanak is infallible. Some would hold that every word and every letter within it were imparted directly by God to the people of Israel in ancient times.5 The view that the Bible (including most of the Apocrypha) is infallible was held as the official position of the Catholic church until recent times. While the Catholic view of infallibility was historically somewhat different from the view of Biblical literalism held by some Protestants, in that Catholics made use of the allegorical or "spiritual" method of interpretation, it is nevertheless the case that in both its literal and spiritual senses the Bible was held to be infallible. The Bible, then, along with church tradition, was held to be an ultimate authority. As indicated above, some Protestants have held that the Bible (Apocrypha excluded) is literally and verbally inspired by God such that it is absolutely without error. Today these groups are sometimes called Fundamentalists and one of their doctrines or beliefs, which most obviously distinguishes them from other Protestant groups, is their belief that the Bible is infallible in all respects.

On the other hand, there are those within each of the three traditions who claim that, while the Bible is inspired by God, it is not infallible in all respects. Such groups include the following: (1) Reform and Conservative Jews, (2) individual "liberal" Catholics and Catholicism generally since Vatican Council II (1962-1965), and (3) liberal and Neo-Orthodox Protestants. These groups tend to emphasize that whatever is accepted as Sacred Scripture is a witness to the

33

revelation (self-disclosure) of God in history. While
the revelation itself is absolute, the witness to the
revelation need not be and indeed is not absolute.
Since these groups do not accept the infallibility or
inerrancy of the Bible, they more readily accept the
method and results of critical and scientific research
in the study of the Bible.

C. The method of studying the Bible which is used
by the large majority of Biblical scholars today, most
of whom teach courses in the Bible in colleges and
theological seminaries, might be designated as the
method of "historical criticism." The term "criticism"
as used here does not refer to a negative attitude, an
attitude of disapproval, but to a process of inquiry.
It means nothing more than applying to the Biblical
material the rational and scientific methods of scholarship which are applied in other fields of study.[6] This
process of inquiry involves several types of investigation. While they are discussed separately here for
the sake of making clear what is involved in the method
of historical criticism, all are essential for the work
of the Biblical scholar. They are as follows:

1. "Lower" Criticism. The purpose of this type
of investigation is to secure (a) the best possible
Hebrew text of the Old Testament and the best possible
Greek text of the New Testament, and (b) with producing
the best possible translations of the Hebrew and Greek
into the vernacular.

(a) Textual Criticism.

This process of inquiry is concerned with
recovering as nearly as possible what the
Biblical authors actually wrote. Obviously,
a scholar who engages in such a task must have
a thorough knowledge of the Hebrew and Greek
languages, but also he needs to have a knowledge of other ancient Near-Eastern languages,
and of the general social and cultural conditions in the ancient Near-Eastern, Greek, and
Roman societies.

The Bible was written over a period of about
twelve hundred years and was completed long
ago. There are no original manuscripts of the
Bible or of any portion thereof, but only
copies of copies of copies, and so on. Also

34

it appears that in early times there were no standard texts of the various books of the Old Testament and of the New Testament which possessed sole authority. Given this fact, along with occasional copyists' errors and scribal emendations, it is not surprising that there were often variant recensions of the same Biblical books.

The task of the textual critic is to carefully analyze the available early Hebrew and Greek manuscripts in order to establish the best possible Hebrew and Greek texts. This requires as indicated previously, a knowledge of the Biblical and other ancient languages. It requires also a comparison of the various available recensions, a familiarity with extra-Biblical literature in order to see how terms are used during the various time periods when the Bible was being written, and a giving of attention to the larger contexts of passages whenever there is any obscurity with respect to one or more of the words used in the passages.

Three examples of the type of analysis engaged in by textual critics are as follows:

In the earliest Hebrew texts of the Old Testament the words contain no vowels but only consonants. In about the sixth century A.D. a school of Jewish scholars known as the Massoretes invented a system of "pointing" Hebrew to indicate the vowel sounds. This Massoretic text has provided the basic Hebrew text for the Old Testament until recent times when other and earlier manuscripts have been discovered such as the Dead Sea (Qumran) scrolls which are centuries earlier than the Massoretic text. The evidence provided by these recently discovered manuscripts indicates that at some points the Massoretic text is faulty and obscure. In Isaiah 33:8, the Massoretic text from which the Authorized English Version (King James) of 1611 A.D. was translated, contains the word "cities" which is meaningless in the context of this verse. The Revised Standard Version (1953) renders the Hebrew word here as "witnesses," for this is the Hebrew word in the

Dead Sea scroll of Isaiah, and "witnesses"
makes sense in the context of this verse.[7]
The reason the later Massoretic text has
"cities" rather than "witnesses" appears to be
due to the fact that in the "unpointed" Hebrew
(without vowels) the word for "cities" is similar in appearance to the word for "witness"
such that in copying it was very easy to substitute one for the other. Given the context
of the verse (Isaiah 33:8) and the evidence
from the Dead Sea scroll of Isaiah, the
textual critic is able to correct the Massoretic text at this point and thus to render the
verse as it was probably intended by the original author.

Another example of a statement in the Massoretic text which is plainly absurd and probably
due to textual corruption is found in Job 21:
24. The King James Version (1611 A.D.) reads,
"<u>His</u> breasts are full of milk and his bones
are moistened with marrow." Geddes MacGregor
has the following to say about this verse:

> This reading is plainly absurd. In
> the Massoretic text the word desig-
> nating the container of milk is,
> however, very obscure, and translators
> from ancient times onwards have made
> wild guesses at it . . . In the King
> James Version the translators were
> apparently eager to have the appro-
> priate part of the human anatomy as
> the milk-container, regardless of
> the appropriateness of the sex of its
> owner. Milk belongs to breasts, so
> breasts it had to be, even though the
> breasts were male ones . . . All these
> wild attempts sprang from the accept-
> ance of 'milk,' plainly given in the
> pointed Hebrew of the Massoretic text.
> This word, in unpointed Hebrew, is
> identical, however, with the Hebrew
> word for 'fat' which, of course, might
> go with almost any part of the anatomy
> and make sense. A much more likely
> hypothesis, therefore, is that the
> Massorites incorrectly vocalized the

36

Hebrew to make it read 'milk' where
it should have read 'fat.'[8]

In light of the context of the entire passage
in Job 21, the word "fat" appears to be the
correct rendering. Thus, the Revised Standard
Version (1953) renders Verse 24, "His body full
of fat, and the marrow of his bones moist."

One final example is taken from the New Testament. The Greek manuscripts of all or of
parts of the New Testament number about 5000.
Of these the most important are about 300,
written on papyrus or parchment and dating
from the second to the eighth century A.D.[9]
As we have seen above, the King James Version
of the Old Testament was based on the late
Hebrew Massoretic text. Similarly, the King
James Version of the New Testament was based
on rather late Greek texts. Thus, in Matthew
5:22, the King James Version reads,

> "But I say unto you, that whosoever is
> angry with his brother without a cause
> shall be in danger of the judgment."

The words "without a cause" are not found in
many of the earliest and best manuscripts.
Thus they appear to have been inserted by a
copyist at a later time. The Revised Standard
Version omits these words and reads,

> "But I say to you that every one who
> is angry with his brother shall be
> liable to judgment."

The examples given above not only illustrate
what is involved in the process of textual
criticism but also demonstrate the significant
contribution which the results of this process
can provide us with respect to a more accurate
knowledge of the contents of the Bible. The
purpose is to recover, as far as may be possible, what the authors of the various portions
of the Bible actually wrote. As J. Philip
Hyatt has said:

> The average reader of the Bible cannot
> concern himself with the details of

textual criticism. He should understand, however, that its purpose is always to recover the very best text possible, and that means the most nearly original text; its purpose is not to improve the Bible and make it say what some modern scholar thinks it ought to say. The average reader benefits from the work of the textual critics, and may be grateful for what they have done to provide him with more accurate versions of the Bible than he would have had without their labors.[10]

(b) Accurate Translation

Since the average reader of the Bible lacks a knowledge of the Hebrew and Greek languages, it is important not only to secure the best texts possible but also to provide the best possible translations of these Hebrew and Greek texts. This requires a considerable amount of skill, for it is not always easy to render the expressions of one language into another. Furthermore, in a "living" language such as English, new expressions are being continually added to the language and old ones become either obsolete or their meanings shift, sometimes just to the opposite of their original meanings. In the King James Version of 1611, for example, "let" means "hinder," "prevent" means "precede," "allow" means "approve," "comprehend" means "overcome," and "allege" means "prove."[11] These are only a few examples of the more than 300 words in the King James Version which are still in constant use but which now convey meanings different from those which they had in 1611.

In light of this fact, it is obvious that the average reader of the Bible should use modern translations in order to acquire as accurate a knowledge as possible of what was actually said in the original languages of the Bible. There are many good modern versions. Among them are The Holy Scriptures, Jewish Publication Society, 1917; new edition, The Torah, 1962; The New Oxford Annotated Bible, Revised Standard Version,

38

Oxford University Press, 1973; <u>The Jerusalem Bible</u>, Doubleday and Company, Inc., 1966. However, given the fact that textual criticism is a continuing process such that further improvements in the texts of the Bible may appear in the future and given the fact that contemporary languages are continually changing and expanding, even these versions cannot be expected to remain adequate for an indefinite future. Indeed, in light of past experience, it seems reasonable to suppose that new versions will be needed in the future, possibly as often as every century.

2. "Higher" Criticism. The method of historical criticism as applied to the study of the Bible also involves what is generally called "higher criticism." The use of the word "higher" in this context does not imply a value judgment, that higher criticism is more important than lower criticism. Rather the terms "lower" and "higher" are used simply to distinguish two types of investigation which are involved in the process of historical criticism. Both are essential, and the two are closely interrelated. While an individual Biblical scholar may concentrate on one more than the other, he cannot ignore the other. Indeed, the "lower" critic must take into account the work of the "higher" critic if he is to do the work of lower criticism adequately. Similarly, the "higher" critic cannot successfully pursue his type of investigation without a knowledge of lower criticism. In short, these two processes of inquiry are inextricably intertwined and are distinguished here only in order to make clear the processes of inquiry contained within the method we have called "historical criticism."

The higher critic raises and seeks the answers to certain specific questions concerning a given book of the Bible, or a portion of the Bible (a part of a book or a group of books together). According to J. Philip Hyatt, these questions are:

> Who wrote it?
> When did he write it?
> For what purpose did he write it?
> To whom did he write?
> What sources did he use?
> What did the first author actually write, and
>   what was added later?[12]

Several methods of analysis or criticism may be used by the higher critic in the attempt to secure answers to these questions. Among them are:

(a) Literary Criticism

This type of analysis distinguishes certain differences in literary style and words and expressions found in a book of the Bible or several books attributed traditionally to a single author. For example, the first five books of the Bible, Genesis through Deuteronomy (the Pentateuch or Torah) were traditionally attributed to Moses. Yet in Genesis there are several proper names denoting God, among which are Elohim and Yahweh. In the passages where Yahweh is used as the divine name there is a distinctive literary style and many character- istic words and expressions. This fact sug- gests that there was more than one author. Also there is other evidence which leads to this conclusion such as the presence of some chronological lapses and anachronisms. Genesis 36:31 reads,

> "These are the kings who reigned in
> the land of Edom, before any king
> reigned over the Israelites."

Under Moses (died about 1250 B.C.), the Israel- ites were wandering, nomadic tribes in the wilderness of the Sinai peninsula, and even after the settlement into Canaan there was a considerable lapse of time before the estab- lishment of the monarchy at the time of King Saul about 1000 A.D. Surely the standpoint of the person who could write, "before any king reigned over Israel," must have been after the establishment of the monarchy.

Facts such as those mentioned above lead the higher critic to the conclusion that there were several authors of the Pentateuch who wrote their accounts in different time-periods, after the establishment of the monarchy. Iso- lating these several sources and analyzing their contents, the higher critic is able to arrive at probable time periods in which each of these sources was written. Given this, the higher critic is able to put the various sources in the larger contexts of the actual historical situations in which the authors lived, to understand better the intentions and purposes of the authors and the issues which were of concern for those to whom the authors were directing their writings, and to arrive at some knowledge of the probable sources used by the authors. That is, by putting these sources in the contexts of the life situations out of which they arose, the higher critic is able to arrive at a fuller understanding of the original meanings contained in the contents of the passages of the various sources.

One further example of the contribution of literary criticism to a better understanding of the Bible will be mentioned here because it is so striking. Scholars have long been aware of the fact that the literary style, characteristic words and expressions, and even some ideas found in Isaiah, Chapters 40-55, are quite different from those found in Isaiah, Chapters 1-39. Given the additional fact that Isaiah 44:28 and 45:1 refer explicitly to Cyrus, King of Persia, to whom Babylon fell in 539 B.C., Chapters 40-55 are attributed to an unknown Jew who was a member of the Jewish community in exile in Babylon. Since the actual historical Isaiah pursued his ministry in Jerusalem from 740-700 B.C., the oracles contained in Chapters 40-55 were written about two centuries later. Thus, the life situations of the authors are entirely different and it is only as this is known that the full meaning of what they said can be understood.

(b) Form Criticism

First used by German scholars, another type of investigation employed by many higher critics is called "form criticism."[13] While it has long been recognized that there are a variety of literary genres or forms in the Bible, it is only recently that they have been studied in and for themselves and used as tools in the analysis of Biblical literature. Previously, the various forms of literature in the Bible

41

had been taken for granted much as we take for granted the various genres in our own literature. Instead of taking the various literary forms of the Bible for granted, the form critic concentrates on them as special objects of study. Roland E. Murphy, in describing what the form critic attempts to do, has used as an analogy of contrast the various forms of literature in a modern newspaper. He says:

> Any newspaper presents its readers with many and various literary genres: Advertisements, obituary notices, editorials, letters to the editor, human interest stories, the comics, etc. In all these cases, fixed written forms can be recognized. Each has its own specific characteristics: Certain expressions or formulae and perhaps even a given structure. The modern reader is oblivious to all these details. He is so attuned to the literary expressions of his own culture that he automatically 'shifts gears' as he moves from one genre to another. But it is a different experience when he exposes himself to a literature as ancient and varied as the Bible. The difference between the peoples of the ancient Semitic world, its way of thinking, and our own style, quickly dawns on us. It would not do to exaggerate these differences, but the fact remains that the mode of expression of biblical times is a challenge to our understanding . . . The reader's task is to ascertain and respect the various literary types, whether historical, epic, saga, or legend, that occur in the Bible; otherwise, he will fail to comprehend the literary riches presented in the various parts of Scripture.[14]

The form critic not only isolates the various literary forms as found in the written material of the Bible but also, using the methods and results of studies in ancient and modern folklore, seeks to gain some knowledge of the functioning and meaning of these forms in their early early oral stages prior to their being put into written form. Studies of folklore in general have tended to provide some evidence for the following claims: (1) Folklore tends to develop certain rather specific and fixed forms (limericks, conundrums, aphorisms, parables, myths, legends, sagas, epics, etc.). (2) The forms are transmitted even orally with little alterations. (3) The forms grow out of the life situations in which traditions were fixed. (4) Much of the history of the tradition itself can be ascertained through an analysis of the origins and functioning of the forms. So the form critic attempts to penetrate the written documents of the Bible to the period of oral transmission lying behind the written records. Using the written records as clues in this quest, he seeks to isolate and classify each individual literary unit according to its form, evaluate it historically, and recover the purposes of the people who created these forms and transmitted them orally.

While in the very nature of the case, form criticism is not as exact a "science" as literary criticism, it has, nevertheless, made a significant contribution to our understanding of the Bible. It provides us with some knowledge concerning the oral "traditions" which lie behind a great deal of the written material in the Bible. With this knowledge, the higher critic is able to ascertain more fully the sources used by the writer of a particular portion of the Bible, how he used these sources, and what purposes and theological views of his own are to be found in what he wrote.

(c) Redaction Criticism

The method of form criticism brought forth another approach, namely redaction or composition criticism. This method studies a document in the Bible in its final form in an attempt to gain a knowledge of the theological point of view of the author who arranged, modified, and edited the traditional material that

43

was available to him. That is, this method
takes into account not only the life setting
when the traditional material was formulated
but also considers the life setting of the
author of the document. Through analyzing the
structure or arrangement of the document and
the modifications contained therein, it provides certain conclusions concerning the
author's own personal theology.

Current higher criticism tends to use all the
methods described briefly above. These methods to not
exclude one another but, in fact, are mutually comple-
mentary. They are not simply intellectual exercises
for the elite, but are used in order to gain as complete a knowledge as possible of what the original
authors sought to communicate in their writings.

Historical criticism (lower and higher criticism
combined) makes possible genuine exegesis, which means
drawing the meaning out of the passage. It assists us
in avoiding one of the most common failings which
plagues interpreters, namely eisegesis which reads a
meaning into the passage. It is often a temptation for
the interpreter to read a passage in the Bible in light
of contemporary presuppositions and perspectives, and
thus unconsciously make the passage mean what he thinks
it should mean. Thus, the meaning of the passage for
the original creator and hearers, or writer and readers,
is obscured or entirely obliterated. Historical criticism, however, helps us to place the various parts of
the Bible in their concrete historical situations, to
permit the authors and speakers in the Bible to speak
for themselves, to place ourselves in the positions
of the various personalities, writers, readers, or
hearers found in the Bible, and to determine what the
words meant to them. It is only after we have done
this--namely interpreting exegetically rather than
eisegetically--that we can adequately understand what
the words can say to us in our own lives in the twentieth century.[15]

Chapter II

[1] Tanak is the traditional Jewish designation for the Jewish version of what Christians call Old Testament. It is actually an acronym of the initials for the threefold division of the Jewish Scriptures: T for Torah (Pentateuch or Five Books of Moses); N for Nabim (Prophets), and K for Kethubin (writings).

[2] J. Philip Hyatt, The Heritage of Biblical Faith (The Bethany Press, 1964), p. 121, cf. Chapter IV, pp. 121-157; cf. Bruce M. Metzger (ed.), The Apocrypha (Oxford University Press, 1965), "Introduction," pp. IX-XXX. Catholic versions of the Bible (see The Jerusalem Bible) contain the books of Tobit, Judith, I Maccabees, II Maccabees, The Book of Wisdom, Ecclesiasticus, and Baruch, as well as some additions to a few Old Testament books. These are not found in the Jewish and Protestant Bibles.

[3] The Interpreter's Dictionary of the Bible, Vol. A-D (Abingdon Press, 1962), pp. 161-166.

[4] Ibid., pp. 165-166.

[5] Milton Steinberg, Basic Judaism (Harcourt, Brace, and Co., 1947), p. 24.

[6] C. H. Dodd, The Bible Today (Cambridge University Press, 1951), p. 23.

[7] The Interpreter's Bible, Vol. 5 (Abingdon Press, 1956), p. 23.

[8] Geddes MacGregor, The Bible in the Making (J. B. Lippincolt, 1959), pp. 51-52.

[9] "Introduction to the New Testament," The New Oxford Annotated Bible, Revised Standard Version (Oxford University Press, 1973), p. 1169.

[10] J. Philip Hyatt, The Heritage of Biblical Faith (The Bethany Press, 1964), p. 22.

[11] cf. "Preface to the Revised Standard Version," op. cit., p. XV.

[12] J. Philip Hyatt, op. cit., p. 24.

[13] The scholars who first used form criticism were Hermann Gunkel, The Legends of Genesis (Schocken Book, 1964) and The Psalms: A Form-Critical Introduction (Fortress Press, 1967), and Martin Dibelius, From Tradition to Gospel (Charles Scribner's Sons, 1935). Another famous form critic of the New Testament was Rudolf Bultmann, History of the Synoptic Tradition (Harper and Row, 1968).

[14] Roland E. Murphy, "Modern Approaches to Biblical Study," The New Oxford Annotated Bible (Oxford University Press, 1973), pp. 1519-1520.

[15] For an excellent discussion of four primary values of the historical approach to the study of the Bible, cf. J. Philip Hyatt, op. cit., pp. 31-38.

SUGGESTIONS FOR FURTHER READING

Briggs, R. C., Interpreting the New Testament Today, Abingdon Press, 1973.

Calwell, E. C., The Study of the Bible, Revised Edition, University of Chicago Press, 1964.

Dodd, C. H., The Bible Today, Cambridge University Press, 1951.

Grant, R. M., The Bible in The Church, Macmillan Co., 1948.

Hyatt, J. Philip, The Heritage of Biblical Faith, The Bethany Press, 1964.

Koch, Klaus, The Growth of the Biblical Tradition, Charles Scribner's Sons, 1969.

MacGregor, Geddes, The Bible in The Making, J. B. Lippincott Co., 1959.

Neill, Stephen, The Interpretation of The New Testament, 1861-1961, Oxford University Press, 1973.

Oxford Annotated Bible, Oxford University Press, 1973, Appendices, pp. 1515-1557.

Rahner, Karl (ed.), Sacramentum Mundi, Vol. I, Herder and Herder, 1968, "Bible," "Biblical Exegesis," and "Biblical Historiography," pp. 160-214.

Rece, E. H., and W. A. Beardslee, Reading the Bible: A Guide, Prentice-Hall, 1956.

Rowley, H. H., The Old Testament and Modern Study, Oxford University Press, 1951.

Sandmel, Samuel, The Enjoyment of Scripture, Oxford University Press, 1972.

Selby, Donald J., and James King West, Introduction to The Bible, The Macmillan Co., 1971.

Steinberg, Milton, Basic Judaism, Harcourt, Brace and Co., 1947.

The Anchor Bible, Vol. I, Doubleday and Co., Inc., 1964.

47

The Interpreter's Bible, Vol. I, Abingdon Press, 1952, "General
    Articles on The Bible," pp. 3-171.

The Interpreter's Dictionary of The Bible, Vol. A-D, Abingdon
    Press, 1962, "Biblical Criticism," pp. 407-418.

Tucker, Gene M., Form Criticism of the Old Testament, Fortress
    Press, 1971.

Willoughby, H. R., The Study of The Bible Today and Tomorrow,
    University of Chicago Press, 1947.

CHAPTER III

THE OLD TESTAMENT

As we have noted in Chapter II, the Old Testament is regarded as sacred scripture by both Jews and Christians. While occasionally some few Christians may speak of the Old Testament as a "Jewish" book, they are, in doing so, departing from the normal Christian view in which the Old Testament is invariably regarded as a part of the Christian canon of Scripture. Indeed, there have been and are some Christians who view the Old Testament as a Christian book. While this view is not correct with respect to the origins of Old Testament writings, it is the case that there is a considerable continuity between the Old and New Testaments, even though the latter was written by Christians. Thus the narratives and messages of the New Testament cannot be fully understood unless viewed in light of Old Testament history and themes. This is especially true with respect to an understanding of the career and teachings of Jesus as sketched in the Synoptic Gospels (Matthew, Mark, and Luke). Whatever else he may have been, Jesus was a Jew, not a Greek nor a Roman. He was born into and grew up in a Jewish environment. He attended synagogue services (Mark 6:1-2; Matthew 13:54; Luke 4:16) and probably attended the synagogue school[1] where he became familiar with the Old Testament (Tanak) in Hebrew and with at least some of the traditions of the Rabbinic sages. A necessary condition, then, for the understanding of Christian beginnings is some knowledge of the Jewish heritage. Thus an understanding of the Old Testament is essential for an understanding of both Judaism and Christianity.

Given the length of the Old Testament, both in terms of pages and time-span, our brief discussion in this chapter can deal only with certain key issues, perspectives, and events.[2] Topics to be considered are as follows: (I) a brief description of Old Testament history; (II) a brief description of the several sources comprising the Pentateuch (Torah-Book) and of a few themes found in each source; (III) an explication of the major Old Testament theme, namely the Convenant theme; (IV) a discussion of how this theme was understood and used by the great Prophets; and (V) a brief characterization of some of the other later writings and perspectives in the Old Testament.

I. A Brief Sketch of Old Testament History

The purpose of the brief sketch below is to give the reader reference points in a time frame such that the discussions concerning the writings, events, and ideas in the Old Testament which follow can be put in their proper historical settings. As indicated in Chapter II, a proper interpretation of the writings, events, and ideas in the Bible depends upon putting them in the actual life situations out of which they arose.

A. The Patriarchal Period (Abraham, Isaac, Jacob, Joseph) Ca. 1800-1600 B.C.

B. Sojourn of Hebrew tribes in Egypt, Ca. 1700-1300 B.C. The exodus of the Hebrew tribes from Egypt, Ca. 1290 B.C.

C. Settlement in Canaan and tribal confederacy, Ca. 1250-1020 B.C.

D. Monarchy, Ca. 1020-587 B.C.

   1. United monarchy, Ca. 1020-922 B.D.

   2. Divided monarchy

      (a) Northern Kingdom (Israel), Ca. 922-721 B.C.

      (b) Judah, Ca. 922-587 B.C.

E. Exile in Babylon, Ca. 597/87-538 B.C.

F. Restoration and Reconstruction in Judah, Ca. 538-63 B.C.

   1. Under the Persians, Ca. 538-333 B.C.

   2. Under the Greeks, Ca. 333-167 B.C.

   3. Independence (Maccabean Kingdom), Ca. 167-63 B.C.

G. Judah under Rome, 63 B.C.

The reader will more readily understand the discussion in the remainder of this chapter if he will refer to this brief sketch from time to time.

II.   The Pentateuch (Torah Book)

The Pentateuch (a term which literally means five
books) is the term used by Christians to refer to the
first five books of the Old Testament (Genesis, Exodus,
Leviticus, Numbers, Deuteronomy).   Jews generally refer
to it as the Torah or Torah-Book.   Traditionally it was
believed that Moses was the author and in ancient times
it was often called the Book of Moses.   Today, however,
the dominant view held by most biblical scholars, Jewish, Catholic, and Protestant, is that the Pentateuch
is a composite work in which several sources or documents, written centuries after the time of Moses, have
been blended together, and that the Pentateuch reached
its final and present form about 400 B.C.

Using the methods of higher criticism, biblical
scholars isolate these sources, label them, and assign
them approximate dates of origin.   Such information is
not to be found in the Bible itself.   Instead one must
consult scholarly textbooks or studies of the Old Testament in order to find discussions of the four Pentateuchal sources and lists of passages which are to be
assigned to each of the sources.[3]   The sketch below
indicates the usual designations of these sources,
their dates, and brief characterizations of their contents.

A.   The earliest of the Pentateuchal sources, generally designated as J[4], was probably written during
the reign of King Solomon (Ca. 961-922 B.C.).   In his
pre-Mosaic narratives (in the book of Genesis), as
well as in his narratives concerning the Mosaic period,
this author used the name Yahweh as the name for God
(sometimes rendered Jahveh; hence, the use of the initial J to designate this source).   Passages which may
be assigned to J are found primarily in the books of
Genesis, Exodus, and Numbers.   When these passages are
isolated from those by other writers, it becomes
apparent that, using the oral traditions or "memory
units" which had for some time been circulating more or
less independently, the J writer with considerable literary skill had combined them into a literary structure
for the first time and produced a great national epic.[5]

It would appear that the J writer was concerned
with preserving the core of Israel's[6] faith which had

51

arisen in the pre-monarchy period of the exodus from Egypt and the wilderness wanderings (the Sinai covenant and Mosaic period), and which had been reconfirmed in the establishment of the tribal confederacy (Joshua, Chapter 24). Undoubtedly he felt that the new situation of the monarchy, with its centralized government and state sanctuary at Jerusalem, might lead the nation to abandon its traditions and faith, the very thing that had brought this people into existence in the first place. So the J writer was concerned not only to preserve the ancient traditions but also to interpret and present them in such a way that they might be seen to be relevant to the new situation. It is only as she understands her past so that it is real in her present that Israel can genuinely exist in the present and fulfill her divine mission in the world.

The central theme of the J epic is the covenant relationship between Yahweh and Israel,[7] a relationship which had brought Israel into existence as a people. Even though the Covenant had been established at Mount Sinai during the time of Moses, the J writer views all history in light of the Covenant theme. According to Bernhard W. Anderson,[8] the J writer writes his epic, as it were, backwards, viewing prior historical experiences from the vantage point of the Covenant. It is as though he had written first Israel's life story from the exodus from Egypt to Israel's arrival at the borders of Canaan, including in this narration accounts concerning Moses, the Covenant making at Sinai, and the wilderness wanderings. Then he adds to this his account of the Patriarchal period, the stories about Abraham, Isaac, Jacob, and Joseph, indicating that the Covenant had been prefigured in Yahweh's call of Abraham and that Yahweh's purpose was that "by you all the families of the earth shall bless themselves" (Genesis 12:3). Given this perspective, it is then appropriate for the J writer to prefix his narrative of Israel's "historical" experiences with an account of primeval "history," that is, the creation (begins in Genesis 2:4b), Garden of Eden, and other narratives which include all mankind.

This third section, then, clearly reveals the J writer's view that Yahweh's covenant with Israel transcended national interests and was intended by Yahweh to serve his history-long and universal purpose of bringing all mankind into the divine-human fellowship. Yahweh had created human beings for life in community (Genesis 2:18-25), but they had rebelled against their creator. Yielding to the pretensions of self, to pride or egocentricity, they had sought to become like God (Genesis 3:22).[9] Thus human community was disrupted and human history became the scene of estrangement or sin. Yet Yahweh had acted time and again, in judgment and mercy,[10] to persuade human beings to return to the divine-human fellowship and thus to what Yahweh had intended in the creation. But estrangement or sin continued to grow until finally Yahweh called Abraham to be the father of a "great nation" through whom "all the families of the earth shall bless themselves" (Genesis 12:3). So the J writer sets the stage for the remainder of his epic dealing with the past traditions of the Covenant community. Clearly with this epic he is encouraging the people of his own day (the time of Solomon) to renew the Covenant faith and to make it vital in the new situation. He is calling upon both the people and the king with his court to abolish whatever violated the Covenant faith (fertility cults, social injustices such as Solomon's high taxation and labor conscription, and power politics) and instead to renew their Covenant faith. It is probably not an exaggeration to say that the J epic was primarily responsible for keeping alive the Covenant faith in a time when there was a very real danger that it would be lost in nationalistic fervor, in pride over the accomplishments, expansion, and power of the nation under Solomon.

B. A second Pentateuchal source is generally designated as E due to the fact that in his pre-Mosaic narratives in Genesis this writer uses Elohim as the name for God.[11] Since he employs a distinctive literary style and characteristic words and expressions, his writing can be generally distinguished from that of J and the other two writers in the Pentateuch. Suggestions in the content of the material assigned to the E writer indicate that he wrote his document approximately a century after the division of Solomon's kingdom into the Northern Kingdom (Israel) and Judah, that is, about 850 B.C. Beginning his account with Abraham (Genesis 15), the E writer follows the general outline of J through the rest of Genesis, Exodus, and Numbers.

In light of the content of his document, it appears that the E writer lived in the Northern Kingdom, perhaps about the time of the prophet Elijah when the Israelites were being especially tempted to abandon their faith and to follow the easy way of religious syncretism. Beginning his document with an account of a Covenant between God and Abraham, the E writer emphasizes the Israelites' obligation to demonstrate radical obedience to God, the sovereign Lord of History. Bernhard W. Anderson has succinctly summarized the major themes of E when he says:

> More so than the Yahwist (J), the Elohist's (E) epic is closely bound to the popular tradition of the ancient Tribal confederacy. . . This epic is essentially an elaboration of the themes of the sacred history: The call of Israel, the deliverance from Egypt, the wandering in the wilderness, and the inheritance of the land. These themes are developed in such a way as to heighten the significance of Yahweh's revelation in the Mosaic period, and to glorify the figure of Moses. . . Thus, the Elohist narrative rehearses the sacred history of Israel, with special emphasis upon the revelation to Moses and the call to the obedience of faith.[12]

C. A third source is generally designated with the initial D. Even though the D writer (or writers) prepared the long history contained in the books of Samuel and Kings, the Pentateuchal material which can be assigned to D is found in Deuteronomy, the fifth book of the Pentateuch. The book appears to report speeches and words of Moses. However, in light of the literary style and theology, it is assigned by most scholars to the period of the Judean king, Josiah (640-609 B.C.). In 621 B.C. Josiah instituted a sweeping religious reform which was celebrated by a Covenant renewal ceremony (II Kings, Chapters 22-23). Apparently Deuteronomy was written just prior to this reform, inspiring it and supporting it. While the contents of this book rest on ancient traditions, it is basically a reaffirmation and reinterpretation of the Mosaic teaching in the light of later historical understanding. It sets before the Israelites what is required in both their worship practices and the concrete affairs of everyday life if they are to maintain faithfulness to Yahweh and the Covenant faith.

D. The fourth Pentateuchal source is generally designated with the initial P. Marked by the style and cultic interests of the priestly circle, this document was probably prepared by a priestly writer or

54

writers during the time of the Babylonian exile, about 550 B.C. or perhaps a little later. Apparently the P writer made use of the JE epic (these two had been put together by an editor after the fall of the Northern Kingdom in 721) as a basis for his own presentation which served as a sort of framework for JE. While Genesis, Exodus, and Numbers contained passages which can be assigned to P, the whole of Leviticus is to be attributed to this source. By 400 B.C. the priestly writers had incorporated D in their work and the Pentateuch was completed.

Even a superficial reading of the passages assigned to the P writer makes one aware of the spirit of worship which pervades this whole work.[13] According to Bernhard W. Anderson:

> The purpose of the Priestly Work is to show that the whole thrust of history, from the time of creation, was the selection of Israel for the 'service' of worship. Israel is conceived as a 'congregation' (_'edah_) or religious community which not only witnesses to Yahweh's redemptive act of the Exodus but articulates the creation's praise of the Creator, as in many of the Psalms. Israel's whole life was to be a 'liturgy,' a service of God.[14]

III. The Covenant Theme and Its Characteristic Features

In the discussion of the Pentateuchal sources in the previous section, reference was made several times to the Yahweh-Israel Covenant. Even though the writers of these sources have different life-settings and thus there are some differences among them with respect to the emphases which they place on certain features of the Covenant theme, it is the case, nevertheless, that the Covenant provides the central and unifying theme of each Pentateuchal document. As we will see later, this is also the case with respect to the writings assigned to the great Prophets of Israel. Given these facts, it is obvious that an essential, or necessary, condition for understanding the Old Testament is an understanding of the significance, meaning and characteristics of the Covenant theme. The discussion in this section, and the one to follow, will hopefully provide a basis for such an understanding.

We now know from extra-biblical writings discovered by archaeologists that covenant making was widely practiced among the peoples of the Ancient Near-East. There were the parity covenants or bargains between equals and there were the suzerainty covenants in which the party of the first part was exceedingly more powerful than the party of the second part. That is, the Suzerain (king) is under no obligation to offer a covenant to people, vassal, or conquered foe. He does so solely out of his benevolence and graciousness. It is clear in the Old Testament descriptions of the Yahweh-Israel Covenant that it was understood as a suzerainty covenant.

An outstanding example of a covenant treaty between a victorious king and his conquered foe is the one made by a victorious Hittite king with his conquered foe, Rameses II (the Pharaoh of the exodus). Copies of this treaty have been found at the site of the ancient Hittite kingdom in Asia Minor and in Egypt. Among the features contained in this treaty are the preamble which specifies the name and titles of the great Hittite king, the historical prologue which describes the king's deeds of benevolence on behalf of the vassal, the loyalty oath in which the vassal pledges obedience to the king, the designation of the witnesses to the treaty (the gods of both countries), and the sanctions for the vassal's loyalty or disloyalty to the Covenant.[15]

There are some obvious similarities between the form of this Hittite covenant treaty and that of the Yahweh-Israel Covenant made at Mt. Sinai under the leadership of Moses (especially as described in Exodus, Chapters 3, 19, and 20). It is possible that Moses may have become familiar with the Hittite covenant treaty during his youth in the Pharaoh's court in Egypt. Even if this were not the case, covenant making was such a wide-spread practice among peoples in the ancient Near-East, the Israelites could hardly have avoided becoming acquainted with such a practice at some point in their historical experience. Whatever may have been the historical causal conditions which resulted in the particular forms or patterns by which the Covenant was structured, the conviction that a God (indeed, the one God) had voluntarily offered a covenant to a people appears to be unique among ancient peoples.

The discussion which follows provides a brief exposition of the major characteristic features of the Yahweh-Israel Covenant. There is no attempt here to distinguish between earlier and later understandings of the Covenant but rather to describe the characteristic features of the Covenant faith as it came to be understood by the faithful in Israel.

A. Basic to the Covenant faith was the view that Yahweh had taken the initiative in delivering Israel from Egypt and in offering her the Covenant. His deed of deliverance had been accompanied by the disclosure of his name (similar to the first feature of the Hittite covenant treaty) and therefore of his nature since in ancient times names were not just arbitrary denotations but were designations indicating something about the nature of the one named (Exodus 3:7-17; 20:2). Since the consonants of Yahweh are similar to the consonants of the Hebrew verb "to be" and this was understood in an active dynamic sense, Yahweh is understood as the active God who is aware of the cries of the distressed Hebrew slaves in Egypt and acts to deliver them. It was not because of their worth but because of his compassion that Yahweh took the initiative and acted to deliver them from Egypt.

While this appears to be implicitly present in the early narratives about the exodus from Egypt and the Covenant of Sinai, it is most explicit in later reflection on the meaning of the Covenant. Thus in Deuteronomy, which inspired King Josiah's Covenant renewal and reform in the 7th century B.C., it is stated:

> It was not because you were more in number than any other people that the LORD (Yahweh) set his love upon you and chose you, for you were the fewest of all peoples; but it is because the LORD loves you, and is keeping the oath which he swore to your fathers . . . Know therefore that the LORD your God is God, the faithful God who keeps covenant and steadfast love with those who love him . . . (Deuteronomy 7: 7-9).

Yahweh offers the Covenant to Israel not because Israel is a great nation nor because Israel merits it, but simply out of his unmerited and self-giving love. No causal explanation can be given for this love other than

57

that it is Yahweh's nature so to love. Though freely given by Yahweh, it possesses the characteristic of steadfastness. Israel from time to time may be faithless and disloyal to the Covenant and thus subject to Yahweh's disciplinary judgment but Yahweh is faithful, keeping covenant and steadfast love. Even his disciplinary judgment of Israel arises out of his steadfast love.

At the heart of the Covenant faith in the Old Testament is the view of Yahweh's love not only for Israel but also for all mankind. We must emphasize this point because there are some outside the Hebrew faith who, because they are impressed with the many laws and the occasional primitive views found in the Old Testament, characterize the God of the Old Testament as a God simply of justice, a stern law-giver who demands conformity to his law. In light of the passage quoted above, and many others (such as Leviticus 19:17-18, 33-34; Hosea 11:8; Isaiah 54:5-10) this view is surely incorrect. God's love is the very foundation of his covenant with Israel. His disciplinary judgments are never unmotivated but arise because of Israel's faithlessness to the Covenant in the everyday affairs of life such as the oppression of the poor, corruption in the courts, and worship of the fertility gods. God does act in judgment-justice but it is never retributive punishment. It is disciplinary, out of his loving concern for change, for a renewal of covenant faithfulness. His justice is in the service of his love. Surely love is not genuine if it does not contain justice. While there may be justice without love, there cannot be love without justice, however much the former may transcend the latter. So the fundamental view of God in the Covenant faith of the Old Testament is not, on the one hand, of a vindictive tyrant nor, on the other hand, of an overindulgent grandfather, but rather of a loving father who disciplines his children for their sake. In the beginning, because of his gracious love and mercy, God took the initiative and through the Covenant brought Israel into existence. He continues to exercise care and compassion for Israel both in his acts of judgment and in his acts of mercy.

B. Another fundamental feature of the Covenant was that it was understood in terms of history. Just as in the Hittite covenant treaty there was a historical prologue which described the king's deeds of benevolence on behalf of the vassal, so also in the

accounts of the Yahweh-Israel Covenant and the later
Covenant renewal ceremonies (cf. Joshua, Chapter 24)
there are historical prologues reciting Yahweh's deeds
of benevolence on behalf of Israel. For example, in
the account of the covenant making at Mount Sinai the
E writer presents a very succinctly stated historical
prologue when he says:

> And Moses went up to God, and the LORD
> called to him out of the mountain, saying,
> 'Thus you shall say to the house of
> Jacob, and tell the people of Israel:
> You have seen what I did to the Egyptians,
> and how I bore you on eagles' wings and
> brought you to myself.' (Exodus 19:3-4)

While many events in the history of Israel are viewed
as Yahweh's gracious deeds of benevolence, the deliverance from Egypt is always primary and always emphasized
in the historical prologues of the accounts of the various Covenant renewal ceremonies.

This discussion reiterates an important point made
in Chapter I in our discussion of some basic perspectives in the Judeo-Christian tradition, namely that
God discloses himself in history (Section III, Point
5). In the Covenant faith Yahweh is viewed not as a
static absolute nor as a nature God (a sun-god or a
storm-god). He may use the powers of nature to accomplish his purposes but history is the primary realm of
his activity. Further, the great events of the past
which were determinative for Israel's existence are not
viewed as unreal or dead, but rather as "living" on in
the present, providing meaning and direction for the
covenant community in its ongoing experiences.

C. A third fundamental feature of the Covenant
perspective, closely related to the first, is that the
Covenant relationship is voluntary. In the Hittite
covenant treaties the Hittite king voluntarily offers
the Covenant to the vassal and the vassal voluntarily
pledges allegiance. So in the Yahweh-Israel Covenant
Yahweh voluntarily elects Israel and Israel voluntarily
takes the loyalty oath. The E writer in Chapter 19 of
Exodus expresses this perspective when he says:

> Now therefore, _if_[16] you will obey my voice
> and keep my covenant, you shall be my
> possession among all peoples . . . And all

the people answered together and said,
'All that the LORD has spoken we will do.'
(Exodus 19:5, 8)

There are important implications in this perspective of the voluntary nature of the Covenant relation, implications which contributed greatly to the uniqueness of Israel's Covenant faith. For one thing, given its voluntary nature, the Covenant is contingent. Since Israel was not forced to accept it nor Yahweh to give it, Yahweh is not forced to bless Israel no matter what she does. Israel is free to break the Covenant and whenever such is the case, Yahweh is free to bring his judgment-justice against Israel. The "if" in the "if you will obey my voice" of the quote above clearly indicates the contingent character of the Covenant. Its existence depends on Israel's faithfulness.

Secondly, the voluntary nature of the Covenant relation provided the basis for the development of ethical monotheism in the religion of Israel. Yahweh was not understood to be tied to Israel by the natural ties of "descent," forces of nature, or geographical location, as so many other peoples understood their gods to be related to them. The factor of choice in the Yahweh-Israel Covenant means that Yahweh cannot be appropriately thought of as limited to any People because they are "descended" from him nor to any of the forces of nature or geographical territories. While he chooses a people for a special task or mission, he is the one creator God of all, totally good in his nature, seeking through the Covenant to make of Israel "a holy nation" and thereby to bring all peoples into a "kingdom" of righteousness and love. While the meaning and significance of ethical monotheism is expounded more fully in later reflection on the Covenant, it does seem to be the case that at least the root of this perspective is present already in the account of the covenant making at Sinai. This claim is supported by Norman Gottwald when he says:

In an age when gods were the natural
patrons of their respective lands, Moses
brought to Israel word about a God who
had chosen those who were not his own
by nature. Yahweh's choice of Israel
and Israel's choice of Yahweh impart to
Mosaic religion its distinctively
ethical elements . . . Karl Budde . . .

60

gave pointed expression to its significance: 'Israel's religion became ethical
because it rested on voluntary decision
which established an ethical relation
between the people and its God for all
time.'[17]

D. Finally, as already implied in the discussion
under C. above, the Covenant is viewed as confronting
Israel with responsibility. That is, Israel was chosen
not for privilege but for responsibility, for service.
In his account of the covenant making at Sinai, the E
writer puts it in the following way: "And you shall be
to me a kingdom of priests and a holy nation" (Exodus
19:6). Further, he indicates the basic ingredients of
Israel's Covenant obligation to be a holy nation in his
account of the Ten Commandments (Exodus 20:1-17).

Given their form and the context in which they
appear, it is obvious that the Ten Commandments do not
comprise a law code. There are, of course, many casuistic type law codes in the Old Testament. They contain specific conditional laws aimed at specific cases
and imposing specific penalties. The form of the
casuistic laws is: if (or whenever) such and such is
done, such and such shall be the penalty. An example
of casuistic law is the following: "If a man seduces
a virgin who is not betrothed, and lies with her, he
shall give the marriage present for her, and make her
his wife" (Exodus 22:16). Many scholars have pointed
out the striking similarities between many of the casuistic laws in the Old Testament and those in the
ancient law code of Hammurabi, King of Babylon about
1700 B.C.[18] The form of the Ten Commandments, however,
is quite different. It is apodictic and unconditional
(Thou shall or shall not), and, according to many
scholars, this feature is unique, demonstrating the
origin of the Ten Commandments within the context of
the Covenant faith. Thus the Decalogue (another designation for the Ten Commandments) is not to be regarded
as some sort of neutral or philosophical ethical code.
Rather it is only understood properly when it is seen
as representing the religious and moral terms of the
Covenant, the stipulations contained within the loyalty
oath which "vassal" Israel made to Yahweh.

Since the Decalogue represents the religious and
moral terms of the Covenant obligation, it is essential to understand its nature and scope in order to

61

adequately understand the Covenant. In what follows we shall present a brief analysis which is based largely on the perceptive discussion of the Decalogue by B. Davie Napier in his book, Song of the Vineyard.[19]

Napier divides the Decalogue into two pentalogues (5 Commandments each). The first pentalogue presents what is required of Israel if she is to maintain the integrity of her understanding of and relationship with Yahweh. It deals, so to speak, with the vertical dimension of the Covenant obligation. The second pentalogue presents what is required in the relationship within the community in order to maintain the integrity of the covenant community under Yahweh. It deals, so to speak, with the horizontal dimension of the Covenant obligation.

Traditionally Christians have taken "You shall have no other gods before me" and "You shall not make for yourself a graven image" (Exodus 20:3-4) as the first and second commandments. Following the Jewish tradition, Napier takes "I am the LORD your God who brought you out of the land of Egypt, out of the house of bondage" (Exodus 20:2) as the first commandment and combines the two verses quoted above into one commandment.

Thus, the first pentalogue is concerned with the following:

1. Yahweh's identity: "I am the LORD your God, etc." According to Napier this is a commandment and means, therefore, that Israel should "know and acknowledge Yahweh as him without whom you, Israel, would not exist . . . Only in Yahweh's identity are you an entity."[20]

2. Yahweh's nature: "You shall have no other gods . . . shall not make . . . a graven image." For Yahweh to condone belief in other gods and their representations would be to deny his very nature. He is God alone, unique.

3. Yahweh's name: "You shall not take the name of the LORD your God in vain" (V. 7). Just as with his identity and his nature, the integrity of Yahweh's name must be preserved. It is perhaps difficult for us today to grasp the full importance of this commandment, for we view a proper name as simply arbitrarily denoting

the bearer of the name. But among many ancient peoples the proper name was thought to contain the real essence of the one named. It was this perspective which was the basis for the magical practice of name incantation. Knowledge of the name and using it orally (generally in certain ritual formulae) brought one power over the god, or demon, or spirit who bore the name. Thus the prohibition against taking Yahweh's name "in vain" is a prohibition against magic, the attempt to control Yahweh. Covenant faithfulness requires that Israel submit to Yahweh's control instead of attempting to control him for her own purposes.

4.   Yahweh's day: "Remember the Sabbath day to keep it holy" (V. 8).   As Napier says: "To 'remember' and to 'keep' the day is to acknowledge Yahweh as creator-sustainer and to affirm that life continues under his reign and providence.   It is an act of trust."[21]   Further, it serves to remind Israel of her Covenant obligations not only to Yahweh and to the community but also the the larger community of all mankind.

5.   Yahweh's claim: "Honor your father and your mother" (V. 12).   Given the context of this commandment as the climax of the first pentalogue which specifies Israel's Covenant obligations to Yahweh in the "vertical" dimension, it would appear that honoring parents is a symbolic act for acknowledging Yahweh's claim on every life.   As Napier expresses it: "Life is his and therefore sacred and holy.   The holiness of life can be upheld only in honor of father and mother through whose joined life the divine image and animating breath are given."[22]

The second pentalogue which is concerned with maintaining the integrity of the community under Yahweh stipulates the following obligations:

6.   The integrity of life: "You shall not kill" (V. 13).   Basic to the life of a community is the integrity of each individual life.   Since Yahweh has a claim on each person's life, that life is to be held as sacred.   Killing violates the integrity of both the human community and the divine-human community.

7.   The integrity of person: "You shall not commit adultery" (V. 14).   The violation of person, as well as life, destroys community.   As clearly seen in the J account of creation, the sexual relationship is

viewed as a divine gift. Although it is not the source of sin, human beings may sin in this relationship as well as in others. The sexual partner may be regarded as an object by means of which to satisfy one's own desire, and thus the dignity or sacredness of the person of the sexual partner is violated. Adultery disrupts both the human and the divine-human community.

8. The integrity of property: "You shall not steal" (V. 15). Since we live in an economically affluent society, it is perhaps difficult for us to grasp the full importance of this commandment. To be understood adequately it must not be separated from the context in which it is integrally related to commandments 6 and 7. In the simple economy of the Israelites in the Wilderness wanderings, the loss of food and/or garment by theft could result not only in the owner's suffering but also even in his death. Thus to steal is as potentially as great a violation of community as murder or adultery.

9. The integrity of reputation: "You shall not bear false witness against your neighbor" (V. 16). While the language here suggests a prohibition against the giving of false testimony in court, the intention would appear to be to prohibit all statements concerning the neighbor which would violate his reputation. Such violation of the integrity of the neighbor's reputation violates both the human and the divine-human community.

10. The integrity of status: "You shall not covet your neighbor's house" (V. 17). The word "house" is used here in a very inclusive sense. It means all that is the neighbor's, his full status. The remarkable emphasis on inner intention and attitude in this last commandment makes of it an appropriate sum and climax of the second pentalogue and indeed of the whole Decalogue. Ultimately genuine community, both the human and the divine-human, depends upon the purity of the inner intentions, motives, and attitudes. As Napier says: "If contemplation is covetous, community is already violated and all possibility of mutuality is crushed."[23]

So the Decalogue succinctly summarizes the religious and moral stipulations which are to provide guidance for Israel concerning the obligation she has assumed in accepting Yahweh's gift of the Covenant.

The importance of the Decalogue in the life of ancient Israel, therefore, can hardly be overemphasized.

IV. The Covenant and The Great Prophets of Israel

The persons and the messages of the prophets were accorded a role of prime importance in the literature and tradition of Israel. One item of evidence supporting this claim is found in the very arrangement of the Hebrew canon of Scripture, the Tanak. In the threefold division of the Tanak (Torah, Prophets, and Writings) the category of the Prophets is placed at the center and this category is viewed as being more inclusive than it is regarded to be by Christians. That is, the Books of Joshua, Judges, Samuel, and Kings, designated as books of history by Christians, are classified as the "Former Prophets" in the Hebrew Scriptures. This reflects the historical fact that the Deuteronomic writers who prepared the historical account contained in these books had been influenced by the message of the prophets prior to their own time. The rest of the prophets are classified as "Latter Prophets" and this classification includes Isaiah, Jeremiah, Ezekiel, and the twelve prophets from Hosea to Malachi.

Since the prophets played such an important part in the development of Israel's traditions and literature, it is absolutely essential that we obtain a clear understanding of the prophets' role and message if we are to gain an adequate understanding of the Old Testament. First of all, we must be clear about the meaning of the word "prophet" as it is used in the Old Testament.

To understand the meaning or signification of the Old Testament usage of the term "prophet" (Nabi), we must eliminate from our thinking the signification of this term in the common everyday usage today. In our common usage, the term means primarily one who predicts the future. Thus we may speak of the weather forecaster on the evening news as a weather prophet. We may say of Jean Dixon whenever she claims to be revealing something about the future destiny of some outstanding leader that she is uttering a prophecy. We may designate as prophets those religious people who claim that having gazed into God's crystal ball they are able to predict the shape of things to come. But this is not the meaning of the Hebrew term Nabi. It means "one who is called" or "one who announces" or both. That is, the prophet is one who is called by God to be his spokesman to the contemporary situation in which the prophet finds himself. He is one who speaks forth for God and thus is the "mouth" of God. In the account of Yahweh's call of Moses, Yahweh is represented as saying, "Now therefore go and I will be with your mouth and teach you what you shall speak" (Exodus 4:12). Of Aaron, Moses' brother, it is said, "He shall be a mouth (Nabi) for you" (Exodus 4:16). The prophet, then, is a forthteller, not a foreteller. As Bernard W. Anderson says:

> Our English word comes to us from the Greek word (Prophētēs), which literally means one who speaks for another, especially for the gods. And this Greek word, in turn, is a fairly accurate way to render the Hebrew 'nabi' which refers to one who communicates the divine will.[24]

Not only must we be clear about the meaning of the word "prophet" if we are to understand the role and message of Israel's great prophets but also we must be aware of the general religious, social, and political conditions of the times during which the great prophets lived. It is impossible here for us to describe these conditions in detail but perhaps a very brief and general sketch will prove helpful as a basis for our summary of the prophets' message which is to follow.

We have referred several times in the sections above to the Sinai Covenant and the wilderness wanderings. Israel's culture during this time was semi-nomadic. While there are accounts in Numbers of some rebellion on Israel's part, it was surely the case that in this historical and geographical setting which required equality and cooperation in order to survive there were not as many nor powerful temptations to be disobedient to the Covenant as there were later on, after the settlement into Canaan and the development of the monarchy. The inhabitants of the land of Canaan into which Israel came were a settled agricultural and trading people organized politically in small city states having "petty" kings. With the entrance into Canaan and during subsequent centuries, Israel's covenant faith was put to the severest test by three powerful temptations having their roots in the old Canaanite culture, namely the temptations of fertility cult, class structure, and power politics.

66

It is evident from passages in the Book of Judges[25] and from archaeological discoveries[26] that the religion of the Canaanites was largely a polytheistic and close to nature fertility cult. Myths concerning the activities of certain fertility gods had a large role to play in this cult. There was Baal, the god of rain and fertility, the warrior goddess Anath (Asherah or Ashtoreth in the Old Testament), Baal's consort-sister, and Mot, the god of summer drought. Mot kills Baal and takes him to the underworld. Because of her great passion for Baal, Anath searches for him and, finding him in the possession of Mot, kills Mot, brings Baal back to earth where he is resurrected and the lovers are reunited. Once again fertility has returned to earth, animals, and human beings. The reunion of Baal and Anath is then celebrated in rites of sacred prostitution. Indeed, these rites were apparently regarded as essential in order that the lovers, Baal and Anath, be motivated by these rites of "sympathetic" magic to engage in sexual intercourse so that fertility returns to the earth.

Since the fertility cult attempts to satisfy two fundamental drives, sex and hunger, it is understandable why Israel would be powerfully tempted by this cult and sometimes yield to this temptation. Apparently this yielding might take one or more of several forms. Yahweh might be thought of as an almighty Baal, a lord of nature rather than of history. Sometimes there were attempts to combine the worship of Yahweh and of Baal in which Yahweh was called upon in times of great national emergencies while Baal was called upon to provide the necessities for everyday living. Even Solomon apparently engaged in such religious syncretism (I Kings 3, 11). Finally, the worship of Yahweh might at times be abandoned as is suggested in the Book of Judges when the writer says:

> And the people of Israel did what was evil
> in the sight of the LORD and served the
> Baals; and they forsook the LORD, the God
> of their fathers who had brought them out
> of the land of Egypt; they went after
> other gods . . . and served the Baals and
> Ashtaroth. (Judges 2:11-13)

Thus the fertility cult posed a very serious threat to the purity of the Covenant faith throughout the early centuries of Israel's existence as a Covenant people.

It should be obvious from the important role played by the fertility cults in Canaanite culture that the economy of this culture was based largely on agriculture. Such an economy made it possible for a class structure to develop in the society. Some of the farmers were able to produce more than they needed for their own families and so obtained resources which enabled them to enlarge their land holdings. Merchants were needed to provide markets for goods and products. Thus a social pyramid developed with the peasants at the bottom, land holders and merchants in the middle, and the princes of the Canaanite city-states at the top. Especially with the development of the monarchy, Israelite society took on a similar class structure with the exception that there was one king with his court at the top of the social pyramid instead of several princes over city-states. Further, with the development of the monarchy, Israel was tempted to engage in the power politics "games" of the ancient Near Eastern nations, to become like the other nations. Just as the fertility cult threatened the integrity of Yahweh, so the class structure and the power politics threatened the integrity of the Covenant community. There was a real danger that the Covenant faith would be lost from the scene of history, and this might have happened had it not been for the appearance of the great prophets. At the very least, it can be said that the prophets more than any group such as priests or kings were responsible for preserving the purity of the Covenant faith for posterity.

It is not possible here to discuss fully the prophetic movement in ancient Israel nor to describe the full scope of the message of each of the great "classical" prophets[27] (Amos, 750 B.C.; Hosea, 745 B.C.; Isaiah, 740-700 B.C.; Micah, 722-701 B.C.; Jeremiah, 626-587 B.C.; Ezekiel 593-573 B.C.; II Isaiah, 540 B.C.). Instead we shall attempt a brief summary of classical prophetism as a whole. As with our discussion of the Decalogue so also this summary of the prophets' message owes much to B. Davie Napier's discussion of the prophets in his book, Song of the Vineyard.[28] According to Napier, the following five concepts were basic in the prophets' perspective and message.

A. Word and Symbol: "Thus Says Yahweh"

As we have seen in Section III above, Israel in accepting the Covenant pledged to do "all that Yahweh has spoken" (Exodus 19:8). Whenever Yahweh acted in history, in deliverance or in judgment, this action was accompanied by his word of revelation. Word and action were inseparably linked. Indeed, the Word itself was thought "to be charged with the power of performance."[29]

It is rather difficult for us today to fully understand this perspective. Given our recent history we tend to regard "talk as cheap." Some would even claim that language in all its forms, and especially when used orally, obscures instead of disclosing truth. Seldom is it recognized that it is by their use of language that human beings exercise some degree of power in the world, either for good or evil.

The perspective held by most ancient peoples was quite different. The uttered word, especially the word or words uttered by consecrated persons, was thought to carry great power. It was regarded as an entity containing the power to bring to pass its content. Thus when the prophet proclaimed "Thus says Yahweh" and then proceeded to deliver an oracle of judgment against the king, he was considered to have sealed the doom of the king and thus to have committed treason (Amos 7:10-11). Not only the spoken word, but also the symbolic acts of the prophets were regarded as charged with the power of performance. So Isaiah is said to have walked for three years through the streets of Jerusalem naked and barefoot (Isaiah 20) and Jeremiah to have worn an ox yoke over his shoulders (Jeremiah 27-28) indicating thereby a captivity to a foreign power.

It may be that this view of the power of the Word had its beginnings in early primitive magic. Whatever its source, the perspective of the prophets is absolutely without any trace of magic. Never is the Word used in the attempt to coerce Yahweh. Rather just the opposite is the case. The Word of Yahweh coerces the prophet. As Napier says:

> In relationship to the prophet himself and his call, we witness the phenomenon of the psychology of captivity--a self-consciousness in vocation characterized by feelings of having been overpowered by the Word of Yahweh.[30]

The feeling of having been overpowered by the Word of

Yahweh is evident throughout the messages of the prophets and accounts for the continual use of "Thus says
Yahweh" to introduce their oracles. It is especially
striking in several narratives recounting the prophets'
call to their prophetic ministry (Amos 7:15, Isaiah 6,
Ezekiel 1, Jeremiah 1). Perhaps the most graphic
illustration of "the psychology of captivity" is to be
found in the words of Jeremiah. In his account of Yahweh's calling him to be prophet, Jeremiah says:

> 'Before I formed you in the womb I knew you,
> And before you were born I consecrated you;
> I appointed you a prophet to the nations.'
>
> Then I said, 'Ah, Lord God! Behold, I do
>   not know how to
> speak, for I am only a youth.' But the
>   LORD said to me,
>
> 'Do not say, "I am only a youth;"
> for to all to whom I send you you shall go,
> And whatever I command you you shall
>   speak . . .'
>
> Then the LORD put forth his hand and touched
>   my mouth;
> And the LORD said to me, 'Behold, I have
>   put my words in your mouth.'
> (Jeremiah 1:5-9)

Later, having experienced bitter opposition from family,
friends, and other people, Jeremiah desired to cease
proclaiming the word of Yahweh but found that he could
not. Concerning this he said:

> If I say, 'I will not mention him or speak
> any more in his name,' there is in my
> heart as it were a burning fire shut up in
> my bones, and I am weary with holding it
> in and I cannot. (Jeremiah 20:9)

B. Election and Covenant

While the prophets seldom use the Hebrew word for
covenant, berith, it is the case that the Covenant
faith is the basic and essential ingredient of the entire prophetic message. Probably they refrained from
using the term berith because it had become associated
in the thinking of some of their contemporaries with

70

the idea that Israel was specially favored by Yahweh, that the Covenant meant privilege instead of responsibility. Yet they used many figures of speech such as son (Hosea 11:1, Isaiah 1:4), bride or wife (Hosea 2, Jeremiah 1:2), and servant (Isaiah 49:3) to designate the Covenant relationship with Yahweh. Everywhere in the message of the prophets, the concept of Covenant is assumed and is fundamental in their interpretation of Israel's historical existence. According to Napier:

> If the prophets speak on behalf of social and economic justice, they do not preach a general abstract morality, but pointedly and specifically proclaim an election/ covenant ethic, the sense of which is something like this: you shall refrain from this practice, or you shall do thus-and-so, because I am Yahweh who brought you up out of Egypt (election) and you are a people voluntarily committed in return to the performance of my righteous will (covenant).[31]

C. Rebellion and Judgment

We have seen that Israel's covenant responsibility required her to be a "holy nation" and that this meant in the terms of the Decalogue that she maintain the integrity of Yahweh and the integrity of the Covenant community under Yahweh. But time and again Israel went after the Baals (the fertility cult), permitted social injustices to arise in the community, and made alliances with foreign kings which meant that the gods of these kings would be recognized and often worshipped even in the central state shrine, the temple in Jerusalem. In all of this the prophets saw a shocking betrayal of Israel's Covenant faith, a rebellion against Yahweh.

Often the prophets speak of Israel's rebellion and Yahweh's judgment in terms of a Covenant lawsuit (most clearly described in Micah 6:1-8, but also suggested in Amos 3:2, 13; Hosea 4:1-3; Isaiah 1:13; Jeremiah 2:9). In this image of the lawsuit, Yahweh is pictured as both judge and prosecuting attorney. He charges Israel with Covenant faithlessness, presents the evidence in support of the charge (worship of foreign gods and social, economic and political injustices), and as judge passes sentence upon the accused.

71

With stunning and shocking (often coarse) language the prophets present the charge and evidence of Covenant faithlessness. Israel is pictured as a rebellious son (Isaiah 1:4; Hosea 11:2) or as a harlot (Hosea 2; Ezekiel 23; Jeremiah 3:8) or as a "people laden with iniquity" (Isaiah 1:4). Such a charge is then supported by numerous references to personal immoralities and to the social, economic, and political injustices being committed in the community of their own times. The prophets' Catalogue of Israel's sins include such things as acts of idolatry (Amos 5:26; Hosea 11:2; Isaiah 2:8; Jeremiah 7:18), oppression of the poor (Amos 2:7; Isaiah 3:14-15), corruption of judges (Amos 2:6; Isaiah 1:23), luxurious living and debauchery (Amos 4:1, 6:4-7; Isaiah 3:16-24, 5:11-12), nationalistic pride and confidence in military forces (Amos 6:8; Hosea 10:13; Isaiah 2:7), and moral blindness and skepticism (Isaiah 5:19-20).[32]

An example of a succinctly described covenant lawsuit is to be found in the Book of Hosea:

> Hear the word of the LORD, O people of Israel;
> for the LORD has a controversy with the
>   inhabitants of the land.
> There is no faithfulness or kindness, and no
>   knowledge of God in the land;
> there is swearing, lying, killing, stealing,
>   and committing adultery;
> they break all bounds and murder follows
>   murder.
> Therefore the land mourns, and all who dwell
>   in it languish,
> and also the beasts of the field, and the
>   birds of the air;
> and even the fish of the sea are taken away.
> (Hosea 4:1-3)

Since the Hebrew word translated "controversy" is a technical term designating a charge or complaint made in a law court, this passage obviously employs the imagery of a Covenant lawsuit. It refers implicitly to social sins and explicitly to personal immoralities as evidence for the charge of Covenant faithlessness. Furthermore, the passage contains two other concepts which must be carefully noted.

First, there is present here, at least implicitly, the ancient perspective of society as a "corporate personality,"[33] the one in the many and the many in the one. Unlike the modern perspective in Western society, there was no concept of an atomic individual. The individual and/or particular groups within the nation were regarded as accountable for the sins of even a few individuals within the nation. Thus the charge of the prophets was against all Israel whether everyone was directly guilty or not. They viewed the sins of even some members of the community as infecting the entire community.

Secondly, the judgment of Yahweh is coming against the community or nation. Often the word of Yahweh's judgment is introduced in the prophet's oracles with a threatening "therefore," and the judgment is described with numerous figures such as the "land mourning" or "They shall return to the land of Egypt" (Hosea 11:5). Generally, the agent of Yahweh's judgment is identified as some conquering power such as the Assyrians or the Babylonians. Even though they are unaware of it, Yahweh is using these nations to bring his judgment against Israel. These foes will devastate the nation. Only a remnant will remain.

It must not be thought that the prophets were sadistic Cassandras who enjoyed their messages of woe. It was with great agony of soul that they proclaimed the message of Yahweh's judgment upon their own people. As they saw it, the callousness and indifference of their contemporaries with respect to the blatant violations of Covenant faithfulness was bringing against them the stringent judgment of Yahweh so as to shock them out of their blindness and rebellion. Perhaps even the message of judgment might accomplish this end. Since Yahweh was merciful and forgiving, the judgment might be averted if Israel would repent and turn to Covenant faithfulness. While such was possible in principle, the propets as practical realists did not anticipate such a change on Israel's part and thought that the judgment must run its course in order that Israel be made fully aware of the extent of her rebellion.

Furthermore, given the sense of corporate personality in ancient Israel, the one in the many and the many in the one, the prophets never regarded themselves as proclaiming their message of judgment from a standpoint apart from the community. As Napier expresses it:

The prophets became not only executioners

73

of Israel but at once their own executioners. In the destructive Word and
Symbol directed at the people they are
themselves destroyed in profoundly realistic psychological meaning.[34]

Surely this contributes to the obvious agony and pathos
with which the prophets proclaim their message of judgment. There is pathos not only for themselves but also
for Israel and for Yahweh. It is not that Yahweh desires to discipline Israel but that, like the perfect
parent, he must do so for the sake of the wayward son.
And, like the perfect parent, such punishment brings
agony to Yahweh himself.

Support for this claim that the prophets viewed
Yahweh's judgment as disciplinary and not retributive
is found even in the very meaning of the Hebrew word
translated as "judgment." According to Napier:

> The Hebrew root shaphat, "to judge," con-
> veys an act by which wrong is righted by
> punishment of the aggressor, by restitu-
> tion to the victim, or by both. Offenders
> of all sorts are to be judged, but so are
> the victims of abuse and misfortune (e.g.,
> Isaiah 1:17). Thus, judgment is the reali-
> zation of justice . . . Prophetism always
> intends to and wants to proclaim judgment
> in the full sense of justice--the setting
> right of the woefully wrong, the reorder-
> ing of that which is tragically awry--so
> that the very objects of judgment are
> restored.[35]

D. Compassion and Redemption

Since for the prophets Yahweh's judgment is not a
vindictive end in itself but wrung out of his compas-
sionate love, they look beyond the judgment in the
confidence that Yahweh will act again for the deliverance and redemption of Israel. It was out of Yahweh's
steadfast love (hesed) that the covenant community,
Israel, was brought into existence. It is out of his
hesed that Israel is judged. And it is out of his
hesed that Israel will be redeemed and the Covenant
itself transformed. No one expressed this any more
vividly than did the great unknown prophet, usually
called II Isaiah, who, living near the end of the

74

Babylonian captivity, proclaimed in the following words
that Yahweh's deliverance is at hand:

> For the mountains may depart and the hills
>   be removed,
> but my steadfast love (hesed) shall not
>   depart from you,
> And my Covenant of peace shall not be removed
> says the LORD, who has compassion on you
> (Isaiah 54:10)
> And the ransomed of the LORD shall return,
> and come to Zion with singing;
> everlasting joy shall be upon their heads;
> They shall obtain joy and gladness,
> and sorrow and sighing shall flee away.
> (Isaiah 51:11)

E. Universal Consummation

We have seen in Section II of this chapter that
the early J writer affirmed that Yahweh's purpose in
covenanting with Israel was that in Abraham/Israel
all the nations of the earth shall be blessed (Genesis
12:3). This emphasis that the Covenant with Israel is
intended by Yahweh to be the means through which he
will realize his ultimate goal of bringing all peoples
into the divine-human fellowship is found also in the
prophets. According to Napier:

> The notion of the historical redemption of
> Israel alone was never able to contain the
> prophetic faith or answer prophetism's
> pressing questions about the meaning of
> Israel's existence. Even, sometimes, where
> the terms are of Israel's redemption, the
> prophetic intensity of feeling and pressure
> of conviction mark the intent to be uni-
> versal . . . The prophetic disposition and
> intention embraces all men.[36]

This prophetic understanding of the universal intent
of the Covenant is explicitly expressed in several
passages in the writings assigned to the prophets.
Among the most beautiful are the following.

> It is too light a thing that you should be
> my servant to raise up the tribes of Jacob
> and to restore the preserved of Israel;
> I will give you as a light to the nations,

75

> that my salvation may reach to the end of
> the earth. (Isaiah 49:6)
> They shall not hurt or destroy in all my
> holy mountain; for the earth shall be full
> of the knowledge of the LORD as the waters
> cover the sea. (Isaiah 11:9)

In this brief summary of the prophets' perspective
we have seen that they felt compelled to proclaim the
Word of Yahweh and that this Word cannot but accomplish
Yahweh's purpose. Basic to the Word is Yahweh's election of Israel as his Covenant community. But Israel
rebelled and so Yahweh must discipline Israel for her
sake. Beyond the judgment, however, is Yahweh's compas-
sionate redemption of Israel. A redeemed Israel will
fulfill her covenant responsibility such that she shall
be a "light to the nations" and Yahweh's salvation
shall "reach to the end of the earth" in universal consummation.

V.   Later Perspectives and Literature

In the centuries following the Babylonian exile,
there were many important developments in the religion,
life, and literature of Israel. There was the return
from exile, the rebuilding of Jerusalem and the temple,
the rule of Persian kings followed by the Greek descended Ptolemies of Egypt and Seleucids of Syria, and
finally the brief period of independence prior to the
Roman domination. There was the appearance of numerous
written works including such canonical books (the Jewish Canon) as Chronicles, Ezra, Nehemiah, Ruth, Jonah,
Esther, Psalms, Wisdom Literature (Proverbs, Ecclesiastes, Job), and apocalyptic[37] literature (Daniel), and
non-canonical wisdom and apocalyptic writings. There
was the appearance of the religious institution known
as the synagogue (the word literally means "gather
together"). Probably having originated during the
Babylonian captivity[38] when the temple lay in ruins,
the synagogue was a place of worship, prayer, and study
but not of sacrifice. It did not require a consecrated
priesthood but could be established wherever there were
ten male Jews. There was the appearance of certain
socio-religious groupings or parties such as the Pharisees who accepted the oral interpretations of the Torah
as being as authoritative as the Torah-book itself, the
Sadducees who accepted only what was written in the
Torah-book, and the Essenes who regarded themselves as
the true Israel preparing for that great event, the end

of the age. Neither the synagogue nor these groups are explicitly mentioned in the Old Testament but, nevertheless, were very important in the religious life of Israel in the late post-exilic period.[39]

It is not possible here to discuss fully all the developments in post-exilic Judaism. Instead, we shall give attention to three important issues and summarize briefly the major responses to these issues.

One such issue was the question as to whether or not the purity of the Covenant community required racial exclusivism. As we have seen, religious syncretism had been a threat to the purity of the Covenant faith in previous centuries. This was even more the case during the exile in Babylon and the post-exilic period when Judah was no longer an independent nation but was a province in subjection to foreign powers. In such a situation there were powerful temptations to forget the heritage of the Covenant faith or to attempt to mix it with elements from foreign religions. Intermarriage tended to breed such syncretism and so it seemed to some that survival of the Covenant faith depended upon maintaining a strict racial purity in the community. In the late fifth and early fourth centuries B.C. of the post-exilic period, Nehemiah and Ezra insisted that membership in the community was determined by birth. Therefore they placed a ban on intermarriage and Ezra went so far as to require that those males who had foreign wives must divorce them. Such extreme measures were not the result of a narrow nationalism or racialism but rather of a passionate loyalty to the Covenant faith.

Yet during this same period there were protests against this exclusivism. According to many scholars, the Books of Ruth and Jonah were written during this time and contain such protests. The delightful story of Ruth concludes with Ruth, who was not Jewish but a Moabitess, as the great grandmother of King David, indicating thereby that God's greatest favor was bestowed upon Israel through a mixed marriage. The humorous story of Jonah concludes with all the inhabitants of the wicked pagan city Nineveh repenting and turning to God as a result of Jonah's preaching.[40]

In the lengthy Book of the Psalms, compiled during the post-exilic period, both emphases are to be found. Some Psalms express an exclusivism (Psalm 9, for

77

example) while others (Psalm 96) assert that the LORD's glory and salvation are to be declared among the nations. So while there were exclusivistic tendencies there were also tendencies other than narrow exclusivism at work in post-exilic Judaism.

Another issue of importance in post-exilic Judaism was the question: does the Covenant, the divine-human fellowship, require strict observance of Torah (both written and oral) or may it be based simply on repentance resulting in a "clean heart" and a "right spirit" (Psalm 51:10)? The Book of Ezra and some of the Psalms (1, 119) emphasize the former while Jonah and other Psalms (51) emphasize the latter. It must not be thought that those who emphasized obedience to the law were narrow-minded legalists. In most cases such obedience is infused with a spirit of devotion and joy. There is no strict dichotomy between emphasis upon obedience to the law and emphasis upon repentance. Indeed, in most cases they are mixed such that it is a matter of degree of emphasis. However there are these differences in emphasis and in the case of the Book of Jonah the inhabitants of Nineveh are accepted by God simply on the basis of their repentance. Further, the Book of Job, among other things, seems to suggest that a moralistic view of salvation is totally inadequate. Job is pictured as the ideally righteous man, and yet this does not guarantee a right relation with God nor protection from suffering as his three "orthodox" friends suppose. Instead, salvation is dependent solely on divine grace.[41]

A third issue which received attention in post-exilic Judaism had to do with the question as to when the conflicts of history would be over and God's universal reign become actual in the world. As we have seen, the prophets looked forward with hope to a universal consummation. Yet for centuries Israel had been under the domination of foreign empires and history remained a scene of conflict. Given this situation there were those who became pessimistic concerning the possibility of human beings ending this conflict. Possibly influenced by Persian Zoroastrianism, they viewed the present age as under the control of an evil power (being) or powers who could be defeated only by a direct intervention of God with supernatural power. Just when this great event, the eschaton, would occur was the subject of much speculation and is generally designated as apocalyptic (uncover the hidden).

While apocalyptic thinking is more fully expressed in rather late non-canonical writings (in the so-called intertestemental period), the canonical Book of Daniel contains apocalyptic emphases.

Not everyone, of course, accepted this apocalyptic thinking. There were those who held that the universal consummation would come about by means of the reign of a righteous human king, a descendent of the house of David who would be adopted by God to accomplish his purposes, and this would be done without a supernatural and cataclysmic upheaval in nature or history. Others, such as the Sadducees in the very late post-exilic period, rejected outright any type of eschatology. Still others were simply silent on this issue. So the writers of the Wisdom literature (Proverbs, Ecclesiastes, Job) deal with the problems and issues which confront individuals in the concrete affairs of life and have little or nothing to say about eschatology. Just as with the other two issues, there were different views in post-exilic Judaism with respect to eschatology.

In concluding this chapter, it is important to emphasize again that in spite of the wide variety of literature and the wide range of historical events recounted in the Old Testament, there is, nevertheless, an underlying and fundamental unity. By way of an analogy, it might be said that the Old Testament (indeed, the entire Bible) resembles a historical drama.[42] God is both the director and the chief actor. That is, the Old Testament is God-centered, and this in itself provides it with a certain unity. But beyond this, there is a "dramatic plot" which underlies all the variety of different kinds of literature, historical situations, and theological expressions and binds them together in a fundamental unity. The plot moves from creation to eschaton. In between is the tragedy occasioned by man's sin, God's election of Israel to be his covenant people through whom he will bless all mankind, Israel's rebellion and God's judgment, his redemption of Israel, and ultimately his redemption of all mankind. In spite of the variety of understandings expressed concerning these particular items contained in the plot (as in the post-exilic period), it is the case, nevertheless, that the main thrust of the plot is always "the working out of God's purpose in spite of all efforts to oppose it."[43]

[1] According to Samuel Sandmel, _Judaism and Christian Beginnings_ (Oxford University Press, 1978), p. 144, "wherever there was a synagogue, there was also a school."

[2] Of necessity, much of importance and interest in the Old Testament must be omitted in our discussion. There are a large number of good introductory textbooks on the Old Testament. Authors and titles of a number of these books are listed in the Suggestions For Further Reading. The student will find it helpful to read one of these in order to supplement the discussion in this chapter.

[3] cf. Walter Harrelson, _Interpreting the Old Testament_ (Holt, Rinehart and Winston, Inc., 1964), Part One, pp. 25-104; Appendix, 487-492.

[4] As indicated in Chapter II, evidence for the J source is the use of the divine name Yahweh in contrast to Elohim in the pre-Mosaic narratives in Genesis and that in the passages in Genesis where Yahweh is the divine name there is a distinctive literary style and characteristic words and expressions used different from those where Elohim is used.

[5] cf. Bernhard W. Anderson, _Understanding the Old Testament_, Third Edition (Prentice-Hall, 1975), Chapter 7, pp. 198-225.

[6] The term "Israel" means literally "may God rule." It is often used in the Old Testament to designate the entire covenant community. However, with the division of Solomon's kingdom into two nations, the term "Israel" is often used as the name for the Northern Kingdom distinguishing it from Judah, the Southern Kingdom. The reader of the Bible, by noting the context of any passage in which the term "Israel" appears, can determine which one of these two meanings the term has in the passage. Here, of course, we are using the term in its first and primary sense, that is, as a designation for a whole people having a special relationship with the God Yahweh.

[7] The Covenant is a central theme not only of the J epic but also of the entire Old Testament. This theme will be discussed more fully in Section III below.

[8] Bernhard W. Anderson, _op. cit._, p. 206.

[9] The fruit of the tree does not symbolize the human sex drive, but human pretension or egocentricity, as Genesis 3:22 clearly indicates. Apparently the J writer associated the "Tree of Knowledge" with knowing good and evil destinies; that is, with divination, witchcraft, etc., which had been a feature in Canaanite culture, which was still manifest in his own day, and which he regarded as a rebellion against Yahweh, the God of the Covenant.

[10] In J's stories about the expulsion from the Garden, Cain and Abel, Noah and the flood, and the tower of Babel, Yahweh is pictured as acting in judgment because of man's sin but also as performing merciful acts precisely for those against whom he has directed his judgment.

[11] In Exodus 3:15 the E writer introduces the name Yahweh which he uses in the remainder of his writing. However, due to his distinctive literary style and characteristic words and expressions, his source can be distinguished from the other sources in the remainder of the Pentateuch.

[12] Bernhard W. Anderson, op. cit., p. 269.

[13] The P writer concludes his account of creation in Genesis, Chapter I, with a statement about the Sabbath. For him this day of rest and worship was as old as creation itself.

[14] Bernhard W. Anderson, op. cit., p. 425.

[15] Bernhard W. Anderson, Ibid., p. 89.

[16] The italics are mine.

[17] Norman K. Gottwald, A Light to the Nations (Harper and Brothers, 1959), p. 132. The quotation from Karl Budde is from Religion of Israel to the Exile (Putnam, 1939), p. 38.

[18] cf. James B. Pritchard (ed.), The Ancient Near East, Vol. I (Princeton University Press, 1958), pp. 138-167.

[19] Harper and Brothers, 1962, pp. 74-82.

[20] Ibid., p. 75.

[21] Ibid., p. 78.

[22] Ibid., p. 79.

[23] Ibid., p. 81.

24 Bernhard W. Anderson, op. cit., p. 226.

25 cf. Judges 2:11-13; 3:7; 6:25-32.

26 Berhard W. Anderson, op. cit., pp. 139-147. Here Anderson describes the fertility cults of the Ancient Near East including the myths and rituals of the fertility gods contained in the Ras Shamra tablets discovered in 1929 on the coast of northern Syria.

27 My discussion of the prophets should be supplemented by reading one or more of the following: Bernhard W. Anderson, op. cit., pp. 259-470, J. Philip Hyatt, Prophetic Religion (Abingdon-Cokesbury, 1947), Stephen Winward, A Guide To The Prophets (John Knox Press, 1969), Abraham J. Heschel, The Prophets (Harper and Row, 1963), Martin Buber, The Prophetic Faith (Harper Torchbook, 1960), Norman K. Gottwald, All the Kingdoms of the Earth (Harper and Row, 1965).

28 B. Davie Napier, Song of the Vineyard (Harper and Brothers, 1962), pp. 296-305.

29 Ibid., p. 297.

30 Ibid.

31 Ibid., pp. 298-299.

32 This list is not exhaustive but simply an illustration of the types of sins which the prophets regarded as evidence of Covenant faithlessness. Further, the Scripture references cited are only a sample. Many more could be given.

33 B. Davie Napier, op. cit., p. 297.

34 Ibid., pp. 297-298.

35 Ibid., pp. 299-301.

36 Ibid., p. 304.

37 The term "apocalyptic" comes from the Greek word "apocalypse" which means "revelation" or "disclosure." Thus, apocalyptic literature contains purported "disclosures" concerning the end of the age or of history which it is thought will occur in the future by virtue of a supernational and cataclysmic intervention in the life of the world.

38 cf. Ezekiel 33:30-31. This passage says that the exiles gathered before Ezekiel to hear his message.

[39] In our discussion of the emergence of Rabbinic Judaism in Chapter V more attention will be given to these groups.

[40] Nineveh was the capital of the Assyrian empire which had dealt so harshly with the Israelites in the seventh century B.C., several centuries before Jonah was written. It had become the symbol of wickedness, paganism, and foreign oppression.

[41] cf. Samuel Terrien, "Introduction to Job," The Interpreter's Bible, Vol. 3 (Abingdon Press, 1954), pp. 877-905.

[42] cf. Bernhard W. Anderson, The Unfolding Drama of the Bible (Association Press, 1953), especially pp. 9-13.

[43] Ibid., p. 12.

SUGGESTIONS FOR FURTHER READING

Anderson, Bernhard W. Rediscovering the Bible, Association Press, 1951.

Anderson, Bernhard W. The Unfolding Drama of the Bible, Association Press, 1953.

Anderson, Bernhard W. Understanding the Old Testament, Third Edition, Prentice-Hall, 1975.

Beebe, H. Keith. The Old Testament, Dickenson Publishing Company, 1970.

Clements, Ronald E. Old Testament Theology, John Knox Press, 1979.

Efird, James M. These Things Are Written, John Knox Press, 1978.

Gottwald, Norman K. A Light to the Nations, Harper and Brothers, 1959.

Harrelson, Walter. Interpreting the Old Testament, Holt, Rinehart and Winston, Inc., 1964.

Hyatt, J. Philip. The Heritage of Biblical Faith, The Bethany Press, 1964.

Kuntz, J. Kenneth. The People of Ancient Israel, Harper and Row, 1974.

McCarthy, Dennis J., S. J. Kings and Prophets, The Bruce Publishing Company, 1968.

Napier, B. Davie. Song of the Vineyard, Harper and Brothers, 1962.

Sandmel, Samuel. The Hebrew Scriptures, Alfred A. Knopf, Inc., 1963.

The Interpreter's Bible, Vol. I. "General Articles on the Old Testament," Abingdon Press, 1952.

THE NEW TESTAMENT

The New Testament is much shorter than the Old Testament in terms of both length and time-span covered. It contains twenty-seven brief books, and its history covers only about a century and a half. Yet it is of central significance for the Christian faith, for it records events and perspectives which are of crucial and enduring importance for Christians. This does not mean, of course, that the Old Testament is of no importance for, as we have seen in Chapter III, it is an integral part of the Christian canon of Scripture. The New Testament presupposes the Old Testament and cannot be understood adequately without an understanding of the Old Testament. There is continuity as well as discontinuity between the Old and New Testaments. Even though the language may be different, there is the continuity of the covenant theme. The words "New Testament" mean literally New Covenant. So the covenant theme continues. But it is the <u>new</u> covenant and hence the discontinuity. The basic <u>theme</u> of the New Testament is that in Jesus Christ God had acted decisively for the redemption of mankind so that the New Age, the New Covenant, had begun to break into the present situation. Those who experience this redemption, Jews and Gentiles, form the community of the new covenant, the church, through whom God will accomplish his purposes for the world. It is the same God with the same purposes who again has acted in history but in so doing has employed means of action which in some respects are similar and yet in other respects are different from the old.

The brief discussion of the New Testament in this chapter[1] will focus on the following points:

I.   The New Testament writings, their composition and characteristics;

II.   The ministry and message of Jesus;

III.   The Apostle Paul's understanding of the Christian faith; and

IV.   Perspectives in the Johannine and other New Testament literature.

I. The New Testament Writings: Their Composition and Characteristics

An important aide to the understanding of the New Testament is a knowledge of approximately when the various books it contains were written. Such knowledge permits us to place the authors in their own actual historical situations and thus to better ascertain what purposes they had in writing. According to most New Testament scholars, the letters of the Apostle Paul are the earliest writings in the New Testament. Written between 50-62 A.D., Paul's letters, with the exception of Philemon, were addressed to churches. The letters in the New Testament which are generally attributed to Paul are I and II Thessalonians, Galatians, I and II Corinthians, Romans, Colossians, Philemon, Ephesians,[2] and Philippians. The next New Testament writing in chronological sequence is the Gospel of Mark, probably written around 65-70 A.D. Mark is followed by the Gospel of Matthew and Luke-Acts which were probably written sometime between 80-90 A.D. The Pastoral Letters (I and II Timothy, Titus), I Peter, Hebrews, James, Revelation, and the Johannine literature (the Gospel of John; I, II, III John) were probably written between 90-110 A.D. The latest works in the New Testament are Jude and II Peter, probably written between 130-150 A.D.

Already it is evident that some of the New Testament writings are real letters addressed to churches or to individuals while others are called Gospels. The term "gospel" is ambiguous. It may be used in a general way to designate the good news of the redemption offered to mankind through Jesus Christ, but it is also used in a specific sense to designate each one of four writings which have something to say about the ministry and message of Jesus, namely Matthew, Mark, Luke, and John.

In characterizing the New Testament writings, it is helpful to distinguish between those which were the result of the telling, retelling, and embellishment of stories about what Jesus did and said and those which were the result of meditation about him, about the significance of his person and career. All the New Testament writings are concerned with the latter category to some extent, but the writings other than the Synoptic Gospels (Matthew, Mark, and Luke[3]) deal solely with such a perspective. The letters of Paul, for example, have very little to say about Jesus' ministry and message but a great deal to say about who and/or what he was. The Gospel of John, although cast in the form of a Gospel, is, according to many scholars, primarily a meditation on the significance of Jesus' person and career. On the other hand, the Synoptic Gospels contain narratives concerning Jesus' actions and teachings.

It is from the Synoptic Gospels that we may gain some information concerning the historical Jesus. While there are a few references to him in some extra-biblical writings[4] and these lend support to his existence as an actual historical person, these writings tell us almost nothing about his career and teachings. Since the same is true with respect to the New Testament writings other than the Synoptics, it is to the latter that we must turn for information about Jesus. Even then, however, the quest for the historical Jesus requires more of us than simply reading the Synoptic Gospels. They must be carefully and critically studied. That is, the method of historical criticism[5] must be employed, and this involves seeking answers to such questions as why, how, when, and to whom were the Synoptics written.

Even a superficial reading of the Synoptic Gospels makes it obvious that the writers were not historians nor biographers in the modern and technical senses of these terms. They did not regard themselves as writing history or biography, and even if they had they did not possess the sources for such writing.[6] There had been no one analogous to a modern newspaper or television reporter following Jesus around and recording everything he did and said. For about a generation, stories about Jesus' actions and teachings circulated orally, and since there were high expectations that Christ would soon come again (the Parousia or second coming) to usher in the eschaton, there was no felt need among the first-generation Christians to put the oral tradition in written form for the sake of future generations. Given these facts, why were the Synoptic Gospels written? Obviously, there was some reason other than that of preserving a historical record for future generations since it was believed that history would come to an end with the eschaton.

According to many New Testament scholars, the Synoptic Gospels were written to serve the church's function of evangelism and teaching. Since they were written during the last thirty years of the first

century, a considerable period of time had elapsed
since the crucifixion and resurrection of Jesus in
about 30 A.D. The Parousia had not occurred. Eye-
witnesses of Jesus' ministry had died. Since the
church had grown considerably both geographically and
numerically, its membership had come to be made up
largely of Gentiles, many of whom lacked an adequate
knowledge of Jesus' Jewish heritage and of his life
and teachings. Debates arose in the church as to the
nature and practice of the Christian faith, and there
was a need for authoritative written works which
could provide a basis for instruction as to Jesus'
attitudes and sayings on important issues. Thus the
Synoptic Gospels were written to serve primarily as
manuals of instruction for church members and new converts. Since this is the case, they naturally reflect
to some extent the faith stance of their authors and
of the church at the time they were written. A careful analysis is required in order to get back through
what is written in the Synoptics to Jesus and his own
actual life situation.

Scholars engaged in the so-called "quest for the
historical Jesus" have used literary (or source), form,
and redaction criticism in their studies of the Gospels. The earliest (and according to some, most basic)
method employed was literary or source criticism. It
has long been recognized that there are striking similarities and yet equally striking differences between
the Synoptic Gospels. Called the Synoptic problem by
scholars, this fact of similarities and differences
raised the question of the manner in which the Synoptics were composed. On what theory of origin could
both the similarities and differences best be accounted
for?

The solution of the Synoptic problem which is
rather widely held among New Testament scholars today
is that taken together the Synoptics contain four
distinct literary sources. That such is the case is
at least hinted at in the beginning of the Gospel of
Luke when the author says:

> "Inasmuch as many have undertaken to
> compile a narrative of the things which
> have been accomplished among us, . . .
> it seemed good to me also, . . . to
> write an orderly account for you, . . ."
> (Luke 1:1-3).

According to source critics, these many include: 1. The Gospel of Mark which as the earliest Gospel was used as a source by the authors of Matthew and Luke; 2. A body of material shared by Matthew and Luke but not present in Mark and called Q (from the German Quelle meaning "source"); 3. Material peculiar to Matthew's Gospel and called "M"; and 4. Material peculiar to Luke and called "L."

There is a considerable amount of evidence in support of the conclusion that Mark was the earliest Gospel and was used as a source by the authors of Matthew and Luke. With the exception of only about nine per cent,[7] the material in Mark is contained in Matthew and Luke, and within this common material there is extensive agreement in vocabulary. In the material parallel to Mark, Matthew and Luke generally agree with the sequence of the narrative in Mark. When one departs from it the other follows it and vice versa. Rarely do they agree with each other whenever the Markan sequence is not followed. Further, the very nature of the occasional changes in language and subject matter common to all three suggest the priority of Mark. Awkward Greek grammatical constructions found in Mark are given a better form in Matthew and Luke. A few changes in subject matter also suggest the use of Mark. For example, in Matthew 9:2 no reason is given for Jesus' remark concerning the faith of the men who brought the paralytic to him, but Mark 2:4 tells of their making a hole in the roof through which they lowered the paralytic as evidence of their faith. Clearly, Matthew's use of Mark is to be assumed here. Much more evidence for the use of Mark by Matthew and Luke can be easily secured by examining a good edition of Gospel Parallels.[8]

An examination of Gospel Parallels will show also that, in addition to material common to all three Synoptics, Matthew and Luke have a common body of material which is not found in Mark. There are about two hundred verses in Matthew and Luke but not in Mark which agree almost word for word and which contain primarily sayings of Jesus. Since, according to most scholars, Matthew and Luke were written at different places and times, this common body of material was not due to the authors collaborating but to a second source, Q (Quelle). Given the different arrangements of the material from Mark and Q in Matthew and Luke, it would appear that Q as well as Mark was a written document.

The other two sources, M (Matthew's special source) and L (Luke's special source) may have been written or oral or a mixture of both.

Source criticism makes it clear that, although the Gospel writer made his own unique contribution to the material he presented in his Gospel, especially in the way in which he organized this material, he did not write his Gospel ad hoc. Instead he transmitted previous traditions and was, in a sense, a kind of editor. Form criticism demonstrates that behind the written Gospels and their written sources there were units of oral traditions in the earliest church. Undoubtedly, these pericopes provided the basis for the Gospel of Mark and the Q source with the writers of these sources grouping them according to certain patterns or structures. Redaction criticism calls attention to the specific organizational structure of each Gospel and the differences with which sometimes the same narrative, parable or saying is reported in different Gospels and thus provides highly probably conclusions concerning the perspectives and purposes of each Gospel writer. In light of such analysis, it is evident that Mark was concerned to present Jesus as one who, even though misunderstood, opposed, and humiliated during his early life, was, nevertheless, the long awaited Messiah. The writer of Matthew was concerned to present Jesus as one who fulfilled Scripture and was thus Messiah but also teacher and founder of the church, the true Israel. Luke presents Jesus as Messiah and teacher but also emphasizes Jesus as the friend of the poor and the outcasts and the savior of the sick in both body and soul. In his total writing, Luke-Acts, Luke emphasizes the universal mission of the church, setting the Gospel in the context of the world-wide and history-long purpose of God.

By taking into account the purposes of each Gospel writer, the modifications they sometimes make, and the actual historical setting of Jesus' ministry, it is possible to arrive at some highly probable conclusions concerning the Jesus of history. While it is not possible to write a full and precise biography nor to construct a detailed chronological account of his ministry, it is possible to gain from the Gospels a fairly reliable "portrait" of the man, his mission, and his message. The presentation of a full analysis of the Gospels on the basis of source, form, and redaction criticism would take us beyond the limits of this introductory study. However, assuming such an analysis as a background, we shall attempt to present here a brief summary of the ministry and message of Jesus.

II. The Ministry and Message of Jesus

While it is the case that a detailed chronological account of Jesus' ministry is not possible, a very general and overall chronological sequence is ascertainable from the Synoptic Gospels. Aside from the birth narratives in Matthew and Luke and Luke's delightful story of the boy Jesus in the temple (Luke 2:41-52), the Gospel narratives begin with accounts of John the Baptist's mission (unlike Matthew and Luke, Mark opens his Gospel with such an account). Jesus is baptized by John the Baptist and after John is put in prison by Herod Antipas, Tetrarch of Galilee and Perea, Jesus is joined by some disciples, and engaged in a teaching and preaching mission in Galilee. The burden of his message, according to Mark, was:

> "The time is fulfilled, and the kingdom of God is at hand: repent, and believe in the gospel" (Mark 1:15)

Attracted by the man and his message, rather large crowds flock to hear him. This gains the attention and undoubtedly the opposition of Tetrarch Herod Antipas. Quite possibly because of Herod's opposition and to escape the great crowds in order to reflect on the future course of his ministry, Jesus and his disciples leave Galilee and spend some time in the regions of Tyre and Sidon and Caesarea Philippi. Having decided that the good news of the kingdom must be proclaimed also in Jerusalem, the Holy city, Jesus and his disciples travel to Jerusalem arriving there a few days before the Passover. The most detailed of all the narratives in the Synoptics is of the Passion Week. Jesus' message arouses the opposition of the "establishment," the religious and civil authorities. He eats a last meal with his disciples, is arrested, charged with treason, and executed by order of Pilate, the Roman Procurator (governor). This is not the end of the story, of course, for each Gospel has some narrative concerning the risen Lord.

In light of this brief sketch of Jesus' public ministry gleaned from the Synoptic Gospels, it appears

91

that this mission took place during a period of time of not more than a year. The truly amazing thing about this is that in such a short span of time Jesus could have had such a profound impact upon his fellow countrymen in general and his disciples in particular. Surely this is due not only to the depth of his personality, his love for God and persons, but also to the simplicity, concreteness, and yet profoundity of his teachings about God and his kingdom.

The traditions about Jesus' teachings as reported in the Synoptic Gospels indicate that the central theme of his teaching was the kingdom of God, a new order of life on earth which is now dawning but which is to come in fulfillment in the future. This concept, if not the precise terminology, was already present in Jesus' religious heritage. As we have seen in Chapter III, the Covenant between Yahweh and Israel was a suzerainty covenant. Emphasis was upon the sovereignty of Yahweh who takes the initiative in offering the Covenant to Israel. Later, in Rabbinic prayers, God is addressed as king of the universe. That is, by virtue of his having created it, God is in reality king of the universe whether acknowledged as such or not. To the extent that it is acknowledged, God's reign accepted, his kingdom (God's reign) is a present reality on earth. But similar to the prophets who had looked forward to a universal consummation in the future so the later Rabbis felt that the kingdom would come in fulfillment sometime in the future.

In Jesus' sayings about the kingdom as reported by the Synoptics there are some in which he clearly speaks of the kingdom as present while there are others in which the kingdom is spoken of as future. Even allowing for some modifications by the early church, it seems fairly certain that for Jesus the kingdom was both present and future. It is present in the sense that there are those who have and are responding to his proclamation concerning the good news of God's gracious acceptance and the life in community which this brings. It is future in the sense that there will be an ultimate universal fulfillment or consummation.[9]

A formal definition of the kingdom of God is nowhere to be found in the sayings and parables of Jesus as recorded in the Synoptics. Yet these teachings do present Jesus' perspective with respect to its nature and the quality of the life style of those who accept it. Even where the expression "kingdom of God" is not explicitly present, the saying or parable can be understood adequately only in light of the kingdom of God theme.

A careful analysis of the parables which eliminates whatever embellishments and modifications which were made by the early church and/or Gospel writers indicates that Jesus used the parables as teaching devices to illustrate his central theme of the kingdom and its coming. Given the important role they play in his teaching, a brief explication of the nature and contents of the parables is essential for an understanding of Jesus' message.

First of all, a necessary condition for understanding the message of the parables is a clear understanding of what a parable is. By definition it is an earthly story illustrating by comparison a meaning in the religious domain. Generally, it makes one, and only one, main point and always contains within it all that is needed for its own explanation. It is different from both a fable and an allegory.

A fable is based on fantasy. It departs from nature and anthropomorphizes animals and even inanimate objects. That is, it attributes human emotions and capacities to them.

An allegory is a literary device (primarily a tool of the writer rather than the speaker) in which a system of ideas is expressed by an entirely different system of ideas. The persons, things, and happenings in the story are supposed to have meanings other than their literal meanings. Unlike a parable in which there are often some features and details whose function is simply that of making the picture more distinct and concrete and for which no explanation is needed, in an allegory every detail is supposed to signify something in another order of abstract spiritual truths. It is, as Maurice Goguel has expressed it, "a kind of algebraical language."[10] Each detail is taken to symbolize some abstract or spiritual truth.

Since the function of comparison is basic to both parable and allegory, they have sometimes in the history of Christian thought been treated as though they were identical. That is, the parables of Jesus have sometimes been interpreted as though they were allegories. Such interpretation gives free reign to eisegesis[11] and opens up a Pandora's box on all sorts of bizarre interpretations. Whenever a parable has been allegorized, the main point of the parable has been obscured or missed altogether.

For example, St. Augustine's (354-430 A.D.) allegorization of Jesus' parable of the Good Samaritan (Luke 10:30-35) simply ignores the point of the parable as told by Jesus. For Augustine, the "certain man" traveling from Jerusalem to Jericho represents Adam. Jerusalem is the city of Peace from which Adam fell and Jericho our human mortality toward which he goes. The thieves are the devil and his angels who strip Adam of his immortality, beat him into sinfulness, and thus leave him half dead. The priest and Levite represent the Old dispensation from which Adam could expect nothing. The Samaritan is Christ, and the beast upon which he places the wounded man represents the incarnation. The inn to which he takes the wounded man is the church, and the innkeeper is St. Paul.[12] Obviously, such allegorization misses the original point of the parable. It would have astounded Jesus who told the parable in response to the lawyer's (Scribe) question, "And who is my neighbor?" Given the context, the point of the parable is quite clear, namely that those who accept the kingdom or reign of God do not ask such a question but rather seek to live neighborly in whatever situation they may find themselves. That is, they seek to live in light of that love which is not restricted, which does not begin by defining its object (who is my neighbor) but which instead ignores absolutely the customary limits of status, race, or location.

Many New Testament scholars who have given special attention to a study of the parables find that they express a few basic concepts of Jesus concerning the kingdom and may be grouped according to these concepts. Employing different images, several parables express the same concept or make the same point and so may be grouped together. Taken as a whole, the parables quite naturally fall into several groupings with the parables in each grouping illustrating a particular point which Jesus made concerning the kingdom of God. Some of the most basic of these points or concepts (with an example for each) are discussed below.[13]

1. The kingdom of God is a gift of God. It cannot

be earned but only accepted or rejected. In the discussion of the characteristics of the Yahweh-Israel Covenant in Chapter III we have seen that the Covenant was understood to be a gift of Yahweh who had taken the initiative in offering it to Israel. It was not because of Israel's merit that Yahweh offered the Covenant but simply because of his gracious love. In light of his religious heritage, it is not surprising that Jesus viewed the coming of the kingdom as God's gracious gift. No one can ever merit such a gift but only gratefully accept it or stubbornly reject it. While this point is made in several parables, a striking example of it is to be found in the parable of the Laborers in the Vineyard (Matthew 20:1-16).

In this parable the owner of a vineyard goes out at sunrise and at an agreed upon wage hires some laborers to work his vineyard. Later, he hires others at 8:00 A.M., still others at noon, and finally hires some about 3:00 P.M. At the close of the day when the laborers come to get their wages he pays them all the same. Those who had worked since sunrise grumbled because they thought they should have received more. But the owner said to one of them:

> Friend, I am doing you no wrong; did you
> not agree with me for a denarius? Take
> what belongs to you, and go; I choose to
> give to this last as I give to you. Am
> I not allowed to do what I choose with
> what belongs to me? Or do you begrudge
> me my generosity? (Matthew 20:13-15)

Obviously many of the details in this parable are there to make it more vivid and concrete and do not require an explanation. Even though this parable presents a very concrete picture of the economic and labor situation in the time of Jesus, it does not present teachings with respect to economics and labor relations. Rather the point is that the kingdom of God cannot be earned, for the kingdom is God's generous gift.

2. The kingdom of God is inclusive. Since God graciously offers to everyone the kingdom as a gift, no one is excluded because of such accidental matters as position or status. Even the outcasts and sinners may receive the gift if they are willing to accept it. That is, God lovingly accepts those who in fact are unacceptable if they are willing to accept his

acceptance. Indeed, it is the self-righteous persons who, taking pride in their own supposed virtue, find it most difficult to accept the freely given gift of the kingdom. This two-pronged point is graphically expressed in the beautiful parable of the Prodigal Son (Luke 15:11-32).

Criticized for his acceptance of the outcasts and sinners (Luke 15:1-2), Jesus responded to this charge with the three parables of the Lost Sheep, the Lost Coin, and the Lost Son. The point of all three is that God accepts the outcasts and sinners. The last of the three, the Prodigal Son parable, is the climax of Jesus' defense of his mission to outcasts and sinners and quite clearly emphasizes the inclusiveness of God's gift of the kingdom. Since its point is of such fundamental importance in Jesus' teaching and life style and since it is such an outstanding example of Jesus' skillful use of the parabolic form of teaching, this parable merits quoting in its entirety:

> And he said, 'There was a man who had two sons; and the younger of them said to his father, 'Father, give me the share of property that falls to me.' And he divided his living between them. Not many days later, the younger son gathered all he had and took his journey into a far country, and there he squandered his property in loose living. And when he had spent everything a great famine arose in that country, and he began to be in want. So he went and joined himself to one of the citizens of that country, who sent him into his fields to feed swine. And he would gladly have fed on the pods that the swine ate; and no one gave him anything. But when he came to himself he said, 'How many of my father's hired servants have bread enough and to spare, but I perish here with hunger! I will arise and go to my father, and I will say to him, 'Father, I have sinned against heaven and before you; I am no longer worthy to be called your son; treat me as one of your hired servants.' And he arose and came to his father. But while he was yet at a distance, his father saw him and had compassion, and ran and embraced him and kissed him. And

96

the son said to him, 'Father, I have
sinned against heaven and before you; I
am no longer worthy to be called your son.'
But the father said to his servant, 'Bring
quickly the best robe, and put it on him;
and put a ring on his hand, and shoes on
his feet; and bring the fatted calf and
kill it, and let us eat and make merry;
for this my son was dead, and is alive
again; he was lost, and is found.' And
they began to make merry. Now his elder
son was in the field, and as he came and
drew near to the house, he heard music and
dancing. And he called one of the servants
and asked what this meant. And he said to
him, 'Your brother has come, and your
father has killed the fatted calf, because
he has received him safe and sound.' But
he was angry and refused to go in. His
father came out and entreated him, but he
answered his father, 'Lo, these many years
I have served you, and I never disobeyed
your command; yet you never gave me a kid,
that I might make merry with my friends.
But when this son of yours came, who has
devoured your living with harlots, you
killed for him the fatted calf!' And he
said to him, 'Son you are always with me,
and all that is mine is yours. It was
fitting to make merry and be glad, for this
your brother was dead, and is alive; he was
lost, and is found.' (Luke 15:11-32)

Obviously, the central figure in the parable is
the father who runs to greet the returning son and is
so joyful over his return that he throws a party for
him. Equally as obvious is that the elder brother is
a self-righteous prig, proud of his virtue, and therefore one who refuses to rejoice at the return of his
brother. Precisely because of that he finds it difficult to accept the graciously and freely given love of
the father.

3. Those who accept the gift of the kingdom demonstrate in the concrete affairs of everyday life a
loving concern for others. This neighborly life style
which is produced by the acceptance of the kingdom is
beautifully illustrated by Jesus in the parable of the
Good Samaritan (Luke 10:29-37). As indicated previously,

97

the point of the parable is not who is my neighbor but rather am I neighborly in whatever situation I find myself. It is this latter question which is of concern to those who accept the gift of the kingdom. Out of gratitude for God's gracious acceptance, they seek to live with neighborly or loving concern for others.

It is surely the case that for Jesus the kind of morality by which the kingdom members live is based precisely on their experience of God's gracious acceptance, his gift of the kingdom. The very nature of God who gives his kingdom as a gift is Agape. Agape is the Greek term which is used throughout the New Testament to designate God's self-giving and self-sacrificial love. Where the English language employs the one word "love" to designate several types of love, the ancient Greek language used three different words.[14] Thus, philia designates mutual love or friendship. Eros designates "love" in the sense of desire, physical attachment, or self-fulfilling love. Agape generally designates gratuitous love, and as used in the New Testament means that freely given love which asks no questions concerning the worth or lack of worth of the one loved. Since it does not bargain nor seek for fulfillment, it transcends both philia and eros. It is not that philia and eros are destroyed by Agape, but rather that in transcending them Agape paradoxically fulfills both philia and eros.

In the parable of the Prodigal Son, Jesus illustrates his view of God agapeistically accepting in his kingdom those who even though unworthy are willing to accept his acceptance. Surely this is the point of the father's embracing and kissing the returning son before the latter can express his entire confession. In the parable of the Good Samaritan, on the other hand, the point is made that those who accept God's Agape will in turn treat others "agapeistically." The author of the first letter of John had certainly clearly understood this perspective of Jesus when he wrote: "Beloved, if God so loved us, we also ought to love one another" (I John 4:11, in the Greek text a form of Agape is used in each instance of the reference to love in this passage).

4. The dawning kingdom ruptures the framework of the old order in the world. The traditional and customary order of the world which is based on position, prestige, power, control of people, inequities is

broken up by the "Agapeistic" lifestyle of those who
accept the kingdom. Using traditional metaphors for
the New Age, the twin parables of the New Cloth and
the New Wine (Mark 2:21-22) make this point. A piece
of unshrunk cloth sewn over the tear in an old garment
will shrink when the garment is washed and make the
tear worse. New wine put into old wine skins will
ferment and cause the inelastic skins to burst so that
the wine is lost. While in themselves these parables
indicate only the danger of the new, and while in the
early church they were undoubtedly used to indicate
that the Christian message cannot be reconciled with
the ceremonial forms of Judaism, in the context of
Jesus' teaching and lifestyle they certainly teach that
the lifestyle of the kingdom cannot be reconciled with
the customary order in the world. Instead it breaks up
this order. Indeed, the dawning of the kingdom inaug-
urates the New Age.

5. The kingdom of God is the supreme value of
life. Certainly Jesus was thoroughly familiar with
the creation narratives in Genesis in which emphasis
is placed upon socialization as a basic and God given
fact of human existence. That is, human beings were
created to live together in community (Genesis 2:18-24),
in love and acceptance. Sin brought estrangement and
disruption in the human community. But the kingdom of
God breaks the power of estrangement and restores that
kind of community for which God had created human beings. Thus the kingdom is of supreme value. The twin
parables of the Hidden Treasure and the Pearl illustrate this point.

> The kingdom of heaven is like a treasure
> hidden in a field, which a man found and
> covered up; then in his joy he goes and
> sells all that he has and buys that field.
>
> Again, the kingdom of heaven is like a
> merchant in search of fine pearls, who,
> on finding one pearl of great value, went
> and sold all that he had and bought it.
> (Matthew 13:44-46)

In interpreting these two parables no importance should
be attached to the ethics of the two men nor to the
method of discovery. These are simply the true to
life details in the parables which require no explanation. The same is true also for what is given up in

99

order to gain the treasure and the pearl. The stress
is solely on what is gained. So also the kingdom is
of greater worth than anything else which one may possess or experience. It is the supreme value of life.

Just as the parables so the sayings of Jesus are
to be understood in light of the kingdom of God theme.
Quite a few of these sayings were compiled by the author of Matthew to form the Sermon on the Mount
(Matthew 5-7). A careful analysis of the Sermon on
the Mount which takes into account the later modifications by the church and/or Gospel writer, and which
attempts to view these sayings in the context of
Jesus' own life situation, indicates that these sayings do not so much comprise an ethical code as a
descriptive design for life in the kingdom. That is,
they are not a set of requirements which must be met
before one can receive the kingdom. No one could fulfill such conditions entirely and anyway, for Jesus,
the kingdom of God is a gift. Rather, the sayings in
the Sermon are descriptive of the lifestyle to which
those who accept the gift aspire. They aspire to this
ideal lifestyle not for prudential reasons but out
of gratitude for the gift. The sayings in the Sermon,
therefore, are to be understood as descriptive rather
than prescriptive.

The Beatitudes (Matthew 5:3-12) describe the
characteristics of those who accept the kingdom. They
recognize their need of God, are sensitive to the
plight of the world, and together are strengthened to
bear the sorrows of the world, are meek to God, yearn
for personal and social righteousness, are merciful to
others, sincere in motives, and act for peace in human
relations. In a world governed by power, greed, hatred,
and estrangement, such a lifestyle inevitably arouses
opposition. Yet, in spite of opposition, the kingdom
members are happy because of their community with God
and with others. While the world may not recognize it,
the kingdom with its lifestyle is the very thing which
can preserve its life and bring light to its darkness
(5:13-16).

In relation to the old religious tradition, the
good news of the kingdom does not abolish it but fulfills it. This is done by transcending the "law and
the prophets" in terms of emphasis on motive and
intention as well as on actual deeds (5:17-20). Those
who accept the gift of the kingdom seek to go beyond

100

simply refraining from murder, adultery, swearing, and retaliation and to develop those inner agapeistic attitudes which make such external moral prohibitions superfluous (5:21-48). Further, their worship is simple and sincere and their ultimate trust and devotion are centered on God alone (6:1-34). Given this, it follows that their love (Agape) is directed to all, even enemies (5:43; 7:1-12). Finally, they do not just make their "professions of faith" but actually engage in the practice of the kingdom life (7:13-17).

As perceived by the early faith witnesses and as presented in the Gospels, the supreme example of the ideal lifestyle of the kingdom of God was Jesus himself. Whatever else may be said about him, he was, to use the words of the young German theologian Dietrich Bonhoeffer, who was executed by the Nazis, "the man in the world totally for others."[15]

III. The Apostle Paul's Understanding of the Christian Faith

Any discussion of the origins of Christianity must give some attention to the career and thought of the Apostle Paul. His importance cannot be minimized for he might well be called "the second founder of Christianity."

Paul's own life situation made him admirably suited to bridge the gap between the Jewish heritage of early Christianity and the Greco-Roman world. Of Jewish descent, Paul grew up in the Greek speaking Gentile community of Tarsus in Asia Minor (Acts 9:11). Not only would he have assimilated aspects of Greek culture (including knowledge of the Greek language) in Tarsus, but also he would have been educated in the Jewish Scripture and Traditions in the Synagogue and Synagogue school, and may even have studied in a Rabbinic Academy in Jerusalem (Acts 22:3; 26:4).[16] Having opposed the early Christian movement, Paul apparently had a dramatic personal experience which changed him from a persecutor to an advocate (Acts 7:54-8:1; 9:1-22; 22:4-16; 26:9-18).

After an interval of time, Paul became convinced that the Christian faith was for Gentiles as well as for Jews. Regarding himself an Apostle to the Gentiles, he engaged in several missionary journeys spreading the Christian Gospel and establishing churches around the

eastern shores of the Mediterranean basin. While in
Jerusalem for the Passover after his third missionary
journey, he was arrested and sent to Caesera to be
tried by the Roman Procurator. After some time of imprisonment in Caesera, he appealed to Caesar (as a
Roman citizen he had this right) and was finally sent
to Rome where we last hear of him under house arrest
awaiting trial (Acts 28:14-30; Philemon 1; Colossians
4:3, 10, 18).

Such a brief description fails to do justice to
the man or his career. Even though apparently he
suffered from some sort of physical infirmity, he was
able to engage in long journeys in a time when travelling was not easy. He endured all sorts of hardships
such as shipwreck, imprisonment, and beatings. Yet
he persisted in preaching the good news of the Christian Gospel in as many places as he could reach. He
was truly an extraordinary man, and his understanding
of the Christian faith has been of considerable influence in the history of Christian thought.

Our task here is to attempt a brief summary of
Paul's theology. This task is complicated by virtue
of the fact that the writings of Paul in the New
Testament are genuine letters most of which were
written to answer specific questions or in response
to specific issues which had arisen in the churches he
had founded. Thus they are not systematic theological
treatises. Even the letter to the Romans which is the
most complete exposition of Paul's theology was, nevertheless, a genuine letter written to gain the goodwill
and support of the Christians in the church at Rome
for his projected missionary activity in Spain. Since
there is no one treatise which presents Paul's theology
fully in a systematic way, we must glean his theology
from his letters in our attempt to summarize his leading theological ideas.[17] In the discussion which
follows, we shall give attention to six major themes
of Paul's thought which taken together provide the
basic structure of his message.

1. All human beings under the conditions of
historical existence are enmeshed in the predicament
of sin from which they cannot extricate themselves.
As Paul himself put it: "All have sinned and fall
short of the glory of God" (Romans 3:23). With respect
to the origin of this predicament, Paul did not say
a great deal. Sometimes he seemed to have suggested

102

that sin originated with the "elemental" spirits or
demonic powers that oppose man and God (Colossians 2:8).
At other times he said that sin began with Adam, the
ancestor of the human race and thus the representative,
typical or essential man. Paul, like other Biblical
writers, believed that man is bound to the human race
as a whole. As in the Old Testament Prophets, there
is the sense of the one in the many and the many in
the one. Thus the story of Adam, with its report of
Adam's attempt to be like God, which entails rebellion
against God (Genesis 3:5), is the story of every man.
It is not something that happened "once upon a time
long ago" but characterizes the human race in every
age. No one can "escape" from the human race but
necessarily participates in the collective guilt of
the human race's rebellion against God.

Of more importance to Paul than the origin of
sin was the present fact of sin, the universal predicament of human beings in the state of estrangement from
God, others, and their own genuine selves. It is clear
that he viewed sin as not just an act or a series of
acts but as the state or condition of estrangement
(Colossians 1:21). The acts (sins) which are performed as a result of this condition are symptoms of
this basic state of sin or estrangement. This fundamental problem of human existence may be characterized
in three ways. It is not that these three characteristics denote three different sins. Rather they are
simply three ways of characterizing sin as a state or
condition of being. First, it may be characterized as
insensitivity to the graciousness of God, distrust,
and the separation of the will from God's will (Romans
1:21). This is only the "other side of the coin" for
the second characterization, namely hubris, or exces-
sive pride. That is, sin has to do with the pretension
of self, with human presumption, with man's attempt to
elevate himself into the sphere of the divine (Romans
1:22). The third characterization is closely related
to the first two. It is the unlimited desire to draw
the whole of reality into one's self, to take the
"sponge" approach to life, to value the world of
nature and other human beings only insofar as they
serve one's own perceived interests, to treat others
as means rather than ends (Romans 1:28).

This view of sin which is the dominant view in
the Biblical perspective, and which has been emphasized
time and again in the history of Christian thought, has

been strikingly and succinctly summarized by the modern theologian, Donald M. Baillie. According to Baillie, sin is the fact that:

> Each person makes himself the centre of his universe, caring little for the fellowship of the whole, but seeing things from his selfish point of view; becoming his own God, and worshipping himself. [It is] each person trying to be a quite independent cell, a self-sufficient atom, dancing on a pattern of its own, instead of joining in the great communal game of universal love.[18]

2. "What the law could never do, because our lower nature robbed it of all potency, God has done" (Romans 8:3, The New English Bible). Given the view that all human beings are caught in the predicament of sin, the question which assumes primary importance is, what is the way of release from this predicament? Paul's Jewish heritage and the opposition of the "Judaizers" (some early Christians who accepted the Jewish law as binding) led him to pose the question as to whether or not such release is to be achieved by means of the law. While Paul sometimes used the term law in the sense of "principle," he generally meant by it the whole Torah in both its ceremonial and moral aspects. Although he had more to say about the law in the sense of the whole Torah, he was convinced that in both senses the law was powerless as a means of delivering human beings from the predicament of estrangement. It was not that the law in itself was evil. Indeed, it was good, a gift of God. It was given in order that human beings might know their genuine natures as children of God and be related to him. But under the conditions of historical existence, in the state of estrangement, human beings pervert the law and make it into commandment. Love cannot be commanded. To talk ethics to one bound to a morally impotent race is a waste of time and grossly misleading. Laws do not make one good. They simply remind one of what is wrong and may even tempt one to break them. Further, any fulfilling of the laws, any accomplishment in this sphere, given the fact of sin, leads only to self-righteousness, the pride of virtue, and so to even worse enslavement in the predicament of estrangement. Thus, because of sin, the law, instead of being what God had intended, a guide to assist human beings in

their relationship with God, has become an idol and an obstruction to a genuine relationship with God (Romans 7:7-25). If there is already a relationship with God, the law, at least in its moral aspects, may function legitimately to provide guidance for actions in the concrete world, but the law itself cannot provide such a relationship nor release one from the predicament of sin. What the law cannot do, God has done through Jesus Christ.

3. "It was God who reconciled us to himself through Christ" (II Corinthians 5:18, The Jerusalem Bible). While Paul had much to say about what God had done through Christ, he never explicitly defined the relationship between Jesus and God. His thinking was not conceptual or theoretical but was action centered. He was concerned with God's action in Jesus. In speaking of this, he did sometimes closely identify Jesus and God but he never said that Jesus is God. The several titles he used in designating Jesus, titles such as Lord, Son of God, and Christ, clearly indicate his conviction that there was an intimate and unique relationship between Jesus and God. The concern for mankind and the selfless attitudes demonstrated in the character of Jesus were regarded by Paul as divine qualities. So he described the death of Jesus on behalf of sinners as "God's own proof of his love towards us" (Romans 5:8, The New English Bible). The Lord Jesus Christ was the one through whom God was working to release human beings from the power of sin and to reconcile them to God.

In the attempt to communicate his understanding of what God had done for mankind through Jesus Christ, Paul used several metaphors. Some of the major terms which he used metaphorically were derived from some of the major institutions or practices of his time, namely slavery, sacrificial rites, and law courts. So he sometimes spoke of God's action in Christ as ransom from bondage. As Paul himself put it: "So through God you are no longer a slave but a son" and "for freedom Christ has set us free" (Galatians 4:7; 5:1, R.S.V.). While Paul believed that God's providing of the means of release had been costly to God himself, the emphasis is upon the release, the freedom from the bondage of the law in the sense of Torah and especially from the "law" of sin and death (Romans 7:23-24).

Another term which Paul uses metaphorically to

describe what God has done in Christ is "sacrifice."
"For God showed him publicly dying as a sacrifice of
reconcilation to be taken advantage of by faith" (Romans 3:25, Smith and Goodspeed, The Complete Bible,
An American Translation). The point here is not that
God is a wrathful or vengeful deity demanding sacrifice,
a scapegoat, for him to be appeased or conciliated.
Paul spoke too often of God's love and forbearance for
that to be the case. It is not that God's attitude
toward mankind needs to be changed but that human attitudes toward God and others need to be changed. In
Jesus utter faithfulness to God, which was demonstrated
in his deep concern for all human beings, his acceptance
of the outcasts and dispossessed, and which aroused
powerful opponents who put him to death, God's merciful
forgiveness is unmistakably shown. Jesus was faithful
unto death (Philippians 2:8), and thus the barrier of
guilt that separated human beings from God has been
broken.

In their book Understanding the New Testament,
Professors Kee, Young, and Froelich have given a good
exposition of what Paul meant by his use of the metaphor "sacrifice" when they say:

> The initiative of God in bringing men into
> the right relationship with himself has
> been fully and finally made known in
> Jesus Christ (Romans 3:25, 26). Up until
> the time of Jesus' coming, God has been
> forgiving toward man, and forbearing
> towards man's sins, but man's sense of
> guilt and spiritual blindness kept him
> from understanding the true nature of God.
> Weighted down by guilt, man fled from
> God's presence and sought peace and safety
> in the worship of false gods. But now
> Jesus has come, completely dedicated to
> God, even to the extremity of death.
> Thus, he has demonstrated once and for all
> that God is One who vindicates the
> oppressed, removes the barriers that
> separate man from him, and brings man into
> relationship with himself.[19]

A third major term which Paul uses metaphorically
to describe what God has done in Jesus Christ is justification. The imagery here is of a court of law in
which an accused person may be acquitted, declared

innocent and reconciled with his accuser. The emphasis
is upon the acquittal. That is, God through Christ
offers acquittal to estranged and sinful mankind, even
though human beings are not innocent. God takes the
initiative and accepts those who are unacceptable if
they accept his acceptance. The appropriation of his
acceptance is by faith (Romans 3:26; Galatians 3:24).
And for Paul "faith" does not mean merely giving mental
assent to a body of doctrines or beliefs. Rather, as
J. Philip Hyatt has said:

> He meant trust in the living Christ,
> confidence in the faithfulness of God.
> In the fullest sense, faith is man's
> wholehearted acceptance of the good news
> that the saving grace of God has been
> freely offered to him in Christ. . . Faith
> is the response of man to the revelation of
> God in Christ. 'For by grace you have
> been saved through faith; and this is not
> your own doing, it is the gift of God--
> not because of works, lest any man should
> boast.' (Ephesians 2:8-9). Faith means
> the abandonment of all dependence upon
> one's self and one's own merit, and com-
> plete reliance upon the grace of God,
> as revealed most of all in Jesus Christ.[20]

4. "Now you are Christ's body, and each of you a
limb or organ of it" (I Corinthians 12:27, The New
English Bible). This quotation emphasizes a dimension
of Paul's thought which sometimes is overlooked. The
Community of the New Covenant, the Church, is an
important aspect of Paul's thought for he never thinks
of persons as being saved merely as individuals, of
Christians existing alone. Since the Christian has a
personal relationship with God, he also has a relationship with others in the community of the new Covenant.

It is sometimes held that the Old Testament is
concerned only with the group while the New Testament
is concerned with the individual. This view is
entirely too simplistic. It is true that the Old Testament deals to a large extent with the Covenant community, but this does not mean that the individual is
ignored. While the message of the New Testament is
directed to individuals, the group is not viewed as unimportant, for the Christian is not expected to live a
solitary life. So one of the important aspects of

107

Paul's thought is his view of the church.

Paul's favorite metaphor for the church is "the body of Christ." As J. Philip Hyatt points out:

> In I Corinthians 12:12-30 and Romans 12:4-8, he uses the figure to emphasize the variety of gifts within the church, the mutual dependence of the members, and the full importance of all the members. In Colossians 1:18 and Ephesians 1:23; 4:16; 5:23, the figure is used to stress the unity of the church and the headship of Christ.[21]

Other metaphors which Paul uses to designate the church are "the temple in which God dwells" (II Corinthians 6:16; Ephesians 2:19-22), "the bride of Christ" (Ephesians 5:23-32), and the "Israel of God" (Galatians 6:16).

5. "If we live by the Spirit, let us also walk by the Spirit" (Galatians 5:25). Paul's emphasis upon justification by faith rather than by the law, his insistence that in Jesus Christ God has freely offered release from estrangement, reconciliation with himself, and the gift of faith which appropriates this release and reconciliation, has led some interpreters, in his own day and since, to think that Paul's perspective was anti-nomian. That is, they interpreted Paul's position as one in which the Christian is free from all law to do whatever he wants to do, that freedom means license. This, however, is a serious misreading and misunderstanding of what Paul said in his letters. In his letters there are often large sections in which he gave specific moral injunctions and admonitions to his readers.

The fact that for Paul one cannot find release from sin and reconciliation with God by the works of the law does not mean that the Christian will not do good works. It means that the _motive_ for doing good works has changed. Instead of doing them in order to win favor with God, the Christian does them because he _wants_ to do them. He does from inward desire what one under the law did from outward compulsion.

The typical way in which Paul expresses this is to say that the life of the Christian is a life "in

Christ," or "in the Lord," or "in the Spirit." His
faith works through love. So Paul himself could say:

> For I through the law died to the law,
> that I might live to God. I have been
> crucified with Christ; it is no longer
> I who live, but Christ who lives in me;
> and the life I now live in the flesh I
> live by faith in the Son of God, who
> loved me and gave himself for me (Gala-
> tians 2:19-20, R.S.V.).

This Christ-mysticism was not that in which one becomes
absorbed in the divine. Instead it was a matter of
reconciliation and fellowship, not absorption. As
J. Philip Hyatt describes it:

> It was an ethical mysticism, in which the
> believer seeks to live a life worthy of
> the Christ with whom he has union . . .
> [So the Christian is] admonished to strive,
> with the help of God, to become that which
> he already is by the grace of God.[23]

Put in another way, it might be said that for Paul
the _imperative_ is based on the _indicative_.[24] The indicative is what God has done for mankind through
Jesus Christ. Wholehearted acceptance of the saving
grace of God freely offered in Jesus Christ is life
"in the Spirit." On the basis of this _indicative_ rests
the _imperative_ to "walk by the Spirit." This means
that good works are not alien to the life of the
Christian but flow naturally out of the Christian's
life of reconciliation with God and others. They are
not done for prudential reasons such as to gain the
reward of salvation, for this is a gift of God. Rather
they are done gratuitously, out of the relationship of
fellowship and love which God has given through Christ.

6. "'Death is swallowed up in victory'" (I Corinthians 15:54, R.S.V.). While Paul spoke of himself
and other Christians as being in Christ, this did not
mean that he thought the reconciliation with God
through Christ made the Christian perfect. True, it
has brought and continues to produce a change in the
life of the Christian. But it will not be complete
until the End of the Age. So Paul said of himself:
"Not that . . . I am already perfect, but I press on
. . . toward the goal for the prize of the upward call

of God in Christ Jesus" (Philippians 3:12, 14, R.S.V.).

In his eschatological views, Paul certainly believed in the second coming of Christ. The Greek word
for "coming" is parousia and means "an arrival," "being
present," "being there." Sometimes it was used in
connection with a king or emperor being present. As
Kee, Young, and Froelich point out:

> It could refer to an actual visit made
> by the emperor to a province, where he
> appeared as the living embodiment of the
> power of the Roman state, or it could be
> his symbolic or representative presence,
> as personified by a governor or pleni-
> potentiary sent by the emperor to carry
> out his work. The most important connota-
> tion of parousia is not the act of coming
> or route of arriving, but the potency of
> the kingly presence. The term was appro-
> priate, therefore, for the triumphant
> Christ at the End of the Age. He will
> embody the power of the New Humanity, and
> will represent the authority of God,
> ruling as God's agent over the whole of
> Creation. Indeed, that kingly authority
> is even now being exercised, although
> invisibly, and that Rule must continue
> to be extended until all the unseen
> forces of the universe, including the
> demonic powers, are brought under Christ's
> control (I Corinthians 15:24-25).[25]

In his early letter, I Thessalonians, Paul seems
to think that the parousia of Christ will take place
in the very near future. While he never gives up his
hope for the parousia, the expectation of the early
return of Christ seems to subside somewhat in his
later letters. But whenever it is to occur, Paul is
convinced that it will result in the ultimate defeat
of sin and death and usher in the New Age, a foretaste
of which is even now to be found in the community of
the "New Humanity," the church.

While one of Paul's major emphases was on the community of the "New Humanity" in the New Age, he also
had words of hope and comfort for individuals. He was
convinced that the physical death of the individual did

not result ultimately in annihilation. Instead there is a post-mortem "life."

In the fifteenth chapter of I Corinthians, Paul dealt at some length with the theme of resurrection from the dead. His expectation of a resurrection life was firmly grounded in his faith in Jesus Christ. As Paul himself expressed it:

> For as by a man came death, by a man has come also the resurrection of the dead. For as in Adam all die, so also in Christ shall all be made alive. But each in his own order: Christ the first fruits, then at his coming [parousia] those who belong to Christ. (15:21-23)

It is obvious from this passage that Paul did not regard the post-mortem life as some sort of natural human endowment. His view was unlike that of the Greek philosopher Plato who, especially in the Phaedo, spoke of the immortality of the soul. For Plato the soul (primarily the mental and volitional aspect of human beings regarded as a substance or entity) was naturally immortal. It was deathless and could not be annihilated. In the Hebraic and early Christian view, death brings the extinction of the total person. However, God then acts to recreate or reconstitute the person as a living person in the post-mortem realm. The "resurrection of the dead," then, has a different meaning from the "immortality of the soul."

Just as God through Christ has broken the power of sin, so also, according to Paul, through Christ God has broken the power of death. Reconciliation with God has come as a result of the gift of faith. Similarly, the resurrection life will be experienced as a gift of God, and it will be experienced by "whole persons." So Paul spoke of being raised as a soma pneumatikon ("spiritual body"). Soma ("body") designates the total person. While it may include the physical body, it designates the entire person as a psycho-physical unity. It does not mean simply that part of a person which is physical. It includes heart, mind, life-principle, and body in a living unity, the whole person. When Paul spoke of one being raised from the dead, he wanted to emphasize that this was an experience of the total person and yet was something more than simply the resuscitation of a corpse. So he spoke of it as a "spiritual

111

body," meaning thereby that the whole person is raised to newness of life, in a different type of "body" appropriate for existence in a realm quite different from this contingent world of material and physical objects. Nothing essential for the whole person is lost. Even the bodily form is recreated but is of a "spiritual" nature appropriate for existence in a "spiritual" or "heavenly" realm.

In this brief discussion of the leading ideas in Paul's theology, we have seen that for Paul: (1) All human beings are caught in the predicament of sin which is estrangement from God, others and their own genuine selves due primarily to the pretension of self; (2) The law, while good, is powerless to provide a means of release from the predicament of sin; (3) What the law could not do, God has done through Jesus Christ in God's disclosing himself to be a loving and accepting God who freely offers to mankind the gift of reconciliation with himself; (4) Those who are justified by faith from the community of the New Covenant, the Church; (5) Those who are reconciled to God or justified by faith seek, with the help of God, to become what they already are by the grace of God, i.e., their good works flow naturally out of their life of reconciliation with God; and, (6) Those who are reconciled with God through faith live with the confident expectation of a resurrection life and an eternal fellowship with God.

IV. Perspectives in the Johannine and Other New Testament Literature

As we have seen in Section I of this chapter, the Johannine literature (the Gospel of John, I, II, and III John), the Pastoral Letters (I, II Timothy and Titus), I Peter, Hebrews, James, and Revelation were probably written between 90-110 A.D. Due to the geographical and numerical growth of the church, the delay of the parousia (second coming of Christ), and the rise of local and empire-wide persecutions of the Christians, several crucial problems had begun to plague the church.

For one thing, the original sense of unity in the church was rendered problematical. While there had never been strict uniformity, there had been a sense of unity in the early days of the church. There had been a deep sense of the presence of the Holy Spirit and of being engaged under His guidance in the common task of preparing for the New Age. But, given the delay

112

of the _parousia_ and the expansion of the church, this sense of unity was put to the severest test. Too many people who claimed to speak in the name of Christ were saying contradictory things. False teachings had arisen, and often the unity of the church was in danger of being sundered by different factions.

Closely associated with this problem of unity was the problem of maintaining the purity of the testimony which had been handed down from the original faith witnesses. As time went on, the purity of this tradition was threatened by false teachings. One body of such teachings, an early form of which is opposed in many of the writings listed above, was the heresy known as Gnosticism (from the Greek word _gnosis_ meaning "to know").[26] Claiming to have superior knowledge, the Gnostics affirmed that _matter_ (the material world) is inherently evil and only _spirit_ is good. So the material or physical world was made by an evil kind of demi-god. Christ had no relationship with this demi-god but came from a higher, purely spiritual deity and was himself a purely spiritual being. That is, Jesus as the Christ was not genuinely human. He was a kind of ghostly apparition who did not have a physical body. His function was to bring mystic knowledge to those who were spiritual enough to apprehend it so that with this knowledge they might escape from the clutches of evil matter.

This threat to the purity of the tradition by false teaching often threatened the practice of the Christian life in the moral dimension. This could take either one of two extreme directions. On the one hand, some Gnostics thought that they should withdraw from the world as much as possible and thus engaged in extreme ascetic practices. On the other hand, the more popular direction was that, since the world and the desires of the physical body are on such a low plane and thus of no worth in the ultimate scheme of salvation, the Christian has no obligation to keep any moral demands.

Several perspectives expressed in the Johannine literature are better understood if viewed in light of the three problems discussed above. It was probably in opposition to an early form of Gnosticism which threatened the unity of the church, the purity of the received tradition, and the full practice of the Christian life that the writer claims in the prologue

113

to his Gospel that in Jesus Christ the pre-existent "Word" (the Greek _logos_ here appears to mean the rational structure by which the world is created and exists) "became _flesh_ and dwelt among us" (John 1:14).[27] Also in the Gospel the writer encourages Christians to preserve the sense of unity in the church. This is beautifully expressed in the prayer for the disciples that they may be one even as Jesus and the Father are one (John 17). The opposition to Gnosticism is even more clearly stated by the writer in his first letter. Here he suggests two criteria for distinguishing false from true teachings. The first is the confession that Jesus Christ, the Son of God, came in the flesh, and the second is the demonstration of love in the practice of Christian life. Whoever denies the former and fails to demonstrate the latter is not of God (I John 4:1-8, 15). While the confession is this writer's answer to the problem of maintaining the purity of the tradition, the second criterion is his answer both to the problem of unity (love of God entails love of brother) and the problem of practicing the Christian life (I John 3:3-6; 4:16-5:5).

As indicated under Section I of this chapter, the emphasis in the Gospel of John is upon the significance of the person of Jesus Christ. The sonship of Jesus with God and the life, light, and truth which have come into the world through him are explicitly and powerfully expressed. These two motifs are introduced in the prologue of Chapter I and are continued throughout the entire Gospel. In the _Logos_ ("Word") made flesh God has sent his Son "into the world, not to condemn the world [as the Gnostics claimed] but that the world might be saved through him" (John 3:17, R.S.V.).

As had Paul, so also the writer of the Johannine literature did not think that the Christian lived a solitary life. Rather he is a part of the church, a fellowship of those who have received new life through Christ. In the church is to be found the _paraclete_ (the Greek word for "legal counselor" or "advocate"), the Holy Spirit or Spirit of Truth, which Christ had promised to the disciples and from whom Christians can receive guidance in the path which leads to life, light, and truth (John 14-16).

Those who believe in Jesus Christ, participate in the fellowship, and receive the guidance of the _paraclete_ are granted God's gift of "eternal life." It is clear from several passages (John 5:24; 6:47; 17:3) that by this expression "eternal life" the writer means primarily a new quality of life which is a present possession of believers. It is similar in meaning to Paul's expression "in Christ" and to his Christ-mysticism which, as we have seen, is a mystical-ethical union with Christ. However, as with Paul, its consummation or full actualization lies in the future (I John 3:2-3).

For both Paul and the writer of the Johannine literature, the gift of God's love as disclosed in Jesus Christ and the call for the acceptance of that love and the practice of it in the Christian life are central motifs. Nowhere are these motifs more beautifully and succinctly expressed than in the following passage from the first letter of John:

> My dear people, let us love one another since love comes from God and everyone who loves is begotten by God and knows God. Anyone who fails to love can never have known God, because God is love. God's love for us was revealed when God sent into the world his only Son so that we could have life through him . . . We are to love, then, because he loved us first. Anyone who says, 'I love God,' and hates his brother is a liar, since a man who does not love the brother that he can see cannot love God, whom he has never seen. So this is the commandment that he has given us, that anyone who loves God must also love his brother (I John 4:7-9, 18-21, The Jerusalem Bible).

In the writings called the Pastoral Epistles the basic problem was that of false teachings which had led to immoral living.[28] One way to combat the false teachings was to develop a more formal system of leadership in the church. Structures of leadership had been and were to continue for some time to be rather fluid. The earliest type seems to have been largely that of travelling preacher and teachers, generally associated with some outstanding figure in the church. But, since this very informal situation permitted all sorts of abuses to arise, there was soon the felt need for establishing some sort of local ecclesiastical structure and authority. Since the Pastoral Letters mention bishops, elders, and deacons, it is obvious that they reflect early attempts to establish ecclesiastical orders.

In comparison with the other writings in the New Testament, the Letter to the Hebrews is unique in that the customary distinction between this age and the New Age receives little or no emphasis. Eschatological thinking did not hold a central place in the thought of this writer. Instead, using the Old Testament sacrificial system as an analogy, the writer places emphasis upon the contrast between the material and spiritual realms, claiming that believers have experienced the latter even though they continue to live in the former. Through Christ, the perfect high priest, forgiveness of sins and new life in faith have been made available for believers. Apparently the author believed that, if one falls away (if one sins after baptism), there is no further hope (Hebrews 10:26).

The Letter of James places emphasis upon practicing the virtues entailed in the life of faith. It has sometimes been thought (i.e., Martin Luther) that its emphasis upon works was inconsistent with Paul's emphasis on faith. This is probably not the case, since the writer of James was speaking to an entirely different situation. It appears that he was speaking to those who regarded faith as a formal set of beliefs to which one simply gave mental assent. In this sense, faith would generally have little impact on actual life for it was not a transforming trust in God as in Paul's view. So apparently it was to people for whom faith was only a kind of intellectual exercise that James was addressing himself when he said: "So faith by itself, if it has no works, is dead" (James 2:17, R.S.V.).

The major problem dealt with in I Peter and Revelation was that of persecution and suffering. In I Peter the persecution seems to have been on a local level. The author exhorts his readers to endure this suffering as Christians, to bear no grudges for anyone, to hold no animosity for the state, and to leave no doubt by the quality of their lives that their suffering is unwarranted. Soon the parousia will come and they will be vindicated.

The Book of Revelation reflects a situation in which Christians were being persecuted by order of the state (the Roman Emperor, Domitian). This persecution arose because the Christians refused to participate in

116

the state-sponsored cult of emperor worship. An example of apocalyptic literature (cf. Section V of Chapter III), this book contains exhortations to Christians to remain faithful under persecution, to refrain from engaging in the cult of emperor worship. The God who has acted in history through his disclosure in Jesus Christ still rules the world and, while the present evil must run its course, its doom is already sealed. Those who would make this book into a time-table for the end of the world miss the point. Its major message to Christians under persecution is that they should remain faithful. True, the author believes that the persecution will soon be ended by Christ's coming again to usher in the New Age in its fullness, but his major emphasis is upon keeping the faith _now_.

In our brief survey of the New Testament, we have seen that as with the Old Testament there is a rich diversity in its message. Yet, just as with the Old Testament, so also in the New Testament there is a _unity_ within this diversity. By way of a concluding summary, we will call attention again to the following unifying themes:

(1) In Jesus Christ God had acted decisively for the redemption of mankind so that the New Age, the New Covenant, had begun to break into the present situation.

(2) Jesus Christ was a real man who lived a completely human life and yet in this man's life, teaching, death, and resurrection, God had uniquely disclosed himself as a loving, gracious, and forgiving God. This love which breaks the power of sin and death has been disclosed especially in the crucifixion and resurrection of Jesus Christ.

(3) Even though expressed in a variety of terms, God's action through Jesus Christ for mankind may be appropriated through humble acceptance such that even now there is reconciliation with God and a foretaste of the New Age. On this basis, the Christian seeks to live a life guided by the highest moral standards, not because of prudential reasons, to gain something for himself, but because of his gratitude for God's acceptance and his love for God and man.

(4) The Christian does not live a solitary life but gladly and freely participates in the "body of Christ," the Church, which is the community of the New

117

Covenant. In this community, guided by the Holy Spirit,
Christians received mutual consolation, support, and
admonition to remain faithful in the pilgrimage of the
Christian life.

(5) There is a goal for this pilgrimage since
most of the New Testament writings give expression to
an eschatological hope. Whether it is to occur in the
near future or later, the parousia hope is never abandoned and provides one of the bases for exhortations
to Christians to purify their lives and to patiently
endure the suffering of persecutions in preparation for
Christ's coming again. Then all suffering, sorrow,
sin, and death will be banished in the consummation of
the New Age.

Having summarized the major themes of the New
Testament, it might be well as we conclude our discussion of the Bible to remind ourselves again of the
considerable continuity between the Old and New Testaments. In the final paragraph of our discussion of the
Old Testament in Chapter III, we stated that much like
a historical drama the message of the Old Testament
moves from Creation to New Creation, from the beginning
to the end of history. In between is the "drama"
of man's sin and God's entrance into history to win
back his lost creation through servant Israel, his
covenant people, so that mankind and the whole of
creation might be redeemed and renewed in the final
consummation of the New Age. Now, in light of our
brief survey of the New Testament, we can see that
for Christians the "drama" has been expanded, a new
"act" has been added. In this "act" God has disclosed
himself decisively through Jesus Christ and through
him has broken the power of sin and death which corrupted and threatened history. He has called into
being a New People who reconciled to him through Jesus
Christ await with hope the consummation of the New Age.
So with the addition of this "act," Christians believe
that the message of the entire Bible moves from Creation to New Creation, from beginning to eschaton. In
between are the themes of human sin and rebellion and
God's acts for the redemption of mankind, beginning
with Israel and culminating in the Christ Event, the
New Covenant community, and the promise for the consummation of the New Age.

CHAPTER IV

[1] One or more of the books on the New Testament listed in the Suggestions for Further Reading should be read as a supplement to the discussion in this chapter.

[2] Scholars disagree as to whether Ephesians was actually written by Paul or by some later unknown person in the Pauline tradition. Where competent specialists disagree, it is the course of wisdom to refrain from pontificating on such matters as authorship and date. So while I am listing Ephesians among the genuine letters of Paul, I regard this issue as one which is not as yet definitely settled and thus is still open to scholarly inquiry.

[3] Matthew, Mark, and Luke are called "Synoptic Gospels" because they contain brief synopses of the ministry and message of Jesus.

[4] Among the extra-Biblical sources which refer to Jesus (or Christus) are the writings of the Romans, Tacitus (ca. 116 A.D.), and Seutonius (ca. 120 A.D.), the Jewish historian, Josephus (Ca. 90 A.D.), and the encyclopedia of Jewish tradition, The Talmud. cf. C. Milo Connick, Jesus, The Man, The Mission, and The Message, Second Edition (Prentice-Hall, Inc., 1974), pp. 58-62.

[5] See above, Chapter II, Section C.

[6] This claim is supported by the fact that unlike modern biographies the Synoptics tell us almost nothing about the formative influences on Jesus during his childhood and youth. Their very content indicates that instead of being historical documents they are faith documents and it is for this reason they are called "Gospels."

[7] D. T. Rowlingson, "The Symoptic Problem," The Interpreter's Dictionary of the Bible, Vol. R-Z (Abingdon Press, 1962), p. 492.

[8] See Burton H. Throckmorton, Jr., Gospel Parallels, Second Edition (Thomas Nelson & Sons, 1957).

[9] The saying of Jesus recorded in Mark 14:25 refers to the kingdom as a future reality while that in Luke 17:21 refers to it as a present reality.

[10] Maurice Goguel, The Life of Jesus (The Macmillan Co., 1933), p. 228.

[11] See Chapter II above, p. 48.

[12] Quaestiones Evangeliorum, II. 19.

[13] This discussion owes much to C. Milo Connick, Jesus, The Man, The Mission and The Message, Second Edition (Prentice-Hall, 1974). See Chapter 14, pp. 202-236.

[14] See Liddell and Scott, Greek-English Lexicon (Abridged) (Follett Publishing Company, 1927).

[15] Dietrich Bonhoeffer, Letters and Papers from Prison (The Macmillan Company, 1953), pp. 237-238.

[16] Acts 22:3 reports that Paul studied at Jerusalem in the Academy of Gamaliel. However, there is no mention of Gamaliel in any of Paul's letters.

[17] Such a brief summary always runs the risk of oversimplification. I have attempted to keep in mind the contexts of Paul's letters and life situation as background for this discussion. However, I would encourage the reader to supplement this discussion by reading one or more of the excellent studies on Paul which are now available. Some of these are included in the list of Suggestions for Further Reading.

[18] Donald M. Baillie, God was in Christ (Charles Scribner's Sons, 1948), p. 204.

[19] Howard Clark Kee, Franklin W. Young, Karlfried Froelich, Understanding The New Testament, Third Edition (Prentice-Hall, 1973), p. 214.

[20] J. Philip Hyatt, The Heritage of Biblical Faith (The Bethany Press, 1964), pp. 232-233.

[21] J. Philip Hyatt, Ibid., p. 241.

[22] J. Philip Hyatt, Ibid., p. 237.

[23] J. Philip Hyatt, Ibid., pp. 237, 239.

[24] Rudolf Bultmann, Theology of the New Testament, Vol. I (Charles Scribner's Sons, 1951), pp. 332-333.

[25] Kee, Young, and Froelich, op. cit., p. 198.

[26] It appears that Gnosticism became a more serious threat to the church in the latter half of the Second Century. It will be discussed again in somewhat more detail in Chapter VI below.

[27] I have italicized the word _flesh_ for the sake of emphasis.

[28] The late and very brief letters called II Peter and Jude also deal with this problem but have been omitted from our discussion since what they have to say is primarily a repetition of what is said in the other writings we have discussed here.

SUGGESTIONS FOR FURTHER READING

Albright, W. F., and C. S. Mann, Matthew, Vol. 26, Anchor Bible, Doubleday, 1971.

Beare, Frank W., St. Paul and His Letters, Abingdon Press, 1962.

Brown, Raymond E., S. S., The Gospel According to John, Vols. 29 and 29A, The Anchor Bible, Doubleday and Company, 1966 and 1970.

Connick, C. Milo, Jesus, The Man, The Mission, and The Message, Second Edition, Prentice-Hall, 1974.

Connick, C. Milo, The New Testament: An Introduction to Its History, Literature, and Thought, Dickenson Publishing Company, 1972.

Craig, Clarence Tucker, The Beginning of Christianity, Abingdon Press, 1943.

Crapps, Robert W., Edgar V. McKnight, and David A. Smith, Introduction to the New Testament, The Ronald Press, 1969.

Dodd, C. H., The Parables of The Kingdom, Charles Scribner's Sons, 1936.

Efird, James M. These Things are Written: An Introduction to the Religious Ideas of the Bible, John Knox Press, 1978.

Enslin, Morton Scott, Christian Beginnings, Harper Torchlight, 1956.

Goguel, Maurice, The Life of Jesus, The Macmillan Company, 1933.

Howard, George E., Paul: Crisis in Galatia, Cambridge University Press, 1979.

Hunter, A. M., A Pattern For Life, Revised Edition, Westminster Press, 1965.

Hunter, A. M., Interpreting the Parables, Westminster Press, 1960.

Hyatt, J. Philip, The Heritage of Biblical Faith, The Bethany Press, 1964.

Kee, Howard Clark, Franklin W. Young, and Karlfried Froelich, Understanding the New Testament, Third Edition, Prentice-Hall, 1973.

Klausner, Joseph, _Jesus of Nazareth_, The Macmillan Company, 1949.

Perrin, Norman, _The New Testament, An Introduction_, Harcourt Brace Jovanovich, Inc., 1974.

Price, James L., _Interpreting the New Testament_, Second Edition, Holt, Rinehart, and Winston, Inc., 1971.

Sandmel, Samuel, _Judaism and Christian Beginnings_, Oxford University Press, 1978.

Selby, Donald J., _Toward the Understanding of St. Paul_, Prentice-Hall, 1962.

Spivey, Robert A., and D. Moody Smith, _Anatomy of the New Testament_, Second Edition, Macmillan Publishing Company, Inc., 1974.

The Interpreter's Bible, Vol. 7, "General Articles on the New Testament," pp. 3-227, Abingdon Press, 1951.

CHAPTER V

THE EMERGENCE OF RABBINIC JUDAISM

Any discussion of the origins and sources of the Judeo-Christian tradition would be inadequate if it failed to give some attention not only to the Bible but also to the perspectives, practices, and institutions associated with what might be called "Rabbinic Judaism."[1] In his his excellent book Rabbinic Judaism in the Making, Alexander Guttmann claims that Rabbinic Judaism became and remains "the mainstream of Judaism from antiquity to date."[2]

Rabbinic Judaism emerged and developed over several centuries from about the fourth century B.C. through the fourth century A.D.[3] Given this time span and the fact that the Rabbinic literature of this era (oral and/or written) presupposes the Tanak or Old Testament (and especially the Torah), however tenuous the actual relation to the Tanak may be in particular cases, it seems appropriate to locate the discussion of Rabbinic Judaism in the section on the Biblical Period.

According to Samuel Sandmel, "the Jewish sages in effect rewrote the Bible."[4] Even though, as Sandmel acknowledges, some of this "rewriting" may seem rather far-fetched to the modern Biblical scholar, in their own perspective the sages thought of their literature (oral and/or written) as thoroughly consistent with the Bible which in their literature was regarded as alive and contemporary. According to the traditional view, the revelation of God which had been granted to Israel in the written Torah had overflowed as a spring overflows into a stream into the other books of the Tanak and from there into Rabbinic literature. Further, it was generally held that when God gave Moses the written Torah at Mount Sinai he also whispered its oral interpretations into his ear. In both forms, written and oral, Moses, it was thought, had handed the Torah on to Joshua and Joshua to the Elders and the Elders to the Prophets and the prophets to the men of the Great Synagogue (aboth I. 1)[5] and these sages to the rabbis. Thus, even though sacred Scripture was accorded a position of prime importance and was, as Sandmel says, "the adhesive that held the Jews together, that fed and nurtured their loyalty to the notion of being Jewish,"[6] the literature of the rabbis came to have a place of great authority.

In light of modern historical scholarship, it must be acknowledged that, while the continuity between the Hebrew Scriptures and the Rabbinic literature is very great, there is also some discontinuity. In Chapter IV we indicated that there was both continuity and discontinuity between the Old and New Testaments. Similarly with respect to the Hebrew Scriptures and Rabbinic literature, there is both continuity and discontinuity. As Alexander Guttman points out:

> In their work of adjusting Judaism to the needs of the day, the rabbis proceeded steadily, but gradually. They kept away from extremes. They did not adhere slavishly to the letter of the law as did some peripheral groups. On the other hand, they did not force the Bible to conform to foreign ideas and philosophies to the extent done by philosophical and sectarian schools . . . To keep Judaism meaningful and livable the rabbis did not merely modify old laws and add new ones but also suspended many an out-of-date law, and shifted a number of laws and practices from the periphery to the center and vice versa.[7]

This suspension of some laws and shifting of some from the center to the periphery is especially obvious after the destruction of the Temple by the Romans in 70 A.D. and the resulting elimination of the sacrificial system from Judaism, since sacrifices could be offered only in the Temple. Authority shifted from the High Priest and the ruling council (the Sanhedrin) to the scholar (Rabbinic sage) and the academy. The religious life of ordinary folk was nurtured by the synagogue in which there was worship and study but not sacrifice. Here then were two institutions, the academy and the synagogue, which were not explicitly described in the Hebrew Scriptures as was the Temple. Thus these two institutions and the practices associated with them, even though they may not be in contradition to anything in the Hebrew Scripture, are not in strict continuity with it either but rather represent a further development.

There are many obstacles which confront us in the attempt to gain even a modest general understanding of Rabbinic Judaism and the literature produced by the rabbis during the eight centuries from about the fourth century B.C. through the fourth century A.D. For one thing there is a vast amount of such literature. The major work, the Talmud, which is the written deposit of centuries of oral traditions, contains eighteen lengthy volumes in a standard English translation.[8] Even if there were no other difficulties, the very extensive content of the Talmud would require a lifetime of study if one would become an expert in it.

Another difficulty is found in the great variety and style of this literature. The Talmud, for example, is a conglomerate of law, legend, folk sayings, medical lore, anecdotes, wise sayings, humor, and subtle arguments. The style is generally one of brevity and succinctness. There are innumerable elliptical expressions with whole sentences often indicated by one word. This presented no difficulty for the rabbis who knew the Scriptures and the sayings of hundreds of rabbis in previous centuries by heart, but this laconic or concise style means that for the modern reader the Talmud is not "easy reading." Furthermore, there are often closely reasoned and subtle arguments which will continue over many pages and which sometimes are in the form of questions and answers with no strict line of demarcation between them. It is no wonder that traditionally those who would study the Talmud are advised to seek the guidance of a Talmudic scholar or sage.

A third obstacle is that when we enter the world of Rabbinic literature we seem to be so often in a world radically different from our own. The same impression is also often experienced by those who engage in a study of the Bible for the first time. It would not be correct to overemphasize this obstacle, and yet it is the case that there is material which has no immediate relevance to the practical concerns of life today. A most obvious case in point here, of course, would be the detailed legislation concerning the proper offerings of sacrifices. As we have seen, the legislation became irrelevant to the rabbis themselves after the destruction of the Temple. In spite of the fact that some material in the Talmud is irrelevant for today's concerns, much of it is relevant to any age such as the admonition to love all mankind. Further, while in many cases the models or examples used in arguments may have no application today, the general principles derived from the arguments for the guidance of human life are relevant in any age. Sometimes the models or examples used by the rabbis had no practical relevance for their own times. Rather they were thought of by the rabbis in their attempt to determine whether or not a principle or a law would be applicable to all conceivable situations. Yet, oddly enough, in some cases these models which had no practical application in the time of the rabbis do have a practical application in our own times. An example of such is a discussion of the rabbis concerning the ownership of a tower which floats off into the air. In our day of airplanes and skyscrapers the issue of ownership of airspace is certainly a relevant issue.

Perhaps the most serious obstacle to an understanding of Rabbinic literature and of Judaism in general during the Hellenistic age is the fact of the relatively widespread misconceptions and prejudical judgments concerning it which must be overcome before Rabbinic Judaism can be understood for what it actually was. Some Christians, due to their ignorance and prejudice,[9] claim that Jesus, even though he was a Jew, opposed a degraded Jewish environment in which the dominant motif was a kind of narrow legalism bereft of any sensitivity for the human condition or of any "heart felt" love for man or God. As over against this, the Christian Gospel, they claim, emphasized that love which both transcends and brings freedom from the law. Such claims misrepresent Judaism in general as well as Pharisaism and Rabbinic Judaism in particular. Even a superficial acquaintance with Rabbinic literature (especially the Talmud) makes it clear that such claims are false. While, as indicated above, there is discontinuity as well as continuity between the Old and New Testaments, it does not follow from this that Jesus was at odds with his environment in the sense that he regarded his heritage as ignoble. As the prophets had done in their times so also Jesus opposed some things in the society of his day, but such opposition was not a rejection of his heritage. Similar opposition is found often in the Rabbinic literature. Indeed, the similarity between many of the sayings and parables of Jesus with those in Rabbinic literature is often rather striking. This fact suggests that the study of Rabbinic literature can contribute to a more complete knowledge of the <u>historical</u> Jesus.

While on the one hand Christian partisans have sometimes (perhaps too often) misrepresented the Judaism of Jesus' day by casting aspersions on it, Jewish partisans on the other hand have sometimes presented an

exaggerated picture in support of it. So Samuel Sandmel says:

> Jewish scholars tended to reply [to
> Christian aspersions] by idealizing
> the Pharisees even beyond the prudent
> yield of the documents. That is to
> say, the difficulties inherent in the
> modern study of ancient documents
> have been compounded by regrettable
> aspersions and defensive retorts.[10]

In the attempt to arrive at a basic general understanding of Rabbinic Judaism, the discussion in the
remainder of this chapter will consider briefly the
following: (1) the major socio-religious groups in
the Judaism of the first century A.D.; (2) the emergence of Rabbinic Judaism; (3) the great product of
Rabbinic Judaism, the Talmud, its background and structure, and (4) some characteristic perspectives contained
in the Talmud.

(1) There is a considerable amount of evidence
which demonstrates the falsity of the claim that first
century Judaism was simply one narrow legalistic religious system. Not least among this evidence is the
fact that there were several socio-religious groups in
the Judaism of the time. While there were some perspectives which these groups held in common such as God's
election of Israel and his guidance throughout her
history, there were also some very important differences
between these groups. This fact alone indicates that
there was considerable variety within first century
Judaism. Perhaps the most important of these groups
were the Essenes, the Sadducees, and the Pharisees.

a. The Essenes

While early historians of Hellenistic
Judaism had known of the Essenes,[11] this knowledge was
greatly augmented in contemporary times by the discovery about thirty years ago of the so-called Dead Sea
Scrolls and the subsequent archaeological discoveries
at Wadi El Qumran, the site of an ancient Essene community on the shores of the Dead Sea near the caves
where the scrolls were found.

In light of the information now available,[12] it
appears that the Essene community at Qumran was founded
about 140 B.C. In that year Simon Maccabeus (Maccabeus

is an honorific title meaning "Hammerer") of the house of Hasmon, who was continuing the warfare against the Seleucid rulers of Syria begun by his father and older brothers, managed to have himself made High Priest and thus displaced the legitimate High Priest of the Zadokite lineage. Such action was a violation of the long tradition going all the way back to Solomon in which the lineage and functions of king and High Priest were kept separate. It is not surprising that this move by Simon aroused opposition not only by those of Zadokite lineage but also by many pious people who felt that now the Temple sacrificial cult was corrupted. So in some of the Qumran scrolls there are references to a Righteous Teacher (a fervent supporter of the Zadokite priesthood and presumably of Zadokite lineage himself) who was persecuted by the Wicked Priest (presumably Simon) and who led a band of followers into exile in the wilderness. It was probably this group which established the Essene community at Qumran.

Given this background, it is understandable why the Essenes believed that they were the true Israel, the true Covenant community. Even though they had a high regard for the Temple and the central place it had held historically in the worship and life of Israel, they rejected the Temple cult of their own times because they viewed it as corrupt. Since the offering of sacrifices at any place other than the Temple was prohibited by the Torah (Deuteronomy 12:1-31), the Essenes did not engage in this practice. However they did observe all the festivals in ways other than actually offering sacrifices, and followed a calendar different from that followed in the Temple. They greatly honored Moses and Aaron, and were diligent in the studying and following of the Torah.

Among the documents found in the caves at Qumran are not only copies in whole or in part of all the Old Testament books but also writings by the Essenes themselves such as the Manual of Discipline and Commentaries on some Old Testament books. In the Commentaries it is evident that a major motif in their interpretations was that Scripture had been written for them, their own times and their immediate future. Given the conflicts of their times and the eschatology which they thought to be expressed in some Old Testament books,[13] the Essenes were convinced that they were living near the end of the age. Soon there would be a great holy war between "the children of light" and "the children of darkness." Led by the Messiah of

Israel, of Davidic descent, "the children of light" would be victorious. But along with this Messiah of Israel there was to come a priestly Messiah of Zadokite lineage, and he would establish the true Jerusalem and the true Temple. With victory over "the children of darkness" and the true Temple the New Age would have arrived.

It was this eschatological conviction, as well as the persecution of the "wicked priest," which led the Essenes to withdraw into the wilderness of Qumran. Israel's existence as a community had begun under Moses in the wilderness, and in Isaiah 40:3 (a copy of the entire book of Isaiah was found in the caves of Qumran) there is the command: "In the wilderness prepare the way of the Lord." The Essenes understood such preparation to entail taking vows of poverty and living a communal lifestyle under a strict discipline. This discipline involved celibacy and other ascetic practices. Such asceticism was not based on the view that the body and its desires were evil. Given their heritage (the story of creation in Genesis, for example), no Jew would have thought this. Rather the Essene asceticism was simply a practical matter of being able to spend all their time, freed from family responsibilities, in preparation for the great advent of the New Age which they thought to be close at hand. Thus, the asceticism of the Essenes might be characterized as a pragmatic eschatological asceticism.

It seems to be the case that the Essenes, probably due to their strong eschatological convictions, became involved in the Jewish resistance against Rome in the late sixties A.D. As a result the Dead Sea community was destroyed by the Romans about 70 A.D., and the Essenes ceased to exist as a socio-religious group. Little or no influence from the Essenes can be detected in subsequent Judaism.

b. The Sadducees

While the Bible is silent with respect to the Essenes and information concerning this group must be gained entirely from extra-Biblical sources, the socio-religious group known as the Sadducees is mentioned briefly in the New Testament (Mark 12:18-27, for example). The Biblical references, however, must be supplemented from extra-Biblical sources such as the writings of the ancient Jewish historian, Josephus (90 A.D.).[14] Even when this is done, however, the currently

131

available information concerning the Sadducees is much less than that which we have concerning the Essenes. There are no extant writings from the Sadducees. Instead all of our information concerning them must be gleaned from the writings of their opponents.

There is considerable obscurity with respect to the origin of the name "Sadducee" and some obscurity with respect to the origin of the group itself. Since in some sources of our information concerning the Sadducees (most notably Josephus) there are suggestions that the Sadducees were wealthy aristocrats whose interests were centered primarily in the Temple and the priesthood, there are some scholars who claim that the name "Sadducees" was probably derived from King Solomon's priest, Zadok. If so, then their name simply is indicative of their priestly interests and the centering of their piety in the Temple cult and not, like the Essenes, of their concern to preserve an unbroken Zadokite lineage in the High Priesthood. Indeed, they were apparently supporters of the Hasmonean High Priest (begun by Simon Maccabeus, as noted above). Whatever the origin of their name, it appears from the descriptions in Josephus that the Sadducees emerged as a party in Judaism during Maccabean times (ca. 167-63 B.C.).

According to the information available, it appears not only that the Sadducees centered their interests in the Temple but also, in the words of Samuel Sandmel, were "literalists, 'stand-patters'"[15] in their interpretations of the Torah-book. Unlike the Pharisees (to be discussed below) who accepted the oral interpretations of the Torah-book as being as authoritative as what was actually written in the Torah-book, the Sadducees accorded authority only to what was actually written in the Torah-book. Perhaps this is one reason why they centered their piety in the Temple (explicitly referred to in Deuteronomy) and apparently had little relation to the synagogue which, originating in the Post-Exilic period, is not mentioned in the five books of the Torah.

The Sadducees' rejection of the "oral" Torah most definitely accounts for their denial of a post-mortem resurrection life, a Messianic age, and predestination. They could not find any of these beliefs explicitly stated in the Torah-book and, since for them only what was actually written there was authoritative, they rejected these beliefs. Interestingly, it was on the question of a resurrection life that the Sadducees, according to Mark 12:18-27, engaged Jesus in a controversy. They attempted to show the absurdity of such a belief, but Jesus, in this case using a typical kind of Pharisee argument, defended the belief in a resurrection life.

According to some scholars, in addition to their activities in the Temple the Sadducees played a dominant role in the "great" Sanhedrin. This was the supreme Jewish council of seventy-one members in Jerusalem having legislative as well as judiciary functions. Given the important roles they played in both the Temple cult and the Sanhedrin, they probably served as the official representatives of the Jews in their relations with Rome. In the latter role, they apparently supported some degree of accommodation and coexistence with the Romans, probably in order to preserve the Sanhedrin and uninterrupted Temple services.16

We have noted above that the Temple was at the center of the Sadducees' interests and activities. It is not surprising, then, that after the destruction of the Temple by the Romans in 70 A.D. the Sadducees ceased to exist as a socio-religious group.

c. The Pharisees

A third important socio-religious group in first century Judaism was the Pharisees. Similar to the case with respect to the Sadducees, the origins of the name "Pharisee" and the group itself are clouded with obscurity. The name may mean either "explainers" or "separators" or both, since the Pharisees explained Scripture and sought to separate themselves from evil or defilement. The origin of the group itself may have had its roots in the Hasidim (the "Pious") who resisted the attempts of a Syrian Seleucid King Antiochus IV, to Hellenize the Jews and by this action precipitated the Maccabean revolt. From the Hasidim it is possible that both the Essenes and the Pharisees developed. The Essenes, disillusioned with the Maccabeans when, as noted above, Simon took over the High Priesthood, withdrew from public life. The Pharisees, however, remained in the public arena and attempted to have a direct influence on the active life of the people.

Throughout the centuries, at least in the popular mind, the Pharisees have had, so to speak, a "bad press." They have been regarded as the epitome of a narrow-minded legalism. Even modern English dictionaries

define the adjective "pharisaic," derived from the noun
"Pharisee," as: "emphasizing or observing the letter
but not the spirit of religious law; self-righteous;
sanctimonious; hypocritical" (Webster's New World Dictionary). This view is surely wrong. Undoubtedly
there were some "pharisaical" Pharisees. No religion
seems to be without some people of legalistic perspectives. But there is abundant evidence that the majority
of the Pharisees were not sanctimonious or hypocritical
legalists. Even in the Talmud are to be found passages
attacking "pharisaical" Pharisees and praising the
Pharisee who, like Abraham, loves God, is humble of
spirit, and diligent in study.[17] When it is kept in
mind that these passages originated either with those
who were Pharisees or felt themselves to be in the
Pharisee tradition, then it is obvious how mistaken it
is to characterize the Pharisees as "pharisaical." Instead there was no other group in the ancient world who
demonstrated a higher standard of righteousness in
personal and social life than did the Pharisees.

Although there were individual differences, the
Pharisees as a group appear to have opposed the Sadducees' political policy of accommodation with the
Romans. In their religious perspectives, however, the
Pharisees were not literalists or "stand-patters" as
were the Sadducees. As Sandmel puts it: "the Pharisees were progressive, innovative, and amenable to
the reasonable adjustment of the legacy of the past
to the needs of the present."[18]

While the Pharisees, like all the Jews of their
times, had a high regard for the Temple, central to
their perspectives was the Torah. Unlike the Sadducees,
for them the Torah incorporated not only the Torah-book
(Genesis through Deuteronomy) but also the rest of Old
Testament Scripture and the oral Torah. The oral Torah
contained the oral interpretations of the Torah-book
which had emerged over the centuries in the synagogues,
synagogue schools, and academies. This oral Torah was
as authoritative for the Pharisees as the written Torah.
It represented the attempt to make what was written in
the Torah-book relevant in any age.

It was due to their acceptance of the oral Torah
that the Pharisees, unlike the Sadducees, accepted such
beliefs as the resurrection, Messianic age, and predestination. While these beliefs were not explicitly
stated in the Torah-book, through subtle arguments they
had been derived from statements in the Torah-book.

For example, in the narrative concerning Moses' encounter with God in Exodus 3:1-6, God says to Moses: "I am the God of your father, the God of Abraham, the God of Isaac, and the God of Jacob." Now the sages reasoned that if God could say to Moses I am the God of these patriarchs whose earthly lives had terminated long before the time of Moses, then it follows that they had been raised from the dead to live on in a post-mortem realm. According to Mark 12:18-27, it was this type of Pharisee argument which Jesus used against the Sadducees who rejected the belief in a resurrection life. Given this and similar types of interpretation, the oral Torah was regarded by the Pharisees as simply making explicit what was already implicitly entailed in the written Torah, and thus it is not surprising that this Torah was regarded as authoritative.

Even though, as noted above, the Pharisees had a high regard for the Temple, the fact that the Temple cult was largely under the control of their opponents, the Sadducees, led the Pharisees to center their activity primarily in the academies and the synagogues. The latter had come into existence as a religious institution in Judaism after the Babylonian exile. Wherever there were ten adult male Jews there could be a synagogue. So there were synagogues not only in the towns and villages of Judah, but also wherever there was a center of Jewish population outside of Judah. As noted earlier, the synagogue was an institution for worship and for study of the Jewish heritage including, of course, the Torah. As Sandmel puts it: "The synagogue was a school for adults."[19] For the instruction of children there was a more or less formal school connected with the synagogue. To quote Sandmel again: "Whenever there was a synagogue, there was also a school."[20] Since the Pharisees wished to have an influence on public life, they undoubtedly participated in the various functions of the synagogue. Also they engaged in "higher education" by means of their participation in the academies established by famous Rabbinic sages. Both the academy and the synagogue survived the war with Rome and the destruction of the Temple in 70 A.D. and became the dominant institutions in Jewish life.

(2) The Emergence of Rabbinic Judaism

Of the three socio-religious groups we have discussed it is rather obvious that the Pharisees alone contributed to the development of Rabbinic Judaism.

They participated in the synagogues and Rabbinic academies and contributed to the growth of the oral Torah.
Indeed, during a certain period of time Pharisaic and
Rabbinic Judaism cannot be distinguished but are
identical. According to Alexander Guttmann:

> Pharasaic--Rabbinic Judaism begins with
> Hillel two or three decades B.C.E. [B.C.].
> Rabbinic Judaism proper commences with the
> destruction of the Temple in 70 C.E. [A.D.],
> and its end is not yet in sight.[21]

As we have noted above, the Pharisees as a socio-
religious group supported certain political perspectives and actions. As a group they apparently
supported the rebellion against Rome which resulted
in the Roman military campaigns against Judah and
Jerusalem and the devastation of the country and the
Temple. After this they ceased to exist as a socio-
religious group. Yet their perspectives and traditions
were preserved and further developed in Rabbinic Judaism.

Samuel Sandmel has described the situation very
aptly and succinctly when he says:

> Pharisaism itself, so I believe, petered
> out, but its thrust persisted, and to
> some extent so did the name. But Rabbinic
> Judaism, deriving as it did from Phari-
> saism, is what Pharisaism developed into,
> and is by no means the same as Pharisaism,
> which was in part a political impulse.
> Rabbinic Judaism, on the other hand, is
> the result of the ascendancy of the non-
> political Academy, the result of the shift
> in authority from the ruling council (San-
> hedrin or Bet Din) to the rule of the
> scholars, the Sages.[22]

(3) The Talmud: Its background, structure and
     style

The major work of Rabbinic Judaism is the
Talmud, a work which has had a profound influence in
the history of Judaism. As Adin Steinsaltz has stated:

> If the Bible is the cornerstone of Juda-
> ism, then the Talmud is the central
> pillar, soaring up from the foundations

and supporting the entire spiritual
and intellectual edifice. In many
ways the Talmud is the most important
book in Jewish culture, the backbone
of creativity and of national life. No
other work has had a comparable influence on the theory and practice of
Jewish life, shaping spiritual content
and serving as a guide to conduct.[23]

Since the Talmud is of such fundamental significance
for Judaism, it is obvious that we must seek to gain
at least a general understanding of it, its origins,
structure, style, and content.

In the discussion concerning the Pharisees (Section l.c. above), it was indicated that the Pharisees
accepted the oral interpretations and traditions which
had been derived from the written Torah. This "oral
Torah" resulted from the Torah study of the Rabbinic
sages or scholars and over the centuries developed
into a massive body of oral material. The term Talmud means literally "study" or "learning."[24] So a
Rabbinic sage engaged in the study and discussion of
Torah and of the decisions of previous rabbis was
engaged in the pursuit of "Talmud" (i.e., learning).
As a result of this study and discussion, which was
centered primarily in the academies, there developed
compilations of the oral laws, ethical teachings,
legends, anecdotes, etc., of the Rabbinic sages. This
material itself, especially after it was put into
written form, came to be called the Talmud. Thus the
Talmud is the written deposit of the compilation of
centuries of oral commentaries.

This compilation took place for the most part in
two stages. The first was the Mishnah,[25] a term the
original meaning of which was "to repeat" but which
came to mean "to relate," "to teach," "to transmit
orally." Thus Mishnah means "oral teaching" or
"instruction in the oral law" as contrasted to reading and studying the written law of the Bible.[26] While
some degree of codification and systematization of the
great mass of oral law was attempted by the great Rabbinic sages Hillel (ca. 30 B.C.-10 A.D.) and Akiba
(50-132 A.D.), it was Rabbi Judah the Prince (135-220
A.D.) who was responsible for the major compilation of
the Mishnah (ca. 220 A.D.). While the Mishnah today
may not be precisely the same as that compiled by Rabbi
Judah, it is basically the same. It is divided into

137

six main sections ("orders" or "series") with each section containing several treatises or tractates such that the total number of tractates in the entire Mishnah is sixty-three.

The second stage in the compilation was the Gemara. This term is derived from the Hebrew verb which means "to finish" or "to complete" and so signifies the "completion" of or "supplement" to the Mishnah. Together Mishnah and Gemara constitute the Talmud. While there are two versions, one compiled in Palestine (ca. 400 A.D.) and the other in Babylon (ca. 500 A.D.), the latter, the Babylonian Talmud, is much larger and generally is regarded as the standard Talmud.

The definitions of a few other terms are necessary for our discussion of the evolution and structure of the Talmud. One of these is the term halakah, which means literally "walking" and by implication designates the provisions, laws, and guides which should be followed in their daily lives by those who would be faithful. Halakah is Rabbinic law supposedly derived from Biblical law (Mitzvah).[27] Yet it also designates all expositions, discussions, and reports which have the object of explaining, establishing, and determining legal principles and provisions. The halakot (plural of halakah) contained within the sixty-three tractates of the Mishnah deal with all phases of human life and activity, with what today we would call both the religious and the secular.

The Mishnah provides what might be called the "skeletal" structure of the Talmud. Its style, however, is very terse with little or no explanation of the halakot or citation of Scriptural bases. So the Gemara attempts to put "flesh" on this "skeleton." This "flesh" is designated haggadah. This term means literally "narrative" but in the sense used here includes much more than "narrative" in the strict sense of the term. Indeed, haggadah includes everything which does not have the character of halakah. It includes historical narratives, legends, parables, humorous sayings and stories, anecdotes about famous rabbis, religious and ethical teachings, and free interpretations of Scripture. In its commentary on any particular legal opinion expressed in the Mishnah, the Gemara uses haggadic material in its exposition in order to clarify the opinion and to recommend its acceptance. While the Gemara is primarily haggadic in nature, the Mishnah is largely halakic. However, there

138

is some haggadic material in the latter, most notably in the tractate which is often called "The Ethics of the Fathers" (Aboth, tractate 9 of Order IV: Nezikin, "Injuries").

Other important terms which should be mentioned in a discussion of the evolution of the Talmud are titles for the sages. While apparently the earliest sages were not given titles, any sage mentioned in the Mishnah came to be called <u>tanna</u>, a term which means one who studies and teaches. The term <u>tanna</u> itself does not appear in the Mishnah, but it is used in the Gemara to designate any teacher mentioned in the Mishnah. For about three centuries after the compilation of the Mishnah (Rabbi Judah, 200 A.D.), any teacher or sage who engaged in the work of interpreting the Mishnah which found its way into the Gemara was called an <u>Amora</u>. This term comes from the verb <u>amor</u> which means to speak, interpret, or expound. As Sandmel points out:

> In the Babylonian Talmud, a tanna is called
> <u>rabbi</u> ('My Teacher'); an amora is called
> <u>rab</u> ('teacher,' pronounced rav) . . . The
> age up to the compilation of Mishna
> is called 'the tannaitic age,' or else
> 'the age of the tannaim' (plural of tanna)
> [first through the second century A.D.];
> the subsequent age [third through fifth
> century] is called either 'the amoraic age'
> or 'the age of the <u>amoraim</u>.'[27]

Unlike the case with respect to the Scriptures (The Tanak) in which an official canon was established by a council of rabbis at Jamnia about 90 A.D., no canon of the Talmud was ever established. Even after the amoraic age at the end of which the Mishnah plus the Gemara had been put in written form, there were Talmudic scholars who introduced minor amendments and additions. According to Adin Steinsaltz:

> No single scholar is named as having
> officially completed the writing and
> editing of the Talmud (as is the case
> with the Mishnah), hence the significant
> saying: 'The Talmud was never completed.'
> There was never a time when intellectual
> activity founded on the Talmud came to a
> standstill, and it continued to take on
> new forms for many generations to come.[28]

In light of this, it is appropriate to speak of
the Talmud as "the living Talmud." Commentaries and
opinions of outstanding Talmudic scholars in the post-
amoraic age were often included in the later written
editions of the Talmud. Among these were the comments
and decisions of the heirs of the amoraim, the geonim.
This title is gained from gaon which initially meant
the head of a great academy and then more imprecisely
any great Talmudic scholar. Also there were commentaries by the great scholar Rabbi Solomon Isaaki,
better known as Rashi (1040-1105 A.D.), the tosafot
("additions") which are commentaries by Rashi's
descendants and disciples, and the commentary on the
Mishnah by the famous Moses ben Maimon, better known
as Maimonides (1135-1204 A.D.).

The diagram on the following page is an attempt
to depict graphically the various stages in the development of the Talmud.[29]

Having discussed the Talmud's evolution and structure, we turn now to a general description of its
style. In our discussion of halakah and haggadah we
have noted already that the Talmud contains a variety
of literary forms such as law, legal decisions, legends,
parables, historical narratives, anecdotes, etc. However, more needs to be said concerning a general characterization of this vast body of literature.

It has been emphasized that behind the written
Talmud were centuries of oral teaching and transmission. This is surely one factor which contributes to
the uniqueness of the Talmud's content, the other
being the rabbis' consuming passion to bring the whole
of life under the specific directives of God. Judah
Goldin has characterized the Talmud's content as
possessing a "non-'literary' quality"[30] and a total
commitment to the discipline of halakah. According
to Goldin:

> The non-'literary' quality of Talmudic
> substance does not mean that in the Tal-
> mud there is an indifference to forms of
> expression or an aloofness to the require-
> ments even of literary grace. The very
> seriousness towards terms, the very striv-
> ing toward precision, is proof to the
> contrary. And there is frequently a
> compactness or sharpness to Talmudic
> passages and sentences that reveals

140

THE TORAH

The "written law" which, according to ancient tradition, was given to Moses at Sinai, who passed it on to Joshua and Joshua to the Elders and the Elders to the Prophets and the Prophets to the Sanhedrin.

THE MISHNAH

Compilation and codification of the "oral law" which for generations had been transmitted by word of mouth. Compiled by Rabbi Judah and his disciples ca. 200 A.D. in Palestine.

THE TALMUD

THE PALESTINIAN GEMARA

Commentaries on the Mishnah by amoraim in Palestine. With the Mishnah this forms Palestinian Talmud. Ca. 400 A.D.

THE BABYLONIAN GEMARA

Commentaries on the Mishnah by the amoraim in Babylonian academies. With the Mishnah this forms The Babylonian Talmud which is much larger than the Palestinian and most widely used. Ca. 500 A.D.

Commentaries such as those by geonim, Rashi, tosafot, and Maimonides. They are primarily though not exclusively dependent on The Babylonian Talmud. The broken line from the Palestinian and the solid line from the Babylonian Talmud indicate the greater dependence on the latter.

141

genuine alertness to style and verbal
effect. But we must never forget that
the Talmud is not a literary treatise
or literary composition brought into
being by an author--who selects a subject,
prepares an introduction, goes on to a
beginning, middle, and conclusion, neatly
(ideally speaking of course) organizes
all he wants to say and artistically
moves either his characters or his ideas
so that they appear with the proper lights
and shadows. In a literary work, you see
things; in the Talmud, you hear voices.
Here is a kind of transcript of the very
words exchanged in the academy or in a
vineyard or on a journey or in a court
session. The scene, the protagonists,
the beginning, middle, end, you must
supply as, on the basis of the conversations, you try to picture what it was all
like and how it developed. The Talmudic
rabbis were not writers of books, but
teachers, by word of mouth creating and
expanding the Oral Torah. We do not so
much read what these great sages said as
hear them in their sessions--but there
are no prepared speeches. What there is
is intellect reacting to intellect.[31]

This "intellect reacting to intellect" was not
done in terms of abstractions. While there was considerable attention given to semantics--that is, word-
meanings and thing-meanings and their relations--and
to logical argument forms, these were based on concrete
cases and models. Even hypothetical examples had the
purpose of providing further illumination for practical
concrete issues. The Talmud possesses vitality not
only because the rabbis were concerned with the issues
of behavior and practice but also because they generally injected some haggadic reflections into the midst
of halakic legal commentaries.

Since in the Talmud we "hear voices" of scholars
and teachers, it is not surprising to find that often
its content is in the form of question and answer with
several answers proposed for a particular question.
Further, there are debates--arguments and counter argu-
ments--between the sages and between different academies. The Talmud contains numerous debates in which
two or more sages holding different opinions contend

with each other. One sage will express his opinion. Another will attack it citing evidence in support of his own argument. Then the first will give a defense for his original theory and the second will attack the defense offered by the first and so on back and forth. Such dialectical reasoning is called <u>pilpul</u>[32] which is a method of approaching even a supposedly settled issue with the query, "But isn't there a different way of looking at it?" or "May not a different conclusion be drawn from the same set of facts or precedents?" Thus in many ways, <u>pilpul</u> is not unlike the dialectical reasoning practiced by the Greek philosophers, most notably Socrates who continually raised questions about what appeared to be the most well established and obvious ideas and practices.[33]

Among the most famous controversies between different academies recorded in the Talmud are those between the schools of Shammai and Hillel. There are some three hundred and sixteen of such controversies[34] with the school of Shammai, in general, taking a more rigorous and the school of Hillel a more lenient view. Generally the opinion of the Hillel school prevailed, as indicated in the statement, "The opinion of Beth ["school"] Shammai when it conflicts with that of Beth Hillel is no Mishnah" (Berakoth 36b). However, this does not mean that the opinions and rulings of Beth Shammai are thought to be <u>absolutely</u> wrong or totally rejected by God. Indeed, there is a story that in the midst of a latter Rabbinic review of the controversies between the two schools a voice from Heaven said: "The opinions of both academies are the voice of the living God; the halacha, however, is to follow the Academy of Hillel."[35] So "the voice of the living God" applies also to the rejected Shammaite view, for it, too, is held to be an expression of divine creativity.

The fact that Shammaite opinions can be considered "the voice of the living God" even though rejected as halakah illustrates another characteristic feature of Talmudic style, namely, a thoroughgoing objectivity. While there are heated debates, this feature is balanced by an objectivity not unlike that of the modern scientist. As Steinsaltz has pointed out:

> When one of the sages ventured to say a
> certain theory was not to his liking,
> he was scolded by his colleagues, who
> informed him that it is wrong to say of
> Torah, 'This is good and this is not.'

143

Such a view is analogous to the case of
the scientist who is not permitted to say
that a certain creature seems to him
'unappealing.' This does not mean to
imply that evaluations (even of appeal)
should never be made; they should, however,
be based on consciousness of the fact that
no man has the right to judge or to
determine that a certain object lacks
beauty from the purely objective point
of view . . . This way of thinking also
engendered the view that no subject is
too strange, remote or bizarre to be
studied.36

The characteristic of objectivity is demonstrated also
in the fact that in a very fair way the Talmud presents
different and even contradictory opinions on numerous
issues. Often the discussion will arrive at what is
to be taken as the accepted halakah but in these cases,
as noted above in the discussion of Shammai and Hillel,
the different and/or contradictory opinions are not
treated with disdain. Sometimes the discussion does
not conclude with a statement of the accepted halakah
(Shabbath 37a). In such cases the issue is left open
suggesting that it is a question still in need of
resolution. Again, this is analogous to the methods
and procedures of the modern scientist who, when he
is unable to solve a problem definitely, presents the
available evidence supporting two or more solutions
and leaves the problem open for further investigation.

The debates, arguments and counter-arguments in
the Talmud demonstrate several types of argument forms.
Among these are the following:

1) Argument from common sense. An illustration of
such an argument is found in a discussion of Leviticus
19:27 which prohibits rounding off the hair on temples
or marring the edges of the beard. It is stated that
women are exempted from such a prohibition. In
response to the query as to how we know this, the
answer is, "by common sense for they have no beard"
(Kiddushin 35b).

2) Argument from authority. As already indicated,
the Torah occupies a position of primary authority
and attempts are made to solve problems on the basis
of Scriptural texts. In addition, there are traditional rulings and precedents which, if accepted by a

144

majority of the sages, are held to have great, even if not _absolute_, authority. Often what is called a "generally accepted rule" is cited in support of an argument (Yebamoth 6a). An example of such is contained in the following quotation: "We have a rule that we may raise an object to a higher grade of sanctity but must not degrade it to a lower" (Berakoth 28a, Yoma 112b).

3) Argument of inference or implication. This is an argument in which a conclusion is drawn on the basis of a careful consideration of the words in which a law or opinion is framed. For example, Mishnah (Shebuoth 3:11 or 29b) states that one is liable for an oath but it must be uttered by his own mouth. Yet in the same passage it goes on to say that one is liable if adjured by the mouth of others. Finally, in this passage it says that if the other says, "I adjure thee," and one responds, "Amen," then the latter is liable. The Gemara discussion points out that there is a contradiction between the first statement (must be uttered by his own mouth) and the second statement (one is liable if adjured by the mouth of others). However, it should be inferred that the first statement refers to a case in which one did not say, "Amen," and the second to a case in which he did say, "Amen." This inference is supported by a reference to Numbers 5:22 where, after having been adjured by the priest, "the woman shall say, 'Amen, Amen'" without herself having actually uttered the oath.

4) Argument from analogy. This type of argument depends upon two cases having a similarity which is the basis for concluding that what holds in one case will hold also in the other. Some of the analogies drawn by the sages are humorous and farfetched. An example of such an analogy occurs in a discussion of the liability incurred by one who borrows an animal which he puts to work. The general principle is that, if the animal is overworked so that it dies, the borrower is liable to make good the owner's loss. However, both in practice and in principle, it is often difficult to determine what constitutes overwork and so the sages would resort to analogies in an attempt to solve a particular case. The following is an example of an appeal to an analogous situation to solve a particular case related to the liability of the borrower:

A man borrowed a cat from his neighbor;

145

the mice formed a united party and killed
it. Now, R. Ashi sat and pondered thereon:
'How is it in such a case? Is it as though
it had died through its work, or not?'
Thereupon R. Mordecai said to R. Ashi:
'Thus did Abimi of Hagronia say in Raba's
name: A man whom woman killed--[for him]
--there is no judgment nor judge (Baba
Mezia 97a).

The point is that a man whom a woman killed is not
really a man so there is no redress. Similarly a cat
whom mice killed is not really a cat and so in such a
case the borrower is not liable.

5) Argument a fortiori ("all the more"). This is
a kind of argument from analogy. It consists in demonstrating that something such as a law or an opinion
holds true in a matter of lesser or negative significance and then arguing that there is even more reason
for it to hold in a similar matter of greater or
positive significance. This is sometimes called an
argument "from the lesser to the greater." The following story contains such an argument:

In a year of scarcity a certain man
deposited a denar of gold [a gold coin]
with a widow who put it in a jar of flour.
Subsequently she baked the flour and gave
[the loaf] to a poor man. In course of
time the owner of the denar came and said
to her, 'Give me back my denar' and she
said to him: 'May death seize upon one
of my sons if I have derived any benefit
for myself from your denar,' and not many
days passed--so it was stated--before one
of her sons died. When the Sages heard
of the incident they remarked: 'If
such is the fate of one who swears truly,
what must be the fate of one who swears
falsely!' (Gittin 35a).

6) Indirect argument or argumentum ad absurdum.
In this type of argument the contradictory of the
position one wishes to establish is assumed for the
purposes of the argument and then shown to have absurd
or damaging consequences. The following illustrates
such an argument:

The question was raised in the Academy:

146

> is it necessary to state the particulars
> of the vow [on seeking annulment] or is it
> not necessary? R. Papa said that it is
> necessary. R. Nahman said that it is not
> necessary, because if you say that it is,
> it may happen that the applicant will not
> state the case fully and the Sage will act
> on what he has been told (Grittin 35b).

That is, the sage may grant release where it should be
withheld or vice versa. Thus, for R. Nahman, the
position of R. Papa would have absurd consequences,
and this demonstrates the validity of his own position
which is the contradictory of R. Papa's.

While numerous instances of these argument forms
are found in the Talmud, there are also numerous counter arguments in which there is the attempt to demonstrate that there are fallacies in particular applica-
tions of these argument forms. Sometimes there is the
attempt to overthrow an argument from common sense by
showing that good common sense requires the contradictory view. Arguments from authority are sometimes
rejected by demonstrating that the arguments are based
on a misreading or misinterpretation of the Scripture
passages or previous legal opinions upon which the
arguments are based. Often arguments of implication
are overthrown by showing that they are what we today
call non-sequiturs. That is, the premises of the
argument do not provide a basis from which the desired
conclusion can be deduced. Arguments from analogy
are countered in some cases by showing that the analogy
is imperfect. That is, the supposed similarity between
the analogates does not in fact hold. In other cases
arguments from analogy are countered by showing that
the conclusion, if admitted, would prove far too much
allowing for something clearly inadmissable. Finally,
argumentum ad absurdum arguments are often refuted by
showing that a similar objection raised against the
contradictory statement may be raised also against the
original statement.

While it is the case that the Talmud's style
reflects the methods employed by great scholars who
undoubtedly enjoyed the very process of inquiry and
argumentation in and of itself, their purpose in using
such a process involved much more than intellectual
exercises for an elite. The dominant purpose was to
keep Torah (the revelation of God) relevant in any age

and to provide a guide for practice and behavior so as to preserve the divine dimension of life. Indeed, the process of study, interpretation, and debate was regarded as a necessary condition for right living. It is said in the Talmud that one learns (both written and oral Torah) in order to practice (Aboth VI.6), and that genuine learning results in such attributes of character as humility, moderation, patience, uprightness, love of God and of his creatures, and "a good heart which does not delight in giving legal decisions" (Aboth VI.5-6).

In Chief Rabbi Dr. J. H. Hertz's Foreword to the eighteen volume Soncino English edition of the Babylonian Talmud is a selection which characterizes both the style and content of the Talmud and which provides an appropriate conclusion for our discussion in this section. The selection from Rabbi Hertz is as follows:

> The Talmud is not an ordinary literary work. It bears no resemblance to any single literary production but forms a world of its own. . . The ancient Hebrew metaphor which speaks of the 'ocean of the Talmud', is helpful to the understanding of its nature. The Talmud is indeed an ocean, vast in extent, unfathomable in depth, with an ocean-like sense of immensity and movement about it. Its great broad surface is at times smooth and calm, at others disturbed by waves of argument and breakers of discussion, stormy with assertion and refutation. And like the ocean, it swarms with a thousand varied forms of life.[38]

4) Some Characteristic Perspectives Expressed in the Talmud

As has been suggested previously, the Rabbinic sages directed their attention to the whole of life. For them there was no such distinction as we often make today between the religious and secular domains of life. The rather commonly held perspective in contemporary western culture is that being religious is something special having to do with the personal and communal practices associated with religious institutions, but that it has little or nothing to do with such common ventures of life as politics, economics, legal proceedings, marriage and the family, social

problems, labor, and recreation. While the Rabbinic
sages viewed the Temple as sacred and insisted on the
faithful observance of sacred days and festivals and
on ritual and cultic purity, they held that doing the
divine will in the other common ventures of life was
just as obligatory. Their purpose was to bring every
aspect of life under the divine will disclosed in Torah.
Since Torah was regarded as encompassing everything
contained in the world, the scope of Talmudic teachings
includes almost every conceivable subject. It was not
that the sages attempted to develop an abstract,
coherent, and total philosophical system. They were
not philosophers but public teachers and expositors
who wanted to reach the masses and influence their
conduct.

In its discourse about God the Talmud quite naturally reflects the views of Scripture. There is no
attempt philosophically to prove the existence of God.
As in the Bible so also in the Talmud the existence
of God is simply assumed. For the sages the existence
of God was just as real as the existence of a neighbor
which certainly requires no abstract proof. Further,
God is the loving Creator of all that is, and Torah
is God's instrument for and fulfillment of all created
things.[39] He is a personal God of compassion and loving kindness toward his creatures. In the very beginning of the world he demonstrated his extraordinary
love for man by creating him in the divine image which,
according to the sages, meant man's capacity for
intelligence and understanding (Aboth III.14).

Not only did the universe come into being because
of God's creative activity but also it continues to
exist because of God's providence. In the view of
the sages, God is not some impersonal absolute. He
is not an absentee God who is unconcerned with what is
going on in the world. Rather he knows what is happen-
ing and is actively concerned. While the sages never
developed a philosophical theory in which divine omni-
science and providence on the one hand and human freedom on the other were coherently combined, they did
insist that both are real and actual. As they expressed
it: "Everything is foreseen, yet freedom of choice is
granted" (Aboth III.15). Commenting on this statement
in the Mishnah, the medieval sage Maimonides said:

> Do not think that because God knows what
> will happen things are predetermined and
> therefore a man is predestined to act as

149

he does. It is not so. Man has the
freedom to choose what he wants to do.[40]

Of course the sages did not think that a particular person could do everything he might _desire_ to do. They
were aware of the accidents of birth, physical strength
or weakness, intelligence, and other circumstances.
Yet they insisted that a person had the freedom to be
either good or bad, righteous or wicked. As one sage
put it: "Everything is in the hands of heaven, except
the fear of God" (Niddah 16b).

Since God is the Creator of all that is, it follows that he is the source of moral duties. As in the
Bible so also in the sages' view God's will is the
ground of human duties and the doing of his will is
the supreme value of life. As one sage put it: "Do
his will as though it were thy will so that he may do
thy will as though it were his will" (Aboth II.4).
Every aspect of life and conduct should be brought
into conformity with the will of God.

Man can do the will of God because he was created
in God's image as an intelligent, free, and moral being.
Created as good, man, under the conditions of actual
existence, finds himself in a struggle between the good
inclination or impulse and the evil inclination. It
was not that the sages thought of man in a dualistic
fashion. They did not regard the physical body and
its natural impulses as evil and the spirit or soul as
good. For them man is one. The physical side of life
as well as intellectual and moral capacities was a
creation of God and so should not be disdained nor
annihilated. To be sure, one who is not in control
of his physical desires but is controlled by them is
in the power of the evil inclination. Release from
this power, however, is not to be achieved through the
destruction of sensuous desires. A Talmudic story tells
of some very pious people who requested of God the
power to destroy sensuous desires and were given the
response: "Beware lest you destroy the world" (Yoma
69b). For the sages the best way to resist evil was
through the doing of good, the following of the good
inclination, bringing one's will into conformity with
God's will.

Since the sages viewed man as a morally responsible being, they were convinced that he was accountable
before God for his conduct. In both this life and the
next, there are rewards for doing God's will and

150

punishments for disobeying his will. Yet the rewards
and punishments should not be the reason or the motive
for one to do the will of God. Instead the sages insisted that one should do the will of God solely for
the sheer love and joy of doing it. So Antigonus
of Soko is quoted as having said:

> Be not like unto servants who serve
> the master in expectation of receiving
> a gratuity, but be like unto servants
> who serve the master without the ex-
> pectation of receiving a gratuity (Aboth
> I.3).

We have noted that the aim of the sages was to
bring all aspects of life under the divine will. Thus
it is not surprising to find that the Mishnaic halakot
are all encompassing dealing with even the most minute
of details involved in both "sacred" and "secular"
matters. Four sections of the Mishnah, the "orders" of
Zeraim, Moed, Kodashim, and Toharot, contain laws dealing with cult or sacred matters. Among them are laws
which have to do with prayers, tithes, sacrifices,
fasting, festival observances, ritual slaughter of
sacrificial animals, ritual cleanliness and uncleanli-
ness, purification rites, diet, and Sabbath observance.
The exacting detail with which the sages formulated
these laws is illustrated by the thirty-nine classifica-
tions of what constitutes work on the Sabbath day, with
each classification broken down into even more activities which are forbidden (tractate Shabbath 73a-75b, in
Order II, Moed). All of this, of course, represented
an attempt to obey faithfully in their own times the
fourth commandment of the Decalogue. Similarly the
dietary laws (primarily in tractate Hulin of Order V,
Kodashim) were intended as guides for those who would
faithfully obey God's will and abstain from idolatrous
worship of other gods. In ancient times certain animals were thought to incorporate the powers and spirits
of certain gods and when worshippers ate their flesh
and drank their blood they were thought to be partaking
of the powers and spirits of these gods. So strict
monotheists abstained from eating such animals. For
example, swine (in Babylon sacred to the God Ninurta)
and mice were venerated in some ancient polytheistic
religions, and that is a major reason why ancient Jewish dietary laws prohibited eating the meat of these
animals (Lev. 11; Isa. 66:17).

Two of the Mishnaic orders, Nashim (number III)

151

and Nezikin (number IV) contain laws governing such things as marriage, adultery, divorce, vows, and contractual obligations, civil cases, crimes, court procedures, judges, evidence, and witnesses. Capital cases, for example, were tried by a court composed of twenty-three judges (the Bet Din or Small Sanhedrin) who were chosen according to strict criteria. They were under standing instruction to refrain, if at all possible, from passing the death sentence. A majority of one was sufficient to clear a defendant while a majority of three was required to condemn him. There must be three witnesses to testify against the defendant, and if even one witness was disqualified, the entire evidence was invalidated (Sanhedrin 8b). Further, circumstantial evidence was not sufficient, the sages claimed, because it is based on conjecture. On this point a Gemara commentary has the following to say:

> Our rabbis taught: What is meant by 'based on conjecture?' He [the judge] says to them: Perhaps you saw him running after his fellow into a ruin, you pursued him, and found him sword in hand with blood dripping from it, while the murdered man was writhing [in agony]: If this is what you saw, you saw nothing (Sanhedrin 37b).

That is, he did not actually witness a murder and indeed such may not have been the case, for there are other possible causes of the observed circumstances. Witnesses can only attest to what they have actually seen with their own eyes, and the courts did not accept conjectures nor hearsay evidence. Regulations such as these are only a very small sample of the vast body of laws developed by the sages in order to insure fair trials.

While the sages developed a large body of laws dealing with all phases of life, it does not follow from this that they were narrow minded legalists who delighted in giving legal decisions. As we have seen the decisions of the more lenient Hillel and his school rather than those of the more rigorous Shammai and his school were regarded as normative halakah in the Mishnah. In his Foreword to the Soncino English edition of the Babylonian Talmud, Rabbi Hertz quotes a passage from I. Zangwill which admirably describes the Talmudic

perspective concerning the relation between law and
spirit, deed and motive. Zangwill characterizes the
Judaism of the rabbis as:

> 'A code which left the intellect and
> the emotions free to speculate and
> wonder . . . but which fettered the
> will, leaving the spirit free to transcend
> the law in love and self sacrifice, but
> not to fall below it; so that even those
> Philistines who for religion--the music
> of life--had no ear, should at least be
> kept sane and strong and mechanically
> moral, centres of happiness to themselves
> and channels for a finer posterity. They
> should be kept from playing wrong notes
> and jarring chords, if they could not
> give us sonatas and symphonies of their
> own.'41

While it is the case that there is a healthy realism in the teachings of the sages, it is surely the
case also that most of them were in tune with "the
music of life" and produced numerous "sonatas and
symphonies of their own." As we have seen, they insisted that the genuine love of God and his creatures
is a gratuitous love which seeks nothing in return.
This is beautifully expressed in the following saying
of the sages: "If love depends on some selfish end,
when the end fails, love fails; but if it does not
depend on a selfish end, it will never fail" (Aboth
V.16).

However sublime the ethical teachings of the sages,
they do not lead to the extreme excesses and austerities
of asceticism. Rather they are compatible with the
best in human nature and with the existence and welfare
of human society. For the sages it was the will of
God that one participate in the common ventures of
life and not only love God and his creatures but also
order his own life wisely. So the tannaitic sage
Hillel remarked: "If I am not for myself, who is for
me, but if I am only for myself, what am I, and if not
now, when?" (Aboth I.14). That is, one should be
self-reliant and cultivate to the fullest all of one's
capacities so that one is not always dependent on
others. While learning is best acquired in a community
of scholars (the sages recommend going to a school),
it rests ultimately upon the desire, initiative, and
discipline of the individual. No one can be forced to

learn nor to seek higher things. Instead he must do
that for himself. Yet being exclusively for one's
self is an unworthy attitude, for one cannot be genuinely human nor genuinely love God without also loving his neighbor in the immediacy of the present
moment. Undoubtedly the Scriptural basis for Hillel's
terse statement was Leviticus 19:18, "You shall love
your neighbor as yourself."

The priority of love for neighbor in Hillel's
perspective is further illustrated in a delightful
story concerning a would-be proselyte who came to
Hillel and said that he would convert on condition
that Hillel teach him the whole Torah while he stood
on one foot. To this request Hillel responded:

> What is hateful to you, do not to your
> neighbor: that is the whole Torah,
> while the rest is commentary thereof;
> go and learn it (Shabboth 31a).

In the perspective of the sages love is not merely
a sentimental or emotional matter. While it transcends
the virtues of justice, truth, peace, and charitable
works, it necessarily entails these virtues. Surely
one who claims to love another but does not treat the
other in terms of justice, truthfulness, peacefulness,
and charitable works has made a false claim. Without
the practice of such virtues, genuine love cannot be
actually expressed in the concrete world of human relations. As Simeon, son of Gamaliel, said: "On three
things does the world [human society] stand: on
justice, on truth, and on peace" (Aboth I.18).

Justice involves treating others with fairness or
equity. Yet it is always viewed in the context of love
which not only motivates one to treat others fairly
and equitably but also leads one voluntarily to do more
than is required by justice in works of charity. Further, works of charity entail more than mere almsgiving
for such is to be accompanied by sympathetic and kind
attitudes and words. Works of charity are most meritorious when done in secret so that they do not put
the recipients under obligations (Baba Bathra 9a.b).

Truth for the sages is sacred and enduring because
it is the seal of God (Shabboth 55a). Thus to seek
truth and to be truthful is a sacred obligation. To
deceive another is sinful, for as Eleazor said: "Whoever dissembles in his speech is as though he had

154

engaged to idolatry" (Sanhedrin 92a).

The primary and basic condition for human welfare and happiness, according to the sages, was peace and harmony in domestic life, social relations, and public affairs. So Hillel said: "Be of the disciples of Aaron, loving peace and pursuing peace, loving mankind and drawing them to the Torah" (Aboth I.12). In the view of the sages those virtues which lead to peace are humility, gentleness, patience, self-control, and love. Those who practice such virtues are called "the friends of God . . . [who] shine forth like the sun in its splendor" (Yoma 23a).

The sages were not simply "arm chair" scholars. The duty of scholarship was combined with the duty of industrious labor and useful activity. Unlike the Greek philosophers who regarded manual labor as degrading, the Rabbinic sages insisted upon the dignity and worth of manual labor. Indeed, they regarded it as a splendid thing which brings honor to men. So Rabbi Gamaliel is quoted as having said: "Excellent is the study of the Torah together with a worldly occupation," (Aboth II.2) and Rabbi Ammi said: "He who lives on the toil of his hands is greater than he who indulges in idle piety" (Berakoth 8a).[42] In light of this perspective it is not surprising that many of the sages made their living by various kinds of handicraft.

Not only did the sages regard the Torah as providing guidance for personal morality, for duties to oneself, to wife and children, to friends and strangers, and to the poor but also as placing one under obligation to participate responsibly in the life of the community. So Hillel said: "Do not isolate thyself from the community and its interests" (Aboth II.4), and Gamaliel proclaimed: "Those who work for the community shall do it without selfishness, but with the pure intention to promote its welfare" (Aboth II.2).[43]

In the view of the Talmudic sages the divine obligation to work unselfishly for the good of the community was not limited simply to the community of Israel. It extended also to the world-wide community of all mankind. No man is to be despised, for love of fellow man extends to all without distinction of creed or race. So the rabbis taught: "It is our duty to relieve the poor and needy, to visit the sick and bury the dead without distinction of creed and race"

(Gittin 61a)[44]. Even though they did attempt to regulate every detail of life in terms of the Torah, the Talmudic sages, nevertheless, expressed a liberal and universal perspective. Moses Mielziner has described this quite well when he said:

> The liberal spirit of Talmudic ethics is most strikingly evidenced in the sentence: 'The pious and virtuous of all nations participate in the eternal bliss' [Tosephta Sanhedrin Ch. XIII], which teaches that man's salvation depends not on the acceptance of certain articles of belief, nor on certain ceremonial observances, but on that which is the ultimate aim of religion, namely, Morality, purity of heart and holiness of life.[45]

We have seen that both Judaism and Christianity incorporate the Janus principle; that is, they look back to past events for revelation and guidance and to the future with the hope provided by revelation (cf. Chapters I, III, and IV). In the Judaism of the centuries following the Babylonian captivity, apocalyptic views of the end of history, although not accepted by everyone, came to play a rather important role in the thinking of some groups (cf. section V of Chapter III and section (1) of this Chapter). Among these groups there was much speculation about what kinds of events would occur in nature and history as signs that the advent of the Messiah and the World to Come was near, and there were many attempts to determine the precise date when this would occur. While the Talmudic rabbis were convinced that the Messiah would come and that there would be an existence beyond history, their teachings on these matters were rather guarded and fragmentary. Moreover, they had little patience with speculations concerning the dating of the eschaton (the end of history). As Sandmel points out, there are several passages in the Talmud in which the rabbis scorned and denounced the "calculators of the Ends."[46] For example, Rabbi Jonathan said, "Blasted be the bones of those who calculate the end. For they would say, since the predetermined time has arrived, and yet he has not come, he will never come" (Sanhedrin 97b).[47] Thus there was a considerable difference between the apocalyptic and the Rabbinic views concerning the World to Come. According to Sandmel, "the doctrine of the Messiah becomes almost peripheral in the Rabbinic

156

literature, for eschatology is of only the most minor of concerns to the Rabbis."[48]

Yet, as Sandmel acknowledges,[49] the Talmud contains many statements concerning the Messianic hope. This Rabbinic Messianic hope is characterized by the following features. First, when the Messiah comes he will deliver Israel from the rule of any foreign nation such as Rome, assume the throne of Israel as the son of David, miraculously gather the dispersed of Israel back to the Holy Land, and establish Israel as God's elect nation. Thus there would follow a period of time which was designated as the "Days of the Messiah." Secondly, salvation in the World to Come is not restricted simply to Jews. The righteous of all nations who observe the so-called "seven laws of Noah" will have a share in the World to Come. (These laws are an expansion of Genesis 9 and include avoidance of idolatry, unchastity in terms of incest and adultery, bloodshed, profaning God's name, robbery, cutting off flesh from a living animal, and the establishment of courts of justice.) Thirdly, the Rabbinic hope for the future is not characterized by an otherworldliness which neglects or ignores the present. While the present is viewed as a time of waiting patiently for the Messiah's advent, this patient waiting is a matter of attitude, and does not mean inactivity but rather active preparation for this great event. According to Seymour Siegel:

> One of the most profound of all Rabbinic stories is that concerning one of the Rabbinic sages who found the Messiah sitting at the gates of Rome as a leprous beggar. He asked the Messiah, 'When will you come?' The Messiah said, 'Today.' The rabbi went back to his colleagues and joyfully proclaimed that the Messiah was soon to arrive. Of course, the day passed and the Messiah did not come. He went back to Rome and asked, 'Why did you mislead me?' The Messiah referred him to the verse in Scripture which promises, 'Today, if you will but hearken to my voice.'[50]

Fourthly, in the Rabbinic view, at sometime after the "Days of the Messiah," he will institute the Great Judgment, thereby establishing the new age, the World to Come. With respect to what is involved in the

157

World to Come and the resurrection life, there is, as Sandmel points out, a notable lack of uniformity in the Rabbinic views.[51] Some teach that individuals are judged immediately after death, with the righteous entering Paradise and the wicked consigned to hell; others, that judgment does not occur until all are resurrected and brought to the land of Israel for the Great Judgment. The result of this Great Judgment is that the thoroughly righteous go immediately to heaven and the thoroughly wicked to hell where, according to some rabbis, they are punished for a period of time and then annihilated. Some rabbis claim that the moderately wicked are purified in hell for twelve months after which they are taken into Paradise; others, that God tilts the scales of justice toward mercy and immediately grants them a place in Paradise. In the view of some rabbis, no one is consigned to hell for an eternity.

Among all the rabbis there was much less emphasis on hell than on Paradise. Their convictions concerning Paradise were elaborated to a much larger extent than those concerning hell. It was the view of some rabbis that in some future time in Paradise there was to be the wondrous Messianic banquet where the meat of Leviathan (the primeval dragon subdued by Yahweh at the dawn of creation, cf., Psalm 74:14; Isaiah 27:1) would be served along with wine preserved since the six days of creation. Yet Rab (a variant form of rabbi) Abba Areka said, "Not like this World is the World to Come. In the World to Come there is neither eating nor drinking, no procreation of children nor business transactions, no envy or hatred or rivalry. The righteous sit enthroned, their crowns on their heads, and enjoy the radiance of the Shekinah [the presence of God]" (Berakhot, 17a).[52] In this spiritual existence in heaven everyone will enjoy the greatest happiness conceivable by the rabbis, namely to study the mysteries of Torah with God himself (cf. Hagigah, 14a).[53] This was the ultimate hope of the rabbis, but it was a hope which did not ignore the present in order to gain the future or abandon the future in order to "save" the present. Indeed, for them the present was hallowed precisely because they understood the meaning of the present in terms of their convictions concerning what God had done in the past (creation and covenant) and what he will do in the future (the sending of the Messiah and the World to Come).

Perhaps no better concluding summary of Rabbinic

Judaism can be found than the one given by Seymour
Siegel when he said:

> The literature of the rabbis may be
> summarized as a plea for Shalom, which
> in Jewish literature means a good deal
> more than peace. Shalom is God's name.
> It is integrity, wholeness, steadfast-
> ness, community, solidarity, and the
> total mobilization of human powers to
> serve the reality which is above and
> beyond us. Therefore, the central word
> in Rabbinic literature is the word
> Shalom. Consequently, it is no accident
> that the whole of Talmudic literature
> ends with that word: 'The Holy One,
> blessed be He, could find no vessel that
> was so full of blessing for Israel and
> mankind as that of Shalom.' [Uktzin 3:
> 12]54

[1] Samuel Sandmel prefers to use the expression, "Synagogue Judaism" to designate the Judaism which emerged in the centuries after the Babylonian exile, expecially during the Greek and Roman periods (from about 300 B.C.-200 A.D.). He feels that this expression is more general in scope such that it includes the speculations of the Apocalyptists, of Hellenistic Jewish philosophers such as Philo and the perspectives of the Qumran community as well as the expositions and disputes of the Rabbinic sages (see Samuel Sandmel, Judaism and Christian Beginnings, Oxford University Press, 1978, p. 16). Sandmel's use of "Synagogue Judaism" has the advantage of not obscuring the varieties and diversities in early Judaism and thus of avoiding oversimplification and reductionism. Rabbinic Judaism was only one strand within early Judaism even though it was (or became) the most dominant. Since we have discussed apocalypticism briefly in Chapter III and will discuss the socio-religious groups in the Judaism of the period under consideration in this chapter, I hope to avoid oversimplification and reductionism even though I do concentrate largely on Rabbinic Judaism. Limitations of space as well as lack of expertise will prevent me from doing full justice to Rabbinic Judaism. Indeed, a whole lifetime of study would hardly be adequate to become an expert in this field. Yet I hope that this discussion, though brief, will be sound.

[2] Alexander Guttmann, Rabbinic Judaism in the Making (Wayne State University Press, 1970), p. XII.

[3] Since the use of the conventions B.C. and A.D. (literally Anno Domini, the year or age of our Lord) to designate the periods before and after Christ arose out of the theology of the Christian Church, many Jewish scholars use B.C.E. (Before the Common Era) and C.E. (the Common Era) instead of B.C. and A.D. Since the latter convention is more familiar and I have used it previously, I will continue to use it in this chapter. There are some Jewish scholars who also use this convention, obviously without any theological implications. One such scholar is Professor Samuel Sandmel in his book, Judaism and Christian Beginnings.

[4] Ibid., p. 18.

[5] References to material in the Talmud, the great work of

Rabbinic Judaism, will be indicated generally with the name and section of the tractate in parentheses immediately following the reference or quotation. I have used the Soncino translation and edition of the Babylonian Talmud.

[6] Sandmel, op. cit., p. 17.

[7] Guttmann, op. cit., pp. XIII-XIV.

[8] The Soncino Press, London.

[9] During the Middle Ages, church authorities often sent armed forces into the Jewish communities to search out and burn all the copies of the Talmud they could find. Fortunately they did not find all of them.

[10] Sandmel, op. cit., p. 14.

[11] The first century Jewish historian, Josephus, in his Antiquities of the Jews and Wars of the Jews, describes the Essenes in several passages (Antiquities XVIII. I. 1; Wars II. VIII. 2-13).

[12] There are many good studies of the "Dead Sea Community" which are available. Some of them are: Frank Moore Cross, Jr., The Ancient Library of Qumran, Doubleday & Company, Inc., 1958; "The Dead Sea Scrolls," Interpreter's Bible, Vol. 12, Abingdon Press, 1957; Kurt Schubert, The Dead Sea Community, Harpers and Brothers, 1959; W. R. Farmer, "Essenes," The Interpreter's Dictionary of the Bible, Vol. E-J, Abingdon Press, 1962.

[13] The Commentary on Habakkuk and the Genesis Apocryphon are highly eschatological in perspective.

[14] See Josephus, Antiquities of the Jews, XIII. V. 9; XIII. XI. 6; XVIII. I. 4 and Wars of the Jews, II. VIII. 14.

[15] Sandmel, op. cit., p. 162.

[16] See C. Milo Connick, Jesus, The Man, The Mission and The Message, Second edition (Prentice-Hall, 1974), p. 48.

[17] Sotah 22b; Berakot 14b; Sotah 20c.

[18] Sandmel, op. cit., p. 162.

[19] Ibid., p. 147.

[20] Ibid., p. 144.

[21] Guttmann, op. cit., p. XV.

[22] Sandmel, op. cit., p. 162.

[23] Adin Steinsaltz, The Essential Talmud (Bantam Books, Inc., 1976), p. 3.

[24] Sandmel, op. cit., pp. 103, 184.

[25] Scholars differ with respect to the transliteration of Hebrew terms. Some use Mishna instead of Mishnah, Halacha instead of Halakah, Aggada or Haggada instead of Haggadah. In each case I will follow the latter usage.

[26] Moses Mielziner, Introduction to the Talmud (Block Publishing Co., 1968), pp. 6-7.

[27] Sandmel, op. cit., p. 106.

[28] Steinsaltz, op. cit., p. 47.

[29] The basic structure of this diagram was suggested to me by a diagram on the evolution of the Jewish law in an article by Rabbi Eugene Lipman, "The Making of the Mishnah," Keeping Posted, Vol. 20, No. 4, January 1975, p. 19 (published by the Union of American Hebrew Congregations).

[30] Judah Goldin, The Living Talmud (The University of Chicago Press, 1957), p. 27.

[31] Ibid.

[32] Steinsaltz, op. cit., pp. 231-232, 241-242.

[33] This statement does not mean, of course, that the sages derived the pilpul method from the Greek philosophers but only that there is some similarity between the two methods of dialectical reasoning. One should always be careful never to assume that similarity between two sets of ideas, practices or methods found in different cultures means that historically one set was borrowed from the other.

[34] Sandmel, op. cit., p. 241.

[35] I have taken this quotation from Sandmel, ibid., p. 241. The reference given by Sandmel is "Jer. Berachot 3a bottom," ibid., p. 459.

[36] Steinsaltz, op. cit., pp. 6-7.

[37] For the classification of argument forms in the Talmud, I am indebted to Moses Mielziner, Introduction to the Talmud, Fourth Edition (Block Publishing Company, 1968), pp. 247-264. The discussion of these forms is primarily my own.

[38] J. B. Hertz, "Foreword," The Babylonian Talmud, Vol. 12, Vol. I of Seder Nezikin (London: Soncino Press, 1935), p. XXVI.

[39] Cf. Judah Goldin, op. cit., p. 141.

[40] This quotation is taken from Goldin, ibid., p. 142.

[41] T. H. Hertz, op. cit., p. XXVI.

[42] In the quote from Berakoth 8a I have used the rendering of Moses Mielziner, op. cit., p. 272.

[43] Also in these quotes from Berakoth 8a I have used the rendering of Moses Mielziner, op. cit., p. 272.

[44] Mielziner's rendering, ibid., p. 279.

[45] Mielziner, ibid., p. 280.

[46] Sandmel, op. cit., p. 189.

[47] Cited by Robert M. Seltzer, Jewish People, Jewish Thought; The Jewish Experience in History (Macmillan Publishing Co., Inc., 1980), p. 308; see pp. 286, 294, 306-309.

[48] Sandmel, op. cit., p. 206.

[49] Ibid., p. 207.

[50] "Rabbinic Foundations of Modern Jewish Thought," Jewish-Christian Relations in Today's World, edited by James E. Wood, Jr. (The Markham Press Fund of Baylor University Press, 1971), pp. 75-76. This story is found in the Talmud, Sanhedrin 98a. Italics are mine.

[51] Sandmel, op. cit., p. 190.

[52] Cited by Seltzer, op. cit., p. 309; also see Sandmel, op. cit., pp. 175, 189-190, 201-202.

[53] Ibid.

[54] Seigel, op. cit., p. 76.

SUGGESTIONS FOR FURTHER READING

A Rabbinic Anthology, C. G. Montefiore and H. Lowe, eds., Meridan Books, Inc., 1963.

Balo, Salo W. and Joseph L. Blau, Judaism: Post Biblical and Talmudic Period, The Liberal Arts Press, Inc., Bobbs-Merrill Co., Inc. 1954.

Danby, Herbert, The Mishnah, Oxford University Press, 1933.

Goldin, Judah, The Living Talmud, University of Chicago Press, 1957.

Goldstein, Morris, Thus Religion Grows: The Story of Judaism, Longmans, Green and Co., 1936.

Guttman, Alexander, Rabbinic Judaism in the Making, Wayne State Press, 1970.

Guttmann, Julius, Philosophies of Judaism, Holt, Rinehart and Winston, Inc., 1964, Part I.

Interpreter's Dictionary of the Bible, Vols. E-J, Abingdon Press, 1962, "Essenes," pp. 143-149.

Interpreter's Dictionary of the Bible, Vols. K-Q, Abingdon Press, 1962, "Pharisees," pp. 774-781.

Interpreter's Dictionary of the Bible, Vols. R-Z, Abingdon Press, 1962, "Sadducees," pp. 160-163.

Mielziner, Moses, Introduction to the Talmud, Fourth Edition, Block Publishing Co., 1968.

Moore, George Foot, Judaism, Vols. I and II, Harvard University Press, 1946.

Neusner, Jacob, ed., Understanding Rabbinic Judaism, Ktav Publishing House, Inc., 1974.

Sandmel, Samuel, Judaism and Christian Beginnings, Oxford University Press, 1978.

Sandmel, Samuel, The First Christian Century in Judaism and Christianity, Oxford University Press, 1969.

Seltzer, Robert M., Jewish People, Jewish Thought: The Jewish Experience in History, Macmillan Publishing Co., Inc., 1980.

Steinsaltz, Adin, The Essential Talmud, Basic Books Inc., 1976.

Strack, Herman L., Introduction to the Talmud and Midrash,
    Meridan Books, Inc. 1959.

The Babylonian Talmud, I. Epstein, ed., The Soncino Press, London,
    18 Vols. published from 1935-1948.

PART III

THE EARLY AND MEDIEVAL PERIODS

In Part II on the Biblical period we attempted a brief survey of the major perspectives contained within the major source book for Judaism and Christianity. The discussion of the emergence and development of Rabbinic Judaism in the final chapter of Part II did carry us beyond the Biblical period as such because Rabbinic Judaism represented a further development on Old Testament perspectives in the ages subsequent to the era in which the Old Testament was written. Since, as we have seen, Rabbinic Judaism became and remained the "mainstream" or dominant form of Judaism, we will not discuss Judaism in Part III. Instead we will return to a discussion of Judaism in Part V on the modern period. In that discussion we will discuss briefly an outstanding medieval Rabbinic thinker, Moses Maimonides, and one medieval Jewish movement distinct from Rabbinic Judaism, for both have had some degree of influence on two of the movements in modern Judaism.

Our task in Parts III and IV is to describe briefly certain fundamental issues, perspectives, and practices which emerged in the history of the Christian church from the end of the Biblical period to the rise of the modern period. A general understanding of the major perspectives which emerged during this long time span is essential as a background for an adequate understanding of the perspectives and issues which arose in modern Christian thought.

While there have been and still are some Christians who claim that they are "Bible believing Christians" in the sense that their beliefs and practices are identical with those recorded in the Bible, this is hardly the case in any literal or exact sense. Just as the Rabbinic sages, in their attempts to make the Torah book meaningful and livable in succeeding ages, modified, developed, and adjusted the Torah to the needs of their own times, so Christian thinkers with the Old and New Testaments as a basis sought to make the Christian faith relevant to the issues and needs of their own times. Unlike the Rabbinic sages, who for the most part remained within the context of Jewish culture, Christian thinkers in the post-Biblical period lived and worked in the different context of the Greco-Roman culture.

Even before the end of the New Testament period, Christianity had spread out of its original Palestinian setting into the Greco-Roman world, and the membership of the church encountered the challenge on the one hand of the popular Greco-Roman polytheistic mystery religions and on the other hand of the theoretical or metaphysical speculations of the philosophers. While a few beliefs and practices in the mystery religions (promises of immortality and baptismal rites, for example) probably had some small influence on the developing theology and practice of the church, the general attitude in the church toward these religions was primarily negative. Given the Christian insistence on monotheism, faithful Christians adamantly rejected polytheism even at the risk of persecution. In the thinking of the philosophers, there were also some perspectives such as, for example, the view of deity as an impersonal absolute which were inconsistent with the Christian faith. Yet there was much in the thinking of the philosophers which was to have a relatively large positive influence on both the modes of thinking and the content of the theological positions which emerged in the church during the early and medieval periods.

The theological positions which came to be regarded as orthodox by the church generally have their roots in the Bible, yet at the same time transcend their Biblical bases. The categories or ways of thinking in the Bible are concrete and personal. However, the theologies, dogmas, and creeds of the early and medieval church generally contain theoretical concepts derived from philosophy. Even though the ancient philosophers had given attention to ethics and human relations, their thinking on these issues had been to a large extent a theoretical mode of thinking. Further, one of their major concerns had been the development of abstract or metaphysical theories concerning the ultimate nature of being or reality. Here was a mode of thought different from that of the Bible but one which had to be utilized by the church if the Christian faith was to be understood by those accustomed to this way of thinking. So even though the theologies, doctrines, and creeds which emerged in the church presuppose a Biblical basis and would have been impossible without such a basis, they nevertheless represent the attempt within the church to express the faith in terms of rational and consistent concepts and theories based on carefully worked out principles. The purpose of such endeavor was twofold, namely that of confessing and of defending the faith so that it could be alive and meaningful in a different cultural context and in successive ages.

CHAPTER VI

THE EARLY PERIOD

We have seen in our discussion of the New Testament in Chapter IV that when the Christian church spread outside of its original Palestinian environment into the Greco-Roman world and increased in membership, it encountered three very fundamental problems. First, there arose the problem of preserving unity in the church. While in the earliest days of the church, there had not been <u>uniformity</u> imposed by ecclesiastical authority, there had been, in spite of individual differences, a sense of unity within the New Covenant Community empowered by the Holy Spirit. But as time went on, the <u>Parousia</u> (second coming of Christ) did not occur, and debates arose in the church, the early sense of unity became problematical. Secondly, there arose the problem of what was an acceptable moral life for Christians and how the church was to deal with those Christians who committed sins of at least a serious nature after conversion and acceptance into the church. Thirdly, there arose the problem of maintaining the essentials of the gospel ("good news of redemption") which had been handed down from the original faith witnesses while at the same time communicating it in meaningful ways to those of a different culture. While these problems arose in the New Testament period (50-150 A.D.) and are dealt with in a preliminary way in some New Testament books, they continued to plague the church in the early centuries after the close of the New Testament period. In its attempt to protect and to preserve its unity, the moral purity of its members, and the authentic or genuine teachings of the faith the church finally developed a canon of Scripture, ecclesiastical orders (i.e., a ministry made up on bishops, priests, and deacons), creedal statements, and prescribed practices.

In this chapter we will deal first with a few of the important post-Biblical early Christian writings in which solutions are proposed for the three problems. Then we will consider briefly the controversies concerning the nature of God and the nature of Christ which finally resulted in the doctrine of the Trinity as formulated by the Council of Nicea (325 A.D.) and the doctrine of Christ ("truly God and truly man") as

formulated by the Council of Chalcedon (451 A.D.).
Finally, we will conclude this chapter with a brief
discussion of certain important aspects of St. Augustine's theological thought, some of which had an influence on subsequent Roman Catholic theology while others
had an influence on the theology of the Protestant
Reformers of a much later time. Of necessity, our discussion will be highly selective and will consider only
a very few representative thinkers who deal in one way
or another with the key issues mentioned above.[1]

The challenge of the first and second problems
(disunity in the church and sins as a continuing reality in the lives of Christians) is quite evident in
two post-Biblical Christian writings from about the
middle of the second century, namely the Didache and
the Shepherd of Hermas.[2]

The sixteen chapters of the Didache, a manual of
church discipline, may be divided into three parts.
The second part describes the proper form for the rite
or sacrament of baptism but the first and third deal
with the issues of moral purity and church unity. In
the first part the author describes the two ways, the
way of life and the way of death. Those who fulfill
their Christian duties, love God and neighbor, avoid
evil in all its forms, are on the way of life. But
those who engage in the telling of lies, the practice
of vice, in hypocrisy and avarice, etc., are on the way
of death. Obviously, this section shows the author's
concern lest Christians drift into moral laxity.

In the third section of the Didache the author
suggests certain criteria in light of which members
of a local church may determine whether or not a traveling teacher who has come to their church is a true
or false "prophet." Leadership in the earliest church
seems to have been without any particular structure.
Those who became leaders did so on the basis of "charis-
matic" authority. Outstanding leaders often engaged
in missionary travels and/or sent out their close
associates on such journeys as had been the case with
the Apostle Paul and the author of the third letter
of John in the New Testament. While it is the case
that in the New Testament Pastoral Letters reference is
made to such local church leaders as bishops, deacons,
and elders (presbyters), these offices are not defined
and very little is said about their official functions
(I Timothy 3, 5). For some time the situation with
respect to leadership seems to have been rather informal

and fluid with both traveling "prophets" and local bishops, deacons, and elders. Given this situation, it was relatively easy for charlatans to get in on the "traveling tours" and by false teachings and immoral behavior to produce divisions among the members of local congregations.

It is in light of such a situation that the Didache advises the churches to test the traveling "prophets" to see if they are of God or not. A "prophet" is known by his behavior. If he asks for money, or orders a table set so that he may eat from it, or does not practice what he preaches, then he is "trading on Christ" and is a false "prophet." However, traveling missionaries, who by their lives show that they are true "prophets" deserve to be accepted and supported by the congregation. While the author of the Didache mentions bishops, presbyters, and deacons, the "office" of the true "prophet" is highly esteemed by him. Later, of course, the "office" of "prophet" disappears, and the church's leadership is formally structured in terms of a hierarchy of bishop, priest, and deacon with those holding such offices regarded as having a special status in the church by virtue of having received the sacrament of ordination. The desire to protect and to preserve the unity of the church was certainly a major reason for this development.

In a collection of commandments, parables, and allegorical visions the author of the Shepherd of Hermas made it quite evident that his major concern was the lack of dedication on the part of some Christians and the problem of what to do with those who committed sins after the purification of baptism. The author of the New Testament book of Hebrews had stated: "For if we sin deliberately after receiving the knowledge of the truth, there no longer remains a sacrifice for sins" (Hebrews 10:26). Apparently there were rigorists in the early church who understood this to mean that there was no forgiveness for sins of at least a serious nature committed after baptism. However, as the high expectations of an early return of Christ began to subside and the church as an historical community continued to be confronted by evils and sins both from without (opposition and persecution) and from within, the rigorists' position became increasingly untenable. If Christians who committed sins after baptism were excluded, the very existence of the church as an institution would become problematical. For the sake of the church's survival there had to be the possibility of forgiveness for post-baptismal sins, and so the church developed a procedure by means of which the penitent Christian sinner could receive divine forgiveness. The position taken in the <u>Shepherd</u> <u>of</u> <u>Hermas</u> represents an early stage in the development of the formal structure of the sacrament of penance.

In his allegory of the church as a tower and in his fourth commandment Hermas indicates that there can be one repentance for post-baptismal sins. According to the allegory, the tower is built on a rock arising out of water. The water symbolizes baptism which is necessary for purification. The stones constituting the tower have arisen out of the water as pure and so represent individual believers taken into the church after repentance and baptism. Some of the tower's stones, however, become marred. Yet they may be repaired at least once. This is clearly stated in the fourth commandment[3] where it is said that there cannot be several but only one repentance for post-baptismal sins. It appears that for Hermas this second repentance could extend to all sins, even "deadly" sins.[4] While the view of the one repentance after baptism was shared by other Christians in the second century, there were those who thought that among the class of serious sins there were three which were unforgivable or "deadly," namely murder, adultery, and apostasy (denying the faith). There was no unanimity of opinion on this issue even in the second century, and later it came to be universally held in the church that all sins were forgivable by means of the sacrament of penance.

It would seem to be the case that at the time of the <u>Shepherd</u> <u>of</u> <u>Hermas</u> the second repentance required of the penitent Christian sinner a public confession before the assembled congregation of the church in which, it was thought, absolving power was divinely lodged. Upon hearing the confession the congregation decided whether or not to declare the sinner absolved of his sins, i.e., forgiven by God and freed from guilt. If absolution were proclaimed, then the congregation might direct the forgiven sinner to make some sort of restitution or engage in some work of satisfaction. Thus, although there were to be some further developments with respect to the sacrament of penance, its basic structure was already a part of the practice of the church as early as the <u>Shepherd</u> <u>of</u> <u>Hermas</u>.

In the next century, Cyprian, Bishop of Carthage from about 249-258 A.D., was largely responsible for

the full development of the sacrament of penance and
also for some lasting distinctive perspectives in the
Catholic Church concerning the nature and role of the
church and the clergy.[5] It is quite evident from his
writings that two of Cyprian's major concerns were with
the problems of post-baptismal sins and church unity.

We have seen that in the second century there
were some Christians who held that among the serious
sins murder, adultery, and apostasy were unforgivable
or "deadly." However, in the early third century,
Callixtus, Bishop of Rome (217-222 A.D.), claimed that
as a successor of the Apostles he could forgive those
offenders who committed the fleshly sins of murder and
adultery.[6] While there was opposition to this practice
on the part of some, many bishops followed it, including Cyprian. Yet at this time apostasy was generally
regarded as unforgivable. With the persecution of
Christians by the Roman emperor Decius (250 A.D.), the
situation changed. While the persecution was in process, many Christians had become apostates (i.e.,
denied the faith), but when it subsided some of them
wished to be forgiven and to be readmitted to the
church. Some of the martyrs (those who had been imprisoned or exiled during the persecution) with the
approval of some priests were serving as "confessors"
for penitent apostates, granting them pardon and re-
admission to the church. Cyprian soon recognized that
this practice was undermining the authority of the
bishop and that the general sentiment was against
his position that apostasy was unforgivable. So he
yielded on this point insisting, however, that adequate
penance must be required and that absolution was a
prerogative of the bishop who alone, as successor of
the Apostles, has the authority to forgive mortal sins
and impart divine grace although he may delegate such
authority to his priests. Even though the distinction
between great and small sins continued to be held,
Cyprian's view that all sins are forgivable came to be
the dominant view in the church. Penance, like baptism and holy communion (the Lord's Supper or eucharist), has become a structured ecclesiastical affair
rather than informal. It has become a sacrament in
the full sense.

In Cyprian's view the bishop is the dominant
ecclesiastical figure. Not only is he the ruler of
the church but also, as the successor of the Apostles,
he is the only "priest." His sovereignty is absolute
because he owes his appointment to God and not man.

The presbyters or priests have no independent gifts but have their priestly functions delegated to them by the bishop. They are his representatives. Apart from the bishop, Cyprian claimed, there is no church. "The bishop is in the church and the church is in the bishop and if anyone is not with the bishop he is not in the church" (Letter 66:1, 4, 8).

One of the major reasons why Cyprian placed great emphasis on the authority of the bishop was to protect the unity of the church. This meant not only the unity of the local church under its bishop but also the unity of all the churches under a collective episcopate. That is, Cyprian insisted on the unity of the church at large under the control of all the bishops together in a united episcopacy in which the bishops consult with one another on matters of importance (On the Unity of the Catholic Church, 5). No one bishop has the right to dictate to other bishops nor to interfere with the internal matters in their churches. Even so, Cyprian claimed, the church at Rome is "the principal church whence priestly unity has sprung" (Letter 59:14). The reason for this is that this church, according to tradition, had been founded by the Apostle Peter. According to Cyprian, the other Apostles had been granted the same priestly authority as Peter, but he was the first to receive this authority and this made him the source of Apostolic unity. So also the church founded by him has a certain priority among the churches as the source of their unity, even though this priority does not grant it nor its bishop authority over other churches. While the church at Rome and its succession of bishops are to be honored as the source of the unity of the church at large, this unity as a continuing reality, Cyprian claimed, is a common property shared by all the bishops. It consists in the common faith and communion of all the bishops among themselves.

In Cyprian's day the unity of the church was threatened not only by heresy but also by schism. That is, there were some "orthodox" Christians who were withdrawing from the Catholic Church with its episcopate and were forming fellowships or "churches" which did not have bishops in the apostolic succession. This greatly disturbed Cyprian who claimed that these schismatics were in a worse state than the apostates. The latter could gain forgiveness through the sacrament of penance and be readmitted to the Catholic Church, but the former did not recognize schism as a sin for which they needed forgiveness. For Cyprian these schismatics

were really heretics no matter how orthodox or righteous they might claim to be, and as heretics they had
forfeited any possibility of salvation (On the Unity
of the Catholic Church, 19).

The reason for Cyprian's uncompromising attitude
toward schism was his view that the one Catholic Church
is more than simply a fellowship of Christians. It
is, he claimed, the sole ark of salvation outside of
which no one can be saved. "He cannot have God as
Father who has not the church as Mother" (On the Unity
of the Catholic Church, 6). While earlier Christians
had emphasized the importance of the church for salvation, Cyprian identified the church with a particular
institution, the Catholic Church, which was founded
upon and had its existence in those bishops in succession from the Apostles. This church alone possesses
saving grace and apart from it there is no salvation
nor anything which is truly Christian (Letter 55:24;
66:8). In it are the sacraments through which grace
is channeled into believers so that they might be truly
Christians. So it is that Cyprian gave shape to a
doctrine of the church which was to have lasting influence in Catholic theology. While it is the case that
later Catholic theology rejected Cyprian's view that
the sacraments are valid only when performed by priests
of good moral character and genuine faith and accorded
greater authority to the Bishop of Rome, it is true,
nevertheless, that in a very real sense Cyprian was,
as A. C. McGiffert has said, "the founder of the
Catholic Church."[7]

As we have seen in the discussion above, a major
contributing factor to the threat of disunity in the
early church was the appearance of heresy or false
teaching. When the church moved into the Greco-Roman
world, it encountered the problem of maintaining the
essential purity of the Christian message as it had
been received from the early faith witnesses. Converts came into the church from different religious
and cultural backgrounds, and such diversity of backgrounds gave rise to various interpretations of the
faith. All of them claimed to be the true understanding of the faith, but many of them contradicted certain
fundamental beliefs of the faith in its traditional
form. The issue then was that of distinguishing between a genuine Christian faith and what was simply
another religion with a few Christian elements.

Two heresies with which the church had to deal in

the Second Century were Ebionism and Gnosticism.[8] The former appears to have had its major source in the thought of Jewish converts to Christianity. Given such a background, it is not surprising that the Ebionites viewed salvation primarily as a matter of obedience to the law (i.e., Jewish or Old Testament law) with the exception of the laws governing animal sacrifices. The significance of Jesus who had come to fulfill rather than abolish the law was that he was merely a man whom God had chosen to proclaim his will. He was not born of a virgin but at his baptism was "adopted" by God and endowed with the power which enabled him to fulfill his mission. This mission was the calling of mankind to obedience to the law which included circumcision of males, Sabbath observance, and following the moral laws of the Old Testament such as those found in the Decalogue. While Ebionism presented a challenge to the church in the first two centuries of her existence, it was never very widespread and disappeared as the church's membership became increasingly Gentile.

By contrast, Gnosticism appears to have gained strength during the Second Century and constituted a very serious threat to the purity of the Gospel tradition and the unity of the church. Even though a brief description of this heresy was presented in Chapter IV on the New Testament, more needs to be said concerning it in order that we may understand more clearly the reasons why the church developed certain "orthodox" creeds and theological positions.

While the sources of Gnosticism were many and varied and there was a bewildering variety of beliefs expressed by the Gnostics, there were certain general traits or characteristics contained in these beliefs. A very basic characteristic of the Gnostics was their fondness for syncretism. That is, they would take beliefs or perspectives from any source regardless of origin or context and try to fit these beliefs into what they regarded as a superior Christian theology or knowledge. The term Gnosticism comes from the Greek gnosis which means knowledge or wisdom and the Gnostics claimed to have superior knowledge. It is evident, however, that many of their beliefs were derived from the philosophers and the mystery religions and were irreconcilable with the received Christian tradition.

In their speculative constructions, the Gnostics viewed the ultimate as one eternal spiritual principle or aeon or being. From this one other principles or aeons are produced in a descending scale of reality and significance until the last one out of envy for the ultimate aeon's productive power produces the evil material world. Thus there is a derivative dualism between matter and spirit. The world of matter since created by an inferior, envious, and evil being is not simply worthless but is itself evil. The God whom the Old Testament claims to have been responsible for the creation of the world is identified as the evil aeon, and the Old Testament is rejected as Holy Scripture. Spirit, on the other hand, does not really belong to this world but is of the ultimate aeon's substance and thus inherently good.[9] Yet spirit, especially in man, has fallen into the material world and become enslaved to matter. Man's nature is viewed by the Gnostics in a dualistic fashion. He is a combination of material body and animal passion on the one hand and of spirit on the other. The innately good spirit is imprisoned in the evil material body. Salvation is a matter of freeing the spirit from the body, and this can be done only be means of saving knowledge (gnosis). Such knowledge consists not only in an understanding of the human situation (the body-spirit dualism and the necessity of freeing the spirit from the body) but also in receiving supernatural revelation (secret gnosis) from the transcendent messenger, Christ, who points the way for the faithful back to the spirit world from which they had originally come.

According to the Gnostics, Christ had descended into the world from the ultimate purely spiritual being or aeon. Since they thought it inconceivable that the ultimate aeon should be present in one who had a real physical body and who really suffered and died, they accepted the position called docetism (from the Greek dokeo which means to seem or to appear). That is, Christ only appeared to have a physical body. He was, in fact, a purely spiritual being. He only appeared to have suffered and died, for a purely spiritual being cannot suffer and die. The purpose of such a charade was to fool the powers who rule the evil physical world and to bring saving knowledge to those who were spiritual enough to accept it.

While Gnosticism enjoyed a degree of popularity in the church during the second century, most Christians felt their faith threatened by it. Gnostic views were opposed to the understanding expressed in the received tradition on the three fundamental doctrines

178

of creation, salvation, and Christology. Traditional
Christian doctrine affirmed that the one totally good
God had created the world, not some lesser being or
demi-god. Since it had been created by the eternal
God who continues to act in history, the world is
essentially good. The principle of evil does not
reside in matter but in willful rebellion against God.
Salvation in the traditional Christian view was not the
negative matter of release from the evil material body
but was a matter of the fulfillment of life including
the body in its glorification in the resurrection from
the dead. Finally, the tradition affirmed that Jesus
Christ was not just some ghostly apparition but had
come in the flesh, had been a real human being who had
really suffered and died. Without this there would
have been no saving divine revelation--no disclosure
of God in actual human life. In denying that Christ
had come in the flesh, the Gnostics had rejected the
heart of the Christian faith.

In response to the challenge of the heresies, the
church soon developed formulae or creeds for testing
the orthodoxy of those who requested admission and baptism. The present Apostle's Creed, for example, is
the end development of some very early baptismal formulae such as the so-called "old Roman symbol" which
emerged in the church at Rome and which undoubtedly
expressed traditional views concerning creation, salvation, and Christology. Even in its present form the
Apostle's Creed is more fully understood if it is
viewed as a defense against heresy. In its final form
the Creed reads as follows:

> I believe in God the Father Almighty;
> Maker of heaven and earth.
>
> And in Jesus Christ his only (begotten)
> Son our Lord; who was conceived by the
> Holy Spirit, born of the Virgin Mary;
> suffered under Pontius Pilate, was cruci-
> fied, dead, and buried; he descended into
> hell; the third day he rose from the
> dead; he ascended into heaven; and sitteth
> at the right hand of God the Father
> Almighty; from thence he shall come to
> judge the living and the dead.
>
> I believe in the Holy Spirit; the holy
> catholic Church; the communion of saints;
> the forgiveness of sins; the resurrection

of the body (flesh); and the life everlasting. Amen.

It is to be noted that the Creed begins by insisting that it is God the Father Almighty and not some
demi-god who created everything that is. It is this
sole deity rather than some ultimate aeon who sent his
Son. In these two claims the Creed reflects a basic
perspective of the Bible, namely that the Creator is
the Redeemer and the Redeemer is the Creator. Creation
and redemption are two functions of the one God rather
than activities of two gods, one good and the other evil.
It is to be noted further that the Creed denies the
Ebionite position when it claims that the Son was conceived by the Holy Spirit. At the same time it rejects
the Gnostic position when it emphasizes that the Son
was <u>born</u>, <u>suffered</u> under Pontius Pilate, was <u>crucified</u>,
<u>dead</u>, and <u>buried</u>. These expressions certainly entail
that Christ was a real human being located in a particular place and in a particular time. The expression of
belief in the resurrection of the body (flesh) certainly
indicates a rejection of the Gnostic view that salvation
is simply a matter of the spirit's release from the body.

The heresies were attacked not only in the church's
creeds but also in the writings of several church "fathers." One of the most significant of the early
"fathers" was Irenaeus (ca. 130-202 A.D.) who became
bishop of Lugdunum (Modern Lyons, France). In his
monumental five-volume work entitled <u>Against Heresies</u>
it is evident that Irenaeus viewed the Gnostic and
Ebionite heretical forms of Christendom as primal forces
bent on the destruction of the "faith once delivered."

In his attempt to defend the "faith once delivered,"
Irenaeus unleashed a scathing attack on the Gnostics.
They lack, he claimed, a unity of perspective and express a bewildering variety of views. These views are
inconsistent, contradicting one another, and yet each
is claimed to be true. But two statements which contradict one another cannot both be true. Further, the
Gnostics reject large portions of Scripture, accepting
only a few of the New Testament writings. Even those
they accept (in some cases only Luke's Gospel and Paul's
letters) they radically revise in eliminating many
things, most notably statements concerning the flesh of
Christ. Finally, they cannot point to any received
tradition or succession of authoritative teachers or
leaders. By contrast, the churches, Irenaeus insisted,
proclaim one and the same faith without inconsistency

or contradiction. They have authentic Scriptures
(Irenaeus likened the four Gospels to the four corners
of the earth) as a source of their faith. They possess a received tradition and a succession of authoritative leaders. With respect to the latter, Irenaeus
claimed that the church at Rome was founded by the
Apostles Peter and Paul and that the twelve bishops of
Rome since that time (Irenaeus listed them by name),
having been in the genuine apostolic succession, had
preserved the apostolic tradition or the "faith once
delivered."10

Irenaeus also attacked the Ebionites for their
adoptionist Christology, their rejection of Paul as a
genuine Apostle, and their acceptance of only Matthew's
Gospel as authoritative New Testament Scripture.11
Again he appealed to authentic scriptures, received
tradition, and apostolic succession in his rejection
of the Ebionite positions. So for Irenaeus unity,
antiquity, and authority were the marks of the Christian teaching which could stand against the heretics.

Irenaeus' defense of the "faith once delivered"
contained not only an attack on the absurdities of
the heretical positions but also an exposition of what
he considered to be an orthodox Christian theology
based on the "rule of faith," the content of which was
similar in many ways to the Old Roman Symbol. In the
brief summary of his theology which follows, it is
rather obvious why Irenaeus claimed that the Gnostic
and Ebionite positions diverged from the received
tradition.12

Of fundamental importance in Irenaeus' theology
is his insistence that God the Father, the Redeemer,
is also the Creator. He has made both the _form_ and the
matter of this world and brought it into being out of
nothing (_ex nihilo_). Its pattern and order he has
established and maintained, and in him justice and
mercy are joined in such a way that they are inseparable from one another.

Man, according to Irenaeus, had been created by
God but not in a finished perfect state in the sense
that he was all that God intended him to be. Adam was
only the beginning of God's purpose in creation. He
was like a "child" whose purpose was to grow into a
closer relationship with God. Irenaeus expressed this
point in terms of distinguishing between the "image"
and the "likeness" of God referred to in Genesis 1:26:

181

"Then God said, let us make man in our image, after our likeness."[13] Even though in the Genesis context "image" and "likeness" are in poetic parallelism and have the same meaning, Irenaeus attributed different meanings to these two terms. By "image" he meant man as a free, personal, and moral being, and this Adam is already. By "likeness" he meant the quality of personal existence which is the finite likeness of God, namely complete moral goodness, fellowship with God, and capacity for eternal life. This likeness of God is the goal which God intended Adam to reach through his free and responsible dealing with life in the world in fellowship with God. But "child" Adam rebelled against his "father" (Creator), and he and his descendents became subjected to the power of sin and death. In this subjection man not only denies God but also his own nature, in that he is stunting his own growth into that which God intended him to be.

In spite of the Fall, God continues to love man and seeks to lead him along the path toward the divine likeness. Out of his love God gave man the law (Great Commandment of Love and the Decalogue) in order to restrain his sinfulness and to serve as his "schoolmaster." Yet obedience to the law is not the final goal of man. Even though opposed to sin, such obedience is servitude and far from being the freely-chosen maturity or likeness to God which is God's loving plan for human life. So in the fullness of time God sent Jesus Christ in order that human nature might be liberated from the power of sin and death (for Irenaeus this is the Devil's power) and granted the power to grow into the divine likeness.

At the center of Irenaeus' theology is his understanding of the nature and work of Christ. Christ is the new Adam who recapitulates in his own life what the Old Adam could have become had he not rebelled against his Creator. That is, Christ recapitulated the perfect man, step by step, so that man might become aware again of his possibilities. So with Christ there is a new beginning. Yet this new beginning is the fulfillment of the original creation, not its destruction. In Christ the mortal nature of man has been united with the immortal nature of God. In him were both the image and the likeness of God. As Irenaeus put it: "And how can man be changed into God unless God has changed into man."[14]

The elevation of man into the divine likeness,

182

according to Irenaeus, can be effected only through the incarnation of the divine life within the limits of a genuinely human life. He was emphatic, terribly emphatic, on that point. Jesus Christ has to be a man. No one other than one who was man could have effected the deification of the race. An alien invader from outside the race could not have done it. It was necessary that the mediator be himself a full-fledged member of the erring group. On the other hand, it was no less necessary that in him human nature should be genuinely united with the divine. Apart from that, there could have been no elevation of the race. So, for Irenaeus, Christ reveals both man as fully grown and God as one who lovingly and at great cost to himself makes it possible that man should be fully rounded out.

The stress in Irenaeus' view of salvation is not on the propitiation or appeasement of God. It is true that Irenaeus speaks of Christ giving himself as a sacrifice for men but this is a sacrifice on their behalf, not in their place. It is not that Christ substituted for men and by his sacrifice satisfied the divine justice. Rather it was by his sacrifice that he fully disclosed the continuous forgiving and sacrificial love of God which is ever seeking to lure men along the pathway to the divine likeness. Irenaeus expressed this beautifully when he said: "Our Lord Jesus Christ who did, through his transcendent love, become what we are, that he might bring us to be even what he is himself."[15]

It is through the faithful acceptance of God's forgiveness and love mediated through Jesus Christ and through seeking by the help of God to follow the model provided by Christ that men may experience the growth interrupted by the Fall and sin, and became finally what God had all along intended human beings to be. In this pilgrimage believers are aided by the community of the New Covenant, the church, and by the divine power communicated through the sacraments of baptism and the Lord's Supper. The ultimate goal of this pilgrimage is the resurrection of the total person unto eternal life.

While Irenaeus had insisted that in Christ the union of God and man achieved its highest goal, he did not explain this union in terms of a combination of two "substances" or "natures." Instead he understood this union in terms of a dynamic or functional relationship. This was the case also with his later contemporary

183

Tertullian (ca. 150-220 A.D.). Tertullian did use the Latin term substantia in his trinitarian formula, "una substantia, tres personae" (one substance, three persons).[16] However, he generally used the term "substantia" in the sense of status instead of in the philosophical sense of "nature," "essence," or "form." For him the fundamental attribute of God is supremacy of status. By "persona" Tertullian meant a functioning unit. In the ancient Greek dramas the masks which the actors wore were called personae. One actor might play several roles indicating a change in role by changing masks. So for Tertullian, the one God eternally "plays three roles" of Father (Creator), Son (Redeemer), and Holy Spirit (Sanctifier) but still is of supreme status in each of these three different functions or roles.

In contrast to Irenaeus and Tertullian, other early Christian thinkers expressed their views concerning the relation between God and Christ and/or the Trinity in terms of Greek philosophical concepts.[17] One such concept was that the ultimate or God was immutable and impassible. That is, he is incapable of changing and of suffering. Another concept was that the fundamental constituents of reality, that which is genuinely real and enduring, are the forms, universals, or "ideas." In Greek philosophy this genuinely real and enduring reality was referred to by the term ousia.[18] Ousia contains such forms or universals as redness, roundness, squareness, but also truth, beauty, and goodness. It is the combination of form and matter which constitutes an actual existing thing. A thing cannot be what it is without possessing, however imperfectly, some form. Without the representation of forms or essences, there would not be a cosmos, a universe, but only undifferentiated matter or potentiality. So ousia is the essence of a thing in contrast to its properties. Perhaps reference to the Catholic doctrine of transubstantiation concerning the elements of Holy Communion might make clearer the distinction between essence (ousia) and properties (accidents). According to this doctrine, in the Mass the bread and wine become the body and blood of Christ. But the bread and wine still retain their properties (accidents), still look, feel, and taste like bread and wine. What has changed is their inner essences such that now they are really the body and blood of Christ under the appearance of bread and wine. Of course this reversed the usual understanding of the relation between essences and properties in which essences are eternal and unchanging while properties are contingent and changing.

The use of these two concepts from Greek philosophy, the immutability of God and ousia, caused problems resulting in the Trinitarian controversy which raged in the church, especially in the early part of the fourth century. The issue was how, in terms of these concepts, could strict monotheism be preserved and yet the divinity of Christ and the Holy Spirit be maintained. This was not a matter simply of speculative interest but was directly related to the question of the nature and means of salvation. Had human nature been genuinely united with the divine nature in Christ such that essential human nature had been remade, making it possible for actual human beings to grow into the divine likeness? But in terms of the ousia concept, how was such a union possible?

A popular priest at Alexandria, Arius[19] (ordained in 312 A.D.), who had studied Greek philosophy, came to the conclusion that it was impossible for the two "substances," human and divine, to be united in one person. God, according to Arius, is one both in substance and in person. His nature is indivisible and cannot be shared by any other being. He is self-existent, eternal, immutable, and impassible. Everything else has been created out of nothing. So the Son of God, the personal Logos, was made out of nothing to be God's agent in the Creation of the World. While the Son of God or the personal Logos was pre-existent and the first of all creatures, he was not eternal. There was when he was not. His nature (ousia or substantia) was not identical with that of God any more than is the nature of any other created thing. God is immutable and impassible. The Son of God was subject to change and suffering. The essence (ousia) of the Son was his own and was identical neither with that of God nor with that of man. Instead he was tertium quid, a third something. As the first of all creatures, the Son or Logos belongs to a higher order than other creatures, whether angels or men. It was this created Son or Logos which became incarnate in the historical Jesus as Jesus' soul, while his body was human. Because of his virtue during his earthly life, his devotion to the divine will, the Son has been given glory and lordship and may be worshipped even though he was not actually God.

Athanasius (ca. 295-373 A.D.), who like Arius had been ordained in the Church at Alexandria and later became its bishop, was one of the first and most important opponents of Arius. For Athanasius, Arianism was

185

inconsistent with the received tradition on three important points. First, since for Arius the Son or Logos
was neither God nor man but a kind of demi-god, his
position, Athanasius claimed, was really polytheistic.
Secondly, Arianism destroyed Christ's mediating function since as created he too would need a mediator.
Thirdly, Arianism destroyed the Christian's certainty
of salvation, since it made redemption dependent on a
created fallible being who was neither genuinely God
nor genuinely man. As Irenaeus had done, Athanasius insisted that Christ, who was genuinely united with God,
really became what we are that we might become what he
is. Arianism stood in contradiction to this truth and
thus must be rejected.

For a while Arianism gained adherents and this
brought not only disunity in the church but also political divisions. So Emperor Constantine convened the
First Ecumenical Council at Nicea in 325 A.D. The
Creed formulated by the Council "fathers" was essentially an affirmation of Athanasius' position. The
earliest form of this creed was probably the following:

> We believe in one God the Father All-
> sovereign, maker of all things visible
> and invisible; and in one Lord Jesus
> Christ, the Son of God, begotten of the
> Father, only-begotten, that is, of the
> substance of the Father, God of God,
> Light of Light, true God of true God,
> begotten not made, of one substance
> [homoouios] with the Father, through
> whom all things were made, things in
> heaven and things on earth; who for us
> men and for our salvation came down and
> was made flesh, and became man, suffered,
> and rose on the third day, ascended into
> the heavens, is coming to judge living
> and dead. And in Holy Spirit. And those
> who say 'There was when he was not,'
> and 'Before his generation he was not,'
> and 'He was made out of nothing,' or
> allege that the Son of God is 'of another
> substance or essence' or 'created' or
> 'changeable' or 'alterable,' these the
> Catholic and Apostolic Church anathema-
> tizes.[20]

It is noted that the Creed insists that the Son is
of the same substance as the Father. Apparently Arius

186

had been willing to say that the Son was of a <u>similar</u>
substance (<u>homoiousios</u>) as the Father but not of the
same substance. The majority of the council fathers
at Nicea, however, decided in favor of using the term
<u>homoousios</u>, which means of one and the same substance.
Furthermore, the anathemas added at the end of the
Creed (beginning with "and those who say 'There was
when he was not.'") make it clear that the intention
of those who formulated and agreed to this Creed was to
leave no room for Arianism which in their view was
heretical. Arianism continued to have a following
for a time, but with the second Ecumenical Council held
in Constantinople in 381 A.D. and its reaffirmation of
the Nicene Creed, Arianism ceased to be an important
factor in theological discussion.

The Nicene-Constantinopolitan Creed, which reaffirmed that Christ was of the same substance as God
and proclaimed that the Holy Spirit proceeds from the
Father and is to be glorified with the Father and the
Son, finally settled the Trinitarian controversy. Once
this issue was settled, there was another question
which theologians had to consider, namely the question
of Christology. The word "Christology" refers to those
theories which attempted to explain how the divinity
and humanity were related in Jesus Christ. After the
Council of Constantinople the controversy which arose
centered not so much on the relation of God and Christ
as on the relationship of the human to the divine <u>in</u>
Christ. Was part of Christ human and another part
divine and what proportion? Did Christ have two centers of personality, a human and a divine, which some-
how managed to cooperate in a kind of loose federation?
Was his human nature completely overshadowed by the
divine such that only his flesh was human? These were
some of the questions involved in the Christological
disputes which resulted in the Council of Chalcedon
(451 A.D.). This Council produced a creed containing
a Christological definition regarded as orthodox. In
the discussion which follows we will attempt to describe briefly three variant Christological theories,
why they were rejected, and what the Christological
definition of the Council of Chalcedon was.[21]

One of the first who attempted a rational solution
to the problem of Christology was Apollinaris, Bishop
of Laodicea (d. 392 A.D.). A hearty supporter of the
Nicene Creed, Apollinaris rejected the Arian view that
the divine Word (Logos) which had been incarnate in
the historical Jesus was created and mutable. He

attempted to develop a Christology in which it could
be shown how the immutable Logos was united with
mutable humanity. Like Athanasius he was convinced
that only a real union or fusion of the divine and
human in Christ made salvation, the growth into divine
likeness, possible. But how was such a union possible?

In the attempt to answer this question, Apollinaris
drew a distinction between human nature and personality.
While it was not possible for there to be a union or fusion of two persons, it was possible for the divine
Logos to take on human nature. This is the case,
Apollinaris argued, because human beings are made up
of body, spirit (psyche), and mind (nous). The mind
contains the personality which distinguishes one
person from another but body and spirit are properties
of human nature as such. In Christ the divine Logos
occupied the place of mind so that in Him human nature
(body and spirit) was united with divine Reason. The
divine Logos could remain immutable and yet at the
same time be the active agent in Christ's life while
his human nature was passive. In this way Apollinaris
thought that on the one hand he had avoided attributing
to Christ two selves or personalities, and that on the
other hand he had retained the two natures and their
union in one person.

However, there were opponents of Apollinaris who
argued that mind is an essential part of human nature,
for man is not a mindless animal. By denying that
Christ had a human mind, Apollinaris had so mutilated
the human nature of Christ that his position was a
kind of semi-docetism.[22] If Christ really became
what we are so that we might become what he is, then
all of his faculties must be genuinely human. That is,
the divine must be united with the fully human.

Among the leading opponents of Apollinaris were
the three Cappadocians, Basil of Caesarea, Gregory
of Nyssa (Basil's brother), and Gregory of Nazianzus.
Among the most outstanding bishops, theologians, and
supporters of monasticism during the second half of
the fourth century, they took up the work of Athanasius
in defending the Nicene faith and prepared the way for
its victory at the Second General Council held at Constantinople in 391 A.D. Similar to Athanasius, they
opposed the Arian homoiousios (of similar but not the
same essence) and insisted upon homoousios (of the same
essence). Yet they explained homoousios in such a
manner as to make it clear that oneness of essence did

not obliterate the distinctions among the members of the Trinity. Thus they used the formula "one ousia in three hypostases," which means "one essence in three substances." While Athanasius had used ousia and hypostasis as synonymous, the Cappadocians attributed a different meaning to hypostasis. In their usage it meant a distinguishable entity, somewhat similar to the Latin persona. Ousia, on the other hand, was used by them in a sense equivalent to the Latin substantia. Thus their formula was not unlike that employed previously by Tertullian. For them, "one ousia in three hypostases" meant that the common essence of the Godhead was possessed by the three individual members of the Trinity, just as three men, though numerically distinct, share a common human essence or nature.

As we have seen, while Apollinaris advocated the Nicene faith, he claimed that the divine essence had supplanted the human mind of Jesus Christ. The Cappadocians were the first to recognize the danger hidden in this Christology, that for all practical purposes it denied the human integrity of Jesus. This, they believed, would destroy what they regarded as essential for the Christian doctrine of salvation. Similar to Irenaeus and Athanasius, they insisted that in Jesus Christ God had assumed humanity so as to enable man to participate in the divine life and to attain deification. In Christ, God truly assumed humanity, not so much to give an example to humanity or to pay man's debt to God, as to defeat the forces of evil that had captured humanity and at the same time to provide the way for the deification of man.

Thus the Cappadocians emphatically condemned the Christology of Apollinaris, insisting that anyone who denied that Christ had a human mind was unworthy of salvation. As Gregory of Nazianzus said:

> For Godhead joined to flesh alone is
> not man, nor to soul alone, nor to both
> apart from intellect, which is the most
> essential part of man. . . . That which
> He [the preexistent Son or Logos] has not
> assumed He has not healed; but that which
> is united to his Godhead is also saved.
> If only half of Adam fell, then that
> which Christ assumes and saves may be
> half also; but if the whole of his nature
> fell, it must be united to the whole

nature of Him that was begotten, and so
be saved as a whole.[23]

Another attempt to solve the Christological issue
was that of Nestorius, Bishop of Constantinople (428-
431 A.D.). Before becoming Bishop, Nestorius had been
a priest and monk in the church at Antioch of Syria.
The leaders of this church had tended to emphasize
the full humanity of Christ in a "Logos-man" type of
Christology, a position which was in opposition to
that of the leaders at Alexandria who emphasized the
deity of Christ in a "Logos-flesh" type of Christology.
Influenced by the position of Antioch, Nestorius was
concerned to emphasize the reality and completeness
of the human nature of Christ as well as of the divine.
It appears that this concern was so strong that it
led him to use language which exceeded that which he
himself probably intended.[24] In his attempt to insist
that in the incarnation each of the two natures retained all of its properties, Nestorius sometimes
spoke of two prosopa ("persons") in Christ. Yet when
he spoke of the conjunction of the two natures he used
the term prosopon.[25] This ambiguity led others to
understand him as saying that there are two natures in
Christ in the sense of two selves or somewhat like
the phenomenon designated in modern psychology as
"split personality" or "multiple selves." Even though
Nestorius probably did not think of the two natures in
precisely this way, he did think that the conjunction
of the two natures in Christ was not an ontological
union but a matter of voluntary cooperation on the part
of each nature. Apparently he thought of the conjunction of natures as being somewhat like the relation of
husband and wife who, while united and one in the
marriage bond, remain separate natures and persons.
Thus it appeared to his opponents that Nestorius had
not spoken of the union of natures in strong enough
terms. If the conjunction of the natures in Christ
is only a matter of will, a kind of moral cooperation,
then essential human nature has not been genuinely
united with the divine so that it has been remade and
growth into the divine likeness made possible.

In opposition to Nestorianism, there arose still
another position on Christology which had its foundation in Alexandrian theology. For Cyril, Bishop of
Alexandria (412-444 A.D.), the humanity of Christ had
no center apart from the Logos. In him the Logos had
taken flesh, had clothed himself with humanity. Unlike
Nestorius, who had insisted on the reality and

completeness of both natures, Cyril viewed Christ as having little more than an _impersonal_ humanity centered in the divinity. His concern, of course, was to emphasize the deity of Christ, the immutability of the Logos. While admitting that the union in Christ was _out of two natures_, Cyril affirmed that the center of Christ's person was the Logos.[26] Since the Logos assumes impersonal humanity, it cannot be said that the historical Christ was an individual man like other men.

Cyril's Christology gave rise to monophysitism, the view that Christ had but one nature and that it was the divine or Logos nature. The most extreme exponent of this view was the monk Eutyches who, though popular, was somewhat lacking in the ability to think carefully and critically on theological issues. He refused to accept the view that there were two natures in the historical Christ. While he was willing to affirm that the Savior was of two natures _before_ the incarnation, there was only one, the divine, _after_ the incarnation. In the incarnation even the body of Christ was deified and so Eutyches denied that Christ was "consubstantial [of the same substance] to us."[27] Obviously, Eutyches' monophysitism contradicted that which was regarded as essential for salvation, namely that Christ be really and fully man, and so it was condemned by powerful opponents including Pope Leo I (440-461 A.D.) in his famous letter (usually called "Tome") to Bishop Flavian.[28] In this letter Leo insisted that the two natures in the historic Christ preserved their characteristics fully and yet there was a genuine union of these two in the one person.

Just as had the Trinitarian controversy, the Christological disputes produced conflict and disunity in both church and state and finally a great ecumenical council was called into session at Chalcedon in 451 A.D. to deal with this problem. Influenced greatly by Pope Leo's Tome, the council produced the following creed:

> Therefore, following the holy Fathers, we all with one accord teach men to acknowledge one and the same Son, our Lord Jesus Christ, at once complete in Godhead and complete in manhood, truly God and truly man, consisting also of a reasonable soul and body; of one substance [homoousios] with the Father as regards his Godhead,

and at the same time of one substance
[homoousios] with us as regards his
manhood; like us in all respects, apart
from sin; as regards his Godhead, begotten
of the Father before the ages, but yet as
regards his manhood begotten, for us men
and for our salvation, of Mary the Virgin,
the God-bearer [Theotokos]; one and the
same Christ, Son, Lord, Only-begotten,
recognized in two natures, without confusion, without change, without division,
without separation; the distinction of
the natures being in no way annuled by
the union, but rather the characteristics
of each nature being preserved and coming
together to form one person and subsistence
[hypostasis], not as parted or separated
into two persons, but one and the same
Son and Only-begotten God the Word [Logos],
Lord Jesus Christ; even as the prophets
from earliest times spoke of him, and our
Lord Jesus Christ himself taught us, and
the creed of the Fathers has handed down
to us.[29]

It is to be noted that this creed provides a
Christological definition so carefully phrased as to
avoid Apollinarism, Nestorianism, and Eutychianism.
The phrases "complete in manhood," "of a reasonable
soul and body," and "like us in all respects" clearly
indicate the rejection of Apollinarism. The insistence
on "one person and subsistence, not as parted or
separated into two persons" is against Nestorianism,
and "recognized in two natures" is against Eutychianism.
In the words of A. C. McGiffert: "Against the former
[Nestorianism] the unipersonality of Christ was asserted; against the latter [Eutychianism], his possession
of two natures, divine and human, each perfect and
unchanged."[30]

Whatever logical problems may be involved in this
creed's Christological definition, it is obvious that
the attempt was to provide a conception of the incarnation which would preserve the doctrine of salvation.
Undoubtedly this is a major reason why the creed has
had a lasting influence in Christian thought. Just
as the Nicene-Constantinopolitan Creed had settled the
Trinitarian controversy and furnished the definition
of Trinity which was accepted by the large majority of
Christians in the subsequent history of the church, so

also the Creed of Chalcedon settled the Christological issue and furnished the definition of Christology accepted by large numbers of Christians since that time.

In our attempt to gain an understanding of the major perspectives which developed in the Christian church, it is necessary to consider briefly the thought of Aureluis Augustine (354-430 A.D.). Standing at the end of the early period, Augustine was the greatest thinker of that period, and further one of the greatest thinkers of all times. His copious writings have had considerable influence on the subsequent intellectual life in Western culture. In terms of the concerns in our study, he is important not only because of the profundity of his thought in itself but also because of the contributions of his thought to Christian theology in both its Catholic and Protestant forms. Some aspects of his theology had a lasting influence on Catholic thought, and yet other aspects of his theology were to wield an influence on the thought of the Protestant Reformers in the sixteenth century.

In our relatively brief discussion of Augustine we will give some attention to each of the following items: his biography and intellectual odyssey, his epistemology (theory of knowledge), his basic theology, and a concluding summary sketching his influence on subsequent Catholic and Protestant theologies.

From his book-length treatise entitled The Confessions[31] (completed about 400 A.D.), we learn that Augustine was born in Tagaste in North Africa of a pagan father and a Christian mother. Although of modest means, his father Patricius managed to provide the financial support for Augustine's education in classical literature at Madua. Patricius soon died, but with the help of a wealthy benefactor Augustine was able to continue his education in advanced studies at Carthage. Here he earned the credentials to be a professor of rhetoric. Much to the distress of his mother Monica, Augustine during the period of his youth refrained from becoming a baptized Christian. Of a rather passionate nature, the young Augustine was unwilling to commit himself to a disciplined Christian life. At age seventeen he took a mistress with whom he lived for fourteen years and by whom he had a son, Adeodatus. A bright boy, Adeodatus tragically died in his seventeenth year.

In Carthage, which was a haven for many religious

sects, Augustine was attracted to Manicheism, a sect
founded two centuries earlier by the Persian prophet
Mani. While the Manicheans spoke of Christ as a great
prophet, they claimed that Mani had brought a later and
superior revelation. This "superior" revelation was
that the universe is a battleground between the two
opposing powers of light and darkness. Light is associated with spirit and goodness, darkness with matter
and evil. Darkness does violence to light by capturing
it in matter. This cosmic dualism is recapitulated
on a lesser scale in man who is a discordant being, a
compound of spirit and body, light and darkness. The
God of light had sent revealors to point out the way.
The last and greatest of these revealors was Mani who,
as the incarnation of the Holy Spirit, was the greatest
Ambassador of light. Receivers were of two kinds, the
hearers and the perfect. The perfect were on the verge
of liberation by virtue of their practice of asceticism.
The hearers, however, lived less strenuously but hoped
to be reincarnated and to achieve liberation in the
next life.

Manicheism appealed to the young Augustine for two
major reasons. First, it provided a relatively simple
solution to the problem of evil. Secondly, as a hearer,
he was not required to give up his life of sensuality.
However, after a period of time, Augustine became disillusioned with Manicheism. He found that the leaders
of this sect were not as intellectually and morally
superior as they claimed to be. Many of them were
making use of astrology (the stars as spirits of light)
to support their claims, but Augustine found undeniable
proof that astrology was false. Furthermore, Augustine
found that no Manichean leader could satisfactorily
answer his question as to how it was that an incorrupt-
able God, the source of light, could be subject to
violence from the realm of darkness.

When Augustine went to Rome in 383, he abandoned
his ties with Manicheism and entered a brief period
of skepticism. This position, which had a long history
in philosophy, denied that human beings can have
certainty with respect to knowledge. All of our judgments, the skeptics claimed, are only relative or
probable, and yet some of them are more probably true
than others. Upon giving this position serious consideration, Augustine came to the conclusion that it
was in error and was ultimately self-defeating. If
some judgments are more probably true than others, then
this implies a prior standard which itself is not

194

probable. The only way one could determine whether
judgment x is more probably true than y is by comparing
x and y with a prior standard which is absolutely true.
If x can be determined to be related to this prior
standard in some way, such as being closely associated
with it or being the effect of it and y cannot, then
x is more probably true than y. Furthermore, the
position of skepticism cannot be consistently stated.
It was not that the skeptics claim that most judgments
are probable or relative but rather than all judgments
are relative. Yet if one says that everything is
relative, then it turns out that this is affirming one
absolute, namely the statement, "Everything is relative." So it seemed to Augustine that skepticism could
not be consistently stated and was a self-defeating
position.

     After a brief period in Rome Augustine was employed
as a municipal teacher of rhetoric in Milan and during
his stay there experienced a decisive turning point in
his life. Having rejected Manicheism and Skepticism,
Augustine engaged in a study of Neoplatonism which was
a pantheistic, mystical, interpretation of Plato's
thoughts. In contrast to Manichean dualism which divided reality between the two powers of light and darkness, spirit and matter, Neoplatonism was monistic.
Ultimately there is only the One and this One is uncre-
ated, indivisible, immutable, perfect, and absolute.
Generous and outgoing by nature, the One pours forth
his essence so that from him emanates everything that
is in a descending scale of existence. Just as light
pours from the sun, so being pours from the One. From
the One comes Nous, the supreme intelligent soul, and
from Nous the world-soul who is the source of rational
human souls, non-rational animal souls, and the rest
of the natural world. The greater the distance from
the radiance of the One the more the white light of the
One fades and the less of true being there is. If it
fades altogether, there is, of course, no being at all.
Matter is not positive substance, corporeal mass, but
a negative limit approached but never reached by being.
As compared with the being of the One, it is not-being.
On this basis, evil is not viewed as a positive substance, as something which exists in itself, as did
the Manicheans but as a deficiency, a privation of
good, a lapse toward not-being. The conquest of evil
occurs when, through disciplined contemplation, the
human rational souls rise to full union with the One.
There is, then, a purpose in the One's emanation or
unfolding, namely that ultimately there will be

refolding of being into the One.

Apparently knowledge of Neoplatonic philosophy made it easier for Augustine to be receptive of the Christian faith and to respond to the sermons and teachings of Ambrose, the great Bishop of Milan. On Easter eve, April 25, 387, much to the delight of his mother who had joined him in Milan, Augustine was baptized by Bishop Ambrose. The year following, after his mother's death, Augustine returned to Tagaste, was ordained a priest for the church at nearby Hippo, and later became its Bishop. While some aspects of Neoplatonic philosophy had a lasting influence on his thinking, Augustine on becoming a Christian abandoned those elements of this philosophy which could not be harmonized with the "received tradition" of the church.

In our attempt to understand Augustine's thought with some degree of clarity, it is important not only to become aware of his life situation and intellectual odyssey but also to gain some familiarity with his epistemology (theory of knowledge). How a thinker views the source and guarantees of human knowledge is often the key which unlocks the door to an understanding of his thought on other issues. This seems to be the case with respect to Augustine.

While it seems evident that Augustine's epistemology owed much to Neoplatonism, it was a Neoplatonism modified by the Christian faith. Unlike the Neoplatonists, Augustine held that God is a personal supernatural being who of his own free will created everything that is ex nihilo (out of nothing) and not a pantheistic One from whom all being emanated. Yet he insisted that God is the source of all truth. Truth is divine illumination, and our knowledge, even though it is a pale reflection of God's knowledge, is a participation in God's knowledge. God is both the source and the guarantor of our knowledge. But how can one arrive at such a conclusion?[32]

In his argument for this conclusion Augustine began with that which certainly seems clear and unquestionable, namely the consciousness of our own existence. A skeptic might assert that, since in the past our knowledge claims have often been mistaken, we might be mistaken also in claiming to know that we exist. To assertions of this type Augustine responded by pointing out that those who would be the ones mistaken would have to exist in order to be mistaken. As he says in On the Trinity: "One who does not exist cannot be deceived, and therefore, if I am deceived, I exist."[33] In the very act of rigorous doubting, including the doubting of one's own existence, one is tacitly affirming his own existence as the doubter. So with respect to the knowledge that one exists there can be no real question.

However, the matter cannot be left at this point. There is still the question as to whether or not we can have knowledge of reality beyond our own personal existence. Can there be certainty with respect to knowledge claims about such reality? The best candidates for such knowledge would seem to be found in the necessarily true propositions of logic and mathematics. Even the skeptics admitted that such propositions are necessarily true, but, they claimed, these truths simply represent arbitrary human conventions and are purely formal. While they may be used in reasoning about the world of actual objects, they are not located in the structure of the actual world. They do not provide us knowledge about the world but only inform us of arbitrary human conventions.

By contrast, Augustine argued that the principles of mathematics and logic characterize the most general structure of reality itself. In this he made use of a modified version of the Neoplatonic vision of the great scale or chain of being. Of all the things we encounter in this world, inanimate objects, plants, animals, beings with rational souls (man), surely the rational soul is the highest. But the rational souls in the world have an awareness or a conception of a rational soul superior to themselves, perfect in being and goodness. Such an awareness could not have been derived from that which is lower in the scale of being nor from other human beings who, however rational they may be, are not perfect. The source must be God himself who, since he is perfect, necessarily exists, for if he were a contingent being, he would not be perfect. Precisely because he is perfect, he is the source of all truth and rational order including the necessary truths of logic and mathematics. So Augustine claimed that logic and mathematics were not created and arranged by men but were discovered because "perpetually instituted by God in the reasonable order of things."[34] It is clear, then, that for Augustine the very content and means of human knowledge rest upon God. Precisely because of this, even though we human beings are sometimes deceived, we can have confidence that in general our knowledge of reality including sensible contingent things as well as the propositions of logic and mathematics is veridical.[35]

We turn now to a consideration of other important aspects of Augustine's thought which are relevant for Christian theology. It has been indicated above that for Augustine God is perfect in being and goodness and thus necessarily exists. This can be said of God alone. The existence of everything else is derivative and dependent, having its source in God's creative activity. All that exists is God and what he has created. The created order is good since created by God out of nothing. However, it is positively rather than perfectly good as is God. It is derivative, dependent, contingent, mutable, and finite.

If all that is, is God and the positively good created order, how can the fact that there is evil in the world be understood and explained? Surely God cannot be the source of evil for then he could not be perfect in being and goodness. So in his theodicy (a term which designates the attempt to justify God in light of the fact of evil), Augustine seeks to locate the source of evil elsewhere. Having rejected Manicheism, he cannot say that its source is an eternal evil power nor that evil is a positive substance. Instead he claims that evil is privation rather than substance and locates its source in Adam's misuse of the free will granted to him in the creation.

Since the created order is contingently and mutably good, it is possible for the good in created things to be increased or diminished. For the good to be diminished is evil. Whether it is natural evil, the physical pain and/or other types of suffering experienced by feeling beings because of events in nature, or moral evil, the pain and suffering of feeling beings caused by human beings, evil is the privation of good. Augustine expressed this very clearly in the Enchiridion when he said:

> For what is that which we call evil but the absence of good? In the bodies of animals, disease and wounds mean nothing but the absence of health; for when a cure is effected, that does not mean that the evils which were present--namely, the diseases and wounds--go away from the body and dwell elsewhere: they altogether cease

to exist; for the wound or disease is
not a substance, but a defect in the
fleshly substance--the flesh itself
being a substance, and therefore something good, of which those evils--that
is, privations of the good which we
call health--are accidents. Just in the
same way, what are called vices in the
soul are nothing but the privations of
natural good. And when they are cured,
they are not transferred elsewhere: when
they cease to exist in the healthy soul,
they cannot exist anywhere else.[36]

Why is it that God permits the privation of good?
The answer to this question, Augustine claimed, is to
be found in what is required for the greater beauty
and harmony of the whole, namely the juxtaposition of
opposites. For example, the beauty of an entire poem
may be enhanced by the side by side presence of certain
antitheses or the beauty of the entire painting may be
enhanced by the side by side presence of light and
dark colors. So God permits evil, both natural and
moral, but only and always for the greater harmony of
the whole. With respect to the evil which men do, God
judged it better to bring greater good out of evil
rather than not to permit such evil to exist.

While it is evident that Augustine's view of evil
as the privation of good owed much to Neoplatonism, he
departed from Neoplatonism in using the Biblical story
of the Fall to account for the source of evil in the
world. Adam and Eve in the Garden of Eden, Augustine
claimed, had been granted by God the power or the freedom either to sin or not to sin (posse peccare and posse
non peccare). They chose to sin and thus lost the gift
which enabled them not to sin. While still free in all
other respects, they no longer possessed the freedom
not to sin. They were free only to sin. Since essential human nature was present in Adam and Eve, the
human race since that time possesses only what fallen
Adam and Eve possessed, namely the freedom to sin.
So Adam and Eve were the source of moral evil in the
world and also of natural evil, for God permits such
as a punishment of sin.

All human beings are caught in the predicament
of sin and for Augustine sin is not simply a matter of
bad deeds. It is a state or condition of being, the
pretension of self, egocentricity, or pride. Sins are

simply symptoms of this more basic fact of <u>sin</u>. The most powerful human faculty, according to Augustine, is the will. Since the Fall the will is infected with the pretension of self or sin and in turn infects the intellect and the emotions. Since it is the will which is a slave to sin, one cannot will himself or herself out of such enslavement. In describing this condition, Augustine said:

> For, as a man who kills himself must, of course, be alive when he kills himself, but after he has killed himself ceases to live, and cannot restore himself to life; so, when man by his own free will sinned, then sin being victorious over him, the freedom of his will was lost.[37]

This loss of the freedom of the will refers only to that original freedom not to sin. Fallen man is still free to will and to do many things, but what he is not free to do is to will himself out of the condition of sin nor to do the good works which would merit him a place in the eternal kingdom. Release from enslavement to sin, salvation, must come from beyond man.

God, Augustine claimed, had taken the initiative to provide release from sin. He has sent Jesus Christ as Mediator and Reconciler. Accepting the church's view of the Trinity and Christology, Augustine viewed the work of Christ as serving two closely related functions. It was a sacrifice to God on our behalf and yet at the same time a channel of the grace of God so that we might be reconciled to God. That is, through Christ we may experience the love of God, learn to love him in return, and ultimately reach eternal beatitude.[38] Yet the acceptance of what God has done for us through Christ is not a matter of our willing to accept it. Faith, which for Augustine is primarily a matter of <u>trust</u> in God through Christ, is not our work. It is entirely a gift of God.[39]

Augustine was very emphatic on the point that fallen man cannot merit the grace of God, and that it is God's free gift. So he claimed that those who have faith have been elected or predestined by God to have faith. This was not a philosophical doctrine of fatalism which views all events as predetermined. Rather it has to do only with salvation. That God had predestined some to salvation, Augustine claimed, was a

mystery but still a fact. Since all of the descendents
of Adam were potentially in him, all men deserve damnation. God's choice of some for salvation is an expression of his mercy. The damned have no basis for complaint since they get what they deserve, and conversely
the saved have no basis for self-congratulation since
their salvation is due to their election by God. Whatever philosophical and/or theological problems there
may be with this doctrine, Augustine's purpose in
formulating it was to testify to the absolute primacy
of God in salvation.

Augustine's positions on original sin and predestination were in part shaped by his controversy with
Pelagius, a British monk who settled in Rome about 400
A.D. Disturbed by the low tone of Roman morals, Pelagius felt that the doctrines of original sin and predestination cut the nerve of moral endeavor and
encouraged indulgence in sins. Unlike Augustine, his
view of human character was atomistic. That is, each
person creates his own character and determines his
own desinty. Adam's fall had an effect only upon himself, not upon his descendents. The sin of Adam did
provide a bad example for his descendents and men do
choose to follow this bad example. Yet they retain the
freedom not to sin. At any moment they can turn to
God and obey. In this they have the help of God's
grace in Christ in experiencing forgiveness of their
sins and in instruction and enlightenment through the
law and the example of Christ. Obviously, Pelagius did
not accept Augustine's understanding of sin as the
willful pretension of self but rather viewed sin as
a matter of sins. Further, as Augustine was quick to
point out, his view of salvation made human decision
primary rather than God's initiative.[40]

Augustine's emphasis on predestination did not
mean that for him the works of believers and the church
of which Christ is the head have no roles to play in
the process of salvation. While God takes the initiative and infuses his grace into the souls of the elect
by means of their hearing the Gospel, the faith thus
received leads them to the church where, through the
sacraments, they receive further grace. Grace is a
power infused into the soul. It operates initially
(sometimes called "prevenient grace") to turn one
to faith and to the church. In the church further
grace (sometimes called "cooperating grace") is infused
through the sacraments such that one is empowered to
complete faith by works of love and to merit eternal

201

life.[41] So for Augustine, God's election, Christ as
mediator, prevenient grace which brings one to faith,
cooperating grace which is received through the church
and its sacraments, and good works are all required to
bring one into the state of ultimate beatitude. In
this state of final blessedness in heaven the elect
transcend the condition of Adam before the fall (posse
peccare, posse non peccare) such that they possess
total freedom from sin (non posse peccare.)[42] Those
who are sanctified in this life will be transported
after death directly into the joyous blessings of
heaven. Apparently those not completely sanctified
will spend a time in purgatory.[43]

In view of the fact that for Augustine the church
is essential for salvation, it is not surprising that
he placed a high valuation on the visible Catholic
Church.[44] Like Cyprian, Augustine was convinced that
apart from the Catholic Church ultimate beatitude was
not possible for only here could believers receive the
true infusion of grace. He opposed the Donatists,
the North African Christian rigorists, who had withdrawn from the Catholic Church. Since some ecclesiastical leaders of the Catholic Church had been unfaithful
in times of persecution, this church, the Donatists
claimed, was impure. Only as the leaders are holy
can the church be truly the church, a congregation of
saints. Sacraments administered by unworthy ministers
are invalid. Since, the Donatists claimed, their own
leaders had been and were pure, only their celebrations
of the sacraments were valid. Augustine, however,
claimed that, since the sacraments are the work of
God rather than men, their validity is not dependent
on the character of the administrator. If there is
proper form and matter, the sacrament is valid. On
this basis, even the sacraments of the schismatics are
valid, and if the schismatics return to the Catholic
Church they do not have to be rebaptized. Yet the
schismatics do not really benefit from their celebrations of the sacraments, for it is only in the Catholic
Church that the sacraments are fully efficacious in
the infusing of grace into the souls of believers.
This is the case because only the Catholic Church
possesses Apostolic succession, catholicity, and unity
which are essential marks of the true church.

Even though the Catholic Church is essential for
ultimate blessedness, Augustine did not believe that
all its members were on the way to this goal. The
Catholic Church is a mixed company. Yet it contains

202

the City of God which stands in contrast to the city of earth.[45] In history the latter is a relative good serving to restrain disorder and to secure a relative peace. But it must pass away. The fall of Rome, which some pagans had blamed on the abandonment of the old gods, was instead a result of Rome's own sin and idolatry and should have been anticipated. Indeed, history is under the direction of God who wills the city of earth to pass away as the City of God grows. Those who make up the City of God are the elect who are within the visible Catholic Church though not all in that church are among the elect. Since the City of God is in the hierarchally organized Catholic Church, the Catholic Church should more and more rule over the world. In this view Augustine laid the basis for the medieval view of a theocratic state. But more importantly, the City of God is eternal and will survive the end of earthly history. Its citizens will go on living truly and joyfully in life eternal while those of the devil will live on in a state of misery.

At the beginning of the discussion of Augustine it was indicated that certain aspects of his thought had an influence on subsequent Catholic thought while other aspects influenced later Protestant thought. As a partial summary of Augustine's views and partial preview of positions to be considered later, we will conclude this discussion of Augustine with a brief sketch of how his thought was influential concerning the following issues:

1. His view of fallen man as enslaved to sin was to influence the Protestant Reformers' (Luther and Calvin) view of fallen man as totally depraved. That is, fallen man's volitions, intellect, and emotions are infected with the pretensions of self. Later Catholic thought, while still speaking of man's original sin and fallen condition, nevertheless tended to be somewhat semi-Pelagian. Since he retains the divine image, fallen man can choose to know a great deal about God and to do a great deal of good even though he cannot know and do the supernatural good necessary for ultimate beatitude without the acceptance of God's revelation and the infusion of divine grace.

2. Augustine's view of the grace of God as an infused power in the two modes of prevenient and co-operating grace, the latter communicated through the church's sacraments which are efficacious quite apart from the character of the administrator, was to remain

important in Catholic theology. For the Protestant
Reformers, the grace of God was understood to be God's
<u>gracious</u> <u>act</u> of forgiveness through Jesus Christ and
the two sacraments, baptism, and the Lord's supper,
witness to and strengthen faith but do not infuse
power into the souls of believers.

3. Augustine's emphasis upon the primacy of the
will in the experience of faith such that faith is
primarily a matter of trust was to influence the
thought of the Protestant Reformers. Later Catholic
thought (especially with Thomas Aquinas) tended to
emphasize the primacy of the intellect and so understood faith as primarily a matter of giving intellectual assent to a set of propositions based on the
deposit of God's Word or revelation as found in both
church tradition and Scripture.

4. The Protestant Reformers followed Augustine
in holding to the doctrine of the divine election or
predestination of believers. The grace of God was
irresistible. Later Catholic thought took a semi-
Pelagian view on this issue claiming that God's grace
was resistible. Even a believer could fall away and
be lost unless he availed himself of the sacrament of
penance.

5. Later Catholic thought followed Augustine in
insisting that faith must be completed by good works in
order for one to merit eternal life. Both faith <u>and</u>
good works are necessary for salvation. The Protestant
Reformers, however, claimed that faith alone is necessary for salvation. Even though faith motivates the
believer to do good works, the works, since relative
and problematical, are not a means of salvation. Salvation is solely a matter of justification by faith.

NOTES

¹ Under Suggestions for Further Reading, I list several good studies on the history of Christianity which the reader may consult for more detailed background information.

² English translations of these writings may be found in the following: J. B. Lightfoot, The Apostolic Fathers (Baker Book House, 1956); Ante-Nicene Christian Library, Vol. I, A. Roberts and J. Donaldson (eds.) (T. and T. Clark, 1870); The Fathers of the Church, Vol. I, Ludwig Schopp (editorial director) (The Catholic University of America Press, Inc., 1947).

³ Ante-Nicene Christian Library, Vol. I, p. 355.

⁴ Williston Walker, A History of the Christian Church, third edition (Charles Scribner's Sons, 1970), p. 92.

⁵ See Ante-Nicene Christian Library, Vols. 8, 13; The Fathers of the Church, Vols. 36, 51; A. C. McGiffert, A History of Christian Thought, Vol. II (Charles Scribner's Sons, 1953), Chapter II; Justo L. Gonzalez, A History of Christian Thought, Vol. I (Abingdon Press, 1970), pp. 244-252.

⁶ A. C. McGiffert, op. cit., p. 27.

⁷ Ibid., p. 34.

⁸ See Justo L. Gonzalez, op. cit., pp. 124-144.

⁹ Some loose similarity of the Gnostic views with Platonism and Neo-Platonism is evident. In Neo-Platonism everything emanates from the One in a descending scale of reality and significance. In Platonism ultimate reality is composed of the universal ideas or forms which are imperfectly manifested in actual objects. True knowledge is a matter of coming to a direct rational apprehension of the pure forms apart from their imperfect representations in the actual world of material objects and sense impressions. In Plato's Phaedo, for example, Socrates claims that the body and its impulses are the source of the ignorance and troubles in the world. So, of all men, the true philosopher should be the least afraid of death for in the search for knowledge he is engaged in the practice of dying. Here, too, is a derivative dualism, an opposition of matter and form, body and soul. Apparently one of the many sources of Gnostic beliefs was Platonic philosophy.

[10] Against Heresies, II. III. 2, 3. Ante-Nicene Christian Library, Vol. V, pp. 261–262.

[11] Ibid., I. XXVI, 1-3, p. 97; III. XV. 1, pp. 320-21; V. I. 3, (Ante-Nicene Christian Library, Vol. 9, pp. 57–58).

[12] See ibid., II. I. II (V. 5, pp. 117-123); II. IX. X (V. 5, pp. 142-146); III. XX. (V. 5, pp. 347-351); III. XXIII. (V. 5, 362-369); IV. XX. (V. 5, p. 439); III. XVI. (V. 5, pp. 323-333); IV. XXXVII-XXXIX (V. 9, pp. 36-45); V. Pref. (V. 9, p. 55), V. I-VII. (V. 9, pp. 55-100); also Gonzalez, op. cit., pp. 160-174; McGiffert, op. cit., V. I, pp. 132-148.

[13] Against Heresies, V. VI. 1.

[14] Ibid., IV. XXXIII. 4.

[15] Ibid., V. Preface.

[16] Adversus Praxean 5, Ante-Nicene Christian Library, Vol. 15. See also my Language, Logic and Reason in the Church Fathers: A Study of Tertullian, Augustine and Aquinas (Georg Olms Press, 1979), Chapter II, Section C, pp. 34-60.

[17] See Gonzalez, op. cit., Chapters IV, VIII, X, and XI.

[18] See W. Windelband, A History of Philosophy (Macmillan Company, 1901), pp. 120-123, 140-143. See also Plato, The Republic, VI. 507 and Aristotle, Metaphysics, Book 1, Chapter 7.

[19] Some sources for the discussion of Arius, Athanasuis and the Creed of Nicea are: Nicene and Post-Nicene Fathers (Wm. B. Eerdmans Publishing Company, 1957), Second Series, Vol. IV; The Library of Christian Classics (The Westminster Press, 1954), Vol. III; Justo L. Conzalez, op. cit., Chapters XI-XII; Documents of the Christian Church, Second Edition, Henry Betten-son (ed.) (Oxford University Press, 1963), Section II. II, IV. V, VII.

[20] See Bettenson, ibid., p. 25.

[21] Some sources for the discussion of Apollinaris, Eutyches, Nestorius, and the Creed of Chalcedon are: Nicene and Post-Nicene Fathers, Second Series, Vols. II, III, VII, XII, op. cit.; Bettenson, op. cit., pp. 44-52; Gonzalez, op. cit., Chapters XVI-XVIII; McGiffert, op. cit., Vol. I, Chapter XV.

[22] See the previous discussion of Gnosticism.

[23] Nicene and Post-Nicene Fathers, Second Series, Vol. VII,

p. 440. Italics are mine. See Gonzalez, op. cit., pp. 311-333, 359-362.

24 See Reinhold Seeberg, Textbook in the History of Doctrines, Vol. I (Baker Book House, 1954), pp. 261-262. Gonzalez, op. cit., pp. 370-374.

25 Gonzalez, ibid., pp. 371-372.

26 See Bettenson, op. cit., pp. 46-47.

27 Ibid., pp. 48-51.

28 Nicene and Post-Nicene Fathers, Second Series, Vol. 12, pp. 38-43.

29 Quoted from Bettenson, op. cit., pp. 51-52.

30 McGiffert, op. cit., p. 285.

31 See Whitney T. Oates, Basic Writings of Saint Augustine, Vol. I (Random House, 1948).

32 See my Language, Logic and Reason in the Church Fathers, op. cit., Chapter III, pp. 62-63.

33 XV. 12. 21, Oates, op. cit., Vol. II, pp. 850.

34 On Christian Doctrine, XXXII. 50; XXXVIII. 56, D. W. Robertson (trans.) (The Library of Liberal Arts, 1950), pp. 68, 70.

35 In addition to the reference cited above, see "On Free Will," II. III. 7 - XV. 39, Augustine: Earlier Writings, Library Christian Classics, Vol. 6 (Westminster, 1963); "The Confessions," VII. 4; "The City of God," XI. 26, VII. 29; "Soloquies," 2, in Oates, Basic Writings of St. Augustine, Vols. I and II (Random House, 1948).

36 Enchiridion, Chapter XI, Oates, Vol. I, p. 662.

37 Ibid., XXX, p. 675.

38 Ibid., XXXI - XXXII, pp. 676-678. Also see The Confessions, VII. XIX, Oates, Vol. I, p. 106; The City of God, XI. II; XXI. XV; Oates, Vol. II, pp. 144-145, 585; On the Trinity, IV. XIV; XV. VII; Oates, Vol. II, pp. 745, 839-842.

39 Ibid. See also On the Spirit and the Letter and On Nature and Grace, Oates, Vol. I.

[40] See *On the Spirit and the Letter*, *On Nature and Grace*, *On the Grace of Christ* and *On Original Sin*, Oates, Vol. I.

[41] See *To Simplician - On Various Questions*, I. 2. 2, *Augustine: Earlier Writings*, *Library of Christian Classics*, Vol. 6 (Westminster, 1963), p. 386.

[42] *Enchiridion*, CV, Oates, p. 720.

[43] *Ibid.*, LXIX, p. 699.

[44] *Of True Religion*, VI. 10-11, VII. 12-13, VIII. 14; *Augustine: Earlier Writings*, pp. 230-233.

[45] See *The City of God*, Oates, Vol. II.

SUGGESTIONS FOR FURTHER READING

Ayers, Robert H., Language, Logic and Reason in the Church Fathers, Georg Olms Press, 1979, Chapters I-III.

Bainton, Roland, Christendom, Vol. I, Harper Torchbook, 1966.

Battenhouse, R. W., Companion to the Study of Saint Augustine, Oxford University Press, 1955.

Berthold, Fred, et. al, Basic Sources of the Judeo-Christian Tradition, Prentice-Hall, 1962, Part Two.

Bettenson, Henry, Documents of the Christian Church, Oxford University Press, 1963, Part I.

Burkill, T. A, The Evolution of Christian Thought, Cornell University Press, 1971, pp. 1-128.

Gonzalez, Justo L., A History of Christian Thought, Vol. I, Abingdon Press, 1970.

Gonzalez, Justo L., A History of Christian Thought, Vol. II, Abingdon Press, 1971, Chapters I-II.

Grant, R. M., Gnosticism and Early Christianity, Columbia University Press, 1959.

Kelly, J. N. D., Early Christian Creeds, Third Edition, Longman, 1972.

Kelly, J. N. D., Early Christian Doctrines, Revised Edition, Harper and Row, 1978.

Lohse, Bernhard, A Short History of Christian Doctrine, Fortress Press, 1978, Chapters 1-4.

Manschreck, Clyde L., A History of Christianity in The World, Prentice-Hall, 1974, Chapters 2-6.

McGiffert, A. C., A History of Christian Thought, Vol. I, Charles Scribner's Sons, 1953, Chapters IV-VIII, XII-XV.

McGiffert, A. C., A History of Christian Thought, Vol. II, Charles Scribner's Sons, 1953, Chapters I-IV.

Oates, Whitney, J. (ed.), Basic Writings of Saint Augustine, Vols. I and II, Random House, 1948.

Pelikan, Jaroslav, The Christian Tradition, Vol. I, University of Chicago Press, 1971.

The Library of Christian Classics, Vols. I-III, V-VIII, Westminster Press, 1963-1966.

Seeberg, Reinhold, Textbook in the History of Doctrines, Vol. I, Baker Book House, 1954.

Walker, Williston, A History of the Christian Church, Third Edition, Charles Scribner's Sons, 1970, pp. 51-172.

CHAPTER VII

THE MEDIEVAL PERIOD

The long medieval period (ca. 6th-15th centuries) was a time during which there were further important theological and practical developments in Christendom. Among these were the growth of monasticism, the increased power and prestige of the church and the papacy in the West, the East-West division of the church, the emergence of mysticism, and the theological synthesis of Thomas Aquinas.

In the previous chapter it was indicated that one of the three major problems confronted by the church as time went on without the return of Christ was how to deal with sins, both within and without the church. Since the early period was one in which Christians were confronted by opposition and were often persecuted by sanction of the Roman government, to live a Christian life required considerable moral courage and purity. It was generally believed that one who suffered martyrdom for the faith immediately received the highest blessings of God. However, when Constantine gained full control of the Roman Empire in 323 A.D. and patronized Christianity, there was an influx of vast numbers into the church and a relaxation of the stringent moral standards required of Christians when under the threat of persecution. Many sensitive Christians were repelled by this moral laxity and sought the isolation of the desert where they could fulfill the "counsels of perfection" which they believed were demanded by the Gospel. While even in the early period there had been those who, indirectly influenced by a Platonic body-soul dualism, had engaged in rigorous ascetic disciplines in order to save their souls, the numbers engaging in such practices now increased. Since martyrdom was no longer possible, monasticism became for many a kind of substitute martyrdom. This situation led to the establishment of a double standard. One was for ordinary Christians who were expected to fulfill only the "ordinary" requirements of the Gospel. The other was for clergy and monastics who, following the counsels of perfection, took vows of poverty, chastity, and obedience.[1]

It was natural that then, as well as now, there

should be the feeling that the clergy should lead lives which would be an example to their flock. Celibacy had long been regarded as belonging to the holier Christian life. Even the Apostle Paul, while not forbidding marriage, had pointed out that in contrast to the married who were anxious about worldly affairs, the unmarried, freed of such anxiety, could give more attention to the affairs of the Lord so as to be holy in body and spirit (I Corinthians 7:32-35). It is not surprising then that celibacy should come to be regarded as a required lifestyle for the clergy (bishops, priests, and deacons). Pope Leo I (440-461) held that even sub-deacons should refrain from marriage.[2] While clerical celibacy was not always universally enforced in the Western church in the Medieval Period, it was the accepted rule and was often strictly enforced by re-forming popes. Finally, it became standard practice in the Roman Catholic Church. However, the Eastern Ortho-dox Church (officially separated from the Roman Catholic Church in the middle of the eleventh century) has been less strict with respect to the celibacy of the clergy. Only celibates can be bishops, but clergy below that rank may marry before ordination.

Not only were the clergy in the Western church sup-posed to live by the counsels of perfection (poverty, chastity, obedience) but also those who entered the monastic life. Apparently Christian monasticism had its beginning in Egypt during the third century.[3] In this early period it was often a matter of individuals becoming ascetic hermits or of small unstructured groups practicing ascetic disciplines. Due to the exam-ples of outstanding leaders such as Ambrose and Augus-tine, the monastic life began to find favor in the West. However, it was Benedict (480-547) who had the greatest influence, for he provided both structure and legisla-tion for the monasticism which became dominant in the Western church. Formed to be self-sustaining and self-contained communities, the Benedictine monasteries were centers of stability, learning, and worship during the upheavals which plagued Western Europe in the early middle ages.

Benedict was born in Nursia and educated at Rome. Disturbed by the low moral standards prevalent in Rome, he became a hermit living in a mountain cave east of the city. Even though he was only a layman, he became famous for his sanctity, and disciples gathered about him in such numbers that finally he founded a monastery at Monte Cassino, the mother monastery of the Benedictine

Order.[4] To it he gave his famous Rule which came to be widely adopted.[5]

From the Rule we learn that for Benedict the best form of monasticism was that practiced in a settled community under the leadership of an Abbot who was regarded as though he were a "general" of this "army" of Christian "soldiers." While the Abbot often consulted with the brothers and was not to rule autocratically, he was to be obeyed in all things. In addition to commanding the Monks to obey the Abbot, the Rule prescribed the practice of such virtues as loving chastity, embracing poverty, hearing of Holy Reading daily, devoting oneself to prayer, loving enemies, helping the poor, etc. Worship was central with seven different periods during the day devoted to prayer and worship. Yet there was also an emphasis on work. The monks were required to do manual labor in the fields and to engage in study. They had to follow rigorous daily schedules which contained stated periods for worship, work, study, and sleep. While it was a strict life which the Rule prescribed, it was not an impossible one for the average man to follow, but his following of it transformed him into a superior man. Among the best men of the times were those in the monasteries. The practicing of the monastic discipline produced individuals who incorporated into their own lives a high regard for manual labor and the physical well-being gained therefrom, the expansion of mental horizons through scholarship, and the spiritual strength acquired through worship and devotional meditation. In the long history of monasticism, not all individual monks, monastic orders, and monasteries lived up to the Benedictine ideals, but those monasteries in which these or similar ideals were operative were havens of peace and worship, centers of industry, and communities of learning. They were beacons of light in troubled times.

It was mentioned above that, with Constantine, Christianity received the sanction of the government. Another important action of Constantine was that he moved his capital from Rome to the rebuilt Byzantium which, in his honor, was renamed Constantinople. This was to have very significant consequences for the Christian church. Among other things, it resulted in the emergence of two centers of authority which contributed to the eventual East-West division of the church and it left the bishop of Rome as the dominant figure in the West.

As pointed out in Chapter VI, from ancient times the Church of Rome and its bishop as the successor of Peter had been held in high esteem. Given the political vacuum created by the move of the capital, the crumbling of the Roman Empire in the West due to the assaults of the barbarians, and the fact that the Roman church managed not only to survive but also to continue its operations, it is not surprising that this church and its bishop came to be accorded even greater authority. While some of the bishops of Rome during this period were men of moderate abilities, several were the strongest leaders of their times, and their leadership resulted in the growth of the religious and political authority of the bishop of Rome. This was symbolized by the fact that the title "Pope" ("Father"), which in ancient times was given to all bishops, came to be used in the West to designate only the bishop of Rome.6 There was, then, the development of a real papacy.

Among the popes who contributed greatly to the elevation of the papacy in the West were Leo I (440-461) and Gregory I (Gregory the Great, 590-604).

Pope Leo I whose Tome (see above, Chapter VI, p. 191) influenced the Christological definition issued by the Council of Chalcedon is important also for the emphasis which he placed on papal primacy. On the basis of Matthew 16:17-19, he claimed that Peter was the first among the Apostles. Reaffirming the tradition that Peter had been the first bishop of Rome and that all subsequent bishops of Rome were in the apostolic succession from Peter, he insisted that, since he too was in this succession, he was the spiritual heir of Peter and was due the honor and recognition accorded to Peter himself. As Peter's successor, the Lord had granted him not only authority over the whole church and all other ecclesiastics but also authority over secular rulers. Anyone who rejected his authority was a sinner on the road to hell. While such claims were not accepted by everyone, even in the West, and undoubtedly were ignored by the ecclesiastical and civil leaders in Constantinople and the East, Pope Leo I did manage to expand the authority of the Pope in the West. Not least of the reasons for this was the fact that in a very practical way, he was able to be of great service to the citizens of Rome when in 452 he persuaded the Huns to abandon their proposed destruction of the city and when three years later he was able to persuade the Vandals to refrain from slaughtering the people of

Rome.[7] It is not surprising then that with Pope Leo I the papacy began to assume political as well as religious authority.

Papal authority over both the Western church and civil society was greatly expanded by Pope Gregory I (590-604). A man of extraordinary administrative talents, strength of character, and leadership ability, he was made prefect or governor of the city in 573 at the age of thirty-three. However, attracted to the monastic life, he soon left this position, used some of his great wealth to establish a number of monasteries, gave the rest to the poor, and entered the monastery of St. Andrew hoping to lead a life of contemplation. His contemplative life was soon interrupted when in 579 Pope Pelagius II sent him as papal envoy to the court of the Emperor at Constantinople. In 586 he returned to Rome to become Abbot of St. Andrew. Four years later by the popular demand of clergy and people, he was chosen to be the Pope, the first monk to occupy that position.

It was a time of trouble in Italy due to famine, pestilence, and the aggression of the Lombards. There was no strong political leadership, for the Emperor was at Constantinople and was too weak to provide any effective help in this crisis. Though nominally subject to the Emperor, Gregory was in fact the actual ruler of Italy. Among other things, he established civil order, collected taxes, appointed governors of certain areas, raised an army to resist Lombard agggression, and made a peace treaty with the Lombards on his own initiative. He so efficiently managed the papal estates that revenues increased and the papacy became the wealthiest institution of the time. Yet he used this money not only for the building of churches, monasteries, and the support of the clergy but also for the welfare of the poor and good works of all kinds. It can be truly said that Gregory made the papacy and the church the guardian of order and spirituality in a time of trouble.

Like Leo I, Gregory insisted that the Pope was the true successor of the Apostle Peter. This succession guaranteed that the papacy had been established by God to oversee all ecclesiastical and political affairs. When the Patriarch of Constantinople claimed the title of "Ecumenical Patriarch," Gregory protested that he had no right to such a title since, as the successor of Peter, the Pope alone had primacy. While Gregory's

215

protest had little effect in the East, it, along with his strong leadership, contributed to the development of papal authority in the West. Furthermore, he did manage to spread his influence to some areas in the West beyond Italy as, for example, in his sending missionaries to the British Isles.

While Gregory did much to increase the power of the papacy, he was of influence also in other areas such as the liturgy of the church, the ascetic discipline of the monasteries, and the theology of the Catholic Church. With respect to theology, Gregory transmitted to medieval thought a kind of semi-Augustinianism. He certainly thought of himself as an advocate of Augustine's theology but, in the judgment of many scholars, he failed to fully understand the profundity of Augustine's thought and often had different emphases than did Augustine.[9] Yet what he did emphasize appears to have suited his own times and that which followed.

In his views concerning the doctrines of God, the Trinity, and Christology, Gregory, as might be expected, followed the traditional definitions put forth by the great Councils. Concerning the nature of the church, he followed Cyprian and Augustine in affirming that the Catholic Church is the one true church outside of which salvation is impossible. In his doctrine of man, Gregory modified Augustine's view with a kind of semi-Pelagianism. Adam's fall had affected all of his descendents but freedom of will, although weakened, has not been entirely destroyed. This weakened condition of man, because of original sin, makes it impossible for him to take even the first step toward the doing of good unless one is rescued from sin by the benefits of the work of Christ which are received in baptism. That is, one must receive the prevenient grace of God. Having received it, believers may cooperate with it and earn merit for themselves. While Augustine had insisted that in rewarding the merits of believers, God is rewarding his own merits (granted to believers in God's grace), Gregory held that God rewards the believers' merits as well. Like Augustine, Gregory spoke of predestination, claiming that the number of the elect is fixed. Yet he seemed to have understood predestination as simply divine foreknowledge. Unlike Augustine, he claimed that God's grace is not irresistible. How the number of the elect could be fixed and yet God's grace be resistible, Gregory failed to explain.

Baptism, Gregory believed, infuses into the believer the prevenient grace of God. Without any merit on his part, the believer is granted forgiveness for pre-baptismal sins, both original and actual, and infused with the power to do good. However, even the baptized believer is not entirely freed from the taint of original sin and will commit actual sins again. Satisfaction must be made for post-baptismal sins, and this may be done by participation in the sacraments of penance and the Lord's Supper or Mass in combination with meritorious works. As in earlier times, penance required the believer to repent of his sins, to confess them to a priest, and to perform the assigned works of satisfaction. The Mass, Gregory claimed, is a repetition of Christ's sacrifice. That is, each time it is offered Christ's redeeming sacrifice is recapitulated so that it is beneficial for both living believers and for those dead believers residing in purgatory. Previous beliefs about purgatory had been rather vague and fluid, but Gregory taught that it was a doctrine essential for faith. Believers who die without the expiation of all sins, even minor ones, must endure the purifying fires of purgatory. However, both Masses and the prayers of the faithful for those in purgatory serve to hasten their exit from purgatory into the blessedness of heaven.

In summary, it may be said that with Gregory the Great there emerged those perspectives, doctrines, and practices in the direction of which the Catholic Church was to grow during the Middle Ages. His support of monasticism, his modifications of Augustine's doctrines of original sin, grace, and predestination, his emphasis on the necessity of meritorious works and of the sacraments of baptism, penance, and the Mass, his insistence that the doctrine of purgatory was essential for faith, and his emphasis on the authority of the Pope in both ecclesiastical and civil matters were emphases which continued in the Western church. In the centuries which followed the popes were not always able to actually exercise this authority. There were occasions when popes and kings were in conflict with the latter appointing ecclesiastical officials in their kingdoms and defying the popes in other matters. Yet the popes did claim that the Pope alone had the authority to appoint persons to ecclesiastical offices and to anoint and crown kings, and in some cases they were actually powerful enough to exercise this authority.

In the discussion above it was noted that Constantine's moving of his capital to Constantinople (330) left a leadership vacuum in the West which was often filled by strong popes and that this move was one of the causal conditions that led to the East-West division of the church. There were other causal conditions, both theological and political, which arose during the centuries between the time of Constantine and the eleventh century when the great schism between the Roman Catholic Church and the Eastern Orthodox Church was officially and formally acknowledged.

There were several theological differences which helped to produce the schism. For one thing the Monophysite Christology had originated and been relatively popular in the East. So there were many Eastern Christians who were dissatisfied with the Christological formula of Chalcedon.[10] They felt that the divinity of Christ should be elevated above his humanity. Indeed, their attention was so focused on the divinity of Christ that they tended to minimize his humanity, and this Christology was at odds with that in the West which had insisted on both the full divinity and full humanity of Christ.

Another theological issue which contributed to the schism was the controversy over the <u>filioque</u> clause which had been inserted into the Nicene-Constantinopolitan Creed in the West. This clause proclaimed that the Holy Spirit proceeded from the Father <u>and</u> the Son. Western theologians, who understood the Holy Spirit as the mutual love which binds the Father and the Son, viewed this clause as appropriate. Eastern theologians, with their emphasis upon the Father as the ultimate source of the Son's being and the Son's subordination to the Father, rejected this clause, claiming that the Holy Spirit proceeds from the Father through the Son. Furthermore, they felt that to interpolate anything into an ancient creed was heretical.

Other issues which contributed to the division between East and West included the East's rejection of such Western practices as fasting on Saturdays, consuming dairy products during Lent, requiring complete celibacy for the clergy, allowing confirmation to be conducted only by holders of episcopal office, and iconoclasm (destruction of sacred images). Even though it was not of long duration, the iconoclastic controversy did result in an increase of tension between East and West. Emperor Leo III (714-774) decreed that the

218

practice of having sacred images in the churches was idolatrous and that the images must be destroyed. There was resistance to this decree in both East and West. Pope Gregory III (731-741), by taking a strong stand against the decree and excommunicating the opponents of pictures, helped to increase the East-West tension.[11]

In addition to the theological differences which alone might not have produced the schism, there were political differences. First, there was a continuing political rivalry between Rome and Constantinople. Secondly, the East differed from the West with respect to church-state relations. While in theory there was supposed to be harmony and mutual cooperation between the spiritual and civil authorities, the Emperor did in fact control the election of the Patriarch who was the head of the Eastern church and could exercise a veto over the decisions of church councils. Ecclesiastical officials in the East were supposed to be concerned solely with the internal matters of the church such as the enrichment of the liturgy and the contemplative life. The church was viewed as a kind of "department" of the state, and unlike the popes in the West the patriarchs did not have absolute authority over even the church. The claims of popes of Rome, such as made by Gregory the Great, were either overtly rejected or simply ignored. Thirdly, the spread of Islam which brought the Eastern church under the continued threat of destruction, and the fact that the West was able to avoid such a threat tended to increase the suspicion and distrust between the Eastern and Western branches of Christendom.

The theological and political differences between East and West finally resulted in Orthodox Patriarch Michael Cerularius (1043-1058) and Pope Leo IX (1049-1054) excommunicating and anathematizing each other. The division of Christendom into a Catholic Church (Roman) and an Eastern Orthodox Church was now fixed. These two churches have remained separated to this day.

The divergent ways of faith which emerged in Eastern and Western Christendom present a bewildering pattern of similarities and differences. Among the similarities are the acceptance of the same scriptures as the major source of Christian teachings, the confession of faith in Jesus Christ as Incarnate Lord and Savior, the use of the Nicene Creed (with its Trinitarian formula) as a summary of the Christian faith, the

219

conviction that the sacraments, especially baptism and the eucharist (Lord's Supper), are essential parts of the Christian liturgy or ordinance, and the affirmation that human beings survive physical death.

In spite of this unanimity in essentials, there are significant differences between the Christian East and West, differences which have kept them rather isolated from each other until relatively recent times. Some of the most important of these differences are the following. First, while in the West the word "orthodox" has been understood as designating proper or correct doctrines or dogmas, in the East it has been understood as designating the praising or glorifying of God in the right spirit. Thus the East has not developed massive doctrinal systems officially sponsored by the Orthodox Churches. To be sure, leading teachers and theologians have given attention to such issues as the nature of God, the nature of the church, the nature of man, of sin and salvation, but their teachings have not been accorded the authority of dogma. Only that which has direct relevance for divine worship has received doctrinal definition.

Secondly, the Eastern view of the church differs from that in the West, a difference which contains several aspects. For one thing, in the West, "catholic" means universal in a geographical sense, and the Catholic Church is regarded as a universal body obeying one head and adhering to the same ritual. In the East, however, "catholic" is understood in the sense of "integrity," "wholeness," and "harmony" of diverse parts, a view which rejects exclusivism and sectarianism. The church is viewed as a divine mystery which stands at the center of history, and the purpose of which is the full deification of humanity (see the discussion of the Cappadocian Fathers in Chapter VI). At the center of the church is the God-man, Jesus Christ, and the church communicates His divine life to its members through the sacraments, especially the eucharist. This sacrament is regarded primarily as a celebration of God's incarnation in Christ rather than as a sacrifice as in the West. The bread and wine become the body and blood of Christ, not as in the Catholic view by transubstantiation, but rather by a transformation due to the operation of the Holy Spirit. Eastern Orthodox Christians have been reluctant to define either the character or exact moment of this change. It is a mystery, a kind of continuation of the Incarnation, the purpose of which is the eventual deification of humanity.

220

Furthermore, Eastern Christians regard the entire Christian community or church as possessing authority. Authority is located neither in an ecclesiastical figure (a pope) nor in the Bible but in the whole church. The infallibility of the Pope in Rome is denied and instead the whole church is regarded as infallible. This means that as long as Christians remain within the Eucharistic Fellowship they will be able to distinguish truth from error. Thus there is no supreme ruler over Eastern Orthodox churches, but each of the several national churches (Russian, Greek, Romanian, Bulgarian, etc.) is self-ruled. At times a kind of informal primacy has been exercised by the patriarchs of Constantinople or of Moscow, but they have had no more power over the Eastern churches than that of persuasion and influence.

Thirdly, the pattern of monasticism in the East has been different from that in the West. Largely due to the influence of leaders like Benedict of Nursia (discussed above), Western monasticism has tended to be more active, having a social orientation and a formative influence on Western culture. In the East, monasticism has been more individualist, more contemplative, and more other worldly. A major reason for this is that mysticism (discussed below) has been much more dominant in Eastern Christendom than in the West. The sense of the presence of God in the soul and life of the individual (the deification of man) is the sole goal of the contemplative Christian life.

In conclusion, Eastern Christians have refrained from identifying Orthodoxy with any one teacher, system of theology, or institution as has so often been the case in Catholicism and Protestantism. Orthodox theology is rooted in eucharistic worship (which is highly developed in both liturgy and devotional art), and therefore is open and experimental. Undoubtedly, this is a major reason why the several Eastern Orthodox churches found it possible to join the World Council of Churches which was established by most of the Protestant denominations soon after World War II. Also after the conclusion of the Catholic Vatican Council II in 1965, the mutual excommunications that were pronounced in 1054 were revoked simultaneously in Rome and Constantinople. Since 1965 there have been several meetings between Orthodox and Catholic leaders for discussions concerning the possibility of achieving closer relations. It now seems that reunion sometime in the distant future is not an impossibility.[12]

It was noted above that the ecclesiastical authorities in the Eastern Orthodox Church were supposed to give attention primarily to matters of the liturgy and the contemplative life. Such emphasis provided a basis for the emergence of mysticism in the Eastern church. Also it was noted above that the monastic orders, wherever located, contained a discipline which included the contemplative or "spiritual" discipline as well as the intellectual and labor disciplines. So from the monastic orders even in the West there emerged some theologians who, like Bonventura and Hugo of St. Victor, sought to combine faith, reason, and mystical vision. Others tended to place emphasis on reason and knowledge in the present practice of the Christian life, reserving the mystical vision to the next life, and still others made primary the acquiring of the mystical vision in this life. For example, both Thomas Aquinas and Meister Eckhart were members of the Dominican Order. Yet Aquinas' theology was not a theology of mysticism in the technical sense of that term (to be defined below), nor was he a mystic in his interpretation of the present life. Meister Eckhart, however, was a mystic of the most thoroughgoing kind.[13]

Although it was never a dominant movement in the history of the church, mysticism of some sort or another has existed in most periods of Christianity and in different parts of Christendom. Apparently it was most widespread in the Western church during the late medieval period. Thus a consideration of this period should give some attention to this phenomenon. In the following discussion an attempt will be made to define "mysticism," to indicate its characteristic features, and to illustrate these features in the perspectives of a few Christian mystics.

The sense in which the word "mysticism" is being used here is not that of simply designating spiritual experiences in general. Rather it is being used in a more specific and technical sense. In this sense "mysticism" designates the view that awareness of spiritual truths and communion with and a final absorption into the ultimate transcendent reality (whether understood as a personal God or as an impersonal One) may be achieved not through human reason but through an intuition acquired by fixed meditation. So, as defined here, the word "mysticism" designates a special type of religious experience.

In his classic study of religious experiences,

William James (1842-1910), doctor, psychologist, philosopher, and Harvard professor, claimed that the mystical experience is marked by four characteristics.[14] The first of these is "ineffability." That is, the subject of the mystical experience "immediately says that it defies expression, that no adequate report of its contents can be given in words."[15] Since it is more like states of feeling that states of intellect, it cannot be imparted to others. It must be directly experienced. The second characteristic is that the mystical experience contains a "noetic quality." Even though similar to states of feeling, mystical states, according to James, "seem to those who experience them to be also states of knowledge."[16] They are supposed to bring knowledge of truths which cannot be gained by means of the intellectual faculty. The third characteristic is "transiency." That is, the mystical state of consciousness cannot be sustained over long periods of time. The fourth characteristic is "passivity." Even though the mystic may engage in rigorous meditative discipline in the attempt to achieve the mystical experience, when he is having it he does not feel that the experience is the result of his own volition but that he has been "grasped and held by a superior power."[17]

In the discussion which follows that concerning the four characteristics, James quotes lengthy passages from the writings of several great mystics, Christian and non-Christian. Not only do these quotations illustrate the four characteristics, but also, since they are from mystics of different religions, they indicate that mysticism as defined is not limited to any particular religion nor to any particular sect within a religion. For the most part the great Christian mystics were traditional as far as doctrine was concerned. Yet in their practices they tended to exemplify the four characteristics.

As already indicated, Christian mysticism was relatively widespread in the late medieval period. Of great influence on the mystics of this period were the writings of an earlier sixth century Christian mystic who published his works under the pseudonym of Dionysius The Areopagite.[18] Influenced by Neo-Platonism, Pseudo-Dionysius conceived of God as One in the absolute sense and of all reality as structured hierarchically. Everything comes from God and leads to him but in different degree according to location in the hierarchical orders. Hierarchical orders are present in both the celestial and terrestrial realms with the most important in the latter being the ecclesiastical hierarchy. Christ, as the Head of both celestial and ecclesiastical hierarchies, is the source of being and illumination of the entire hierarchical orders. The purpose of these orders is that the soul might return to God by means of the higher orders. According to Justo L. Gonzalez:

> It is at this point that Pseudo-Dionysius introduces the doctrine of the three ways, which would be very influential in later mysticism. These three ways or three mystical stages are the purgative or cathartic, in which the soul is rid of its impurity; the illuminative where the soul receives the divine light; and the unitive, in which the soul is united with God in an ecstatic vision—a vision that, because of the absolute transcendence of God, is not 'comprehensive,' but rather 'intuitive.' While following these three ways, the soul is aided by the various hierarchies. This they do through the sacraments, although the notion of sacrament found here is very extensive, and includes not only such things as baptism, the eucharist and ordination, but actually the entire process by which all hierarchies reflect the One from whom they come.[19]

Whatever differences in particulars there may have been among the later medieval mystics, they all show the influence of Pseudo-Dionysius' three ways. This is nowhere more evident than it is in the famous devotional classic, The Imitation of Christ, traditionally attributed to Thomas à Kempis (1380-1471 A.D.), a member of the Brethren of the Common Life. The Brethren not only were concerned to reform the church of its "worldly attachments" but also they represented a mystical tradition. They sought to follow the three ways. So in The Imitation of Christ there are numerous passages which urge the reader to follow step by step the three ways. An example of each is quoted below:

1. Purgation or purification

Vanity of vanities, and all is vanity, except to love God, and to serve Him only. This is the highest wisdom, by contempt of the world to press forward

224

towards heavenly kingdoms.

Vanity therefore it is, to seek after
perishing riches, and to trust in them.
Vanity also it is to hunt after honours,
and to climb to high degree. Vanity it
is to follow the desires of the flesh,
and to long after that for which thou
must afterwards suffer grievous punishment. Vanity it is, to wish to live long,
and to be careless to live well. Vanity
it is to mind only this present life,
and not to foresee those things which are
to come. Vanity it is to set thy love
on that which speedily passeth away, and
not to hasten thither where everlasting
joy abideth. . .

Endeavor therefore to withdraw thy heart
from the love of visible things, and to
turn thyself to things invisible. For
they that follow their own sensuality,
defile their conscience, and lose the
grace of God.

Behold! in the Cross all doth consist,
and in our dying thereon all lieth; for
there is no other way unto life, and unto
true inward peace, but the way of the holy
Cross, and of daily mortification. Walk
where thou wilt, seek whatsoever thou wilt,
thou shalt not find a higher way above,
nor a safer way below, than the way of the
holy Cross.[20]

2. Illumination

O good Jesus, enlighten Thou me with the
clear shining of an inward light, and remove away all darkness from the habitation
of my heart. Repress Thou my many wandering thoughts, and break in pieces those
temptations which violently assault me. . .

Send out Thy light and Thy truth, that they
may shine upon the earth; for I am earth
without form and void, until Thou enlighten
me. Pour forth Thy grace from above, shower
upon my heart the dew of Heaven, supply
fresh streams of devotion to water the face

225

of the earth, that it may bring forth
fruit good and excellent. Lift Thou up
my mind which is pressed down by a load
of sins, and draw up my whole desire to
things heavenly; that having tasted the
sweetness of supernal happiness, it may
be irksome to me to think of earthly
things.[21]

3. Unification or absorption into God
    (the goal which is sought in pursuing
    the first two steps)

This I beg, this I long for, that I may
be wholly united unto Thee, and may withdraw my heart from all created things,
and by means of Sacred Communion, and the
frequent celebrating thereof, may learn
more and more to relish things heavenly
and eternal. Ah, Lord God, when shall
I be wholly made one with Thee, and lost
in Thee, and become altogether forgetful
of myself? Thou in me, and I in Thee;
so also grant that we may both continue
together in one.[22]

Since achieving the mystic or ecstatic vision (the
beatific vision) in this life was not a practical possibility for the majority of Christians, the dominant
perspective in the late medieval church was that this
was the goal which would be reached in the next life.
Life in the church which mediated God's grace was
regarded as a preparation for the beatific vision of
the next life. Through the sacraments further divine
grace was infused into the souls of believers, and
this grace was the source of meritorious works. The
goal of good works was righteousness of life on earth
and the beatific vision in heaven. At death those who
had made full use of the grace offered in the church
went immediately into heaven. Those who had imperfectly availed themselves of the means of grace (the
large majority of Christians) had to undergo a longer
or shorter period in purgatory. With this position
the great medieval thinker, Thomas Aquinas (1225-1274),
was in agreement. One of the great thinkers of all
time, Aquinas developed a profound theology which has
been of great influence on Catholic thought from his
day to ours.

Of the noble family of Aquino in central Italy,

Thomas received a good education in the Benedictine school at Monte Cassino. Despite the bitter opposition of family and friends, he joined the newly founded Dominican Order. His superiors in the Order soon recognized his outstanding intellectual ability and sent him to study with Albertus Magnus, the foremost Dominican scholar of the time. It was Albert who introduced Thomas to the thought of the ancient Greek philosopher, Aristotle, whose writings and the commentaries on these writings by some Moslem philosophers of Spain had recently been translated into Latin. After finishing his studies with Albert, Thomas became a teacher, lecturing at such places as Paris, Naples and Rome. In a lifetime of less than fifty years he wrote some sixty books. Among these were both philosophical and theological works, including commentaries on Aristotle, on Scripture, and on previous thinkers. Undoubtedly the two most influential of his works were the Summa Contra Gentiles and the Summa Theologiae.

By the time of Thomas the word "Summa" had come to designate a comprehensive treatise which gave an orderly presentation of a whole field of learning. In his summae Thomas sought to use the whole range of the learning of his day in an orderly presentation and defense of Christian doctrines. Both are among the great classics of Christian literature. While some traces of mysticism may be found in them, the major emphasis is on a synthesis of reason and revelation, natural and revealed theology. Aquinas' life and writings have been characterized appropriately in the following way: "Personally he was a simple, deeply religious, prayerful man. Intellectually his work was marked by a clarity, a logical consistency, and a breadth of presentation that places him among the few great teachers of the church."[23]

In order to understand the basic ingredients of Aquinas' theological synthesis, it is necessary to be aware of the general cultural and intellectual environment of his time. In a certain sense, the culture of Western Europe in late medieval times was a Christian culture. That is, the views concerning the realms of nature, society, government, business, education, marriage and the family, the arts, etc., were permeated with Christian perspectives, and these views were incorporated into a total Christian world-view. While in principle possible, in practice it was almost impossible for anyone to think outside the context of a Christian world-view. Due to the influence of

227

Augustine (see Chapter VI) and others, a modified form of Platonism and Neo-Platonism informed the ontology (theory of being as such) and the epistemology (theory of knowledge) of this world-view.

In the ontology of this world-view all that there is is God and what he has created. The beings and objects of the created order are the traces, signs, or replicas of the divine ideas or forms, of God's plan and structure for the created order. In the epistemology of this world view God is the source and guarantee of human knowledge. Human beings can have no genuine knowledge whatsoever without beginning with God. True knowledge does not come from experience and cognition of the sensible world, for that attains only reflections. True knowledge comes only from a direct reception of light coming from the spiritual world. Truth is divine illumination. Such an epistemology was congenial to the mystics and the Franciscans for whom the knowledge of God had its source only in inspired Scriptures and the direct encounter with God in the individual soul. It is not dependent on a knowledge of creatures derived from the senses. Indeed, it is only as one has knowledge of God that he can understand the true symbolic values of creatures in relation to God.

The reappearance of Aristotle's philosophy presented a challenge to the fundamental aspects of the Augustinian world-view. For Aristotle the world was simply a thing of movement and causes imitating the eternal circular motion of the prime mover, the unmoved mover. Given certain causal conditions, creatures are continually actualizing the potentiality appropriate to them. They exist in their own right, not simply as symbols of something else, and may be investigated in terms of their own natures. While he held that existing creatures or objects are combinations of form and matter (matter providing potentiality), Aristotle denied that the forms are real, apart from existing creatures. Instead, the forms have objective reality only in actually existing creatures or objects. Conceptual knowledge of the forms, then, can be gained only through a knowledge of actual creatures, and this requires sense experience. For Aristotle, knowledge begins with sense experience, for it provides the data upon which reason operates. Reason extracts intelligible elements from the data, and it classifies and structures the data such that there is knowledge of the world and of the nature of things.

228

As might be expected, Augustinians tended to view Aristotle as "a master of errors,"[24] and to reject his philosophy as a threat to the Christian faith. Others fully accepted his philosophy but kept their philosophy and their theology separated into different realms. A part of Thomas Aquinas' genius was that he, like his teacher Albert, recognized that Aristotelianism had come to stay and must be reckoned with by the Christian theologian. If Christianity was to retain the confidence of the intelligent and educated classes, it simply could not ignore Aristotelian philosophy nor seek to banish it. Instead it should be used as far as possible in the quest of faith seeking for understanding. So Thomas did not view Aristotelian philosophy as a threat to the Christian faith. While for him revelation and faith rather than philosophy are primary, the role of Aristotelian philosophy was that of providing "faith with the means of constructing a rational bridge to man's normal circle of knowledge."[25]

Thomas, of course, was as convinced as the Augustinians that all things must be referred to God. As Creator as well as Redeemer, God is the source of beings and truth. Unlike the Augustinians who felt that no worthwhile knowledge can be obtained from creatures, from the natural order, Thomas felt that in his wisdom God had provided the human intellect with the ability of acquiring some knowledge of the nature of things. True, only God's knowledge is perfect since, as the source of everything, he sees all things in himself. God does not have to reason from things better known to things which are less well known, as do human beings, with all the possibility of errors which this process entails. Human knowledge is far from perfect, but if faith is to become understanding, there should be a quest for knowledge in both the natural and the supernatural realms. In this quest, both need to be considered not only in terms of their source but also in terms of their defined natures.

The knowledge of such supernatural manifestations of truth as the Trinity, incarnation, infused grace, divine judgment, and immortal life requires revelation and faith, and the role of human reason is simply that of indicating their probability and of developing a rationale for them. With respect to the natural order, it is the knowledge of the laws and nature of things which enter into the theological synthesis. Reason is primary and Aristotle provides the "means of producing a human copy of God's science."[26] Sense experience

229

provides the data from which reason derives intelligible elements. With some modifications the Aristotelian categories of cause, essence, substance, potency, movement, and habit are used. It is not that for Thomas there are two kinds of truth, one natural and the other supernatural. Since God is the source of all, there is only one kind of truth even though it has these two different manifestations. Aquinas himself expressed it in the following way:

> The gifts of grace are added to nature in such a way that they do not blot it out but rather perfect it . . . and even though the human intellect is incapable of discovering what is revealed to it by faith, nevertheless it is impossible that what is divinely given us by faith should be contrary to that which has been given us by nature. This latter view must be false, for otherwise, since both are given us by God, God Himself would be the author of falsity, which is impossible.[27]

So, while the manifestations of God by means of the revelation transmitted through Scripture and church transcend the natural order and cannot be discovered and known by the reasoning of the human intellect, they do not contradict that which can be discovered and known by reason. Indeed, they fulfill and perfect that which can be known of God by means of reasoning about the natural order. As Aquinas says: "Natural reason ascends to a knowledge of God through creatures, and, conversely, the knowledge of faith descends from God to us by a divine revelation . . . [but] the way of ascent and descent is still the same."[28] That is, they are the same in terms of their source although the directions, methods, and adequacy of knowing differ.

In the diagram on the following page an attempt is made to indicate Aquinas' understanding of the relation between the natural and the supernatural and the ways of knowing these manifestations of God.

SUPERNATURAL			
Revelation and faith provide knowledge of supernatural truths neces- sary for sal- vation	Trinity Christ Church	sacraments God's Judgment beatitude	<u>Divine law</u> faith hope charity

----

NATURAL			
Sense percep- tion and intellection provide nat- ural knowledge which points to the exist- ence of God and his providence	Unmoved mover First cause Necessary being Designer Perfect	eternal unchanging simple intelligent love	<u>Natural law</u> wisdom courage justice temperance

For Thomas the natural level (that which is below
the broken line) is what faith affirms and reason can
investigate or demonstrate.[29] The supernatural level
(that which is above the broken line) is what faith
affirms and reason cannot investigate nor demonstrate.[30]
This does not mean that on this level reason has no
role to play. While it cannot prove the articles of
faith, reason is needed in order to communicate them
intelligibly, to defend them from attack by unbeliev-
ers, to show that they are not impossible, and to draw
valid conclusions from them.[31]

The two levels are not contradictory nor mutually
exclusive (this is the significance of the broken line
between them). While the upper level transcends the
lower and therefore is not logically entailed in the
lower, the lower is logically entailed in the upper.
One who knows only that which is in the lower level
can never gain a knowledge of that which is in the
upper level, but one who accepts the upper believes all
that is contained in the lower. The lower is that which
in principle reason can learn from nature through sense.
Even the intelligent unbeliever who applies his reasoning capacity to the data received by his senses can
obtain <u>some</u> knowledge about God and values. So Thomas

presents five demonstrations for the existence of God, each one of which begins with a certain feature of the sensible world which can be perceived by anyone, and from that proceeds by a valid argument to a conclusion such as "and this everyone understands to be God."[32] The motion and efficient causes which are experienced in the sensible world, if they are to exist at all, require a first unmoved mover and a first uncaused cause. The contingent things of the sensible world which can be thought of as not existing require for their existence a necessary being or no thing would exist now. The fact that degrees of goodness, beauty, and truth can be predicated of things in the sensible world requires a maximum goodness, beauty, and truth or no such predication of degrees could be made. The fact that in the sensible world objects without intelligence nevertheless demonstrate purpose or order requires a purposer or designer. In contrast to Augustine, Thomas does not seek to demonstrate the existence of God on the basis of analyzing the concept of perfection. Rather he begins with features of the sensible world which everyone experiences and on this basis seeks to demonstrate the existence of God. In all five of the arguments there are conclusions from characteristics of this world to something which makes this world possible. God's existence is proved from his effects.

While for Aquinas knowledge of God's essence, of God as he is in himself, is impossible, the five arguments do provide knowledge of God's existence and to some extent of his qualities. If it can be said that God is the unmoved mover, the first uncaused cause, the absolutely necessary being, the absolutely perfect being, and the intelligent designer, then it follows that it can be said that essence and existence, thought and will, are one in him--that he is pure actuality. From this it follows that God is not a composite being but simple in the sense of being one, and that he is eternal, unchanging, intelligent and perfect. His thought and will are set on perfection which entails that they are set on goodness and love-- the seeking of good for all. Reason, then, can show that the primary nature of God expresses itself in love for all being. Yet for Aquinas, this enterprise of reason is not just a matter of philosophical or intellectual interest. Instead it has the important function of making understandable the relevance of faith to the world of human experience.

232

Although it is of importance in the total theological enterprise, for Thomas natural reason's ascent to a knowledge of God through creatures is inadequate for two major reasons. First, it cannot provide the knowledge necessary for salvation. Even in the state of pure nature, man's capacity for knowledge is proportionate to his nature, and so even in this state he could never know the supernatural truths contained in the articles of faith. The knowledge of faith comes by means of divine revelation. As Thomas declared in the Summa Theologiae:

> It was necessary for man's salvation that there should be a doctrine founded on revelation, as well as the philosophical sciences discovered by human reason. It was necessary, in the first place, because man is ordained to God as his end, who surpasses the comprehension of reason . . . Men must have some foreknowledge of the end to which they ought to direct their intentions and actions. It was therefore necessary that some things which transcend human reason be made known through divine revelation.[33]

Secondly, revelation was necessary even with respect to those things which in principle could be discovered by human reason because only a few have the capacity to understand the demonstrations and to avoid errors. According to Thomas:

> It was necessary also that man should be instructed by divine revelation even in such things concerning God as human reason could discover. For such truth about God as could be discovered by reason would be known only by the few, and that after a long time, and mixed with many errors. Now the whole salvation of man, which lies in God, depends on the knowledge of this truth. It was therefore necessary that men should be instructed in divine things through divine revelation, in order that their salvation might come to pass more fittingly and certainly. . . Faith presupposes natural knowledge as grace presupposes nature, and as perfection presupposes what can be perfected. There is no reason, however, why what is

233

in itself demonstrable and knowable
should not be accepted in faith by one
who cannot understand the demonstration
of it.[34]

While in Aquinas' thought revelation and faith hold
the commanding position, believers who can do so should
seek to understand the demonstrations possible for natural reason in order to relate faith to all realms of
human experience and to strengthen faith itself by
understanding. Faith is the giving of intellectual assent to the propositions of revelation. As Aquinas
expressed it: "to believe is an act of the intellect
as moved by the will to give its assent."[35] The giving
of assent by the intellect can be strengthened by
enlarged understanding. So Aquinas said:

> When a man has a ready will to believe,
> he rejoices in the truth which he believes,
> thinks about it, and turns it over in his
> mind to see whether he can find a reason
> for it. A human reason which thus follows
> the will to believe does not exclude merit.
> Rather it is a sign of greater merit.[36]

An important basis not only for Aquinas' epistemology but also for his views of salvation was his doctrine of creation. Like everything else, man was created by God. But, unlike the other creatures, Adam
(man) was created in both the image and the likeness
of God.[37] The image of God, according to Aquinas,
was Adam's intellectual and rational capacity. The
likeness was an added gift, the supernatural endowment
of grace.[38] Before the Fall, Adam was in submission to
God and possessed the divine virtues. The perfection
of that state was limited only by virtue of the fact
that it did not extend to the vision of the divine
essence nor to the possession of final beatitude. Presumably, however, this could have been achieved by
Adam through his doing of supernatural good had he not
lost this power in the Fall.

In the Fall of Adam man lost the likeness of God
but retained the image of God, even though in a weakened form. It was precisely because fallen man retained the image of God that the man apart from faith
in principle could know some divine truth and do some
good including that of the natural law. For Aquinas
the ultimate basis of law is the very mind of God
himself.[39] The pattern which exists in the mind of

God for the creation and governance of the world he called the "eternal law." This pattern projected into the created world he called the "natural law." The natural law, then, is not different in kind from the eternal law which exists in the rational nature of God. It is eternal law in a different mode, namely that of being applied to created beings. With respect to rational creatures, the natural law is the demand for equity in human relations, and it contains the Aristotelian virtues of wisdom, courage, justice, and temperance. Natural law is objective in the sense that it is constitutive of the created order. Men may reject it but if they do so, they must suffer the consequences. On the other hand, men may consciously and voluntarily acquire the virtues of the natural law. Human or positive law should be the translation of natural law into the specific decrees of governments. But, since these are formulated by fallible human beings, mistakes appear in statutory, positive laws. They may be corrected bit by bit as men learn more of what the natural law requires.

In order to aid men in recognizing and interpreting natural law and also to provide believers with guidance in the doing of supernatural good, God, according to Aquinas, revealed the divine law. Unlike the natural law, which is discernible to reason, the divine law can be known only through revelation. Divine law is positive law revealed in Scripture (includes such things as the Decalogue, beatitudes, golden rule, faith and love, etc.). While the divine law has to do with supernatural virtues and thus transcends the natural law, the latter is logically implied by the divine law. In the following diagram an attempt is made to depict Aquinas' understanding of law in its various modes.

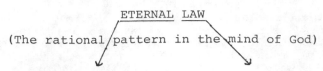

ETERNAL LAW

(The rational pattern in the mind of God)

The natural law ←——————————→ The Divine law

(Eternal law projected into
the created order, applied
to creatures. It contains
the acquired virtues of
wisdom, courage, justice,
temperance.)

Human or positive law

(i.e., the laws of states)

(Revealed in Scripture
and logically entails
the natural law. But
it transcends the nat-
ural law in that it
contains the infused
supernatural virtues
of faith, hope, and
love which are required
for ultimate beatitude.)

According to Aquinas, it is the grace of God which
empowers the believer to practice supernatural virtues.
Grace is a supernatural thing, a force from God, which,
like a blood transfusion in current medical practice,
is infused into the souls of believers. Fallen man
needs this for two reasons, namely in order to be
healed and in order to receive the power to practice
the supernatural virtues required for reaching ultimate beatitude.

As had some of the earlier church fathers, Aquinas
distinguished two modes of God's grace, prevenient and
cooperating.[40] This does not mean that Aquinas believed that there are two kinds of grace. There is only
the one grace of God but it is in two modes and has two
different effects. This grace God has made available
through Jesus Christ. By his sacrificial death, Jesus
Christ (both divine and human) made God's forgiveness
of sins available to human beings. But, because of
his transcendent dignity, his death not only constituted
a superabundant satisfaction for human sins but also
conferred a superabundant grace on his body, the church.
Grace in its prevenient mode turns one to faith and
to the church. In baptism the believer's sins are forgiven. In this and the other sacraments further grace
(cooperating or sanctifying grace) is infused into
the souls of believers. Grace is the source of supernatural good works, and the goal of such good works
in both righteousness of life on earth and eternal life
in heaven. This point was stated clearly by Aquinas
when he said:

236

Actions which lead to an end must be commensurate with the end. But no action
transcends the limits of the principle
by which a thing acts. Thus we see that
no natural thing can produce, by its own
action, an effect which is greater than
its own active power, but only an effect
commensurate with this power. Now eternal
life is an end which exceeds what is commensurate with human nature. . . It follows
that a man cannot, by his natural powers,
produce meritorious works commensurate
with eternal life. A higher power is
needed for this, namely, the power of
grace. Hence a man cannot merit eternal
life without grace, . . . If one is to fulfill the commandments of the law in the
adequate way which is meritorious, grace
is indispensable.[41]

The higher power of grace is to be found in the
church. Not only was the superabundant grace of Christ
granted to the church but also since some of the saints
and martyrs earned more merit than they needed for
eternal life, this merit (the power of grace) is contained in the church and may be transferred to others
by means of the sacraments. By the time of Aquinas
seven sacred actions had come to be regarded as sacraments, namely baptism, confirmation, eucharist or
Lord's Supper, penance, ordination, marriage, and extreme unction. Aquinas held that they were efficacious
ex opere operato in the sense that the effect arises
from the actual performance of the sacramental act in
which there is proper form and matter. All of them convey grace from Christ to the members of his mystical
body, the church. The eucharist (Mass or Lord's Supper)
is the greatest of all the sacraments, for it is the
goal toward which the others are directed. The doctrine
of transubstantiation, which Aquinas defended, affirms
that the essences of the bread and wine are changed
into the essences of Christ's body and blood, even
though the accidental properties of the bread and wine
are retained.[42] Thus the eucharist is both a sacrifice
and a communion, and it is appropriate, according to
Aquinas, to call the celebration of this sacrament the
sacrifice of Christ. It represents the passion of
Christ, and it enables the believer to share in the
benefits of His sacrifice. So each time the mass is
celebrated, the bread laid on the altar and the words
of institution spoken by the priest, the bread becomes

the body of Christ which is held up as an offering on
behalf of the people. But also with the blessing of
God, that which has been offered on their behalf is now
received with the benefits which the power of God has
instilled into it. Believers guilty of mortal sins
must first receive absolution in the sacrament of
penance before they can receive the benefits of the
eucharist. Indeed, Aquinas affirmed, it is through
penance, and for one near death, extreme unction,
that the believer is made ready worthily to receive
the body of Christ.[43]

At their deaths believers who have made full use
of the grace offered in the church go at once to
heaven. The wicked go to hell which is endless and
from which there is no release. Those believers who
imperfectly have accepted the grace available in the
church must spend a longer or shorter period of purification in purgatory.[44]

Aquinas, like others in his time, approved the
granting of indulgences. This practice had come into
existence because of the sacrament of penance and was
the remission of a part or the whole of the temporal
penalty (work of satisfaction) assigned by the confessor to the penitent. On the basis of his views of
the unity of the church, the church's possession of
superabundant merit, and the power of the keys granted
to the Pope and by him delegated to the lesser clergy,
Aquinas defended the use of indulgences.[45] Apparently
he was reticent about the applicability of indulgences
to punishment in purgatory. As applied to earthly
penance, a duly authorized indulgence provided mandatory relief, since the church had full jurisdiction
over its living members. But as applied to the purga-
torial punishment of departed believers, an authorized
indulgence could not provide mandatory relief. It
could serve only as the basis of prayer that the
punishment of the departed souls should be lightened
or remitted. The excesses of a later time (to be
discussed in Part IV, Chapter VIII) in which it was
claimed that indulgences authorized by the Pope could
be purchased, and that they did provide mandatory relief for the departed in purgatory, would have found
no favor with Aquinas.

In light of the descriptions above, it is obvious
that for Aquinas the church is essential for man's
salvation, for his eternal life in heaven. The Scripture, of course, is important since it is the source of

238

God's revelation. But due to the heresies, the Scripture requires authoritative interpretation and needs to be supplemented by final definitions of faith. So the church requires a final authority, the Pope. Since he is in the apostolic succession from the Apostle Peter, the Pope is the head of the church and the source of the authoritative definitions of the faith. Thus subjection to him is necessary for salvation. While papal infallibility did not become a formal and official dogma until 1870, it seems to be implicit in some of Aquinas' statements.[46]

Aquinas' great syntheses of Aristotelian philosophy and Christian theology was not very popular during his lifetime and shortly thereafter. Indeed, it was comdemned by "conservatives" as heretical. However, its apologetic value became more and more recognized and its popularity increased until in 1323 Aquinas was canonized by Pope John XXII. Ever since then, Aquinas' thought generally has been regarded by Catholics not as a threat but as the strongest defense for the Catholic faith.

It was the Council of Trent (1545-1563)[47] which exalted much of the late medieval Catholic theology influenced by Aquinas to the position of ecclesiastical dogma such that it became fixed in the outlook of the Catholic Church. While a major purpose of this Council was to assert the Catholic answer to the Protestant Reformation, it would be too simple merely to interpret it as an answer to the Reformation. It did exclude the Protestant position, but also it rejected some positions which had been permitted in medieval Catholicism. In its legislation it rejected some abuses such as simony, inheritance of ecclesiastical offices, and the sale of indulgences. So it was an answer also to the desire for an inner moral and spiritual renewal of the Catholic Church. Since this is the case and since it reflected many of Aquinas' views, it is appropriate to consider the Council of Trent as the conclusion of our discussion of the medieval period, even though it was held after the Reformation period had begun.

As indicated above, Aquinas affirmed that Scripture requires authoritative interpretation. So also in the Canons and Decrees of the Council of Trent it was declared that the Vulgate edition of Scripture (includes the Apocrypha) is authentic and that it is the prerogative of "holy mother Church . . . to judge of the true sense and interpretation of the Holy

Scripture."[48] Saving truth and moral discipline, it was held, are contained not only in Scripture but also in the "unwritten traditions" of the church. As the Council Fathers said:

> [The Synod] following the examples of the orthodox Fathers, receives and venerates with an equal affection of piety and reverence, all the books of the Old and of the New Testament--seeing that one God is the author of both--as also the said traditions, as well as those appertaining to faith as to morals, as having been dictated, either by Christ's own word of mouth, or by the Holy Ghost, and preserved in the Catholic Church by a continuous succession.[49]

Apparently the words "continuous succession" refer to the Pope's succession from Peter which confers on him the final authority in the interpretation of Scripture and the "unwritten traditions." Both tradition (ancient creeds, etc.) and Scripture are viewed as important sources of revelation and doctrine. While this position is a continuation and formal confirmation of an earlier view, it is, in part, a reaction against the Protestant position of sola Scriptura (the sole authority of Scripture).

In its views of human nature and sin the Council of Trent echoed positions held by Aquinas. In the Fall, Adam "lost the holiness and justice wherein he had been constituted" and in his "original sin" injured both himself and his posterity, for original sin "was transfused into all by propagation."[50] While all of Adam's posterity have inherited Adam's original sin so that they cannot be justified either by the force of nature nor by the letter of the law, they are not so totally depraved as to have lost all freedom of will. Unlike Augustine for whom sin was a state or condition of being in which the will was infected with the pretension of self such that after the Fall there was no freedom not to sin, the Council Fathers themselves said: "Free-will, attenuated as it was in its powers, and bent down [after the Fall], was by no means extinguished in them."[51] This view seems to reflect the perspective of Aquinas that man was created in the likeness and image of God. In the Fall he lost the likeness but retained the image.

240

Also in its view of justification (salvation) the Council seems to have echoed Aquinas' position. There was an emphasis upon the grace of God as a power infused into the soul, upon the necessity of both prevenient and cooperating (sanctifying) grace, and upon the necessity of completing faith by good works so as to be justified by God (i.e., merit eternal life). The Council Fathers expressed these points rather clearly when they said:

> The beginning of the said Justification is
> to be derived from the prevenient grace
> of God, through Jesus Christ, that is
> to say, from his vocation, whereby, without
> any merits existing on their parts, they
> are called; that so they, who by sins
> were alienated from God, may be disposed
> through his quickening and assisting
> grace, to convert themselves to their own
> justification, by freely assenting to and
> co-operating with that said grace; in
> such sort that, while God touches the
> heart of man by the illumination of the
> Holy Ghost, neither is man himself utterly
> inactive while he receives that inspiration,
> forasmuch as he is also able to reject it;
> yet he is not able, by his own free will,
> without the grace of God, to move himself
> unto justice in his sight. . . Justifica-
> tion . . . is not remission of sins
> merely, but also the sanctification and
> renewal of the inward man, through the
> voluntary reception of the grace, and of
> the gifts, whereby man of unjust becomes
> just, and of an enemy a friend, that so
> he may be 'an heir according to hope of
> life everlasting' . . . Man, through
> Jesus Christ, in whom he is ingrafted,
> receives, in the said justification, to-
> gether with the remissions of sins, all
> these [gifts] infused at once, faith,
> hope and charity. . . [Believers] through
> the observance of the commandments of
> God and of the Church, faith co-operating
> with good works, increase in that justice
> which they have received through the
> grace of Christ, and are still further
> justified.[52]

The Council Fathers' perspective on the church was

241

similar to that of Aquinas. It is the custodian of salvation. It possesses the seven sacraments which are necessary in order that further or sanctifying grace be infused into the souls of believers so that they complete their faith by good works and thus merit eternal life. In its discussion of the eucharist the council reaffirmed the doctrine of transubstantiation and declared the mass to be a propitiary sacrifice which obtained merits for both the living and the dead. The doctrine of purgatory was reasserted, and it was claimed that help may be given to souls in purgatory by the good works of those still living and by the sacrifice of the mass. Also the efficacy of indulgences was supported on the basis of the claim that Christ had given indulgences to the church. However, moderation in the granting of indulgences should be exercised, and the abuses which had become associated with the granting of indulgences abolished.[53]

While there were some of the Council Fathers who supported a greater degree of collegiality (all the bishops having joint responsibility for the entire church), the majority held to the view that the Pope is the supreme and absolute authority of the church. It is his prerogative to appoint, endow, and ordain bishops at his will without the consent of other authorities or of the people. One of the articles in the creed formulated by the Council refers to "the primacy of the Roman Pontiff and his infallible teaching authority."[54] Thus at Trent the papacy received a mandate of absolutism which finally was made explicit in the formal doctrine of papal infallibility promulgated by Vatican Council I in 1870.

In light of this brief sketch it can be seen that the Council of Trent elevated much of medieval theology to the position of ecclesiastical dogmas. These dogmas were to dominate the Catholic Church's theology and practice in succeeding centuries. Indeed, they were not to be significantly questioned until Vatican Council II (1962-1965).

NOTES

[1] T. A. Burkill, The Evolution of the Christian Faith (Cornell University Press, 1971), p. 79 and Williston Walker, A History of the Christian Church, Third Edition (Charles Scribner's Sons, 1970), pp. 105-106.

[2] Letters V. XX, The Nicene and Post Nicene Fathers, Second Series, Vol. XII, (Wm. B. Eerdmans Publishing Co., 1964), p. 18.

[3] Walker, op. cit., pp. 125-126.

[4] Ibid., p. 127.

[5] Fred Berthold, Jr. (et al.), Basic Sources of the Judeo-Christian Tradition (Prentice-Hall, 1962), pp. 177-180.

[6] Sacramentum Mundi: An Encyclopedia of Theology, Vol. 5 (Herder and Herder, 1970), pp. 40-41.

[7] Clyde L. Manschreck, A History of Christianity in The World (Prentice-Hall, 1974), p. 101.

[8] For a more detailed discussion of Pope Gregory's life and thought see Walker, op. cit., pp. 172-175; Manschreck, ibid., pp. 107-109; Justo L. Gonzalez, A History of Christian Thought, Vol. II (Abingdon Press, 1971), pp. 69-72, 139-140; A. C. McGiffert, A History of Christian Thought, Vol. II (Charles Scribner's Sons, 1953), Chapter VI.

[9] See Walker, ibid., p. 174; McGiffert, ibid., p. 149, Gonzalez, ibid., p. 70.

[10] See the discussion of Christology in Chapter VI above, pp.

[11] See Walker, op. cit., p. 149.

[12] See Manschreck, op. cit., pp. 110-120; Nichols Zernov, Eastern Christendom (G. P. Putnam's Sons, 1961), pp. 227-237.

[13] See Burkill, op. cit., chapter 24; Gonzalez, op. cit., pp. 173-176, 247-253, 322-323; McGiffert, op. cit., pp. 241-248, 295, 359-377.

[14] The Varieties of Religious Experience (Longmans, Green and Co., 1903), pp. 379-429.

[15] Ibid., p. 380. Italics are mine.

[16] Ibid.

[17] Ibid., p. 381.

[18] See Gonzalez, op. cit., p. 92; Burkill, op. cit., pp. 129-131, 218-222.

[19] Gonzalez, ibid., pp. 92-93.

[20] The Imitation of Christ (Grosset and Dunlap), pp. 16-17, 109.

[21] Ibid., pp. 174-175.

[22] Ibid., p. 310.

[23] Williston Walker, op. cit., p. 245.

[24] Yves M. J. Congar, O. P., A History of Theology (Doubleday and Co., Inc., 1968), p. 104.

[25] Ibid., p. 113.

[26] Ibid., p. 109.

[27] In Boetium de Trin., q. II, ad 3um. I have taken this quote from Congar, ibid., p. 109. The italics in the quote are mine.

[28] Summa Contra Gentiles, IV, ch. 1, N. 11, in St. Thomas Aquinas: On the Truth of the Catholic Faith (Doubleday and Co., Inc., Image Books, four vols., 1955-1957).

[29] Ibid., I, ch. 9, N. 3.

[30] Ibid., IV, ch. 1, N. 3, 9, 10.

[31] Ibid.

[32] Summa Theologiae I, Q. 2, A. 3, in Basic Writings of Saint Thomas Aquinas, Anton C. Pegis (ed.) (Random House, 1945,), Vol. I, p. 22.

[33] Ibid., I, Q. 1, A. 1, quoted from A. M. Fairweather, ed., Aquinas On Nature and Grace, Vol. XI, Library of Christian Classics (Westminster Press, 1954), p. 36. See also II - II, Q. 2, A. 3, p. 245.

[34] Ibid., I, Q. 1, A. 1; Q. 2, A. 2, Fairweather, ibid., p. 36.

[35] Ibid., II - II Q. 2, A. 2, Fairweather, p. 243.

[36] Ibid., II - II Q. 2, A. 10, Fairweather, p. 258.

[37] Ibid., I. Q. 93, Articles 1, 2, 3, 4. Also Summa Contra Gentiles, Book II, ch. 85.

[38] Ibid., I, Q. 95, A. 1-2; Q. 102, A. 4.

[39] Ibid., I - II, Questions 91, 93-95.

[40] Ibid., I - II, Q. 111.

[41] Ibid., I - II, Q. 109, A. 5.

[42] Summa Contra Gentiles, IV, chapters 63-64; Summa Theologiae, III. Q. 75, 65, A. 3.

[43] Ibid., IV, chapters 61-72; Summa Theologiae, III. Q. 65, 83, A. 1, 79, A. 2, 5.

[44] Ibid., IV, ch. 91.

[45] Ibid., IV, ch. 76.

[46] Ibid., IV, ch. 25.

[47] The Council was convened on Dec. 13, 1545. There were interruptions of rather long duration and the Council did not finish its work until December, 1563. Protestants did not participate in the Council.

[48] "The Canons and Dogmatic Decrees of the Council of Trent," Creeds of the Churches, John H. Leith (ed.) (Aldine Publishing Co., 1963), p. 404.

[49] Ibid, p. 402. Italics are mine.

[50] Ibid., p. 405.

[51] Ibid., p. 407.

[52] Ibid., pp. 409, 410, 411, 413. Italics are mine.

[53] See Reinhold Seeberg, Text-Book of the History of Doctrines, Vol. II (Baker Book House, 1954), p. 444. Pages 427-449 contain a good summary of the Council of Trent.

[54] Leith, _op. cit._, p. 441.

SUGGESTIONS FOR FURTHER READING

Ayers, Robert H., _Language_, _Logic_ and _Reason_ in the Church Fathers, Georg Olms Press, 1979, Chapter IV.

Bainton, Roland, Christendom, Vol. I, Harper Torchbook, 1966.

Bainton, Roland, The Medieval Church, Anvil Paperback, 1962.

Berthold, Fred, (et al.), Basic Sources of the Judeo-Christian Tradition, Prentice-Hall, 1962, Part Two.

Bettenson, Henry, Documents of the Christian Church, Oxford University Press, 1963, Part II, Sections I - VII.

Burkill, T. A., The Evolution of Christian Thought, Cornell University Press, 1971, pp. 129-222.

Congar, Y. M. J., A History of Theology, Doubleday and Co., Inc., 1968, Chapters Two - Four.

Cunliffe-Jones, Hubert (ed.), A History of Christian Doctrine, Fortress Press, 1980, pp. 181-286, 403-409.

Ferm, Robert, Readings in the History of Christian Thought, Holt, Rinehart and Winston, Inc., 1964.

Gonzalez, Justo, A History of Christian Thought, Vol. II, Abingdon Press, 1971.

Kempis, Thomas A., The Imitation of Christ, Grosset and Dunlop.

Latourette, Kenneth Scott, Christianity through the Ages, Harper and Row, 1965, Chapters IV - VII.

Lohse, Bernhard, A Short History of Christian Doctrine, Fortress Press, 1978. Chapter V.

Manschreck, Clyde L., A History of Christianity in the World, Prentice-Hall, 1974, Chapters 7-13, 15.

McGiffert, A. C., A History of Christian Thought, Vol. II, Charles Scribner's Sons, 1953, Chapters V - XVII.

Pegis, Anton C. (ed.), Basic Writings of Saint Thomas Aquinas, Random House, 1945.

Pelikan, Jaroslav, The Christian Tradition, Vol. 3, University of
    Chicago Press, 1978.

Petry, Ray C. (ed.), A History of Christianity, Prentice-Hall, 1962,
    Chapters IV - X.

Seeberg, Reinhold, Textbook in the History of Doctrines, Vol. II,
    Baker Book House, 1954.

The Library of Christian Classics, Vols. IX, X, XI, XII, XIII,
    Westminster Press.

Walker, Williston, A History of the Christian Church, Third Edi-
    tion, Charles Scribner's Sons, 1970, pp. 172-297.

Zernov, Nicholas, Eastern Christendom, G. P. Putnam's Sons, 1961.

PART IV

THE REFORMATION PERIOD

Our task in Part IV is to describe as briefly and
clearly as possible the major perspectives in a new
movement which appeared in Christendom in the sixteenth
century, namely the Protestant Reformation. As with
any major socio-religious movement, the factors which
contributed to the emergence of the Reformation were
many and varied. Some of the more important of these
factors were the following:

First, there was the undermining of Aquinas' theological synthesis, since for many it was no longer tenable. Three movements contributed to this undermining
of the Thomistic synthesis.

1. One of the movements was mysticism. As indicated in Chapter VII, the mystics sought to achieve
the beatific vision in this life through following step
by step the three ways of purification, illumination,
and unification or absorption into God. Obviously,
the mystics were convinced that the individual who
followed the three ways could have an immediate or
direct experience of God. By contrast, the Thomistic
theological synthesis had supported the view that the
knowledge of God was mediated, primarily through the
church as the sacramental agent. In spite of this
contrast the mystics were not regarded as a threat to
the life of the church, nor did they intend to undermine its authority. Apparently they intended to renew
its life and witness. However, their emphasis upon
the individual's immediate relationship with God did
present an alternative perspective to that of the church
and contributed to the undermining of its authority.
While Protestantism is not to be equated with mysticism
nor its theology adequately understood only in terms of
an emphasis upon the individual's immediate experience
of God, it is surely the case that mysticism was one of
the causal conditions which helped to prepare the way
for the Reformation.

2. Another movement which contributed to the
undermining of the Thomistic theological synthesis
was Nominalism. In Part III we have seen that an
important concept in early and medieval theology,

derived from Greek philosophy, was that of universals, essences or forms. In spite of differences among theologians as to how universals have existence and are known, there was general agreement that universals are real. Hence the term realists is used to designate these thinkers. Even Aquinas, who like Aristotle emphasized the importance of particulars, was a moderate realist. Structure, order, patterns of rational thought were for him inherent in reality itself. The nominalist of the late medieval period, however, claimed that the universals or essences are only names or terms which people use to talk about various collections of individual things. Individual things alone are objectively real. Universals have no reality other than that of being names or terms, either mental, spoken, or written. In light of this, the fourteenth century nominalist, William of Occam (sometimes spelled Ockham), formulated his famous axiom which is generally designated "Occam's razor," namely, "Entities are not to be unnecessarily multiplied."[1] That is, universals are superfluous entities with respect to knowledge of the actual world. They are only general terms, a kind of shorthand way of talking about groups of individual things which have "family" resemblances.

In its emphasis upon particulars and individuals, Nominalism tended to undermine the Thomistic synthesis based on a moderate realism. It was not that the nominalists like Occam rejected the Catholic faith and Church. Indeed, Occam regarded himself as a devout believer. But he divorced philosophy and theology, affirming that theology must be based entirely on divine revelation.

While Protestantism is not to be equated simply with an emphasis on the individual nor with the extreme rejection of rationality in theology, it is the case that Nominalism was one of the causal conditions which helped to prepare the way for the Reformation.

3. A third movement which tended to undermine the Thomistic synthesis and the church's hold on the life of the times was Renaissance Humanism. In the fifteenth century there was a renewal of interest in and study of the classics of Ancient Greek and Latin literature. This created a view favorable to the concerns of this life in and for themselves. The invention of the printing press made it easy to produce large numbers of copies of ancient documents (including the Bible) in their original languages. And this

contributed to the producing of critical editions of the writings of antiquity. Also such textual criticism raised questions about the purported antiquity of some writings. For example, on the basis of a textual analysis, Lorenzo Valla demonstrated that the so-called Donation of Constantine, which was supposed to be Constantine's last will and testament bestowing his temporal power upon the Pope, was a forgery. The language and style was that of centuries later rather than of the Latin used at the time of Constantine.[2]

A second major factor among the causal conditions which led to the Reformation was the breakdown of the feudal social system. Feudalism was hierarchically structured and authoritarian. In such a society it was possible for the Catholic Church to exercise a considerable degree of control over the lives of people. The Emperor of the "Holy Roman Empire" (it has been said often that it was neither Roman nor holy) who owed his consecration to the Pope was supposed to function as a kind of secular arm for the church. In principle, if not always in practice, he ruled over the nobles and wielded the "temporal" sword. But this "temporal" sword was supposed to be subservient to the "spiritual" sword of Rome (the Pope), the final authority in both spiritual and civil affairs. With the rise in the sixteenth century of nation states, cities, commerce, a monetary economy, and a middle class, feudalism began to crumble and the power of the ecclesiastical hierarchy to decline.

A third factor which helped to prepare the way for the Reformation was the situation within the Catholic Church itself. In its attempt to control all aspects of life the church had overextended itself and to a large extent had become secularized. Also the view that the doing of good works was necessary if one was to merit eternal life produced a view of piety as being primarily an objective, quantitative, and relative matter. It was objective in the sense that there were prescribed deeds to be performed, quantitative in the sense that the larger the number of good deeds done the more merit one achieved, and relative in the sense that the kind of good deeds to be done was relative to one's station in life. Associated with this perspective was the view of the church as a treasure house of merit which could be drawn upon by the purchase of indulgences (see Chapter VII above). As we have seen, this situation disturbed many sensitive believers. It was one of the conditions

251

that led not only to the Reformation but also to the Catholic Council of Trent.

Fourthly, not least among the factors which produced the Reformation was the thought and work of a great leader, namely Martin Luther. It is probably the case that Luther's work would not have resulted in the Reformation had it not been for the ideational, social, economic, political, and institutional conditions described above. About a century prior to Luther, John Wycliff (England) and John Huss (Bohemia) had held theological positions somewhat similar to those of Luther. But the conditions described above were not in effect, and so both were condemned and burned at the stake. This is not to suggest that these conditions alone would have produced the Reformation. Undoubtedly, it would not have occurred without a Luther or some leader of his stature. Apparently, as sometimes happens in history, a great leader appeared when the time was right and served as the catalyst of a new movement.[3]

CHAPTER VIII

MAJOR PERSPECTIVES OF LUTHER AND CALVIN

While many far-reaching forces converged in the
sixteenth century to make the Protestant Reformation
possible, its immediate cause consisted in the struggle
of Martin Luther (1483-1546 A.D.) to find assurance
of salvation and tranquility of mind. Therefore, the
first part of the discussion in this chapter will contain a brief description of Luther's intellectual and
spiritual odyssey. This description will be followed
by a summary of the major theological perspectives
of both Martin Luther and John Calvin (1509-1564).
There were other important leaders and movements in
the Reformation, but these two stand out above all
other leaders and movements. Luther sometimes has
been called the "father" of Protestantism. Calvin
might be called the younger "brother" of the "father."
In spite of some differences there are striking agreements between the two. While they never met, Calvin
always treasured his friendship with Luther, and he
did have personal conversations with Philip Melanch-
thon, a close associate of Luther.[4]

Martin Luther was born on November 11, 1483 in
the Saxony Village of Eisleben, the son of Hans and
Margaretta Luther who apparently were very strict
parents. While they were of peasant stock, they had
sufficient means to provide Martin with a good education. He received the Bachelor's (1502) and the Master's (1505) degrees from the University of Erfurt.
Then, since his parents desired it, he began studying
for a career in law. Shortly thereafter, when returning from a visit with his parents, Luther was caught
in a sudden violent thunderstorm, and terrified by
the thought of dying without being prepared, he made
a vow that if spared he would become a monk. Two
weeks later, at the age of twenty-two and against
the wishes of his father, Luther entered the Augustinian monastery at Erfurt. After a two-year probation
period he received the sacrament of ordination.

Having committed himself to the monastic life,
Luther gave himself to it completely. He sought,
through the wholehearted practice of medieval piety,
to gain a sense of tranquility in the face of the

wrath of God, the judgment of Christ and the terrors
of hell. He sought to purge himself of sinful inclin-
ations by rigorous acts of self denial which included
vigils, fastings, and scourgings. As Roland Bainton
has said: "Curiously, the reform that was to convulse
Christendom was initiated by a Catholic monk and priest
interested only in reforming himself."[5]

Try as he might, Luther could not gain the assurance that he had done enough to merit God's favor.
Even his good works, it seemed to him, were infected
with the pretensions of self, egocentricity or self-
love. However, the church claimed to provide a means
of release from the burden of sin in the sacrament of
penance, provided the conditions of contrition, confession, and satisfaction were fulfilled. With typical vigor Luther engaged in this practice. According
to Bainton:

> He believed, together with the leading
> theologians of his day that sins, to be
> forgiven, must be recalled, confessed
> and absolved one by one. Luther pro-
> ceeded to confess for six hours on end
> and was utterly disconcerted to find that
> after leaving the confessional, he re-
> called some trivial offense he had over-
> looked. Then he would return again and
> again until his confessor grew impatient
> and told him to go and do something worthy
> of being confessed.[6]

The problem for Luther was not whether his sins were
great or small but whether he had confessed them all.
It seemed to Luther that man's sin is so deep that no
introspection can bring one to recognize all that is
wrong. So he came to feel that no one can be sure
that his contrition is so thorough as to be genuine
nor that the satisfaction one can make is enough to
merit God's favor.

It was at this point in 1510 that, due to the
need for the Pope to settle a dispute which had arisen
in the Augustinian order, Luther's monastery sent him
with a fellow monk to Rome, the eternal city. Luther
had high hopes that the sojourn of a month in Rome
would provide him with such spiritual benefits that
he would be released from his inner spiritual turmoil.
Instead, he was deeply disappointed, disillusioned,

and shocked by the worldliness in Rome, the ignorance, levity, and skepticism of the Italian priests, and the abuses associated with the means of attaining merit. According to Bainton: "Luther commented that he had gone to Rome with onions and had returned with garlic."[7]

Upon returning from Rome, Luther engaged in a thorough study of the Bible in preparation for an appointment as Professor of Theology at the University of Wittenberg and in 1512 received the Doctor of Theology degree. From 1513 to 1517 he gave lectures on the Psalms and on Paul's letters to Romans and Galatians. This experience was to be the turning point in Luther's spiritual odyssey. He had tried the way of medieval piety and found that it brought him no assurance of God's mercy and acceptance. The thought of God's glory, majesty, justice, and wrath had filled him with dread and hatred. How could such a holy and righteous God be appeased by a man like Luther who knew himself to be an unholy sinner? Was there another way of understanding God's relationship with the world and miserable human beings? Passages in the Psalms and Paul's letters suggested that there was another way.

In his study of Psalms, Luther came to the first glimmer of hope that there was another way which provided release from the predicament of estrangement from God and hopelessness with respect to his eternal destiny. Like all interpreters of his time, Luther understood the Old Testament as a foreshadowing of the New Testament and so interpreted the Psalms Christologically. When he came to the twenty-second Psalm, which Jesus himself had begun to recite on the cross, "My God, my God, why has thou forsaken me," it dawned on Luther that Christ himself had suffered the same sense of abandonment by God and desolation which he, Luther, suffered. Even though without sin, Christ had identified himself with mankind, taken upon himself the sins of mankind, and participated in human alienation. He was not only the righteous judge but, because he had identified himself with the accused, he also was the forsaken one on the cross. This desolation and suffering of Christ on the cross was for all, including Luther. In this vicarious suffering of Christ, God had disclosed his love and mercy and offered redemption to mankind.

In light of these thoughts, Luther found that the phrase in Psalms 31, "Deliver me in thy righteousness,"

became a source of insight. Formerly the "righteousness of God" had been understood to mean God's fearful,
demanding, and judicial justice. In this Psalm, however, "righteousness" is associated with "deliverance."
Did this mean that God's righteousness is not only
justice but also mercy? Is it the case that in some
mysterious way the justice and mercy of God are united,
that his justice is to be understood in terms of his
mercy?

Luther's study of Paul's letter to the Romans
led him to the insight that mercy is the primary and
fundamental ingredient in God's righteousness or
justice. In Romans 1:17 Paul said: "For in it [the
gospel] the righteousness of God is revealed through
faith for faith; as it is written, 'He who through
faith is righteous shall live'" (R.S.V.). As he
pondered on this passage, Luther came to the conviction that God without demanding any sign of merit
extends his mercy to those who know they are not
worthy. No one can gain righteousness by means of his
achievements. One must relinquish reliance upon himself, and trust God rather than himself and his own
activities. All human attempts to calculate and
measure merit are false notions in relation to God.
The issue is not how can one be actually righteous in
the sight of God. It is that God is righteous in that
although he does not ease his demand upon man, he extends his forgiving and accepting mercy to man. The
emphasis now is upon the mercy which is gracious and
accepting. The experience of this mercy is by faith.
"He who through faith is righteous shall live." This
means that one is released from the terrible and impossible demand to become actually righteous. Instead,
one who accepts God's mercy and acceptance offered in
Christ is accounted righteous by God precisely because
of his faith or trust and thus is reconciled with God.
Using the Apostle Paul's terminology, Luther called
this process of reconciliation "justification by
faith."

Concerning the passage in Romans 1:17, Luther
wrote the following:

>I greatly longed to understand Paul's
>Epistle to the Romans and nothing stood
>in the way but that one expression,
>"the justice of God," because I took it
>to mean that justice whereby God is just
>and deals justly in punishing the unjust.

256

My situation was that, although an im-
peccable monk, I stood before God as a
sinner troubled in conscience, and I had
no confidence that my merit would assuage
him. Therefore I did not love a just and
angry God, but rather hated and murmured
against him. Yet I clung to the dear Paul
and had a great yearning to know what he
meant.
     Night and day I pondered until I saw
the connection between the justice of God
and the statement that "the just shall
live by his faith." Then I grasped that
the justice of God is that righteousness
by which through grace and sheer mercy
God justifies us through faith. Thereupon I felt myself to be reborn and to have
gone through open doors into paradise. The
whole of Scripture took on a new meaning,
and whereas before the "justice of God" had
filled me with hate, now it became to me
inexpressibly sweet in greater love. This
passage of Paul became to me a gate to
heaven. . . . .
     If you have a true faith that Christ
is your Saviour, then at once you have a
gracious God, for faith leads you in and
opens up God's heart and will, that you
should see pure grace and overflowing love.
This it is to behold God in faith that
you should look upon his fatherly, friendly
heart, in which there is no anger nor un-
graciousness. He who sees God as angry
does not see him rightly but looks only
on a curtain, as if a dark cloud had been
drawn across his face.[8]

     It is not surprising that having gained liberation
from his inner turmoil and a sense of reconciliation
with God, Luther sought to share his hard won insight
with others. To this end he published his 97 theses
entitled Disputation Against Scholastic Theology.[9] His
purpose was to create a debate which would draw attention to his hard won insight. This was not to be the
case, for the 97 theses attracted little attention.
Yet they are important because they reflect the positions at which he had now arrived concerning man, sin,
works, law, grace, and election. In this Disputation
he questions medieval rationalism based on Aristotelian
presuppositions and the natural theology of the

Scholastics. He emphasizes the bondage of the will to sin, claiming that the natural man seeks to be God himself and is totally depraved. Salvation cannot be gained by good works, for even they are infected by sin due to the fact that men take pride in them. The law, while good in itself, is corrupted by the evil wills of men and thus is powerless to save. Salvation is by God's gracious act of forgiveness in Jesus Christ. It is faith in this grace of God which alone justifies one, and the preparation for such faith is the eternal election of God. Commenting on Luther's Disputation Against Scholastic Theology, James Atkinson has said:

> Luther saw, and knew for himself, that it was possible for a man to range through the whole gamut of the religious process the medieval church prescribed and yet never know what pardon, sin, repentance, forgiveness and grace really meant as offered in and by Christ. Its whole system was semi-Pelagian at heart and was based on human self-righteousness or works-righteousness. . . . [For Luther] Christianity in its real intent sought to open men to the gravity of sin in order that they may be moved to repent and see and accept God's grace and mercy.[10]

Justification by faith was already the central point of Luther's theology when he posted his 95 theses, Disputation on the Power and Efficacy of Indulgences, on the door of the Castle Church in Wittenberg, October 31, 1517. He expected them to serve as a basis simply for scholarly debate with intellectuals, but they received immediate and widespread attention. So from relative obscurity Luther soon became a personality known throughout Germany and beyond. Undoubtedly the reason for this is that the 95 theses expressed the pent-up grievances of many people and attacked the vested interests of powerful ecclesiastical figures.

At the time of posting the 95 theses, Luther still regarded himself as a loyal son of the Catholic Church. His intent simply was to evoke debates which he hoped would lead to the elimination of the abuses which had become associated with the practice of granting indulgences. As indicated in Chapter VII, indulgences which originally had been simply the remission of temporal penalties assigned to penitents by confessors had come to be regarded as releasing departed souls from purgatory. The particular case that touched off Luther's protest was the sale of indulgences in the territory of Albert of Brandenburg. Albert wanted to be Archbishop of Mainz in order to extend his power in Germany. Pope Leo X (1513-1521) needed money for the building of the new St. Peter's church in Rome. So the two made a bargain. In return for appointing Albert Archbishop of Mainz, the Pope would receive a large portion of the proceeds from a sale of indulgences authorized by the Pope in Albert's territories. The stakes were high, and the indulgence was promoted with appeals and fanfare similar in many respects to a contemporary advertising campaign.

One of the most eloquent of the indulgence preachers was the Dominican monk Johan Tetzel. A sample of his type of preaching is the following excerpt from one of his sermons:

> Listen now, God and St. Peter call you.
> Consider the salvation of your souls and
> those of your loved ones departed. . .
> Consider that all who are contrite and
> have confessed and made contribution
> will receive complete remission of all
> their sins. Listen to the voices of
> your dear dead relatives and friends,
> beseeching you and saying, 'Pity us,
> pity us. We are in dire torment from
> which you can redeem us for a pittance.'
> Do you not wish to? Open your ears.
> Hear the father saying to his son, the
> mother to her daughter, 'We bore you,
> nourished you, brought you up, left you
> our fortunes, and you are so cruel and
> hard that now you are not willing for
> so little to set us free. Will you
> let us lie here in flames? Will you
> delay our promised glory?'
>
> Remember that you are able to release
> them, for
>
> > As soon as the coin in the coffer rings
> > The soul from purgatory springs.
>
> Will you not then for a quarter of a florin
> receive these letters of indulgence through
> which you are able to lead a divine and
> immortal soul into the fatherland of paradise?[11]

This was too much for Luther. In the 95 theses he charges the indulgence preachers with committing abuses by spreading abroad the dangerous notion that salvation can be bought. The power of the Pope does not extend to purgatory, for he does not have at his disposal a treasury of credits which can be transferred for the remission of penalties to those in purgatory. The true treasure of the church is the gospel of God's grace. Indulgences are concerned only with the penalties of sacramental satisfaction established by man. If the Pope has the power to release souls from purgatory, why doesn't he for the sake of holy love and the dire need of the souls there empty purgatory and use his own money for the building of St. Peter's? The ecclesiastical hierarchy cannot pardon the guilt of the least of sins. God alone forgives the guilt of sin. Only the declaration of what God does belongs to the hierarchy. The emphasis should be upon the preaching of the Word of God (the revelation of God's grace in Jesus Christ) rather than upon the preaching of indulgences. Men do not become better by indulgences but by love and the works of love. Money spent on the purchases of indulgences would be used better if it were given to the poor.[12]

The 95 theses gained Luther powerful opponents, including Pope Leo X. In the controversy which followed Luther came to the position that indulgences must be rejected outright and that in light of his new insight concerning the nature of faith the church needed to be radically reformed. It may be said, then, that in posting the 95 theses Luther took the first step along the pathway which led to his final break with the Catholic Church and the establishment of Protestant Christianity.

It was fortunate for Luther that Prince Frederick of Saxony, founder of the University of Wittenberg and an elector of the Holy Roman Empire, looked upon Luther as a protege and so protected him from powerful opponents. In June of 1520 Pope Leo X issued a papal declaration demanding that Luther recant or be excommunicated, and Luther responded by publically burning this document. He then wrote three treatises (published in August, October, and November of 1520) which called for an even more radical reform of the church.

The first of these treatises, To the Christian Nobility of the German Nation Concerning the Reform of the Christian Estate,[13] called upon the nobles to

260

overthrow three walls erected by the "Romanists." These walls, according to Luther, were the claims that the spiritual power (the Pope) was superior to the temporal or secular power (the nobles), that the Pope alone was the final interpreter of Scripture, and that only the Pope could call a reforming council into session. Luther also enunciated his important doctrine of the priesthood of all believers and called for drastic reforms. Since all believers are "priests" they can interpret Scripture for themselves and through Christ have direct access to the spiritual realm. So the Pope and ecclesiastical hierarchy are not superior to Christian nobles in either the spiritual or temporal realms. It is the Christian nobles who should institute the much needed reforms in the church.

The second treatise, The Babylonian Captivity of the Church,[14] dealt with three captivities in the practice and views of the "Romanists" from which the church should be freed, namely the withholding of the cup from the laity in the sacrament of the Lord's Supper, the concept of transubstantiation, and the view of the mass as a re-presenting of Christ's sacrifice and a good work which enlarged the church's treasure house of merits. Luther claimed that since all believers are "priests," the laity as well as the clergy should receive communion in both kinds. Transubstantiation, upon which was based the notion that in every mass Christ's sacrifice is re-presented, is a false doctrine. The mass is neither a sacrifice nor a good work but a sign of the promise of the remission of sins made to us by God.[15]

In the third treatise, On Christian Liberty (The Freedom of a Christian),[16] Luther presented a positive and unequivocal statement concerning the meaning of justification by faith and the priesthood of all believers as applied to Christian life. Works are powerless to save but they do flow naturally from Christian faith and love. The meaning of the priesthood of all believers was stated succinctly by Luther in the following famous paradox:

> A Christian is a perfectly free lord of
> all, subject to none.
> A Christian is a perfectly dutiful servant
> of all, subject to all.[17]

This is to say that every believer is a priest in the sense that he can have direct access to the forgiving grace of God through Christ and in the sense that precisely because he experiences this grace of God he seeks to be a servant ("priest") of others. In light of this, it is clear why Luther in his earlier treatises had rejected the three "walls" and the three "captivities" of the "Romanists."

Shortly after the appearance of the three treatises Luther was summoned by the imperial decree of Emperor Charles V to appear before a gathering of imperial and ecclesiastical dignitaries at the Diet of Worms (April, 1521). There he was called upon to recant his "heretical" views and made his famous reply:

> Therefore, your most serene Majesty and your Lordships, since they seek a simple reply, I will give one that is without horns or teeth, and in this fashion: I believe in neither Pope nor councils alone; for it is perfectly well established that they have frequently erred, as well as contradicted themselves. Unless then I shall be convinced by the testimony of the Scriptures or by clear reason, I must be bound by those Scriptures which have been brought forward by me; yes, my conscience has been taken captive by those words of God. I cannot revoke anything, nor do I wish to; since to go against one's conscience is neither safe nor right: here I stand, I cannot do otherwise. God help me. Amen![18]

His fearless refusal to recant his doctrines resulted in Luther being placed under the imperial ban by Emperor Charles V.

Having been excommunicated by the Pope and placed under the ban by the Emperor, Luther's break with the Roman Catholic Church was now complete. Due to the protection of Prince Frederick, he escaped execution. For about a year he was kept in protective custody by Frederick in his castle at Wartburg. Then he returned to Wittenberg where for more than twenty years he continued to teach, preach, and write concerning his views on such issues as sin, justification by faith, predestination, the life of the Christian as saint and sinner, the priesthood of all believers, the church as a fellowship of believers with the two sacraments of Baptism and the Lord's Supper, the authority of

Scripture over that of the church, and the central role of the preaching of the Word of God in the life of the church. By the time of Luther's death on February 18, 1546, the Protestant Reformation had spread throughout Germany and into many other areas of Europe. Also by this time it had become clear that even though Protestants were divided by nationalisms and some theological differences, Protestant Christianity had become a permanent feature of Christendom.

As stated previously, the two most outstanding leaders of the Reformation were Martin Luther and John Calvin. While Luther was the creative pioneer, Calvin was the skillful systematizer and organizer. In extensive writings he produced for Protestant Christianity a comprehensive and systematic presentation of doctrine and the Christian life. His skill at clarifying and systematizing is nowhere more evident than it is in his work, Institutio Christianae Religionis (Institutes of Christian Religion). Written in Latin, this book was greatly expanded in successive editions. The Latin word institutio contained in the title generally meant "instruction" or "education" and was often used in the title of any comprehensive treatise which dealt with various topics in a systematic way.[19]

Calvin was born on July 10, 1509, the son of a secretary to the Bishop of Noyon, France. Early in his life he demonstrated superior intellectual ability and was able to study in the distinguished universities of Paris, Orleans, and Bourges. While he graduated in law, he was even more interested in humanistic studies. He managed to acquire a rather extensive knowledge in the disciplines of rhetoric, dialectics, philosophy, and languages (Latin, Greek, and Hebrew). His first book, Commentary on Seneca's Treatise On Clemency, was an erudite work of a learned humanist. It did not touch on religion. However, sometime within a two year period after its publication in 1532, Calvin experienced a "sudden conversion" in which he vividly became aware of the glory of God, the sinfulness of man, and the necessity of justification by faith.

After the conversion experience Calvin not only turned his attention to the study of religion but also supported those persons who were calling for reform and a return to the pure gospel. Such reform movements brought persecution from Francis I, King of France (1517-1547). In defense of the persecuted, Calvin published in 1536 the first edition of the Institutes of the Christian Religion which he prefaced with a plea to Francis to end the persecution of his subjects. The Institutes gained Calvin a great deal of attention as a champion of French Protestants and made it dangerous for him to remain in France. After some traveling about he was persuaded by a friend to settle in Geneva, Switzerland. With the exception of a three year period, he remained in Geneva until his death in 1564.

While Calvin sought neither honors nor high position for himself, was not actually ordained, and was but one of the preachers and teachers in the city, his influence soon became dominant in Geneva. Under his guidance many reform programs were instituted, education was improved, and new industries were established to provide jobs for the citizens. Yet Genevan life was brought under the control and minute supervision of a Consistory (12 laymen and 6 ministers) that heard reports once a week concerning any moral infractions committed by any citizen. Indeed, Calvin sought to make Geneva a model of a perfected Christian community. His influence, however, was not limited simply to Geneva. Through his extensive correspondence, his numerous writings, and the many Protestant refugees who found sanctuary in Geneva, his influence spread abroad. He often has been credited with preventing the Catholic Counter-Reformation (see Chapter VII) from overwhelming the emerging Protestant churches. Surely the importance of his contribution to the establishment of Protestantism was second only to that of Luther.[20]

The discussion so far has sketched briefly the careers of Luther and Calvin and briefly described the major experiences which led them to an understanding and practice of the Christian faith different from that of the Catholic Church. While references have been made already to the major Reformation issues, these issues will be explicated more fully in the remaining discussion of this chapter. This discussion will summarize the major theological perspectives of the two reformers. Such a summary of the theologies of these two in one exposition seems warranted in light of the fact that justification by faith is a basic concept for both, and that the implications which they derive from this basic concept are very similar. As previously noted, while there are some differences between the two, the agreements are extensive and impressive. In the following exposition, major attention will be given to the agreements with a few differences noted where appropriate.[21]

1. "Knowledge" of self and "knowledge" of God

A great irony of human existence is that no matter how far man extends his knowledge and control over objective powers and processes, he rarely ceases to be deeply puzzled by himself. While he knows that he is, he does not know what he is. Man is a mystery to himself.

For Luther and Calvin this is precisely the situation in which the person without faith finds himself. Apart from God, man is not himself and does not know himself. The "knowledge" of God and the "knowledge" of self are inseparable. Calvin, for example, in the opening sentences of the Institutes wrote:

> Nearly all the wisdom we possess, that is to say, true and sound wisdom, consists in two parts: the knowledge of God and of ourselves. But, while joined by many bonds, which one precedes and brings forth the other is not easy to discern.[22]

On the one hand, a true knowledge of self in which one is conscious not only of his abilities and gifts but also of his ignorance, vanity, and insufficiency makes one aware of his need to seek for a knowledge of God from whom, as creator, all gifts flow. But on the other hand, due to human pride, self-righteousness, and deception there can be no genuine knowledge of self without a knowledge of God. So Calvin said: "As long as we do not look beyond the earth, being quite content with our own righteousness, wisdom, and virtue, we flatter ourselves most sweetly, and fancy ourselves all but demigods."[23] That is, the self does not truly find itself unless it becomes aware that it is apprehended from beyond itself in God's redemptive work.

Quite clearly, Luther, too, held to this perspective. He regarded the knowledge of self and the knowledge of God as closely interrelated polarities which necessarily are involved in the proper response to the problem of the human condition. In his own spiritual odyssey he had found that it was only as he understood God and himself in a new light that he had received the peace of "sound and true wisdom." So Luther said: "For, because man does God the honor of regarding and confessing Him as true, He becomes to him a gracious God, who in turn honors him and regards and confesses him as true."[24]

In light of the above quotations from Calvin and Luther, it seems obvious that, while both polarities are involved in their perspectives, the major emphasis falls on the knowledge of God. The proper place for true wisdom concerning the self to begin is the knowledge of God. It is only in light of the answer to the problem and mystery of human existence that one receives the wisdom and courage to see himself as he is.

For the reformers the "knowledge" of God required for true wisdom is not "mere" or purely objective knowledge. It is what might be designated as knowledge by acquaintance such as when one says, "Yes, I know Jim" or "I know Susie." Both distinguish between the knowledge that God is and the knowledge of who God is and of his gracious acts on behalf of mankind. The latter is revealed "knowledge" and is the more important because it has to do with the "knowledge" necessary for salvation. So Luther said:

> There is a twofold knowledge of God:
> the general and the particular. All
> men have the general knowledge, namely,
> that God is, that He has created heaven
> and earth, that He is just, that He
> punishes the wicked, etc. But what God
> thinks of us, what He wants to give and
> to do to deliver us from sin and death
> and to save us--which is the particular
> and the true knowledge of God--this men
> do not know. Thus it can happen that
> someone's face may be familiar to me but
> I do not really know him, because I do
> not know what he has in his mind. So it
> is that men know naturally that there is
> a God, but they do not know what He
> wants and what He does not want.[25]

While there is a natural or general knowledge of God as evidenced by the fact that all races are aware that there are gods or divinity above them, this knowledge does not constitute a genuine understanding of God. The God whose existence has been established by the philosophers through reasoning about the realm of nature is not the true God. Even though nature provides proofs for the existence of God, such proofs, according to Luther, are hardly worthy of notice.[26] The person of faith may discern signs of God in the

266

order of nature, but nature in itself is not revelatory of the true God. Nature is as terrifying, if not more so, as it is beneficient. The "face" of God discerned in nature is that of terrible majesty and wrath in which "the inscrutable goodness of the divine will is hidden (as is God himself) from the Old Adam" (the person apart from faith).[27] Genuine knowledge of God is found only in the revelation of his will in his Word, Jesus Christ. As Luther said: "He who does not know Christ does not know God hidden in suffering. . . . God can be found only in suffering and the cross."[28]

Calvin also held to the view that there is in the human mind by natural instinct a certain awareness of deity of which even the worst of men cannot be rid.[29] Less paradoxical than Luther in his view of nature, Calvin stressed the evidence of God's handiwork in the beauty and order of nature and in the products of man's thought and skill such as in the disciplines of physics, logic, mathematics, rhetoric, astronomy, etc. He regarded these disciplines as the excellent gifts of God and said: "If we regard the Spirit of God as the sole fountain of truth, we shall neither reject the truth itself, nor despise it wherever it shall appear, unless we wish to dishonor the Spirit God."[30] The divine imprint in the human mind and the order of nature renders man inexcusable, but, due to sin in the human heart, it cannot produce true knowledge of God. Such knowledge can come only through the acceptance of God's revelation of his will in his Word, his everlasting Wisdom, Jesus Christ.[31] This "knowledge" or faith consists in assurance that one is accepted by God.[32] On such a basis the imprint of God in the human mind and the order of nature may be understood properly, and all the disciplines used for a richer understanding of God, self and the world.

In the view of the reformers, then, it is only because God has taken the initiative to disclose or reveal his will in his Word, Jesus Christ, that there can be a true "knowledge" of God, a proper understanding of the natural order, and a genuine wisdom concerning the self.

2. Man as sinner

As stated above the reformers believed that it was only in light of the "knowledge" of faith that a person can receive the wisdom to see himself as he is. While a being created in God's image and thus possessing

267

gifts which transcend those of the animals, at the same time man is a sinner who stands in estrangement from God, others, and his own genuine self. It is not that human nature as such is evil. Since God created ex nihilo, everything as created is good. So human nature is good. It is its defect which is evil. Under the conditions of historical existence it became infected with sin, and this "defect that is in man by inheritance . . . infects the depth of his nature, so that, from his selfish disposition, he seeks even in God only himself and his own."[33] The wisdom and courage to acknowledge fully that one is a sinner in a state of estrangement from God is found only in faith, for without faith one is prone always to think of himself more highly than he ought to think. So in the Treatise On Christian Liberty Luther explicitly claimed:

> The moment you begin to have faith you learn that in all things you are altogether blameworthy, sinful, and damnable, as the Apostle says in Romans 3 [:23], 'Since all have sinned and fall short of the glory of God', and 'none is righteous, no, not one . . . All have turned aside, together they have gone wrong' (Romans 3: 10-12).[34]

Calvin, too, believed that human nature in itself is good. Sin is not "natural" in the sense that it is an innate quality of human nature as created. Man was created in the image of God, but under the conditions of historical existence man willfully rebelled against his Creator and so corrupted the divine image. Even though the image was not totally destroyed, it "was so corrupted that whatever remains is frightful deformity."[35] Just as one who has seen only dark objects will judge a dirty white object to be whiteness itself,[36] so one without the light of faith will not see himself as he is. It is only from the perspective of faith that one gains a genuine understanding of himself as a sinner.

For the reformers, the human condition of sin was depicted truly in the Genesis account of the fall of Adam. Before the fall Adam had enjoyed God's supernatural gifts and was inclined only to good. He could have chosen to remain in a state of fellowship with God, but in pride and ingratitude he chose to disbelieve what God told him and to disobey God's commands. That is, he chose self rather than God and

268

became a sinner estranged from God. This original sin infected not only Adam but also all of his posterity who have inherited his sinful character.

In their view of the condition of fallen man, the reformers differed from the dominant view expressed in late medieval Catholic theology. While Aquinas and the Council of Trent had spoken of original sin, they understood it as a loss of the likeness of God (supernatural righteousness), and they had affirmed that fallen man retained the image of God even though in a weakened condition (see Chapter VII). On such a basis, late medieval Catholic theology had tended to be semi-Pelagian in its view of sin. Sin was equated with sins. As acts, sins may be offset by other acts which are good. Luther and Calvin, however, held that with the fall of Adam the "image of God has been lost by sin" (Luther) or "so corrupted that whatever remains is frightful deformity" (Calvin). So the state of fallen man may be characterized as that of total depravity.[37]

In the thought of the reformers, "total depravity" designates two closely related features of the human condition since the Fall. First, all human beings are sinners. Their sin is not to be equated simply with specific acts of sin. Sinful acts are but reflections of the more basic state or condition of sin. Similiar to the Apostle Paul and Augustine, the reformers understand sin as the pride and pretension of self which prompts one to seek to build the world around himself, to become a self-sufficient "atom," and so to become his own god. As Calvin says, "the human heart has so many crannies where vanity lurks, so many holes where falsehood lurks, is so decked out with deceiving hypocrisy, that it often dupes itself."[38] Thus it boasts of its own goodness and divinity. To be sure, fallen man may do some good deeds, but even these good deeds are infected with the disease of sin because man is conscious that they are his deeds and takes pride in them. To believe at all in the merit of one's own deeds or goodness is pride or sin. So Luther says: "All that is done apart from faith, or in unbelief, is false; it is hypocrisy and sin, no matter how good a show it makes."[39] The crucial issue, then, is not so much what is done but how and why it is done. On the basis of his own activities, fallen man is incapable of instituting a relation with God.

Secondly, the reformers viewed the depravity of fallen man as total. This did not mean, as previously

stated, that fallen man could not do deeds which are
good when viewed externally. It meant that even the
good deeds are infected with sin because all human
faculties are so infected, and the good deeds are done
with wrong motives. That is, fallen man's will, intellect, and emotions are infected with the pretension
of self or sin. Calvin expressed this view rather
vividly when he said:

> At first man was formed in the
> image and resemblance of God in order that
> man might admire his Author in the adorn-
> ments with which he had been nobly vested
> by God and honor him with proper adknowl-
> edgement. But, having trusted such a
> great excellence of his nature and having
> forgotten from whom it had come and by
> whom it subsisted, man strove to raise
> himself up apart from the Lord. Hence
> man had to be stripped of all God's gifts
> of which he was foolishly proud, so that,
> denuded and deprived of all glory, he
> might know God whom man, after having been
> enriched by his liberalities, had dared to
> despise. As a result, this resemblance
> to God having been effaced in us, we all
> who descend from the seed of Adam are born
> flesh from flesh. For, though we are
> composed of a soul and a body, yet we feel
> nothing but the flesh, so that to whatever
> part of man we turn our eyes, it is im-
> possible to see anything that is not
> impure, profane, and abominable to God.
> The intellect of man is indeed blinded,
> wrapped with infinite errors and always
> contrary to the wisdom of God; the will,
> bad and full of corrupt affections, hates
> nothing more than God's justice; and the
> bodily strength, incapable of all good
> deeds, tends furiously toward iniquity.[40]

Given this view of total depravity, it is not surprising
that Luther and Calvin were convinced that none of our
works is perfect, without some stain of sin.

As had the Apostle Paul, the reformers viewed the
"law," especially in its Old Testament form, as serving
a function in the total gospel message. To be sure,
it is powerless to save. It cannot create faith, but
it can convict one of sin by disclosing the righteous

270

demands of God so clearly that one cannot avoid seeing himself as a sinner. In this sense the "law" is a preparation for the gospel in that it continually makes one aware of his constant need for the forgiving grace of God disclosed in Jesus Christ. For the person of faith the "law" is a constant reminder of his sinfulness and of his constant need for God's grace.[41]

3. The Work of Christ

We have seen that for the reformers, natural theology (speculations about God derived from the natural order) can yield only abstract conclusions concerning God's existence as Supreme Ruler and man's general responsibility to him. It cannot yield knowledge of the real God. The real God can be known only because he has chosen to reveal himself in Jesus Christ. In Christ is disclosed the ways and works of God.

With respect to the doctrines of the Trinity (Christ's relation to God) and of Christology (the relation of the divine and human in Christ), the reformers accepted the traditional formulas of Nicea and Chalcedon (see Chapter VI). While Luther was impatient somewhat with the metaphysical speculations contained in these creeds, he still accepted them as authoritative. Calvin explicated them in more detail than did Luther, but he did so in their defense.[42] Unlike the situation in the early church, the most controversial issues in the sixteenth century were not the relation of Christ to God or of the human and divine in Christ but the issues of sin and justification. The traditional doctrines of the Trinity and of Christology were accepted by the reformers as part of the received faith which did not require reformation. They were not as much concerned with definitions concerning the person of Christ as they were with a consideration of the work of Christ. It may be said that central to the theology of the reformers was a Christology in which the major emphasis was on the work of Christ for the sake of man's salvation.

For Luther and Calvin the work of Christ is that of mediator and savior. In him the divine eternal Word was actualized in a divine-human life in earthly history and so became the Word of reconciliation addressed by God to man. The whole of Christ's life, death, and resurrection discloses God acting in free and sovereign love. In Christ, God identifies himself with man's sin, permits himself to be judged in man's

271

place, transforms man's condition from within, and conquers sin and death. As Luther said:

> Christ is God and man in one person. . . By the wedding ring of faith he shares in the sins, death, and pains of hell which are his bride's. As a matter of fact, he makes them his own and acts as if they were his own and as if he himself had sinned; he suffered, died, and descended into hell that he might overcome them all. Now since it was such a one who did all this, and death and hell could not swallow him up, these were necessarily swallowed up by him in a mighty duel; for his righteousness is greater than the sins of all men, his life stronger than death, his salvation more invincible than hell. . . Who can understand the riches of the glory of this grace? Here this rich and divine bridegroom Christ marries this poor, wicked harlot, redeems her from all her evil, and adorns her with all his goodness. Her sins cannot now destroy her, since they are laid upon Christ and swallowed up by him.[43]

With this understanding of Christ's work Calvin was in essential agreement.[44]

Luther and Calvin differed to some extent in what they had to say concerning the way Christ assumed the sin of man. Calvin tended to emphasize the majesty of Christ in the roles of prophet, king, and priest. The role of priest did entail Christ's offering of himself as a sacrifice by which he made satisfaction for our sins, but this suffering was a prelude to his glory.[45] Luther tended to emphasize the paradox of God's majesty in the lowliness of human form, of God's strength hidden in weakness. Of necessity, the abso- lute love of God can be expressed in human history only in powerlessness and lowliness. This is the strange work of God, hidden to all but those with the eyes of faith. So Luther had a great fondness for Luke's nativity story of the Christ child in the manger, for to him this constituted a graphic message of God's strength hidden in weakness.[46] This differ- ence between Luther and Calvin was not fundamental because they were agreed that Christ had taken upon himself the sin of man, had been judged in man's place, had conquered sin and death, and had transformed man's

272

inner condition. Therefore Christ opened the way to man's justification.

4. Justification by faith

We have seen that for Luther and Calvin fallen man is caught in the predicament of sin, of total depravity. His will is in bondage to sin, and thus he cannot gain release from this bondage by willing himself out of it.[47] Deliverance must come from beyond, and God has taken the initiative in providing the word of deliverance in Jesus Christ. This word is the heart of the Christian gospel. Using the Apostle Paul's terminology, the reformers called it justification by faith.

In his commentary on Chapter Three of Paul's letter to the Romans, Luther claimed:

> He is dealing in that passage with the main point of Christian doctrine, viz., that we are justified by faith in Christ, without any works of the law, and he cuts away all works so completely, as even to say that the works of the law, though it is God's law and his Word, do not help us to righteousness. He cites Abraham as an example and says that he was justified so entirely without works, that even the highest work, which had then been newly commanded by God, before and above all other works, namely circumcision, did not help him to righteousness, but he was justified by faith, without circumcision and without any works at all. . . But when works are so completely cut away, the meaning of it must be that faith alone justifies.[48]

Justification by faith, then, is not based on something that we achieve or do, nor on the prospect of our future achievements. It is not based even on the effort to believe nor on something God finds in the believer, for not even faith itself is a good work. Instead it is based solely on God's mercy, on the loving, forgiving declaration by God in Jesus Christ that we are accepted in spite of the fact that we are sinners. That is to say, on the basis of our faith God accounts us as righteous, declares us to be just, in spite of the fact that we are not objectively just. Our sins are absolved, and Christ's righteousness is

273

imputed to us. By faith the sinner "puts on" the righteousness of Christ and clothed in this "garment" is declared to be righteous. As Calvin said: "Justified by faith is he who, excluded from the righteousness of works, grasps the righteousness of Christ through faith, and clothed in it, appears in God's sight not as a sinner but as a righteous man."[49] Justification does not eliminate sin nor make the Christian perfect. The Christian is at once justified and sinner. Yet justification by faith is the beginning of the Christian life in which, reconciled to God, the Christian enters the pilgrimage of the Christian life, seeking out of gratitude for God's acceptance to become by the help of God what God had intended human beings to be, i.e., actually righteous.

The true and sole function of faith for the reformers was the acceptance of God's acceptance. Faith cannot be manufactured. It is a gift of God. When it occurs the believer confesses that it was not his own doing but God's work in him, no matter how much he may have sought it. While Calvin maintained that there was a cognitive element in faith, since "faith rests not on ignorance but on knowledge,"[50] he was as insistent as Luther that faith is primarily a matter of trust. So Calvin said: "Faith is a firm and solid confidence of the heart, by means of which we rest surely in the mercy of God which is promised to us through the Gospel,"[51] and Luther affirmed: "Faith is a living, daring confidence in God's grace, so sure and certain that a man would stake his life on it a thousand times."[52]

It is in the context of their understanding of justification by faith that the reformers' doctrine of predestination is to be understood. It is not a general doctrine of fatalism. Its foundation is not in a general view of God's governance of the world but in the doctrine of salvation. As we have seen, the reformers insisted that faith cannot be created, is not a good work, but is a gift of God. Predestination is a powerful reinforcement of this insistence on faith as God's gift. It is a guarantee against the notion that salvation is by works and that faith itself is a good work which brings merit to the believer. So it banishes any notion of justification which leads to pride and reinforces the insistence on humility as the proper attitude of one whom God has justified.

For the reformers, then, predestination was a

liberating doctrine. It had to do with the merciful
and trustworthy character of God. God did not require
the impossible for salvation, namely that one become
actually righteous before he could be justified. Instead, in his mercy he freely grants faith to those
whom he has elected. Since it was not one's own efforts
but God who has brought one to faith, one can trust God
and be confident of his salvation even when the inner,
subjective experience of faith is at a low ebb.[53]

On the issue of whether God has predestined those
who are damned as well as those who are saved, Luther
and Calvin differed. Luther believed that predestination had meaning only for believers, and so he held only
to "single" predestination. That is, he felt that apart
from faith he could not make any judgment concerning
God's activity, and faith knows only of God's gracious
choice. Speculation concerning the reason as to why
there are those who are lost is fruitless, for the
believer knows only that the responsibility for his
election belongs to God. So Luther rejected "double"
predestination, the notion that God has predestined
some to damnation and others to salvation.

In contrast to Luther, Calvin insisted upon double
predestination. He admitted that it was a dreadful
decree,[54] and yet he affirmed that it was true even
though human minds could not comprehend it. So in
Instruction on Faith Calvin said:

> For, the seed of the word of God takes
> root and brings forth fruit only in those
> whom the Lord, by his eternal election,
> has predestined to be children and heirs
> of the heavenly kingdom. To all the
> others (who by the same counsel of God
> are rejected before the foundation of
> the world) the clear and evident preach-
> ing of truth can be nothing but an odor
> of death unto death. Now, why does the
> Lord use his mercy toward some and
> exercise the rigor of his judgment on
> the others? We have to leave the reason
> of this to be known by him alone. For, he,
> with a certainly excellent intention,
> has willed to keep it hidden from us all.[55]

In spite of the fact that Calvin supported double
predestination and tended toward a deterministic view
of God's operation in the world, he was as certain as

Luther about the foundation of predestination in the doctrine of justification by faith. He did not move from a deterministic view of God's operation in the world to faith but from faith to predestination. Double predestination was for him a way of reinforcing the view that God alone is the author of faith and that works and merits are worthless with respect to the issue of salvation. It was for him a last drastic guarantee against the notion that salvation may be earned by works.

5. Faith and works in the life of the Christian

In their views of justification by faith and the nature and function of works in the life of the Christian, the reformers were in fundamental disagreement with Catholic theology. As indicated in Chapter VII, Catholic theologians held that salvation, eternal life, could be gained only through merit acquired by the doing of supernatural good. The process of acquiring merit was possible because God infuses his grace (prevenient and cooperating) into the souls of believers enabling them to do good works. Since this grace or divine power was infused into believers through the sacraments, the church was necessary for salvation. In it are stored merits which, through the sacraments, are available to believers. Through partaking of the sacraments and the doing of good works, believers finally may acquire that righteousness of life which merits salvation. Sanctification precedes justification.

The reformers rejected this view and replaced it with the doctrine of justification by faith alone. Only on the basis of the faith granted to him by God can a person genuinely "know" God. One can be confident that faith is more trustworthy than one's own nature and actions. So Luther declared: "Since faith alone justifies . . ., it ought to be the first concern of every Christian to lay aside all confidence in works and increasingly to strengthen faith alone and through faith to grow in the knowledge, not of works, but of Christ Jesus."[56] Calvin also insisted that justification is by faith alone and claimed: "For justification is withdrawn from works, not that no good works may be done, or that what is done may be denied to be good, but that we may not rely on them, glory in them, or ascribe salvation to them."[57]

Works, then, are not trustworthy with respect to

salvation. Since they are infected with sin, they are
always relative and problematical. Even the works of
the Christian are problematical since there is no work
which is absolutely perfect and free from all stain.[58]
The Christian is both a sinner and a saint; that is,
he is a sinner justified by faith. It is by faith
alone that not only the Christian himself but also his
works are justified.[59] This is why the Christian makes
no claim for his works. He takes no credit for them
but gives the credit to God. He is aware that even the
best of his aspirations and actions can stand only on
the basis of the forgiving grace of God. Indeed, it is
precisely because he has encountered God's grace and
has been justified by faith that the Christian recog-
nizes the relative and problematical nature of his
works and of his continual need for repentance. True
repentance is based on faith and should be an accompanying corollary of faith throughout the life of the Christian.[60]

While Luther and Calvin rejected the notion that
both faith and works are necessary for salvation, they
did believe that works belong to the life of faith.
In their view, justification by faith most certainly
did not mean that the Christian was to be passive,
indifferent, and remiss with respect to morality. Faith
was not a sanction for moral license. The reformers
were not opposed to the Christian doing good works,
but rather encouraged it. Instead they were opposed
to what they regarded to be a false understanding of
the place of works, namely that works are necessary for
salvation.[61] The Christian does good works not to
earn merit for himself but because, having experienced
the grace of God, he desires to do them. The motive
for the doing of good works is not prudential but
gratituous. They are done for the sheer love and joy
of doing them. So Luther insisted that the Christian
"does good works out of spontaneous love in obedience
to God."[62]

For the reformers, the experience of the forgiving,
accepting grace of God was actually the presence of
the living Christ in the hearts of believers, and this
moves them to act on behalf of others. Luther was
rather ecstatic in his account of the transformation
which occurs in the Christian's life when, prompted
by Christ, he gratuitously does even more than the law
requires. In one of the most beautiful passages in
all of his writings, Luther declared:

> Behold, from faith thus flow forth
> love and joy in the Lord, and from love
> a joyful, willing, and free mind that
> serves one's neighbor willingly and takes
> no account of gratitude or ingratitude,
> of praise or blame, of gain or loss. For
> a man does not serve that he may put men
> under obligations. He does not distin-
> guish between friends and enemies or
> anticipate their thankfulness or unthank-
> fulness, but he most freely and most
> willingly spends himself and all that
> he has, whether he wastes all on the thank-
> less or whether he gains a reward. . . As
> our heavenly Father has in Christ freely
> come to our aid, we also ought freely to
> help our neighbor through our body and
> its works and each one should become as
> it were a Christ to the other that we may
> be Christs to one another and Christ may
> be the same in all, that is, that we may
> be truly Christians. . . We conclude,
> therefore, that a Christian lives not in
> himself, but in Christ and in his neighbor.
> Otherwise he is not a Christian. He lives
> in Christ through faith, in his neighbor
> through love.[63]

Luther, of course, was aware that the Christian often
falls short of this qualitative transformation of life.
Whenever faith is weak experientially the law (both
biblical and civil) provides both restraint and some
guidance. Its major function, however, is that of
reminding the Christian that he too is a sinner standing constantly in need of God's forgiveness.

Calvin also placed emphasis on the transforming
power of Christ in the life of the Christian,[64] and
yet he was somewhat more sober in his account of it
than was Luther. Justified by faith, the Christian,
though imperfect, may make at least some small progress
each day along the path to sanctification.[65] More
positive in his view of the "law" than Luther, Calvin
held that the law serves not simply to convict of sin
but also to provide positive guidance to the Christian
in his attempt, with the help of God, to become what
he already is by the grace of God.

For Luther there was no special class of signs
which automatically indicated the directing presence of

Christ in the life of the believer. Since works, even
the works of the law, are always infected with sin and
thus relative and problematical, the Christian is not
bound to express his faith in any particular type of
works. Instead, inspired by the presence of Christ
and given the possibilities of the situation in which
he finds himself, the Christian seeks to act in that
situation in terms of the closest possible approximation to the love of Christ. Works and the results of
works are not to be taken as signs of faith and election. Calvin, however, did believe that works and
their results could be regarded by the believer as a
sign of his faith and of his election by God. Consequently, Calvin declared:

> Those who by faith are righteous prove
> their righteousness by obedience and
> good works, not by a bare and imaginary
> mask of faith. . . When we rule out reli-
> ance upon works, we mean only this: that
> the Christian mind may not be turned back
> to the merit of works as to a help
> toward salvation but should rely wholly
> on the free promise of righteousness.
> But we do not forbid him from undergirding
> and strengthening this faith by signs of
> divine benevolence toward him.[66]

In spite of this difference of emphasis, Luther
and Calvin were agreed that central and necessary to
the Christian life was faith in God's loving acceptance
through Christ. It is faith which liberates the believer from calculation, fear and the pretension of
self, and which frees him, though still a sinner, to
love his neighbor and to act responsibly in the world.

6. The Word of God and the Bible

The reformers were convinced that all theology
must have a starting point in the Word of God. By
"Word of God" they did not mean simply the Bible.
Indeed, they used this expression in three senses.
While sometimes they did use it to designate the Bible,
they used it also to designate the preaching function
of the church based on the Bible. Most often, however,
they used "Word of God" to designate the eternal second
person of the Trinity who was incarnate in Jesus Christ.
This was its primary meaning for them, and the other
two were derivative from and secondary to this primary
one. The Bible, then, is a witness to the Word of God

279

in Jesus Christ. It is a work inspired by God but not
in the sense that God had dictated or whispered its
words directly to the authors. The book and God's revelation are not one and the same thing. The Bible gains
its authority only in light of its central message, the
Word of God in Jesus Christ, and it is to be interpreted
in light of the gospel message concerning the revelation
and salvation of God to which it points. In keeping
with much traditional interpretation, the reformers believed that the Old Testament prefigured Christ, and
thus the Old Testament as well as the New Testament witnesses to the Word of God. As Luther affirmed: "The
Whole of Scripture, if one contemplates it inwardly,
deals everywhere with Christ, even though in so far as
it is a sign and a show, it may outwardly sound differently."[67]

The Word of God, then, can be discovered through
the Bible. The Bible is capable of communicating the
Word of God to believers when they read it under the
inspiration of the Holy Spirit.[68] With the guidance of
the Holy Spirit, each believer can read, interpret, and
understand Scripture for himself. He is not bound to
follow the traditional interpretations of the church or
of ecclesiastical authorities. Yet he must understand
that since the Spirit is the source of Scripture, the
"revelation" of the Spirit in his heart will not teach
anything other than what is witnessed to in Scripture.
The Word lives through the Spirit, but genuine life in
the Spirit will be harmonious always with the content
of Scripture. To insure such harmony, allegorical interpretations generally should be rejected in favor of
the "plain" meaning of Scriptural passages.

The reformers insisted on the authority of Scripture over the church and its traditions. The church
owes its existence to Scripture rather than Scripture
owing its existence to the church. Scripture receives
its authority from God and not from the church. For
Calvin this meant that even the canon had been established by God.[69] Thus, there is a fundamental unity
in the Bible and everything in it is inspired of God
in the sense of witnessing to his Word. Luther, however, admitted that the church had established the
canon.[70] The authority of Scripture resides not in the
canon but in the Word of God witnessed to in Scripture.
It is Christ, the Word of God, who is finally important,
and it was he who had established the church.

It was on the basis of taking the Word of God in

Jesus Christ as the key principle of Scriptural interpretation that Luther felt free to hold critical
opinions concerning the Bible. According to him, the
writings in the Bible are not of uniform value. It
would have been better had the book of Esther been
omitted from the canon. James, Jude, and Revelation
were not written by Apostles and are to be distinguished
from the truly important books of the Bible. James contradicts Paul in ascribing justification to works and in
failing to teach of the crucifixion, resurrection, and
spirit of Christ upon which justification by faith rests.
Thus, on one occasion, Luther confessed to his students
an inclination to remove the letter of James from the
canon.[71] Further, he admitted that the work of redac-
tors (editors) is evident in the writings of the prophets, that the books of Kings are more trustworthy
than Chronicles, that the question of the authorship
of Genesis is a matter of indifference, and that it is
doubtful that Solomon wrote Ecclesiastes.[72] It is
clear, then, that Luther was not a biblicist in the
contemporary sense of that term.

While Calvin was less free than Luther in dealing
with the Bible and insisted on the validity of almost
everything in it, he, too, was not a biblicist. According to Dillenberger and Welch:

> Calvin identified the Bible with the
> word of God only in the sense that faith
> in Christ attested to its authenticity
> . . . He did not move from a conviction
> of verbal inspiration to faith, but from
> faith in Christ, grounded in the Bible,
> to a concept of total inspiration.[73]

In spite of their differences, Luther and Calvin
were convinced that, since the Word of God is discovered through the Bible, the Bible is the final
authority for doctrine and practice. It is the standard in light of which the church always must assess
its message and practice. All purported revelations
of God in other sources must be evaluated in terms of
how well they correspond with the Scriptural witness
to the revelation of God in his Word, Jesus Christ.

7. The priesthood of believers, the church,
    and the sacraments

We have seen that in his spiritual odyssey Luther
came to view all believers as priests. Calvin, too,

281

held to this doctrine of the universal priesthood of believers. In the thought of both, it was derived from, and was an important corollary of, their doctrine of justification by faith. Since the experience of faith granted to the believer by God is the presence of the living Christ (or Holy Spirit) within his heart, the believer can have direct access to God and be taught by the Spirit. In this sense, the believer is not subject to anyone. This does not mean that the believer lives a solitary life, for God through Christ moves him to act on behalf of others. Every Christian is a priest to others, "for as priests we are worthy to appear before God to pray for others and to teach one another divine things."[74]

Thus Luther and Calvin did not hold to an individualistic view of the Christian life, but insisted upon the corporate nature of Christianity. One who is genuinely a Christian accepts the honor and responsibility of "priesthood" which entails his participation in the community of believers, the church. The reformers rejected the Catholic hierarchical structure of the church and the Catholic view that the church is a storehouse of merit. They viewed the church as a fellowship of believers, a community of forgiven sinners instead of a community of sinless saints. The church was not founded on any human authority but on the Word of God disclosed in Scripture. Only in a community where the Word of God is rightly preached and the two sacraments of baptism and the Lord's Supper rightly administered is there a true church.[75]

For the reformers the universal priesthood of believers did not mean that all believers should seek to be ministers. As Luther said: "Although we are equally priests, we cannot all publically minister and teach. We ought not to do so even if we could."[76] The preaching of the gospel is an awesome responsibility which requires that one be called by God and chosen by the Christian community for this task. Yet the status of the minister is not superior to that of the laity. Since all believers are priests, no one in the church possesses superior status to anyone else. Whatever differences there are among believers are simply functional and vocational. The status of the layman who, under God, demonstrates Christian responsibility in any decent and useful calling is not one bit inferior to that of the minister. In the fellowship of believers clergy and laity perform roles of equal distinction for the mutual strengthening of faith and Christian living and for the spread of the gospel.[77]

We have seen that for the reformers the Word of God disclosed in Christ is witnessed to in Scripture and in the preaching of the church. The sacraments also are witnesses to God's Word, signs of his promises. As the true signs of God's grace, they are another form in which the Word is heard in faith. Only those acts instituted by Christ and connected with the promises of the gospel witnessed to in Scripture qualify as sacraments. Thus there are only two sacraments, baptism and the Lord's Supper. Their purpose is twofold, namely to serve and to fortify the faith of the partaker and to provide a means of confessing the faith before others.

Baptism is a true sign or symbol of justification, of the remission of sin, of the "death and resurrection" of the believer with Christ, and of union with him. It is not only the beginning of the Christian life, but also the sign under which the Christian should live his entire life. It does not infuse grace into the soul nor is it merely a symbol of the decision for faith. Instead, it is a true and efficacious sign in which the Word of God is present serving the faith of the participant. In light of the conviction that God's gift of his Word is present in the sacrament, and in light of the faith of the congregation, the initiation of children into the Christian fold through baptism is advocated by both Luther and Calvin.[78]

Both reformers viewed the sacraments as the true signs of God's grace and thus as another form in which the Word of God is heard in faith, but they differed in their understandings of how Christ was present in the sacrament of the eucharist or Lord's Supper. We have seen above that Luther rejected the practice of withholding the cup from the laity, the view of the mass as a good work, and the doctrine of transubstantiation. While he denied that the substances of the elements, the bread and wine, change into the body and blood substances of Christ, he affirmed that the body and blood substances were present with and in the bread and wine. That is, he held to what has been called consubstantiation. For this to be possible, Luther thought, the risen body of Christ is not confined to heaven like a bird in a cage. True, it is at the "right hand of God" but, since the right hand of God is everywhere, Christ's risen body is ubiquitous. Calvin, however, took the ascension of Christ quite literally and denied that his

risen body is ubiquitous. It is in heaven and not
locally present. It does not descend to the believer
in the sacrament. Yet in some mysterious way too great
for the human mind to understand, the Spirit raises the
believer to the body of Christ so that in the eucharist
he is joined to that body and receives its benefits.
In this sense, then, Christ's body as well as his
spiritual presence is available by means of the sacrament.[79]

Obviously, the difference between Luther and Calvin concerning the sacrament was relatively small.
It was another Swiss reformer, Ulrich Zwingli (1484-
1531), who held a view of the eucharist radically different from that of Luther and in important respects
different also from that of Calvin. Zwingli claimed
that the words attributed to Jesus in the New Testament
accounts of the Last Supper, "This is my body," mean
"this signifies my body." Thus he denied that Christ's
corporeal presence in any sense is present in the celebration of the Lord's Supper. Furthermore, he placed
emphasis on Jesus' command quoted in the Apostle Paul's
version of the Last Supper (1 Cor. 11:20), "Do this
in rememberance of me." These words, he thought, meant
that the eucharist is of the nature of a memorial ceremony. Yet it involves more than simply a bare memory
of Jesus Christ. According to Dillenberger and Welch:

> He meant that through this act, instituted
> in the New Testament, the believer is
> graphically reminded of and participates
> in the total drama of God's redeeming
> activity in Jesus Christ. One is nourished
> in faith as he engages in an act which
> vividly recalls the total meaning of the
> life, death and resurrection of Christ.
> This act is a visible sign in which is
> telescoped the total gospel in a way words
> could not convey. The remembrance is a
> dramatic presentation of the whole of
> that which is at the basis of faith.[80]

While Zwingli's view was to gain acceptance by
many groups in the subsequent history of Protestantism,
the views of Luther and Calvin also remained within
the Protestant fold. Undoubtedly, the reason for this
is that all three views insist on associating the Lord's
Supper with God's gracious activity in the forgiveness
of sin, a central motif of Protestant thought.

284

8. The Christian and the state

For the reformers the Christian finds his life in the two realms of the spiritual and the temporal or the religious and the civil. Both realms are orders of creation. The civil order was established by God to restrain the wicked. It is a gift of God providing for order and relative peace in the common life. Therefore, the Christian is not to despise the state nor to interfere with its legitimate functions. He is to honor and obey it. This entails obedience to the authorities or rulers of the state who are under divine obligation to govern wisely and justly or otherwise they will pay the penalty before God.

Even though the reformers viewed the state as ordained of God, they were very realistic in their appraisal of actual governments. On the basis of their view of man's sin, they were aware that governments are easily corrupted. Rulers, even Christian rulers, often stray from the right path either in weakness or in the prideful struggle to gain, maintain, and exercise power. They often become tyrants and inflict their subjects with injustices.

Luther held that, since rulers have their authority from God, even evil rulers must be obeyed. Man's obedience to God is more ultimate, of course, than his duty to the government. However, this means only that the Christian, like the prophets of old, should confront evil rulers with the proclamation of God's judgment. That is, evil rulers should be called to account by the Word of God. As private citizens, Christians are not justified in actively resisting or rebelling against even an evil government. They must suffer its injustices and not rebel against it.

Calvin, too, maintained that magistrates have their authority from God and should be obeyed. Yet he permitted two very significant exceptions to this general rule. First, since Christians' first loyalty is to God rather than man, Calvin, unlike Luther, believed that they should refuse to regard magistrates who violated God's commands revealed in Scripture as duly constituted authorities. Secondly, even though he denied the right of private Christians to resist the authority of their rulers, Calvin affirmed that lower magistrates have the duty of resisting unjust magistrates of higher rank and of restoring justice and order to the state. These two exceptions may be understood differently under different conditions, and thus, in spite of Calvin's own rather conservative attitude, they provided a basis for later Calvinists to participate in those revolutionary movements which brought modern democracies into existence. Also, Calvin's recommendation concerning the distribution of power in the state because magistrates, as everyone else, are infected with sin and must be restrained from abusing power probably had some influence on modern political perspectives in Western society. In a statement which may not be entirely unrelated to the American Constitution, Calvin said:

> Therefore, men's fault or failing causes it to be safer and more bearable for a number to exercise government, so that they may help one another, teach and admonish one another; and, if one asserts himself unfairly, there may be a number of censors and masters to restrain his willfulness.[81]

9. Eschatology and resurrection

As was the case in Scripture and most Christian thought, so also the reformers incorporated the "Janus" principle in their theologies. That is, they looked backward to God's revelation in Christ as the source of faith and the Christian life and precisely because of this faith looked forward to the future in the conviction that God eventually would consummate his kingdom. They viewed the Christian life as a pilgrimage which would find its ultimate fulfillment in the kingdom of God. Luther thought that the turmoils of his own times was an indication that the world would not survive for more than a hundred years, and thus the advent of God's kingdom in consummation was close at hand. Calvin spoke of the manifestation of the Christian life in the church as the beginning of the kingdom of God. Its consummation would occur in heaven. Both Luther and Calvin held to the notion of the resurrection life. The total person (body and soul) is raised from the dead. The elect enjoy the blessings of heaven and the damned suffer the torments of hell.[82]

While the reformers believed that the doctrine of the resurrection life was an essential part of the Christian faith, neither one was obsessed by it. In this life the Christian should center his attention on God's word, on faith, and living the Christian life.

286

He should not engage in too much speculation about the future life nor constantly and selfishly be concerned about getting himself into heaven. In a reply to a letter from Cardinal Sadolet, Calvin chided the Cardinal for having engaged in too lengthy a speculation about eternal life. Eternal life is a theme worthy of meditation, Calvin affirmed, but this theme may be abused in self serving ways. Thus Calvin said:

> It is not very sound theology to confine a man's thoughts so much to himself, and not to set before him as the prime motive of his existence zeal to show forth the glory of God. For we are born first of all for God, and not for ourselves. . . It certainly is the duty of a Christian man to ascend higher than merely to seek and secure the salvation of his own soul. I therefore believe that there is no man imbued with true piety, who will not regard as in poor taste that long and detailed exhortation to a zeal for heavenly life, which occupies a man entirely concerned with himself, and does not, even by one expression, arouse him to sanctify the name of God.[83]

For the reformers then, the Christian, in response to the gift of God's acceptance and love, will be assured of his eternal destiny in God's heavenly kingdom, but he will center his attention and efforts in this life on glorifying God through the loving service to others. As Calvin said: "Everything undertaken apart from love and all disputes that go beyond it, we regard as incontrovertibly unjust and impious."[84]

The theologies of Luther and Calvin which have been summarized above were influential to a greater or lesser extent in the several Protestant churches which emerged after the Reformation. Obviously, their influence was greatest in those churches which regarded either Luther or Calvin as the "founding father," namely the Lutheran Church and the Reformed and Presbyterian Churches. Other Protestant churches rejected some elements of the reformers' theologies, and modified other elements. For example, Anglicans (Episcopalians) sought to retain more of catholicity, church tradition, and natural theology than did the reformers. Baptists rejected infant baptism, insisting that only those who already have experienced faith may be baptized. They held to only a mild form of election (once saved always saved), and, along with the Congregationalists, advocated local autonomy and congregational authority in the governance of churches. Methodists rejected the doctrine of predestination, and John Wesley, at least, seemed to have suggested the possibility of ultimately attaining full devotion to Christ or Christian perfection in the Christian life. Yet, in spite of the fact that some elements of the reformers' theologies dropped out of sight, other elements in varying forms and emphases were retained. Among these elements were the reformers' doctrines concerning man as a sinner, the work of Christ, faith as trust in God's gracious activity of redemption, the Christian as a forgiven sinner who seeks with the help of God to grow in righteousness of life, the Word of God contained in Scripture as the ultimate authority for the church's message and life, the universal "priesthood" of believers, the church as a community of believers, and the assurance of eternal life. These elements have been and are the most fundamental aspects of the way in which most Protestants view the Christian movement.

[1] Quoted from T. A. Burkill, The Evolution of Christian Thought (Cornell University Press, 1971), p. 195. Also see Williston Walker, A History of the Christian Church, Third Edition (Charles Scribner's Sons, 1970), pp. 251-252; Armand A. Maurer, Medieval Philosophy (Random House, 1962), pp. 284-285; Justo L. Gonzalez, A History of Christian Thought, Vol. III (Abingdon Press, 1975), pp. 16-18.

[2] See Burkill, op. cit., pp. 80, 228.

[3] The discussion in this introduction to Part IV is supported in general by Justo L. Gonzalez, op. cit., pp. 11-24, and also by John Dillenberger and Claude Welch, Protestant Christianity (Charles Scribner's Sons, 1954), pp. 1-16.

[4] See Hugh Thompson Kerr, Jr. (ed.), A Compend of Luther's Theology (Westminster Press, 1943), Foreword, pp. V-XVI and Walker, op. cit., p. 353.

[5] Roland Bainton, Christendom, Vol. II (Harper Colophon Books, 1966), p. 9.

[6] Ibid., p. 10.

[7] Roland Bainton, Here I Stand (Abingdon Cokesbury, 1959), p. 51.

[8] Quoted from Bainton, ibid., p. 65. The primary source can be found in the "Preface to the Latin Writings," Luther's Works (Concordia and Fortress Press, 1955-1968), V. 34, pp. 336-337, and Martin Luther's 95 Theses, Kurt Aland (ed.) (Concordia Publishing House, 1967), pp. 31-32.

[9] Luther: Early Theological Works, James Atkinson (ed.), Library of Christian Classics, Vol. XVI (Westminster, 1962), pp. 251-273.

[10] Ibid., p. 264.

[11] Quoted from Bainton, op. cit., p. 78.

[12] See Kurt Aland (ed.), Martin Luther's 95 Theses, op. cit., pp. 50-58, for a copy of all the theses.

[13] See _Three Treatises_, Martin Luther (Fortress Press, 1960), pp. 3-111, or _Luther's Works_ (Concordia and Fortress Press, 1955-1968), V. 44, pp. 123-217.

[14] See _Three Treatises_, pp. 115-260.

[15] _Ibid._, pp. 137-138, 155, 161-163.

[16] See _Three Treatises_, pp. 262-316 or _Luther's Works_, V. 31, pp. 329-377.

[17] _Three Treatises_, p. 277.

[18] See Fred Berthold, Jr., _et al._, _Basic Sources of the Judeo-Christian Tradition_ (Prentice-Hall, 1962), p. 252.

[19] See John T. McNeill (ed.), _Calvin: Institutes of the Christian Religion_, V. 20, _Library of Christian Classics_ (Westminster, 1960), pp. XXXI, XXXIII.

[20] For brief summaries of Calvin's biography see Walker, _op. cit._, pp. 348-357 and Clyde L. Manschreck, _A History of Christianity in the World_ (Prentice-Hall, 1974), pp. 216-221.

[21] Of the many excellent summaries of the two reformers' perspectives I found that Gonzalez, _op. cit._, pp. 25-62, 120-161, Dillenberger and Welch, _op. cit._, pp. 15-57 were especially helpful to me in the task of formulating this summary.

[22] _Institutes_, I. I. I, _op. cit._, p. 35.

[23] _Ibid._, I. I. 2, p. 38.

[24] See Hugh Thompson Kerr, Jr. (ed.), _A Compend of Luther's Theology_ (Westminster, 1943), p. 32.

[25] _Lectures on Galatians, Luther's Works, op. cit._, V. 26, pp. 399-400. Also see Calvin's _Institutes_ III. II, 15, _op. cit._, pp. 559-560.

[26] Kerr, _op. cit._, p. 26.

[27] Theodore G. T. Appert (ed.), _Luther: Letters of Spiritual Counsel_, V. XVIII, _The Library of Christian Classics_ (Westminster, 1955), p. 69.

[28] _Heidelberg Disputation_, Thesis 21, _Luther's Works_, V. 21, _op. cit._, p. 53.

[29] _Institutes_, I. III. I, _op. cit._, p. 43.

[30] Ibid., II. II. 15, pp. 273-274.

[31] Ibid., I. XIII. 7, 21, pp. 129-130, 145-146.

[32] Ibid., III. II. 14, pp. 559-560.

[33] William Pauck (ed.), Luther: Lectures on Romans, V. XV, The Library of Christian Classics (Westminster, 1961), p. 182. See also p. 238.

[34] Three Treatises, op. cit., p. 281.

[35] Institutes, I. XV. 4, op. cit., p. 189.

[36] Ibid., I. II. 2, p. 38.

[37] See Kerr, op. cit., pp. 81-82; Pauck, op. cit., pp. 165-166, 173; Institutes, I. XV, 4-8, op. cit., pp. 189-196.

[38] Institutes, III. II. 10, op. cit., p. 554.

[39] Berthold, et al., op. cit., p. 268. See also Calvin's Instruction in Faith, Berthold, ibid., p. 279.

[40] Ibid., p. 279.

[41] Pauck, op. cit., pp. 106 ff., 148, 171. Institutes II. VII. 6-9, op. cit., pp. 351-358.

[42] Institutes, I. XII. 1-29; II. XIV. 1-8, op. cit., pp. 120-159, 482-493.

[43] Treatise on Christian Liberty, Three Treatises, op. cit., pp. 286-287.

[44] See Institutes, II. XVII. 5-6; III. IV. 26-30, op. cit., pp. 532-533, 652-658.

[45] Ibid., II. XV. 1-6, pp. 494-503.

[46] See "Sermon on the Afternoon of Christmas Day" (1530), Luther's Works, op. cit., V. 51, especially pp. 211-218.

[47] E. Gordon Rupp (ed.), Luther and Erasmus: Free Will and Salvation, V. XVII, Library of Christian Classics (Westminster, 1969), Part III, pp. 293-294.

[48] Kerr, op. cit., p. 101.

[49] Institutes, II. XI. 2, op. cit., pp. 726-727. See also III. XI. 1, 3-7, pp. 725-726, 727-734; Luther, The Disputation Concerning Justification, V. 34, Luther's Works, op. cit., pp. 151-196; Lectures on Galatians, V. 26, Luther's Works, op. cit., pp. 4-11, 122-141; Lectures on Romans, V. XV, Library of Christian Classics.

[50] Institutes, III. II. 2, ibid., p. 545.

[51] Instruction In Faith, Berthold, et al., op. cit., p. 281.

[52] Preface to the Epistle to the Romans, ibid., p. 267.

[53] For the reformers' views on predestination see: Calvin, Institutes, III. XXI - XXIV, V. XXI, The Library of Christian Classics, op. cit., pp. 920-987; Luther, Lectures on Romans, op. cit., pp. 246-277; Letters of Spiritual Counsel, V. XVII, The Library of Christian Classics (Westminster, 1955), pp. 115-117; Lectures on Galatians, op. cit., pp. 69-71.

[54] Institutes, III. XXIII. 7, ibid., p. 955.

[55] Berthold, et al., op. cit., p. 281.

[56] Treatise on Christian Liberty, op. cit., p. 281.

[57] Institutes, III. XVII. 1, op. cit., p. 803. Italics are mine.

[58] See Calvin, Instruction In Faith, Berthold, op. cit., p. 283.

[59] See Calvin, Institutes, III. XVII. 9, op. cit., p. 813.

[60] Ibid., III. III. 2, p. 594.

[61] Luther, Treatise on Christian Liberty, op. cit., p. 311.

[62] Ibid., p. 295. Italics are mine.

[63] Ibid., pp. 304-305, 309.

[64] See J. K. S. Reid (ed.), Calvin: Theological Treatises, V. XXII, The Library of Christian Classics (Westminster, 1954), pp. 106-107.

[65] Institutes, III. VI. 5, op. cit., p. 689.

[66] Ibid., III. XVII. 12, p. 816 and III. XIV. 18, p. 785.

[67] Lectures on Romans, op. cit., p. 288.

[68] Luther, The Bondage of the Will, V. 33, Luther's Works, op. cit., p. 28; Calvin, Institutes, I. IX. 3, op. cit., p. 95.

[69] Institutes, I. VI. 1, IV, IX. 14, ibid., pp. 74-75, 1177-1178.

[70] See Gonzalez, op. cit., pp. 42-43.

[71] Ibid., pp. 43-44.

[72] See Reinhold Seeberg, Textbook of the History of Doctrines, V. II (Baker Book House, 1954), pp. 300-301.

[73] Dillenberger and Welch, op. cit., pp. 47-48.

[74] Luther, Treatise on Christian Liberty, op. cit., p. 290. Also see Calvin's Institutes, II. XV. 6, IV. XIX. 28, op. cit., pp. 501-502, 1476.

[75] See Luther, Explanations of the Ninety-Five Theses, V. 31, Luther's Works, op. cit., pp. 215-216, The Babylonian Captivity of the Church, Three Treatises, op. cit., pp. 243-245; Calvin's Institutes IV. I. 1-4, 16-17, 20-21, 23-29, op. cit., pp. 1011-1016, 1030-1032, 1033-1041.

[76] Treatise on Christian Liberty, op. cit., p. 292.

[77] See Luther, Babylonian Captivity of the Church, ibid., pp. 244-245.

[78] See A Compend of Luther's Theology, op. cit., pp. 163-170 and Calvin's Institutes IV. XIV - XVI, op. cit., pp. 1276-1359.

[79] See A Compend of Luther's Theology, ibid., pp. 170-176, Babylonian Captivity of the Church, op. cit., pp. 145-178; Calvin's Institutes IV. XVII, ibid., pp. 1359-1428.

[80] Dillenberger and Welch, op. cit., p. 52.

[81] Institutes IV. XX. 8, op. cit., pp. 1493-1494. Some sources for the reformers' views of the Christian and the state are: A Compend of Luther's Theology, op. cit., pp. 213-232; Calvin's Institutes IV. XX, op. cit., pp. 1485-1521; Dillenberger and Welch, op. cit., pp. 53-56; Gonzalez, op. cit., pp. 60-62, 157-158.

[82] Some sources for the reformers' views of eschatology and resurrection are: A Compend cf Luther's Theology, op. cit., pp.

235-249; Calvin's Institutes, III. XXV, op. cit., pp. 987-1008.

[83] "Reply to Sadolet," Calvin: Theological Treatises, op. cit., p. 228.

[84] Institutes, IV. XX. 21, op. cit., p. 1509.

SUGGESTIONS FOR FURTHER READING

Aland, Kurt, Martin Luther's 95 Theses, Concordia Publishing
House, 1967.

Ayers, Robert H., "Language, Logic and Reason in Calvin's Institutes," Religious Studies, Vol. 16, No. 3, September, 1980.

Bainton, Roland H., Christendom, Vol. II, Harper Torchbook, 1966.

Bainton, Roland H., Here I Stand, Abingdon, 1950.

Bainton, Roland H., Women of the Reformation, Augsburg Publishing
House, 1977.

Berthold, Fred, Jr., et al., Basic Sources of the Judeo-Christian
Tradition, Prentice-Hall, 1962, pp. 238-319.

Burkill, T. A., The Evolution of Christian Thought, Cornell University Press, 1971, Part V.

Dillenberger, John and Claude Welch, Protestant Christianity,
Charles Scribner's Sons, 1954.

Forell, John W., The Protestant Faith, Prentice-Hall, 1960.

Gonzalez, Justo L., A History of Christian Thought, Vol. III,
Abingdon, 1975.

Kerr, Hugh T., Jr. (ed.), A Compend of the Institutes of the
Christian Religion by John Calvin, Westminster, 1939.

Kerr, Hugh T., Jr. (ed.), A Compend of Luther's Theology, Westminster, 1943.

Leith, John H., Creeds of the Churches, Aldine Publishing Company,
1963, pp. 61-399.

Lohse, Bernard, A Short History of Christian Doctrine, Fortress
Press, 1966, Chapters 6 and 8.

Manschreck, Clyde L., A History of Christianity in the World,
Prentice-Hall, 1974, Chapters 12-17.

McGiffert, A. C., Protestant Thought Before Kant, Charles Scribner's
Sons, 1917.

Pelikan, Jaroslav and Helmut T. Lehmann (eds.), <u>Luther's Works</u>, Concordia and Fortress Press, 1955-1968.

Seeberg, Reinhold, <u>Textbook of the History of Doctrines</u>, Vol. II, Baker Book House, 1954.

<u>The Library of Christian Classics</u>, Vols. XV, XVI, XVIII, XX, XXI, XXII, Westminster, 1954-1962.

<u>Three Treatises, Martin Luther</u>, Fortress Press, 1960.

Walker, Williston, <u>A History of the Christian Church</u>, Third Edition, Charles Scribner's Sons, 1970, Part Six.

PART V

THE MODERN PERIOD

The predominant world-view in Western culture during the medieval period and for about the first century
of the Protestant era may be characterized in a general
way as rather static and stable. It provided its adherents with a secure "world." In spite of differences
between Jews, Protestants, and Catholics, there was no
question of God's existence, of his creation of the
world, and of his final authority over it. Events in
the world were thought to have their ultimate source in
final causality. That is, they were caused in terms of
God's ends or goals. God was, so to speak, at the apex
of the vault of heaven guaranteeing the security of the
whole. Through the religious institution and/or the
Scripture, God's plan for human life had been made known
such that there was no quandary concerning its origin,
nature, purpose, and destiny. The major institutions
of church, home, school, and government were viewed as
the supporting elements in this static and stable
"world." In spite of differences between Jews, Catholics, and Protestants as to the precise nature and
function of these institutions, they were regarded as
instituted by God and a means through which he accom-
plishes his purposes in the world. Their true natures
are actualized only when they are directed according
to his purposes.

The modern period, the beginnings of which are
difficult to determine but which certainly had begun by
the latter part of the seventeenth century, brought a
serious challenge to this dominant world-view. Indeed,
in this period the religious institutions and concepts
of the West have had for their environment the most
dynamic and changing civilization in history. Traditional perspectives often not only have been questioned
but also some or all of them openly rejected. In
response to this, numerous developments of interest
have occurred within Judaism, Catholicism, and Protestantism. It is impossible to consider all of these
developments, but instead attention will be centered
on major trends.[1] First, in this introduction to
Part V, two basic components of the modern challenge
to the traditional perspectives of the Judeo-Christian
tradition will be described. Then, the three chapters

297

which follow will deal with major trends which have emerged within Judaism, Catholicism, and Protestantism as they sought to respond to the challenge.

One of the most potent movements which effected a change in the traditional world-view and presented a challenge to the religious concepts and institutions of the West was the scientific movement. In the physical sciences, for example, final causality was replaced with efficient causality, the view of nature as God's handiwork was replaced with a view of nature as operating in terms of natural regularities which may be discovered by observations of the sequences of causes and effects, and the geocentric view of the solar system was replaced with the heliocentric view. For some, these and other results of the physical sciences meant that there was no longer a need for the "God-hypothesis" to account for the operations, sequences, and order of the natural world. Isaac Newton (1642-1727) had held that there was a need for intervention by God from time to time in order to adjust the irregularities of motion which occurred in the solar system over a long period of time. However, Pierre Laplace (1749-1827), a French mathematician and astronomer, demonstrated that the "irregularities" were based in part on faulty observations, and that whatever irregularities existed would cancel each other out eventually so that the whole system was self correcting. There is a story that Napoleon on meeting Laplace remarked, "You have written this huge book on the system of the world without once mentioning the author of the universe," and that Laplace replied, "Sire, I have no need of that hypothesis."[2]

Not only in the physical sciences but also in the biological and psychological sciences efficient causality is a basic methodological principle. In addition, biology gave rise to another basic principle of scientific explanation, namely that all nature is in a state of flux. It is characterized throughout by change and evolutionary process. This includes, of course, all forms of life, plant, animal, and human. In the biological and psychological sciences human life is investigated in terms of its organic and psychological interdependence with its natural and social environment. Thus in the psychological sciences there has been a tendency to view religion as simply the end product of certain psychological processes rather than of rational thought and of revelation. Some psychologists have viewed the concept of God as originating in the human desire for security and belonging in face of the threatening aspects of nature. God, then, is a projection of human desires rather than an objective reality.

Similarly, in the historical and social sciences efficient causality and evolutionary process have been accepted as basic methodological principles, and thus there has been a tendency to explain religion in naturalistic terms. The origins of religions and the differences between them are explainable in terms of people's particular geographical conditions, evolving histories, and intercultural involvements.

These and other developments in the physical, biological, psychological, and social sciences led some to believe that religion was but a fossilized remainder of ancient times obstructing man's progress into a brave new world. The lot of mankind would be improved when the dead hand of religion was eliminated from human life. At the opposite extreme were those who viewed the scientific movement as though it were the work of the devil, seeking to destroy their most cherished convictions concerning the significance and meaning of the world, human existence, and ultimate destiny of the human soul. From time to time throughout the modern period extremists on both sides have engaged in what often has been called "the warfare between science and religion."[3]

In addition to the scientific movement, another basic factor which brought about a transformation in the dominant perspectives and atmosphere of Western culture was the emergence of what might be called the bourgeois or middle class spirit. In large part the result of science, technology, and industrialization, the bourgeois spirit is characterized by different assumptions and attitudes from those held in the medieval period. It may be that most individuals generally are not aware consciously of being imbued with these assumptions and attitudes and of reacting to the issues of life in terms of them. Yet a critical analysis would seem to indicate that the bourgeois spirit generally tends to be secular, anti-authoritarian, individualistic, tolerant or indifferent with respect to theological issues, devoted to technology, optimistic, and urban oriented. That is, the bourgeois spirit tends to center attention on the tangible and human affairs of this world, to magnify the individual's authority in religious matters such that he does not

feel bound to external authorities, to support tolerance or indifference with respect to theological
issues, to have a high regard for technology as the
means of solving problems, to be optimistic in the
sense of holding utopian views concerning history, and
to be pervaded with urban values and attitudes rather
than rural.

Given the scientific movement and the bourgeois
spirit, modern Western man obviously lives in a "world"
quite different from that of his medieval ancestors.
In light of this fact, an important issue for thought-
ful Jews and Christians became that of how to maintain
their faiths and yet at the same time to relate them
meaningfully to universal truths and contemporary
culture. We have seen in Part III that the early Christians confronted the problem of communicating the faith
in ways which could be understood by persons of a different culture while at the same time preserving the
essential and distinctive characteristics of the faith.
Similarly, modern Jews and Christians encountered the
problem of how to communicate their faiths in concepts
which are meaningful in the "world" of modern man without eliminating essential perspectives of these faiths.
In general, three major responses to this challenge
emerged. There were some who attempted to hold on to
traditional concepts and formulations in spite of the
challenge. They took what might be called a "right-
wing" approach. That is, they tended to ignore or
reject any scientific discoveries or modern perspectives
which they thought to be inconsistent with traditional
formulations. Others sought to harmonize their faiths
with modern culture. They took what might be called
a "left-wing" approach. That is, while not abandoning
Judaism or Christianity, they greatly modified and/or
abandoned traditional formulations of these faiths.
Still others took a more moderate approach. They did
not ignore or reject scientific discoveries or modern
perspectives as did the "right wingers" nor give up
as much as did the "left wingers." Instead they sought
to retain essential historical perspectives of these
faiths while modifying to some extent traditional
formulations. At the risk of some oversimplification,
the diagram on the following page is an attempt to
depict in a very general way these three major responses
in modern Judaism, Catholicism, and Protestantism.

300

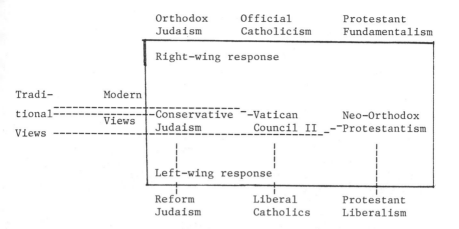

	Orthodox Judaism	Official Catholicism	Protestant Fundamentalism
	Right-wing response		
Tradi- Modern	Conservative -Vatican	Neo-Orthodox	
tional---- Views	Judaism Council II _--Protestantism		
Views ----			
	Left-wing response		
	Reform Judaism	Liberal Catholics	Protestant Liberalism

Perhaps one feature of this diagram requires further explanation, namely, the broken lines. They are used in an attempt to indicate that the groups in the center of the diagram have been influenced by the left-wing groups but have sought to recover more of the traditional views than those of the left wing. In some cases, adherents of the groups in the center came out of left-wing groups. They continued to accept some aspects of left-wing thought but reacted against other aspects of this thought which they regarded as destructive of essential and distinctive elements in the Jewish or Christian faiths.

The discussion in the following chapters on Judaism, Catholicism, and Protestantism will be structured largely in terms of the three major responses to the challenge of modern culture.

[1] Some studies which deal with the modern challenge and/or the responses to it are: Roland Bainton, Christendom, V. II (Harper Colophon Books, 1966), Chapters XI-XIII; George C. Bedell, et al., Religion in America (Macmillan Publishing Co., Inc., 1975); Roger A. Johnson, et al., Critical Issues in Modern Religion (Prentice-Hall, 1973); Will Herberg, Judaism and Modern Man (Farrar Straus and Young, 1951); James C. Livingston, Modern Christian Thought (The Macmillan Company, 1971); W. T. Stace, Religion and The Modern Mind (I. B. Lippincott Company, 1952); J. Paul Williams, What Americans Believe and How They Worship (Harper and Brothers, 1952).

[2] Roger A. Johnson, et al., op. cit., pp. 36-37.

[3] Some good studies concerning the relation of science and religion are: Ian G. Barbour, Issues in Science and Religion (Prentice-Hall, 1966); Robert A. Johnson, et al., op. cit.; Harold K. Schilling, Science and Religion (Charles Scribner's Sons, 1962).

CHAPTER IX

JUDAISM IN THE MODERN WORLD

Chapter V of our study contained a discussion of the emergence and perspectives of Rabbinic Judaism. In that discussion we indicated that, according to Alexander Guttmann, Rabbinic Judaism became and remains "the mainstream of Judaism from antiquity to date."[1] Certainly it is the case that ancient Rabbinic perspectives and exegetical methods have had a great influence in Judaism throughout the ages. Yet there did emerge other influences, philosophical and/or mystical, which to a greater or lesser extent have been correlated with the ancient Rabbinic views. With some modifications, Rabbinic Judaism continues to live in modern Orthodox Judaism and to a lesser extent in Conservative Judaism. It is least influential in Reform Judaism.

Before turning to a consideration of the perspectives in modern Orthodox, Conservative, and Reform Judaism, we will discuss briefly one extraordinary Jewish medieval thinker and the Jewish mystical movement which emerged in medieval times.[2] Both are of importance as a background in light of which certain perspectives in modern Orthodox and Conservative Judaism may be more fully understood.

The thinker was Moses ben Maimon, better known as Moses Maimonides or simply Maimonides (1135-1204). He was born in Cordova, Spain, a great center of Jewish learning and general Islamic culture. In this environment the Maimonidean family for several generations had produced distinguished scholars, rabbis, and judges. Moses' father was a prominent judge and distinguished scholar. In Maimonides' early youth Spain was invaded by a group of fanatical Moslems, and the Maimonidean family was forced to leave the ancestral home. After many years of wandering in southern Spain, northern Africa, and Palestine, Maimonides settled in Cairo, Egypt, where he spent the rest of his life. In spite of the years of wandering, he managed to become an erudite scholar in philosophy and in the whole corpus of Talmudic and cognate literature. As had been the case with the ancient rabbis for whom it was a duty to combine Torah study with a worldly occupation and active concern for the community (see Chapter V above),

Maimonides was not content to be simply an "arm chair" scholar. He earned his livelihood by practicing medicine and was appointed one of the court physicians to the Moslem ruler of Egypt. Also he became the leader of the Jewish community in Cairo, combining the duties of rabbi, judge, and administrative supervisor. Yet he continued his studies and produced copious writings on Rabbinic literature and philosophy. His reputation spread abroad among the Jews in many lands who came to regard him as the authority on Rabbinic law. In his own lifetime it was said of him, "From Moses to Moses [Maimonides] there has arisen none like unto him."[3] The contemporary scholar, Jacob Neusner, claims that Maimonides "stands at the pinnacle of Jewish theology," and describes him as "a truly protean figure, and the quintessential rabbinic Jew."[4] It is not surprising then that Maimonides continues to have an influence in modern Judaism.

What the later Thomas Aquinas was to do for Christian thought (see Chapter VII above), Maimonides had done already in the twelfth century for Jewish thought, namely correlate Aristotelian philosophy with theology. Like Aquinas, he recognized that Aristotle's philosophy presented such a rationally defensible and total understanding of reality that it must be reckoned with by the theologian. So he sought to reconcile philosophy as taught by Aristotle and religion as taught in the Torah and Torah Tradition. Since the Torah was a revelation from God, it is necessarily true. Apart from some details such as the eternality of matter and an impersonal God (the unmoved mover) which, in Maimonides' view, were not demonstrable, Aristotelian philosophy is proved by reason and also must be true. But, since truth cannot contradict truth, philosophy and religion must agree. The challenge of a rationally "purified" Aristotelianism required a philosophical purifying of Judaism in which the rational status of the religious beliefs and legislation of the Torah and Torah Tradition is clarified. While Maimonides' lifelong purpose of reconciling philosophy and religion is evident in his massive studies of Talmudic and cognate literature, it dominates his philosophical work entitled The Guide of the Perplexed.[5]

Using Aristotle's metaphysics and his semantical and logical analyses,[6] Maimonides presents in The Guide of the Perplexed a complete system of thought which takes into account all aspects of reality. This includes arguments for the existence of God, such as the

argument from efficient causes to first uncaused cause
and the argument that the existence of contingent things
requires a source in that which necessarily exists.
Such arguments entail the traditional attributes of God
and his unity and incorporeality. Thus anthropomor-
phisms in Scripture are not to be taken literally but
are figures of speech designating the effects of God
in the universe, his merciful dealings with his creatures. While admitting that miracles are logically
possible, Maimonides tends to explain the miracle stories in Scripture as either poetical descriptions of
natural events or allegorical prophetic visions. While
Scripture is the source of God's revelation, it presents
this revelation in varying forms in order to meet the
intellectual capabilities and needs of both the common
man and the sage. Sometimes the revelation is presented by means of metaphors and symbols which the common man comprehends. So Maimonides seems to suggest,
for example, that the sacrificial system was a divine
concession to the mentality of ancient times, a means
of educating the unlearned in the worship of the one
true God. The sage seeks to understand, and to assist
the common man to understand, the rational truths indicated by the signs, symbols, and metaphors. In addition, Scripture presents divine revelation in terms of
the truths of the divine law. It was through the prophet Moses that God gave the perfect law to Israel.
As a whole, Mosaic law has a twofold purpose, namely
to bring men to a knowledge of God and to perfect the
social order so that the goal of man's spiritual fulfillment may be reached.[7]

Maimonides' intellectual quest for God was not for
him simply an interesting intellectual exercise. As
had always been the case in Rabbinic Judaism, his purpose was to understand, clarify, and systematize the
Torah Tradition so that the "law" might remain always
a relevant guide for life. As had the earlier Rabbi,
Judah the Prince (see Chapter V above), Maimonides in
Mishneh Torah sought to present a comprehensive survey
and codification of halakah ("law") up to his time. In
another work on the Talmud which he wrote over a period
of ten years, the Mishnah Commentary, he presented the
halakic decision for each paragraph of the Mishnah and
an introduction to each tractate. The introduction to
the Sanhedrin tractate contains the famous thirteen
principles which Maimonides considered essential for
the Jewish faith.

While neither intended nor accepted as dogmatic

pronouncements in the sense of creedal statements, the thirteen principles gained prestige as a succinct summary of what a faithful Jew believes. For many Jews, especially Orthodox, they continue to function as a convenient standard of orthodoxy, and are still given a prominent place in several Jewish prayer books. The version quoted below is the one found in the <u>Authorized Daily Prayer Book</u>.[8]

> 1. I believe with perfect faith that the Creator, blessed be his name, is the Author and Guide of everything that has been created, and that he alone has made, does make, and will make all things.
>
> 2. I believe with perfect faith that the Creator, blessed be his name, is a Unity, and that there is no unity in any manner like unto his, and that he alone is our God, who was, and is, and will be.
>
> 3. I believe with perfect faith that the Creator, blessed be his name, is not a body, and that he is free from all the accidents of matter, and that he has not any form whatsoever.
>
> 4. I believe with perfect faith that the Creator, blessed be his name, is the first and the last.
>
> 5. I believe with perfect faith that to the Creator, blessed be his name, and to him alone it is right to pray, and that it is not right to pray to any being besides him.
>
> 6. I believe with perfect faith that all the words of the prophets are true.
>
> 7. I believe with perfect faith that the prophecy of Moses our teacher, peace be unto him, was true, and that he was the chief of the prophets, both of those that preceded and of those that followed him.
>
> 8. I believe with perfect faith that the whole Law, now in our possession, is the same that was given to Moses our teacher, peace be unto him.
>
> 9. I believe with perfect faith that this Law will not be changed, and that there will never be any other law from the Creator, blessed be his name.

10. I believe with perfect faith that the Creator, blessed be his name, knows every deed of the children of men, and all their thoughts, as it is said. It is he that fashioneth the hearts of them all, that giveth heed to all their deeds.

11. I believe with perfect faith that the Creator, blessed be his name, rewards those that keep his commandments, and punishes those that transgress them.

12. I believe with perfect faith in the coming of the Messiah, and, though he tarry, I will wait daily for his coming.

13. I believe with perfect faith that there will be a resurrection of the dead at the time when it shall please the Creator, blessed be his name, and exalted be the remembrance of him for ever and ever.

Even though Mainmonides' influence was very great, he was not without some critics. Some felt that his views were too liberal. Others felt that Neo-Platonism provided a better foundation for their religious perspectives than did Aristotelianism, and they were not attracted by Maimonides' "rationalism." This was the case with respect to most of those who took a mystical approach to their religious heritage.[9] While there had been some mystics and mystical tendencies in earlier times, mysticism per se seems to have reached its most complete development in Judaism in the late medieval period. Even though not a dominant movement, it did have considerable influence, and it continues to have some influence today in Orthodox and Conservative Judaism.

Just as in the mysticism of other religions, so also in Jewish mysticism there was emphasis on attaining direct and immediate communion with God. Such immediate experience of God required strenuous preparation. The medieval Jewish mystics understood both the preparation for and the vision of God in terms derived from their own religious heritage and from their own "secret" traditions. Thus medieval Jewish mysticism came to be known as Kabbalism, a term which means "tradition." It is "tradition" not in the sense of a system of doctrines but in the sense of a religious movement.[10]

307

Unlike Maimonides, the Kabbalists were not concerned with reconciling Judaism with science and Aristotelian philosophy, with logical analyses of religious ideas to make them consistent with scientific thought. Rather they sought to transcend reason, to reconstruct what analyses dissects, and to see all things as a unity. Although this attempt was not a denial of the mind's rationality, it was an attempt to transcend it in an immediate experience of the Ultimate.[11]

Widely accepted by the Kabbalists was the Neo-Platonic view of all reality as consisting of emanations from the one spiritual Absolute.[12] Thus all things in this world are but the outward representations of the unseen spiritual Absolute. Whether aware of it or not, every person is involved in the realm of the unseen. So, through strenuous discipline, the Kabbalist sought to recognize the deeper symbolic significance of everything, to become aware of his involvement with the unseen, and to strive for the goal of the reabsorption of himself and of all reality into God.

For the Kabbalist, the Torah and Torah Tradition were the primary sources of his spiritual discipline. While he acknowledged the importance of the literal signification of the Torah words and verses, he felt that their symbolic meaning was much more important. They were the clues to the unraveling of divine secrets, guideposts leading one to awareness of the unseen realm. So the Kabbalist interpreted the words and verses of the Torah allegorically. Unlike Maimonides, for whom Biblical metaphors were symbols for rational principles, the Kabbalist regarded them as signs pointing to a deeper spiritual order. Every word must be pondered over again and again until one was fully aware of its spiritual significance. Not only Torah study but also scrupulous fulfilling of its precepts, the refining of moral conduct, and the endowment of the common ventures of life with spiritual significance were involved in the Kabbalists' way of life. Abraham Heschel, the distinguished scholar of Jewish mysticism, with his typical eloquence has characterized the Kabbalist in the following statements:

> A longing for the unearthly, a
> yearning for purity, the will to holiness,
> connected the conscience of the cabbalists
> with the strange current of mystic living. . .
> Their intention was to integrate their
> thoughts and deeds into the secret order, to

assist God in undoing the evil, in redeeming the light that was concealed.
Though working with fragile tools for a
mighty end, they were sure of bringing
about at the end the salvation of the
universe and of this tormented world.[13]

Although as a movement Kabbalism did not continue
to flourish, its influence has played a role in the
varying forms of mysticism which have had some degree
of expression in Judaism. In the eighteenth century
there emerged what might be called a revival of mysticism. This revival first appeared in the villages of
the Polish Ukraine in the movement known as Hasidism.
The term "Hasidism" was of ancient origin and means
"the pious" or "the godly." Eighteenth century Hasidism, however, should not be confused with ancient
Hasidism (see Chapter V). The former, influenced to
some degree by Kabbalism, was a mystical movement, while
the latter was not.

According to Hasidic tradition, the founder of
the movement was Israel ben Eleazer (1700-1760). Born
of poor parents in a village in southern Poland, he
was left an orphan in childhood. During his youth he
managed to eke out a meager living by doing menial
jobs such as serving as an assistant to a Hebrew teacher. It seems that he became learned in the Kabbalah
but did not acquire extensive knowledge of the Talmud.[14]
Repulsed by any form of ostentation, intellectual or
otherwise, he sought a genuine simplicity of life, and
felt more at home with peasants, children, and forest
creatures than with scholars. He and his wife lived
for a while in the Carpathian mountains where he
gained a knowledge of therapeutic herbs. The effective
use of this knowledge, along with his deep sympathy for
the lowly and the troubled, brought him fame as a
healer of those who were sick in body and/or soul.
Thus he became known as the Baal Shem TOV (the Master
of the Good Name, usually abbreviated as Besht).

Influenced by Kabbalism, Besht insisted that God
is everywhere present, in the heart of man and in every
object, no matter how insignificant. The presence of
God may be sensed in even the smallest, lowliest, and
most mundane of objects and activities. The most
effective means of communion with God, of course, is
intense and enthusiastic prayer, but there is no set
form or technique for praying. One does not have to
be a Rabbinic sage in order to pray effectively. Morris

Goldstein has illustrated this point by recounting the following delightful story from Hasidic tradition:

> Besht tells of an ignorant shepherd lad
> who, when taken to the synagogue on the
> holiest day of the religious year, was
> overcome with an urge to open his heart
> to God, but he was not sufficiently
> learned to pray. He had to do something.
> In the crowded synagogue, during the hush
> of an awesome moment, the lad could no
> longer restrain himself. From his pocket
> he yanked out a reed-pipe; he put it to
> his lips and on it he sounded a shrill
> blast. Consternation swept through the
> entire congregation--all but Besht.
> "This impulsive act," he defended, "took
> the place of prayer. The simple lad
> served God in the only way he knew.
> God wants the devotion of the heart;
> to Him this tune was more acceptable
> than formal prayer."[15]

While the Besht emphasized a heartfelt devotion
to God which was not limited to particular forms, he
and his followers remained within the Jewish community,
emphasizing the responsibility of all the Jews to each
other. The illumined saint does not live as a hermit
but seeks to perpetuate his experience in the life of
the community. So there emerged in Hasidism the concept of leadership as centered in the person of extraordinary spiritual gifts (the Zaddik). He exercises
leadership by involving himself in the people's daily
cares and anxieties, counseling with them, strengthening
their faith, and praying to God on their behalf. These
and other activities of the Zaddik were thought to be
possessed of mysterious significance. He was not simply
a teacher of Torah but the living incarnation of the
Torah. Even though early Hasidism was rather permissive
with respect to Talmudic halakah, later Zaddik often
combined expertise in Talmudic studies with mystical
experience and dynamic leadership.[16] So there emerged
in Hasidism the tradition of bringing a mystical fervor
to the exacting study of Torah and Talmudic literature
and commandments and to the faithful observance of the
commandments.

Dissastisfaction with modern secularism which ignores the divine dimension of life has contributed to
the revival of Hasidism from time to time in modern

Judaism. Often with revivalistic fervor, Hasidic Jews
call upon Jews to return to a traditional observance
of the commandments. Due to their emphasis upon the
scrupulous observance of the commandments, modern
Hasidic Jews generally are classified as Orthodox. This
does not mean, of course, that all Orthodox Jews are
Hasidic Jews. In post-World War II United States and
Israel there are some relatively small Hasidic enclaves
which are active within the fold of Orthodoxy.[17] In
addition, Hasidism has had and continues to have some
influence in Conservative Judaism.

The differences between the rationalists like Maimonides and the mystics like the Kabbalists and the
Hasids indicate that within the overall Jewish religious
heritage there was room for varying perspectives and
religious styles. It is not surprising then, that
with the challenge of modern western culture there
emerged different movements, of which the three major
ones are Orthodox, Reform, and Conservative. Furthermore, since Judaism has never been in the strict sense
a creedal religion, there is not a strict or absolute
uniformity of beliefs among the adherents of each of
these three movements. Yet there is sufficient concen-
sus among most of the adherents of each group such that
a general characterization of each one is possible. In
the discussion below, we will sketch briefly the major
perspectives which characterize the Orthodox, Reform,
and Conservative movements which represent the right
wing, the left wing, and the moderate responses respectively to the challenge of modern culture.

A. Orthodox Judaism

We have seen that modern Orthodox Judaism includes
within its fold both the Hasidic Jew who brings a mystical fervor to his study and observance of Torah, and
the Orthodox Jew who, like Maimonides, takes a non-
mystical approach. The latter, of course, is as strict
and strenuous in his study and observance of the "law"
as is the former. Both accept Maimonides' thirteen
principles as a standard of orthodoxy. Probably most
Jews (we are using the term "Jew" in the religious
sense) accept the first five and the tenth of Maimonides' principles. That is, they believe that God exists,
is creator, an indivisible unity, incorporeal, eternal,
omniscient, and alone worthy of being worshipped. But
Orthodox Jews adhere strictly not only to these six
principles but also to the other seven. In the following discussion we will seek to indicate these and other

perspectives and practices which are distinctive of Orthodox Judaism.

1. Taking the term Torah in its most inclusive sense as incorporating not only the Torah-Book but also the Torah traditions which emerged in the Talmud and other commentaries, it may be said that the piety of the Orthodox Jew is centered in the Torah. The whole Torah is viewed as God-revealed and therefore as absolutely valid throughout. It provides divine guidance for all areas of life, religious, intellectual, moral, and social. With respect to the Torah-Book itself, Orthodox Jews tend to hold to a view of verbal or literal inspiration and infallibility. In the most extreme form of this view it is held that every word and every letter (Hebrew, of course) was given by God either directly to the whole people of Israel at Mount Sinai or indirectly through Moses. Yet God's revelation did not exhaust itself in the Torah-Book. Milton Steinberg has described this Orthodox perspective on revelation as follows:

> It suffuses the writings of the prophets after Moses, overflows into the rest of Scripture, thence into classical Talmudic literature; thence again, though in diminishing degree, into later rabbinic writings. In other words, the mainstream of the Tradition everywhere possesses something of the authority of the Torah-Book--much in the same fashion as inferences in logic, carry over, if only they are drawn accurately, the authority and certainty of the premises from which they are drawn. Or to put the point as does the Talmud itself: "Whatsoever any earnest scholar will innovate in the future, lo this was already spoken at Sinai."[18]

It seems clear then, that Orthodox Jews hold fast to Maimonidean principles six, seven, eight, and nine in which it is declared that the words of the prophets and of Moses, the chief of the prophets, are true, divine, and immutable. While this entails the view that Judaism is not susceptible to subsequent change, it does not result in a situation which is absolutely static. The ancient Talmudic rabbis (see Chapter V), while holding that the Torah in both written and oral forms had a divine source, had been receptive of reinterpretations so long as these reinterpretations could

312

be shown to be consistent with the Torah. So in modern
Orthodox Judaism some reinterpretations are possible
as long as they remain within the framework of the
Torah. The final standard, in light of which the reinterpretations and, for that matter, the truth and goodness of anything is to be tested, is always the Torah.

2. Given the very great authority of the Torah,
the Orthodox Jew seeks to follow it fully in all of
life's activities, and this includes what Milton Steinberg has called "the daily regimen," "the sacred round,"
and "the life cycle."[19] The daily regimen involves a
rigorous discipline of daily devotional practices from
awakening in the morning until retiring at night. On
first awakening the Orthodox Jew utters a prayer of
gratitude to God for the return of consciousness.
Then, with each act in the process of getting up, wash-
ing, dressing, etc., he recites an ordained prayer.
Next, he prepares for formal worship by wrapping himself in the prayer-shawl and by attaching one of the
teflin to his left arm and the other to his forehead.
The teflin are two small boxes containing the Scripture passages Ex. 13:1-10, 11-16; Deut. 6:4-9; and
Deut. 11:13-21. Fastening them to the left arm and
forehead is symbolic of loving God with heart and mind.
So prepared, he goes to the synagogue, and if there is
a quorum (minyan) of ten adult males present, participates in the worship which consists of prayers and the
reading of selected passages from Scripture and Rabbinic
literature. If there is not a minyan, privately he
engages in formal worship. It is only after this worship that he partakes of the breakfast meal. Prayers
and other ritual acts are involved in the preparation
and eating of this and other meals. The kosher regulations and other dietary laws (see Chapter V) are
followed faithfully.[20] At two other times during the
day, in the afternoon and at dusk, the Orthodox Jew
engages in formal worship. Upon retiring at night
he again recites traditional prayers.

In addition to the daily regimen, the Orthodox
Jew seeks to observe faithfully the sacred round. That
is, he seeks to follow fully the Tradition in his
observance of the various festivals and holy days which
occur during each year. None of them may be skipped
nor abbreviated. The primary festivals and holy days
are as follows:

a. The Sabbath, which is the seventh day of the
week extending from sundown Friday night to sundown

Saturday night is a weekly celebration of God's creation
and his deliverance of Israel from Egypt. In order to
preserve the sanctity of this day and to keep it as a
day of rest, the Orthodox Jew follows the Tradition's
prohibitions concerning labor on the Sabbath. Yet
the Sabbath is an occasion for joyous worship in both
home and synagogue. In the synagogue service there is
total adherence to the historic prayer-book, the almost
exclusive use of the Hebrew language, and the absence
of instrumental music. The men follow the custom of
covering their heads which derives from that prescribed
for the priests of the temple in Exodus 28:40-42. Men
and women are segregated during the service.

b. The New Year (Rosh Hashanah), which comes late
in September, is the beginning of the Jewish religious
year. It is a time of reaffirming the sovereignty of
God and of pious reflection on one's deeds during the
past year. The first ten days of the new year are
days of penitence.

c. The Day of Atonement (Yom Kippur) occurs on
the tenth day after Rosh Hashanah and is a day of
fasting and repentance in the quest for regeneration.

d. The Feast of Booths (Succoth), which comes
in the late Autumn, is an eight day thanksgiving festival associated with the thought of God's providential
care in the days of Israel's wilderness wanderings and
in providing nature's harvest.

e. A high point in the sacred round is the festival of Passover (Pesah), which occurs in the Spring
and is a celebration of Israel's deliverance from Egypt.
An important part of the Passover observance is the
home service called the Seder, during which the Passover meal is eaten. Important elements in the Seder
include the father's reciting the story of Israel's
deliverance from Egyptian bondage and the participation
of the children who are urged to observe the various
ceremonies and to ask for their explanations.

f. Fifty days after Passover is Pentecost
(Shebuoth), which celebrates the giving of the Torah
on Mount Sinai.

g. Two other festivals, not based directly on
the ancient Mosaic tradition, are the Festival of
Lights (Hannukkah) and the Day of Lots (Purim).
Hannukkah, which occurs in December, is the celebration

314

of the cleansing of the temple at the time of the
Maccabean revolt. Purim, which comes in late winter,
is associated with the Biblical book of Esther and is
a celebration of the deliverance of Jews from persecution.

Undoubtedly, for most Jews this sacred round,
whether fully observed or not, serves as a means of
expressing the religious perspectives and value system
of the Jewish faith. For Orthodox Jews the full observance of all of the sacred round is one of the ways
of preserving the distinctiveness of the Jewish faith
in the modern world.

Another way in which the Orthodox Jew seeks to
preserve the distinctiveness of the Jewish faith is by
following the prescriptions in the Torah Tradition
concerning the rites associated with the various stages
in the life cycle of each person. These include the
rites at the birth of a child, the major one of which
is circumcision of each male symbolizing thereby God's
Covenant with Israel and the individual's membership
in the Covenant community. A girl is named at the
service in the synagogue on the Sabbath following her
birth. There is the Bar Mitzvah ceremony for boys following their thirteenth birthday symbolizing their
assumption of the obligations of the Torah Tradition.
There are rites associated with marriage, with the
dedication of a new home (the Mezuzah containing Deut.
6:4-9, 11:13-21 are attached to the doorposts of every
room), and with death and mourning. While all religious
Jews engage in some rites associated with the various
stages in the life cycle, Orthodox Jews seek to incorporate all of the traditional rites in their observances.[21]

3. Not only does the Orthodox Jew seek to sanctify
the whole of life in the present but also he looks to
the future with hope. In this he is guided by the Torah
tradition which, although it avoided the excesses of
extreme apocalypticism, held to the coming of the
Messiah (Principle twelve of Maimonides) who would
actualize the kingdom of God on earth. While there
have been some variations in the Messianic views held
by Orthodox Jews, generally they regard the Messiah
who is to come as a man who is a descendent of King
David. He will be endowed by God with extraordinary
power to purge the world of evil, to establish his kingdom among men and nations, and to reconcile the entire
cosmos with its creator. In the meantime, as they wait

for his coming, the faithful must do whatever they can
for the regeneration of men and the transformation of
society.[22]

4. The hope for the coming of the Messiah is
closely related to the hope for the ultimate return
of all Jews to the Holy Land (Palestine). The latter
is known as Zionism ("Zion" is a Biblical term designating Jerusalem, II Sam. 5:9; I Kings 8:1). For the
Orthodox, Zionism is rooted in the promise contained
in the Biblical narrative of God's Covenant with Israel
that Israel would possess the Holy Land. As we have
seen in Chapter III, the Covenant entails not only
promises but also obligations and hardships. The
centuries-long dispersion of Jews throughout the world
is regarded by the Orthodox as part of Israel's mission
to be a light to the nations that redemption might come
to all. When that goal is accomplished, the long
dispersed and persecuted children of Israel will be
reassembled in the Holy Land, the Temple will be rebuilt, and they will live in peace and security.

Zionism in modern times has extended beyond the
fold of Orthodoxy. In large part this has occurred
as a response to anti-semitism which found its most
horrible expression in the Holocaust perpetrated by
the Nazis. Such experiences gave added force to the
conviction that the only hope of permanent security
for Jews lay in the establishment of a national home
in Palestine. Thus Zionism took on political significance, and the establishment of a Jewish state in
Palestine was advocated by even many non-religious Jews.
With the establishment of the state of Israel, Zionism
has been supported to some extent by most Jews, even
those who, regarding themselves as loyal citizens of
the country in which they live, do not desire to live
in Israel, and for whom Zionism is not an article of
religious faith. For the Orthodox, however, it has
been traditionally an article of faith. From the
beginnings of modern Zionism in the nineteenth century,
Orthodox Jews have been among its strongest supporters.[23]

5. We have seen that Maimonides' thirteenth
principle was an affirmation of faith in the resurrection of the dead. This was in keeping with the perspective concerning life after death held by the
ancient Pharisees from whom it passed on into the
Rabbinic traditions (see Chapter V). It continues to
be held in modern Orthodox Judaism. There is some

316

variety of views with respect to the precise nature of the resurrected bodies, of heaven, and of the nature and duration of hell. Yet the tradition to which the Orthodox are committed insists, according to Steinberg, "that a Jew shall hold to faith in Recompense, Immortality, and Resurrection. Nor may he believe in them as vague allegories. They must at the least mean for him something akin to what they seem to say."[24] So even though Orthodox Judaism has always placed great emphasis upon sanctifying life in the present, there is also the view that sometime in the future the bodies and souls of all the dead will be raised, reunited, appear before God to receive his judgment of bliss or damnation, and then live on in either heaven or hell.

6. In the discussion of Rabbinic Judaism in Chapter V it was indicated that, with the destruction of the Temple in 70 A.D., the synagogue remained as the primary institution for worship and prayer, and that authority shifted to the Rabbinic sages. The rabbi was neither a priest nor an ecclesiastical figure endowed with special status by virtue of ordination. He was a layman especially learned in Scripture and Talmud, and thus competent to function in the roles of teacher and judge. Whatever status he gained he won by virtue of his knowledge and wisdom.

Still today there is no ecclesiastical hierarchy in Judaism. While there are national associations and conferences of congregations and rabbis in the Orthodox, Reform, and Conservative movements, each congregation is autonomous. It is free to choose its rabbi and to determine its policies democratically. The rabbi does not enjoy any special status by virtue of his ordination to the rabbinate. While rabbis in Reform and Conservative circles have taken on some functions similar to those performed by Christian clergymen, the Orthodox tend to follow the traditional model more closely.

The learning required for the rabbinate in Orthodox Judaism is almost exclusively Hebraic, including Scripture, Talmudic literature, and the codes regulative of Jewish thought and practice. To gain knowledge in these areas requires years of study, analogous to that of earning a Ph.D. in other fields. An outstanding Orthodox seminary in the United States is the Rabbi Isaac Elhanan Theological Seminary of Yeshiva (the ancient Hebrew name for Academy) University in New York. This school has been, according to Robert Seltzer, "the major focus of modern American Orthodoxy."[25]

In order to be recognized as rabbis, students graduating from theological schools customarily are ordained. This ordination is performed by a rabbi or by their professors. In some cases, when called to serve a congregation, they do so without compensation. Instead they earn their livelihood in secular occupations (like Maimonides and other ancient rabbis). In some cases they seldom preach to the congregation, this function being performed by laymen who specialize in popular preaching. The major duties of the Orthodox rabbi are those of chief scholar and judge. It is to him that the members of the congregation refer difficult and complicated issues for clarification and judgment.[26]

Morris Goldstein has written a succinct evaluation of Orthodox Judaism which can serve as a concluding summary for our sketch. According to Goldstein:

> The strength of the Orthodox position is the same which preserved Judaism through the centuries. On the basis of the unquestioned supernatural revelation [in the Torah], the Orthodox Jew believes that God is guiding him--whatever happens, that of all the peoples of the earth he is the elect of God, that immortality [resurrection] will be his in the realm beyond, and that ultimate victory and vindication will be his for all his sufferings. Such belief and trust, if sincerely held, makes religion the most important thing in life--worthy of every sacrifice, of the utmost loyalty, of martyrdom even.[27]

B.   Reform Judaism

As indicated in our organizational schema (see diagram in the Introduction to Part V), Reform Judaism represents a "left-wing" response to the challenge of modern culture. It had its beginnings during the eighteenth century Enlightenment in Germany. The Enlightenment's emphasis upon the rule of reason and toleration began to break down the old barriers which had isolated Jews in the ghettos. Increasingly during the eighteenth and nineteenth centuries, Jews were able to participate in the mainstream of the educational,

318

economic, social, and cultural life of the times. Many who did participate began to call for a reformation in Judaism. Among them were secularly educated rabbis who, in several conferences held from 1844 to 1846, called for reconciling Judaism to the "spirit of the age." The perspective of these rabbis was aptly characterized by Rabbi Samuel Holdheim of Berlin when he said:

> All the talk about a Talmudical Judaism is an illusion. Science has decided that the Talmud has no authority dogmatically or practically. Even those who will not acknowledge this go beyond the Talmud. The question is, who gives us the right to change the liturgy? This question requires an unequivocal answer. [The ancient rabbis] have authority only in their age; what they ordained was timely, and on this the sanction of their ordinances rested. We have the same authority for our age, [but] even though the Talmud is not authoritative for us we do not wish to disregard the intellectual activity of two thousand years. We say merely this: Anything which upon unbiased, careful criticism contradicts the religious consciousness of the present age has no authority for us.[28]

Due in part to the migrations from Europe, Reform Judaism quickly spread to the United States. In the United States it made such rapid strides that the United States soon replaced Germany as a center of Reform Judaism. Among the causal conditions for this development were not only the favorable social and political conditions in the United States but also the energetic leadership of some outstanding rabbis. Two of these leaders were Isaac M. Wise (1819-1900), the founder of Hebrew Union College in Cincinnati (a Reform theological school) and the leader of the Central Conference of American Rabbis; and Kaufmann Kohler (1943-1926), whose writings provided a theological basis for the Reform movement. Due largely to the efforts of these two men there was a conference of Reform rabbis in Pittsburg in 1885. This conference adopted a set of principles that came to be known as the "Pittsburgh Platform." Since it has been of considerable influence in the American Reform movement, it is worth quoting in full:

First--We recognize in every religion an attempt to grasp the Infinite One, and in every mode, source or book of revelation held sacred in any religious system the consciousness of the indwelling of God in man. We hold that Judaism presents the highest conception of the God-idea as taught in our holy Scriptures and developed and spiritualized by the Jewish teachers in accordance with the moral and philosophical progress of their respective ages. We maintain that Judaism preserved and defended amid continual struggles and trials and under enforced isolation this God-idea as the central religious truth for the human race.

Second--We recognize in the Bible the record of the consecration of the Jewish people to its mission as the priest of the One God, and value it as the most potent instrument of religious and moral instruction. We hold that the modern discoveries of scientific researches in the domains of nature and history are not antagonistic to the doctrines of Judaism, the Bible reflecting the primitive ideas of its own age and at times clothing its conception of divine providence and justice dealing with man in miraculous narratives.

Third--We recognize in the Mosaic legislation a system of training the Jewish people for its mission during its national life in Palestine, and today we accept as binding only its moral laws and maintain only such ceremonials as elevate and sanctify our lives, but reject all such as are not adapted to the views and habits of modern civilization.

Fourth--We hold that all such Mosaic and Rabbinical laws as regulate diet, priestly purity and dress originated in ages and under the influence of ideas altogether foreign to our present mental and spiritual state. They fail to impress the modern Jew with a spirit of priestly holiness; their observance in

our day is apt rather to obstruct than
to further modern spiritual elevation.

Fifth--We recognize in the modern era
of universal culture of heart and intellect
the approach of the realization of Israel's
great Messianic hope for the establishment
of the Kingdom of truth, justice and peace
among all men. We consider ourselves no
longer a nation but a religious community,
and therefore expect neither a return to
Palestine, nor a sacrificial worship
under the administration of the sons of
Aaron, nor the restoration of any of the
laws concerning the Jewish state.

Sixth--We recognize in Judaism a
progressive religion, ever striving to be
in accord with the postulates of reason.
We are convinced of the utmost necessity
of preserving the historical identity
with our great past. Christianity and
Islam being daughter religions of Judaism,
we appreciate their mission to aid in the
spreading of monotheistic and moral truth.
We acknowledge that the spirit of broad
humanity of our age is our ally in the
fulfillment of our mission, and therefore
we extend the hand of fellowship to all who
co-operate with us in the establishment of
the reign of truth and righteousness among
men.

Seventh--We reassert the doctrine of
Judaism, that the soul of man is immortal,
grounding this belief on the divine nature
of the human spirit, which forever finds
bliss in righteousness and misery in
wickedness. We reject as ideas not rooted
in Judaism the belief both in bodily
resurrection and in Gehenna and Eden [hell
and paradise], as abodes for everlasting
punishment or reward.

Eighth--In full accordance with the
spirit of Mosaic legislation which strives
to regulate the relation between rich and
poor, we deem it our duty to participate
in the great task of modern times, to
solve on the basis of justice and

321

righteousness the problems presented by
the contrasts and evils of the present
organization of society.[29]

Even though the Pittsburg Platform has been important in Reform Judaism as a kind of general direction
for its theology and practice, it has never been regarded as a dogmatic creedal statement. In the history
of the Reform movement there have been those who have
modified to some degree one or more of these principles.
In our discussion it is not possible to describe these
modifications in detail. Instead, in order to characterize Reform Judaism more adequately, some further
elaboration both of the principles of the Pittsburg
Platform and of some other perspectives and practices
will be presented. Our discussion will follow the
order of topics presented in the discussion of Orthodox
Judaism, and where appropriate will contrast the positions of the Reform with those of the Orthodox.

1. Unlike the Orthodox for whom piety is centered in the Torah such that it is the standard in
light of which the truth and value of things is judged,
Reform Jews tend to judge the Torah by the standards
of reason and experience. It is noteworthy that the
terms Torah and Torah Tradition are not used in the
Pittsburg Platform. Indeed, Reform Jews reject the
view that the revelation of God requires an infallible
book. They tend to be rather eclectic in their approach
to the Torah. That is, they accept only that which is
in accord with reason and experience, with the "spirit
of the age." So in the Pittsburg Platform the Reform
rabbis declared that they reject the ceremonies, customs, and laws of the "Mosaic legislation" which cannot
be "adapted to the views and habits of modern civilization," that they "accept as binding only its moral laws,"
that they hold to "modern discoveries of scientific
researches in the domain of nature and history," and
that Judaism is "a progressive religion."

It is clear, then, that Reform Jews accept biological evolution and the doctrine of progress in the social and religious realms. Since the revelation of
God is received by fallible human beings, it unfolds
within the manifold limitations of human minds. As
human understanding in the scientific, philosophical,
and historical realms grows, so does the understanding
of God's revelation. In this sense revelation is progressive, a view which, as we will see in Chapter XI,
is similar to the view of revelation held by Protestant

liberals. The Word of God is not simply the written letter of the Torah but those divine truths which, given the guidance of reason and experience, may be extracted from Scripture or elsewhere. The method used in Reform theological schools to determine the truths of Scripture is the modern method of higher and lower criticism.[30] Thus most Reform rabbis accept the view that the Torah-Book or Pentateuch did not come into existence all at one time through Moses. Rather it was the product of several authors who wrote at different times during a period of several centuries so that the completion of the Torah-Book was the result of a very long process. The piety of Reform Jews, then, is not centered in the Torah. It is based on the moral and spiritual truths contained in the Torah-Book, the great Prophets (who often were critical of the sacrificial system and of ceremonies), the rest of Old Testament Scripture, and in later teachers so long as these truths are consistent with reason and experience in the modern world.

Furthermore, Reform Jews do not limit all revelation of God to Judaism. Most agree with the first principle of the Pittsburg Platform that all religions express "the consciousness of the indwelling of God in man." As we will see in Chapter XI, this is similar in some respects to the position of an early "left-wing" or liberal Protestant theologian of Germany, Friedrick Schleiermacher (1768-1834). According to Schleiermacher all human beings, although differing in the degree of their awareness of it, possess the sense of absolute dependence or God consciousness. Therefore religions should not be judged as either true or false but should be evaluated or ranked according to the adequacy of their expressions of the God consciousness. Since the feeling of absolute dependence logically entails the existence of only one personal deity, the monotheistic religions (Judaism, Islam, and Christianity) rank higher than the polytheistic and pantheistic religions. Of the monotheistic religions, Schleiermacher thought that Christianity in the person of Christ had provided the highest expression of the God consciousness.[31] In contrast to Schleiermacher, the Reform rabbis at Pittsburg proclaimed that "Judaism presents the highest conception of the God-idea."[32] However their declaration that there is "in every religion an attempt to grasp the Infinite, and in every mode, source or book of revelation held sacred in any religious system the consciousness of the indwelling of God in man," agreed with Schleiermacher's claim that all human beings possess the God consciousness.

2. Given the fact that for Reform Jews the Torah
does not possess absolute authority, it is not surprising that their practices with respect to the daily
regimen, the sacred round, and the life cycle differ
considerably from those of the Orthodox. While they
are not disdainful of the traditional practices, Reform Jews tend to be rather casual and relaxed with
respect to the observance of these rites. Viewing
Judaism as a progressive religion, they have not hesi-
tated to abandon and/or modify traditional practices.

In general, Reform Jews do not regard the observance of the daily regimen as mandatory. They either
ignore it altogether or practice only a minimum of
its rites. For example, the weekday formal service of
worship (the minyan), for the most part, has disappeared in both its public and private forms. Dietary
laws are not regarded as binding. According to Steinberg: "Modernists [Reform] range in their attitudes
and behavior concerning the dietary code all the way
from total disapproval and nonobservance to complete
assent and adherence."[33]

The sacred round also has been greatly modified in
Reform Judaism. Due in large part to the efforts of
Isaac M. Wise, a new prayer book was prepared for the
use of American Reform Congregations.[34] Called the
Union Prayer Book, it represented the consummation of
Reform thought on synagogue ritual and practice. It
was almost entirely in English and placed emphasis on
social consciousness and tolerance. The ritual for
Sabbath services in the temple (the term Reform Jews
customarily use to designate the synagogue) was simplified. Among the changes were a reduction in the number
of prayers and lessons from Scripture, the permission
for men to worship with uncovered heads and without
the prayer-shawl, the employment of organs and mixed
choirs, and the permission for families to sit together
during worship. In terms of form, the Sabbath services
in a Reform temple do not differ greatly from the Sunday services in a Protestant church. That is, there
are prayers, hymns, Scripture readings, anthems by a
choir, and a sermon. Also in the Reform observance
of the Sabbath the traditional code prohibiting work
was abandoned. With respect to the yearly festivals,
Reform Jews tend to eliminate some and abbreviate
others. In the early days of the Reform movement, the
observance of Hannukkah, Purim and Succoth were

324

virtually non-existent.[35]

In the life cycle observances, Reform Jews have
followed the practice of circumcising male children
and of naming both boys and girls in a temple service.
There was a tendency to replace the bar mitzvah ceremony for adolescent boys with a confirmation ceremony
and to have an analogous confirmation for girls (sometimes called bas mitzvah). Marriage and funeral rites
were simplified as well.

In recent years, as evident in the latest version
of the Union Prayer Book, there has been somewhat of
a mild trend in the direction of traditional practices.
For example, the tradition of the Kiddush (the sanctification of God's name), the lighting of the Sabbath
candles, and traditional Sabbath melodies have been re-
instated in the Sabbath observances. The more traditional form of the bar mitzvah for boys has been made
optional. Hannukkah, Purim, and Succoth celebrations
are more in evidence. Often Reform congregations spon-
sor a public and interfaith seder during Passover, a
practice which tends to vitalize this celebration.[35]

3. The traditional Messianic expectations have
been revised considerably in Reform Judaism. Instead
of expecting a personal Messiah to come sometime in
the future as do the Orthodox, Reform Jews tend to believe in a Messianic Age. The Messiah is not to be one
man. Instead all men of faith and goodness are "mes-
siahs" whose cooperative endeavors will bring the kingdom of God near. Louis Finkelstein has described the
typical Reform Messianic expectation as follows:

> The Messianic age will come about through
> the gradual enlightenment of men, and
> through the work of many thinkers and
> teachers. All agree that the age will
> be one of profound and universal faith
> in God, recognition of human brotherhood,
> and an unprecedented knowledge of the
> universe. There will be no discrimina-
> tion between persons because of sex,
> origin, faith, occupation, nationality,
> or any other reason. The evils of human
> origin will have been overcome; those
> inherent in Nature will be mitigated
> through further knowledge and increased
> piety. In this world of brotherly love,
> there will be no room for pride in

325

achievement, nor for memories of past
bitterness and oppression.[36]

4. We have seen that in Orthodoxy, Messianic and
Zionist's hopes are closely related. This is not the
case in the Reform perspective. In the early days of
the Reform movement there was an explicit rejection of
Zionism as indicated in principle five of the 1885
Pittsburg Platform. This principle clearly states:
"We consider ourselves no longer a nation, but a religious community, and therefore expect neither a return
to Palestine, nor a sacrificial worship under the sons
of Aaron, nor the restoration of any of the laws concerning the Jewish state." One leader in the early
days of the Reform movement went so far as to say,
"America is our Zion, Washington our Jerusalem."[37] In
light of this, it is not surprising that early Reform
prayer books almost invariably eliminated references
to a personal Messiah and a restoration to Zion.

However, with the resurgence of anti-semitism in
western nations and the rise of Hitlerism in Germany,
Reform rabbis discarded the anti-Zionist formula. In
the 1935 convention of the Central Conference of American Rabbis they adopted a resolution to take no
official stand on Zionism, leaving it up to the individual members of the Conference to either support or
reject, it. Yet there was also in the resolution an
announcement that the Conference would continue to
cooperate in the upbuilding of the Jewish community
in Palestine.[38] This support became intensified, of
course, in reaction to the Nazi Holocaust and the
establishment of the state of Israel.

Will Herberg has presented a rather perceptive
analysis of the attachment which most Jews have for
the Jewish community in Palestine when he said:

> Most American Jews feel, and I think
> very justly, that their bond with the
> State of Israel and its Jewish community
> is of unique and profound significance.
> But why? What is this bond? It is cer-
> tainly not "racial" or national. Nor is
> it in any important sense cultural if
> that term is used with any precision.
> Just as little is it "religious" in the
> sense of adherence to the same religious
> denomination. . . . The bond that unites
> us with the Jews of Israel and their

326

national community goes far deeper. It
is compounded, I think, of the solidarity
which every Jew, whether he knows it or
not, feels with his fellows under the
covenant and of the deep and utterly non-
nationalistic "love of Zion" that is so
ingrained in Jewish spirituality and is
itself an aspect of covenant-existence.
These factors are operative in the lives
of many Jews who make no conscious religious
affirmation and in whom they come to expression in strange and often distorted
and contradictory forms. But they are
there, and it is out of them that, at
bottom, is generated the tie, as unmis-
takable in its workings as it is hard to
define, which binds the American Jew to
the State of Israel and its Jewish community.[39]

5. In Reform Judaism as in Orthodox there is the
belief in life after death. However the Reform understanding of this state of being is quite different
from that of the Orthodox. In principle seven of the
Pittsburg Platform the rabbis rejected the doctrines
concerning the <u>resurrection</u> <u>of</u> <u>the</u> <u>body</u> and of a
<u>literal</u>, <u>spatial</u> heaven and hell. Instead they pro-
claimed a belief in the <u>immortality</u> <u>of</u> <u>the</u> <u>soul</u>. That
is, they believe in the deathlessness of the human
spirit, not simply in the naturalistic sense of a person being remembered, but also in the sense of his
self or soul surviving death. While they affirmed
the belief that there will be recompense for the soul
in the next life, the rabbis, other than rejecting
the notion of eternal damnation, refrained from specu-
lating about the precise nature of this recompense and
its attendant circumstances.

6. The rabbi, in Reform as in Orthodox Judaism,
is not thought to have a special <u>status</u> by virtue of
his ordination to the rabbinate. Ordination simply signifies that he has acquired the knowledge necessary
for functioning in the role of rabbi. College and Rabbinic School degrees are required. The Rabbinic School
of Hebrew Union College, for example, requires a five-
year program of study beyond the undergraduate degree.
There is a heavy concentration of studies in the Bible,
the Talmud, the Midrashim (ancient commentaries on
Scripture passages), and Jewish history. The method
used in these studies is the historical-critical method

rather than the traditional method of Orthodoxy. In addition, the student is required to take some courses in philosophy, theology, liturgy, education, human relations, homiletics (the art of preparing sermons), speech, and practical rabbinics.[40]

The rabbinate in Reform Judaism is regarded as a profession for which one must become prepared and from which one derives a livelihood. While even in Orthodox circles today there has been a tendency for rabbis to engage more in preaching and pastoral functions, this always has been the case in Reform circles. Rabbis preach, administer congregational affairs, direct the religious education program of the congregation, perform pastoral functions (counseling, weddings, funerals, etc.), engage in community causes, and so on. In very recent times some women have been ordained to the rabbinate in the Reform movement.

Our discussion of the Orthodox and Reform movements has indicated that there are considerable differences between the two. Yet these differences have not led to the kind of sectarian schism in which one group regards the other as outside the fold of Judaism and/or damned by God. According to Louis Finkelstein:

> Although the difference in practice between the traditional [Orthodox] and Reform groups is considerable, each accepts the other as being within the fold of Judaism. It is possible for them to do so, because of the principle that even an unobservant or a heretical Jews does not cease to be a member of the covenant made between God and Israel at the time of the Revelation. . . . So long as a follower of the Jewish faith has not by overt act or word and of his own free will declared himself a member of another religion, other Jews are bound to regard him as one of their own faith, and to seek his return to its practices and beliefs.[41]

It has been said of Orthodoxy that its strength lies in its tendency to preserve the distinctiveness of Judaism. With respect to Reform Judaism, it may be said that its strength lies in its emphasis on the freedom of thought and action which keeps Judaism relevant in the modern age. Paradoxically, this is not

328

inconsistent with the underlined{general} underlined{approach} or underlined{method} of the
ancient rabbis who sought by their interpretations to
keep the Torah relevant in their own ages.

C. Conservative Judaism

In our organizational schema we have indicated
that Conservative Judaism is a moderate response to
the challenge of modern culture. Historically, it
arose in the latter half of the nineteenth century due
to the secession from the Reform camp of several
leaders who felt the Reform movement had abandoned too
much of the Jewish heritage. While later on some
Orthodox came into the Conservative camp, this movement
was not a return to Orthodoxy. Milton Steinberg succinctly described the origin and perspective of
Conservative Judaism when he said:

> Conservative Judaism had its origin
> simultaneously in America and Western
> Europe among those Jews who either in
> theory or practice could no longer be
> orthodox, and who yet refused to accept
> what they regarded as the extreme non-
> traditionalism of Reform. . . . Two motifs
> dominate conservative Judaism. The first
> is the assertion of the centrality of
> religion in Jewish life. . . . The second
> theme, heavily underscored, is the sense
> of tradition, of history, of the continuity
> of Jewish life both through time and in
> space. It is this feeling of the organic
> unity of one Jewry with other Jewries which
> Professor Solomon Schechter, the leading
> figure in American Conservatism, caught in
> the phrase "Catholic Israel." This phrase
> is more than a description. It is intended
> to serve as a norm for the guidance of
> behavior. That shall be done by Jews, it
> implies, which is normal to Catholic
> Israel: . . . to hold on to the traditional,
> to sanction modifications slowly, reluc-
> tantly, and, if at all possible, within
> the framework of Jewish law.[42]

Along with the Reform, Conservatives do not accept
the view that the Torah is infallible. The Torah contains the Word of God, is a witness to it, but the
detailed precepts, phrases and words of Scripture are
not understood as literally the underlined{words} of God. In the

Jewish Theological Seminary in New York (Solomon Schechter was its first president) higher criticism is employed as a method of studying Scripture and Tradition. Emphasis is placed on knowledge of and reverence for tradition, but this does not entail naive literalism and legalism. Rather it encourages a process of re-evaluating the past in light of the present and the evaluation of the present in light of the past.

Occupying a position between Orthodox and Reform, Conservative Jews observe more of the traditional practices with respect to the daily regimen, sacred round, and life cycle than the Reform but not as much as the Orthodox. For example, in the synagogue services families sit together, some prayers in English are included, and often there is instrumental music. Yet the prayer text is quite traditional, the Hebrew language predominates, and men cover their heads. The daily week day services are held (if there is a minyan) and the prayer-shawls and teflin are worn. In short, the tendency in Conservatism is not to abolish ceremonial practices, but to revitalize them.

Unlike the Reform movement, Conservative Judáism has been Zionist since its beginnings. The Zionism of Conservatives, however, lacks the literalistic and apocalyptic elements sometimes present in Orthodox Zionism. According to Solomon Schechter, "Zionism is an ideal, and as such is indefinable."[43] It is, of course, a sense of solidarity with the living people of Israel, and this sense of solidarity is viewed as contributing to the continuation of the Jewish faith. In Schechter's view it is desirable that there be a homeland in Palestine for at least a portion of Jews who would have an independent national life there, for such is a bulwark against that assimilation which would destroy the identity of the Jewish faith.[44]

In contrast to the Reform, Conservative Judaism has tended to be more appreciative of the mystical element in religious experience. Solomon Schechter, for example, recommended the infusion of mystical piety into the life of the modern Jew.[45] Hasidism has influenced such outstanding Jewish philosophers and theologians as Martin Buber and Abraham Heschel, both of whom emphasized the personal and experiential nature of encounter with God.[46] Heschel, who was professor of Jewish Ethics and Mysticism at the Jewish Theological Seminary, wrote eloquently about the nature of the divine-human encounter in many books, among which was <u>Man's Quest For God</u>. A brief selection on prayer which illustrates his perspective and the beauty of his literary style is quoted below:

> <u>To pray is to take notice of the wonder</u>,
> <u>to retain a sense of the mystery that ani-</u>
> <u>mates all beings, the divine margin in all</u>
> <u>attainments</u>. Prayer is <u>our</u> humble <u>answer</u>
> to the inconceivable surprise of living.
> It is all we can offer in return for the
> mystery by which we live. Who is worthy
> to be present at the constant unfolding of
> time? Amidst the meditation of mountains,
> the humility of flowers--wiser than all
> alphabets--clouds that die constantly for
> the sake of His glory, <u>we</u> are hating, hunt-
> ing, hurting. Suddenly we feel ashamed of
> our clashes and complaints in the face of
> the tacit glory in nature. It is so embar-
> rassing to live! How strange we are in the
> world, and how presumptuous our doings!
> Only one response can maintain us: grate-
> fulness for witnessing the wonder, for the
> gift of our unearned right to serve, to
> adore, and to fulfill. It is gratefulness
> which makes the soul great. . . .
>
> Trembling in the realization that we
> are a blend of modesty and insolence, of
> self-denial and bias, we beseech God for
> rescue, for help in the control of our
> thoughts, words, and deeds. We lay all
> our forces before Him. Prayer is arrival
> at the border. The dominion is Thine.
> Take away from me all that may not enter
> Thy realm.[47]

A recent development in the Conservative movement has been the rise of what is called <u>Reconstructionism</u>. Based on the thought of Mordecai Kaplan, a professor at The Jewish Theological Seminary, Reconstructionism sought to combine a liberal and rather naturalistic theology with a more traditional view of Jewish culture and ways of worship and observance. It emphasized the view that Judaism is an evolving <u>civilization</u> created by the Jewish people in light of <u>its highest</u> conscience. It has called for the establishment of all-embracing, "organic" Jewish communities around the world that would ensure the survival of Jewish identity and develop secular as well as religious aspects of the

Jewish heritage (art, music, poetry, philanthropy, etc.). While it has not become a mass movement, Reconstructionism has appealed to many intellectuals and has had some influence with respect to Conservative thought and practice.[48]

Of the three movements in American Jewry, Conservatism has grown more in recent years than either Orthodoxy or Reform. Sometimes it has been able to unify whole communities on the basis of its middle-of-the-road approach. Today, the number officially enrolled by the Orthodox and Reform congregations is about a million each, but the enrollment in the Conservative movement is well over a million. Furthermore, recent studies of religious preference, in contrast to formal affiliation, indicate that about half of the Jews in America regard themselves as Conservative.[49]

[1] _Rabbinic Judaism in the Making_ (Wayne State University Press, 1970), p. XII.

[2] Among the many good studies of the history of Judaism which provide information concerning medieval Judaism are: Morris Goldstein, _Thus Religion Grows_ (Longman, Green and Co., 1936); Jacob Neusner (ed.), _Understanding Rabbinic Judaism: From Talmudic to Modern Times_ (Ktav Publishing House, Inc., 1974); Robert M. Seltzer, _Jewish People, Jewish Thought: The Jewish Experience in History_ (Macmillan Publishing Co., Inc., 1980).

[3] This quote is from Goldstein, _ibid._, p. 210.

[4] Neusner, _op. cit._, p. 185.

[5] See _The Guide of the Perplexed_, translated by Shlomo Pines (University of Chicago Press, 1963).

[6] According to Maimonides, "It was Aristotle who taught mankind the methods, the rules and the conditions of demonstration," _ibid._, p. 290.

[7] In addition to _The Guide_, A. Cohen, _The Teachings of Maimonides_ (Ktav Publishing House, Inc., 1968) and Isadore Twersky (ed.), _A Maimonides Reader_ (Behrman House, Inc., 1972) are good presentations of Maimonides complete system of thought.

[8] Ninth American Edition, tr. by S. Singer (Hebrew Publishing Company), pp. 89-90. For other, somewhat longer, versions see _The Standard Siddur Prayer Book_, compiled by S. Schonfeld (J. S. S. Books, London), pp. 74-76, and Twersky, _op. cit._, pp. 417-423.

[9] There were exceptions. One notable one was the thirteenth century mystic, Abraham ben Samuel Abulafia, who combined his mystical theory with the doctrines of Maimonides. This is one more indication that Rabbinic Judaism has tended to be the "mainstream" within Judaism throughout the ages. See Gershom G. Scholem, _Major Trends in Jewish Mysticism_ (Schocken Books, Inc., 1946), p. 126.

[10] _Ibid._, pp. 18, 20.

[11] See Abraham Heschel, "The Mystical Element in Judaism," in Jacob Neusner, _op. cit._, pp. 277-300.

333

[12] See the discussion of Augustine and Aquinas in Chapters VI and VII above for brief descriptions of Neo-Platonism.

[13] Heschel, op. cit., p. 294.

[14] Seltzer, op. cit., p. 488.

[15] Thus Religion Grows, p. 265.

[16] See Scholem, op. cit., pp. 342-348 and Neusner, op. cit., pp. 315-335.

[17] See Seltzer, op. cit., p. 496, and Jacob Neusner, American Judaism (Prentice-Hall, 1972), p. 120.

[18] Basic Judaism (Harcourt, Brace and Co., 1947), p. 24.

[19] Ibid., Chapter VII, pp. 116-134.

[20] Ibid., pp. 125-128.

[21] In addition to Steinberg's Basic Judaism some other sources containing discussions of the daily regimen, the sacred round, and the life cycle are: Philip S. Bernstein, What the Jews Believe (Farrar, Straus and Young, 1950); Louis Finkelstein, "The Jewish Religion: Its Beliefs and Practices," The Jews: Their History, Culture, and Religion, ed. Louis Finkelstein, Vol. II, Third Edition (Harper and Brothers Publishers, 1960), Chapter 42, pp. 1739-1801; Louis Finkelstein, et al., The Religions of Democracy (The Devin-Adair Co., 1945), Chapters V-IX, pp. 36-85.

[22] See Steinberg, Basic Judaism, pp. 167-179; Finkelstein, The Religions of Democracy, pp. 86-87.

[23] See Steinberg, ibid., pp. 91-93; Seltzer, op. cit., pp. 626-709; Jacob Neusner, American Judaism (Prentice-Hall, 1972), pp. 87-116; Bernard Martin, A History of Judaism, Vol. II (Basic Books, Inc., 1974), pp. 319-348.

[24] Ibid., p. 162.

[25] Seltzer, op. cit., p. 728.

[26] See Steinberg, op. cit., pp. 155-156; Finkelstein, The Jews: Their History, Culture, and Religion, Vol. I, pp. 524ff and Vol. II, pp. 1743-1745.

[27] Goldstein, op. cit., p. 325.

334

[28] Quoted from The Jew in the Modern World, eds. Paul R. Mendes-Flohr and Jehuda Reinharz (Oxford University Press, 1980), p. 143.

[29] Quoted from Bernard Martin, op. cit., pp. 300-301. The original source is Yearbook of the Central Conference of American Rabbis, Vol. 1 (Cincinnati, 1891), pp. 120-122. The Pittsburg Platform is quoted in many other studies of Judaism among which are: Jacob B. Agus, Guideposts in Modern Judaism (Block Publishing Company, 1954), pp. 53-55; Goldstein, op. cit., pp. 302-304; Mendes-Flohr, op. cit., pp. 371-372.

[30] For example, the late Samuel Sandmel, for many years president of Hebrew Union College, used this method in his book, The Hebrew Scriptures (Alfred A. Knoph, Inc., 1963). See Chapter II above for a discussion of higher and lower criticism.

[31] See The Christian Faith, eds. H. R. Mackintosh and J. S. Steward (T. and T. Clark, 1960).

[32] Italics are mine.

[33] Steinberg, op. cit., p. 128.

[34] See Bernard Martin, op. cit., p. 293.

[35] See Moshe Davis, "Jewish Religious Life and Institutions in America," in Finkelstein, op. cit., p. 553.

[36] The Religions of Democracy, p. 86. Also in The Jews: Their History, Culture and Religion, p. 1754.

[37] Moshe Davis, op. cit., p. 526.

[38] Ibid., p. 554.

[39] Judaism and Modern Man (Farrar Straus and Young, 1951), p. 278.

[40] See Hebrew Union College-Jewish Institute of Religion Catalogue, 1979-81.

[41] "Jewish Religion: Its Beliefs and Practices," op. cit., p. 1745. Italics are mine.

[42] My source for this quotation is John B. Noss, Man's Religions, Sixth Edition (Macmillan Publishing Co., Inc., 1980), pp. 409, 410. Also see Solomon Schechter, Seminary Addresses and Other Papers (reprint edition 1969 by Arno Press, Inc.), pp. 9-33;

and <u>Studies</u> in <u>Judaism</u>, Vol. 1 (The Jewish Publication Society of America, 1945), pp. XI–XXV.

[43] <u>Seminary</u> <u>Addresses</u> <u>and</u> <u>Other</u> <u>Papers</u>, p. 91.

[44] See <u>ibid</u>., pp. 91–104.

[45] <u>Studies</u> <u>in</u> <u>Judaism</u>, Vol. 1, pp. XI–XXV, 1–45.

[46] See Jacob B. Agus, <u>Guideposts</u> <u>in</u> <u>Modern</u> <u>Judaism</u> (Block Publishing Company, 1954), pp. 102–113; Martin Buber, <u>I</u> <u>and</u> <u>Thou</u> (Charles Scribner's Sons, 1970).

[47] (Charles Scribner's Sons, 1954), pp. 5, 6.

[48] See Agus, <u>op</u>. <u>cit</u>., pp. 125–133; Seltzer, <u>op</u>. <u>cit</u>., pp. 748–752.

[49] See Jacob Neusner, <u>American</u> <u>Judaism</u>, <u>op</u>. <u>cit</u>., pp. 119–120.

SUGGESTIONS FOR FURTHER READING

Agus, J. B., Guideposts in Modern Judaism, Block Publishing Company, 1954.

Berthold, Fred, et al., (eds.) Basic Sources of the Judeo-Christian Tradition, Prentice-Hall, 1962, pp. 343-369.

Cohen, A., The Teachings of Maimonides, Ktav Publishing House, Inc., 1968.

Epstein, Isidore, Judaism, Penguin Books, Inc., 1959.

Finkelstein, Louis (ed.), The Jews: Their History, Culture, and Religion, third edition, 2 vols., Harper and Brothers Publishers, 1960.

Goldstein, Morris, Thus Religion Grows, Longmans, Green, and Co., 1936, Chapter III.

Herberg, Will, Judaism and Modern Man, Farrar, Straus and Young, 1951.

Hertzberg, Arthur (ed.), Judaism, George Brasiller, Inc., 1961.

Heschel, Abraham J., Man's Quest For God, Charles Scribner's Sons, 1954.

Maimonides, Moses, The Guide of the Perplexed, translated by Schlomo Pines, University of Chicago Press, 1963.

Martin, Bernard, A History of Judaism, Vol. II, Basic Books, Inc. Publishers, 1974.

Mendeo-Flohr, Paul R. and Jehuda Reinharz (eds.), The Jew in the Modern World, Oxford University Press, 1980.

Neusner, Jacob, American Judaism, Prentice-Hall, Inc., 1972.

Neusner, Jacob (ed.), Understanding Rabbinic Judaism From Talmudic to Modern Times, Ktav Publishing House, Inc., 1974.

Noss, John B., Man's Religions, sixth edition, Macmillan Publishing Co., Inc., 1980, Chapter 13.

Philipson, David and Louis Grossman (eds.), Selected Writings of Isaac Mayer Wise, Arno Press, Inc., 1969.

Rosten, Leo (ed.), <u>Religions</u> <u>in</u> <u>America</u>, Simon and Schuster, Inc., 1963, pp. 103-111.

Schechter, Solomon, <u>Seminary</u> <u>Addresses</u> <u>and</u> <u>Other</u> <u>Papers</u>, Arno Press, Inc., 1969.

Schechter, Solomon, <u>Studies</u> <u>in</u> <u>Judaism</u>, First Series, The Jewish Publication Society of America, 1945.

Scholem, Gershom G., <u>Major</u> <u>Trends</u> <u>in</u> <u>Jewish</u> <u>Mysticism</u>, Schocken Books, Inc., 1946.

Schwarz, Leo W. (ed.), <u>Great</u> <u>Ages</u> <u>and</u> <u>Ideas</u> <u>of</u> <u>the</u> <u>Jewish</u> <u>People</u>, Random House, Inc., 1956, Chapters 11-18.

Seltzer, Robert M., <u>Jewish</u> <u>People</u>, <u>Jewish</u> <u>Thought</u>: <u>The</u> <u>Jewish</u> <u>Experience</u> <u>in</u> <u>History</u>, Macmillan Publishing Co., Inc., 1980, Part Three - Part Four.

Steinberg, Milton, <u>Basic</u> <u>Judaism</u>, Harcourt, Brace and Company, 1947.

Twersky, Isidore, <u>A</u> <u>Maimonides</u> <u>Reader</u>, Behrman House, Inc., 1972.

CHAPTER X

CATHOLICISM IN THE MODERN WORLD

Given the nature of Catholic doctrine, practice, and ecclesiastical structure, the three responses to the challenge of modern culture, right-wing, left-wing, and moderate, have not been as obvious and distinct in modern Catholicism as in Judaism and Protestantism. Unlike the case in Judaism, distinct organized movements have not emerged in Catholicism. For the most part, the right-wing response has dominated the official position of the Roman Catholic Church, yet Catholicism as a whole has not been without some expression of the other two responses. Thus our discussion of Catholicism in the modern world will be structured in terms of the three-fold response to the challenge of modern culture, namely right-wing, left-wing, and moderate.

A. The Right-Wing Response of Catholic Orthodoxy

As we have seen, in the sixteenth century the challenge of Protestantism and the desire for reform within the Catholic Church itself led to the Council of Trent (see Chapter VII). This Council not only brought about internal reforms, but also exalted medieval Catholic theology to the position of ecclesiastical dogmas. These dogmas, with some further explications and some additions, were to have a dominant place in Catholic thought and practice throughout most of the modern period.

Even though the Council of Trent was discussed in Chapter VII, some of its basic doctrines will be mentioned again because of their influence in the modern period. The perspective of Trent included the following: The ecclesiastical hierarchy is the sole interpreter of Scripture, and church tradition is of equal authority with Scripture. The image of God, though weakened by the fall of Adam, is retained by man such that he is not so depraved as to have lost all freedom of will. He may will to give intellectual assent to the propositions of revelation. The grace of God is an infused power which is available primarily through the seven sacraments. Since the ecclesiastical hierarchy is the dispensary of sacramental grace and supernatural

power, it is the "gatekeeper" of the celestial world.
Thus the Catholic Church, of which the Pope is the
supreme authority, is the only true church and only
"ark" of salvation. Faith must be completed by the
doing of good works which the faithful, with the help
received from the added grace infused through the
sacraments, can will to do. Since the highest good
is supernatural and thus spiritual, the ascetic way of
life is the most effective way of attaining beatitude.
However, in the doctrine of purgatory and the prayers
and masses for the dead, the faithful who cannot or do
not practice the ascetic way are provided with the
assurance of ultimately reaching supernatural beatitude.

From time to time in the modern period, these doctrines have been reaffirmed by various popes and constitute at least an important part of the official
position of the Catholic Church. Thus the official
position has tended to emphasize the value of traditional views in contrast to the new--a trend which
reached its pinnacle in the explicit condemnation of
modernism in 1907. Clearly, then, official Catholicism
has taken a right-wing response to the challenge of
modern culture. The following discussion presents a
few examples of this right-wing response.

An outstanding representative of the right-wing
response was Pius IX (1846-1878). He demonstrated such
a response in the following three ways.

First, after consulting with the bishops, Pius IX
in 1854 issued the bull (official Papal document)
Ineffiabilis Deus in which he proclaimed, on his sole
authority, the immaculate conception of the Virgin
Mary. This doctrine, he affirmed, was revealed by
God and was to be believed firmly and constantly by all
the faithful. In issuing such a decree, Pius IX went
beyond the decrees of the Council of Trent. While Mary
had long been venerated by Catholics, there had not
been a uniform perspective concerning the manner of
her conception. Some (for example, Anselm of Canter-
bury, d. 1109) had viewed Mary as having been conceived
in sin and thus subject to original sin as was everyone
else with the exception of Christ. Others had held to
the immaculate conception of Mary, but prior to Pius IX
it had not been defined as a dogma necessary for faith.
This is precisely what Pius IX did in Ineffiabilis Deus,
proclaiming "the Blessed Virgin Mary to have been, from
the first instant of her conception, by a singular grace
and privilege of almighty God, in view of the merits

of Jesus Christ the Saviour of Mankind, preserved free
from all stain of original sin."[1] It is important to
note that Pius IX elevated the immaculate conception
of the Virgin Mary into a dogma necessary for faith
on the basis of his own authority. Because of this,
the significance of this decree went beyond its content. For the first time in the history of the church,
a dogma was issued officially without its having been
considered previously by a Council. The view that the
authority of the Pope was sufficient for the promulga-
tion of a dogma now appeared. It was but a short step
from this position to that of promulgating the dogma
of Papal infallibility.

Secondly, the right-wing response of Pius IX was
nowhere more clearly set forth than in his encyclical
(a letter sent by the Pope to all the clergy) Syllabus
errorum or Syllabus of Errors. The Syllabus covered a
wide range of topics in eighty succinct paragraphs which
were stated negatively, indicating emphatically what
the Pope rejected. In some of them he condemned things
which most Christians oppose, such as pantheism, natur-
alism, absolute rationalism, and absolute nationalism.
But he also repudiated other things which many Christians accept and some of which provide the foundation
for modern states. Among the repudiations of the Pope
were the denial of the temporal power of the Pope and
of his absolute authority over the Church, the rejection
of Catholicism as the only true religion, the claim that
Protestantism is but another form of the same true religion, the toleration of varieties in religion, the
rejection of the Church's authority with respect to
marriage and divorce, the separation of church and
state, and the non-sectarian schools which had arisen
in Western nations. In the final paragraph the Pope
clearly and succinctly summarized his negative perspective on modern culture when he condemned the claim that
"the Roman Pontiff can and ought to reconcile himself
to and agree with progress, liberalism, and civilization as lately introduced."[2]

Thirdly, the right-wing response of Piux IX was
demonstrated in the decree concerning papal infallibility. It was the most important result of Vatican
Council I which, under the close supervision of
Pius IX, met during 1869-1870. The Council's dogmatic
decree concerning papal infallibility said in part:

> Therefore faithfully adhering to the
> tradition received from the beginning of

341

the Christian faith, for the glory of
God our Savior, the exaltation of the
Catholic religion, and the salvation
of Christian people, the sacred Council
approving, we [i.e., Pope Pius IX] teach
and define that it is a dogma divinely
revealed: that the Roman Pontiff, when
he speaks ex cathedra, that is, when in
discharge of the office of pastor and
doctor of all Christians, by virtue of his
supreme Apostolic authority, he defines a
doctrine regarding faith or morals to be
held by the universal Church, by the divine
assistance promised to him in blessed
Peter, is possessed of that infallibility
with which the divine Redeemer willed that
his Church should be endowed for defining
doctrine regarding faith or morals; and
that therefore such definitions of the
Roman Pontiff are irreformable of themselves, and not from the consent of the
Church.[3]

It should be noted that this decree concerns the
office rather than the person of the Pope. It is not
stated that the Pope is free from personal errors or
that all of his pronouncements are infallible. Infallibility is limited by three conditions, namely
that the Pope's decision is ex cathedra, that its
content deals with a doctrine concerning faith or
morals, and that it is intended for the whole church.
However, since it is not stated precisely when all
three of these conditions are met, a certain ambiguity
remains in this dogmatic decree. It is not surprising,
then, that, even though the decree was not intended
as such, many Catholics tend to view all statements
of the Pope which deal in any way with faith or morals
as possessing an aura of infallibility.

The decree gave dogmatic status not only to the
infallibility of the Pope under the conditions noted
above, but also to his universal episcopate. This is
stated clearly in the following section of the decree:

Hence we teach and declare that by
the appointment of our Lord the Roman Church
possesses a superiority of ordinary power
over all other churches, and that this
power of jurisdiction of the Roman Pontiff,
which is truly episcopal, is immediate;

342

to which all, of whatever rite and dignity, both individually and collectively, are bound, by their duty of hierarchical subordination and true obedience, to submit not only in matters which belong to faith and morals, but also to those that appertain to the discipline and government of the Church throughout the world, so that the Church of Christ may be one flock under one supreme pastor through preservation of unity both of communion and of profession of the same faith with the Roman Pontiff. This is the teaching of Catholic truth, from which no one can deviate without loss of faith and of salvation.[4]

We have seen that in the medieval period and in the Council of Trent there was a growing tendency to emphasize the authority of the Pope. With Pius IX and Vatican Council I this process culminated in the triumph of absolute papal monarchy over the Catholic Church.[5]

Not all of the popes were quite as extreme in their repudiation of modern culture as was Pius IX. The scholarly Leo XIII (1878-1903) did declare that the theology of Aquinas was the standard for Roman Catholic instruction, yet he sought also to apply Christian standards to the emerging social and economic patterns. He opposed slavery, championed the right of workers to organize unions, advocated social justice, and established "Catholic Action," a network of Catholic associations for social, benevolent, economic, and political purposes. Furthermore, he urged the study of the Bible and opened the treasures of the Vatican to historical scholars. Yet at the same time, he warned against the "misuse" of modern discoveries in Biblical studies. He did not disavow explicitly any of the positions taken by Pius IX in the Syllabus of Errors. He supported the ideal of a Catholic state, and on occasion warned against what the next Pope, Pius X, condemned as "modernism."[6]

Pius X (1903-1914) was as adamantly opposed to adjusting the Catholic faith to modern thought as had been Pius IX. In part, this opposition arose from what he regarded as a threat to the traditional faith from a few Catholic scholars who were espousing a "modernist" view. These scholars (some of whom are discussed later in the section on the left-wing response) were urging, among other things, a revision of the idea of dogma that would be compatible with the conclusions of modern Biblical criticism and with the idea of progress in nature and history. In 1907 Pius X issued the decree _Lamentabili_ in which he repudiated sixty-five "modernist" propositions. Prominent among them were the claims that divine inspiration does not extend to all of sacred Scripture, that scientific exegesis and textual criticism should be applied to the study of Old and New Testaments, that the Roman Church became the head of all the churches because of political conditions rather than divine providence, that scientific progress demands the readjusting of Christian doctrines, and that modern Catholicism can be reconciled with science only if it is transformed into a non-dogmatic Christianity.[7] Also in 1907 Pius X issued his encyclical _Pascendi_ which contained a thoroughgoing condemnation of modernism. Modernism, he claimed, placed science above faith and was nothing more than agnosticism, and the most stringent measures in rooting it out were justified. Two Catholic Biblical critics and theologians, Alfred Loisy and George Tyrrell, were excommunicated. Bishops were required to enforce the study of Aquinas, to be vigilant in censoring proscribed books, and to require all clergy and Catholic teachers to take an anti-modernist oath. This anti-modernist oath was reaffirmed in 1918 during the pontificate of Benedict XV (1914-1922) as obligatory for all clergy and teachers.[8]

In spite of the upheavals of World War II and its aftermath, Pope Pius XII (1939-1958) sought to hold the official position of the Catholic Church on its traditional doctrinal course. Even though in _Divino Afflante Spiritu_ (1943) he admitted that the use of scientific methods might be helpful in determining more accurately the original texts of the Bible, he urged the use of the exegesis employed by the Church Fathers (primarily allegorical) in the interpretation of the Scriptures. In the encyclical _Mystici Corporis Christi_ (1943) he proclaimed that the universal church as the mystical body of Christ is one, indivisible, and _identical_ with the Roman Catholic Church. In _Humani generis_ (1950) he repudiated efforts to find a basis for Catholic theology in some system of thought other than Scholasticism (basically Aquinas' theology) and traditional doctrines, and he condemned modernism, Marxism, and rationalism. Perhaps of most significance was his apostolic constitution

<u>Munificentissimus</u> <u>Deus</u> in which he reaffirmed the dogma of the immaculate conception of the Virgin Mary and defined Mary's bodily assumption into heaven as a dogma necessary for faith. As we have seen, the veneration of Mary as the mother of God had long been a part of popular Catholic devotion. This was the case also with respect to the belief that Mary had been taken bodily into heaven, but previously it had lacked official definition as a dogma. There had been some pressure at Vatican Council I (1870) for such an official declaration, but it was not promulgated until Pius XII did so in 1950. This was the first dogmatic decree to be issued officially since the decree of Vatican Council I concerning papal infallibility, and it said in part:

> Therefore the majestic Mother of God, from all eternity united in a mysterious way with Jesus Christ by one and the same decree of predestination, immaculate in her conception, in her divine motherhood a most unspotted virgin, the noble ally of the Divine Redeemer who bore off the triumph over sin and its supporters, finally achieved, as the supreme crown of her privileges, that she should be preserved immune from the corruption of the tomb, and, like her Son before her, having conquered death, should be carried up, in body and soul, to the celestial glory of Heaven, to reign there as Queen at the right hand of her Son, the immortal King of the ages. . . .

> Therefore we . . . declare and define, as a dogma revealed by God, that the immaculate Mother of God, ever-Virgin Mary, on the completion of the course of her earthly life, has been taken up, in body and soul, to the glory of heaven.[9]

In some ways Pius XII sought to adjust to the modern world. He advocated social justice, sought for peace in troubled times, was more favorably disposed toward political democracy than his predecessors, made use of the new media for mass communication, and warned against the dangers of nuclear armaments. However, as indicated above, in the theological realm he continued, developing even further in some respects, the right-wing response to the modern world of his predecessors.[10]

B. The Left-Wing Response of Catholic Modernism

While the _official_ position of the Roman Catholic
Church throughout most of the modern period may be
characterized as a right-wing response to the challenge
of modern culture, there were _some_ earnest and thought-
ful men (both priests and laymen) who sought to interpret Catholicism in terms of the modern intellectual
world. As we have seen, they were called "Modernists"
by Pope Pius X. The term "Modernism" is not used as
frequently today as it was about a generation ago, but
for those who used it, whether Protestant or Catholic,
it signified the attempt to reconcile the essentials
of Christian doctrine with scientific methods and
results and with the spirit and assumptions characteristic of the modern world (see Introduction to Part V).
In general, Modernism represented not so much a precise
system of thought as a liberal attitude of mind which
was not linked necessarily to any single inheritance
of faith or practice. However, in this section an
attempt will be made to describe briefly the basic
features of Catholic Modernism.

In his encyclical _Pascendi_ (see above) Pius X
described Modernism as though it were a movement or
"school" of agnostic thinkers bent on destroying Catholicism. Yet the Modernists did not found a sect,
organize a formal association, meet together in conferences, or publish an official journal. They regarded
themselves as Catholics seeking only to make the church
relevant in the modern world, and even those who were
excommunicated did not seek for a haven in Protestantism.
Thus George Tyrrell declared, "Modernists wear no uniform nor are they sworn to the defense of any system:
still less of that which his Holiness [Pius X] has
fabricated for them."[11] In 1908 the modernist, Alfred
Loisy, wrote the following concerning the Pope's encyclical, _Pascendi_:

> The so-called modernists are not a
> homogeneous and united group, as one
> would suppose if one consulted the
> papal encyclical, but a quite limited
> number of persons, who share the desire
> to adapt the Catholic religion to the
> intellectual, moral, and social needs of
> the present time. . . .
>
> The pope's exposition of the modernist
> doctrines is practically a fantasy of the

346

theological imagination, whereas he has
ignored what is the most important, one
might say the only essential, question.
. . . Pius X attributes to (the modernists)
a system conceived after the manner of
the scholastic theories, where not one
of them will recognize himself, and he
condemns them en bloc in the name of
his own system. . . . The fact is that
they have never formed in the Church a
sect nor a party, nor even a school;
that they have worked on very diverse
fields . . . and that, if they have
found themselves in agreement on certain
points, and in the first instance on the
necessity of a reform of Catholic teaching, it is because they have entered by
different routes into the current of contemporary thought, and that, through
varied experiences, they have reached the
same conclusion. . . . This state of things
is misconceived from the beginning to
the end of the papal encyclical.[12]

While there was much diversity in thought among
the Modernists with some holding to more "radical"
positions than others, there was a unity in their basic
orientation. This basic orientation had three foundations. First, there was an emphasis on freedom of
thought as a necessary condition for meaningfully relat-
ing the Catholic faith to the modern world. Secondly,
the historico-critical method of studying the Bible
and church history was advocated as a legitimate and
fruitful method of inquiry in these fields. Thirdly,
there was the acceptance of some form of evolutionist
view with respect to nature and history. As illustra-
tive of Modernism the positions of two famous Modernists who were contemporaries with Pope Pius X will be
described briefly in the following discussion.

The French Biblical critic and theologian, Alfred
Loisy (1857-1940), is viewed by many as the first great
intellectual leader of Modernism. Educated and ordained for the priesthood, Loisy served as parish priest
for a brief period, and then continued his studies at
the University of Paris, where he earned the Doctor of
Theology degree. In his written thesis for this degree,
History of the Old Testament Canon, he clearly opposed
the traditional teaching on the inspiration of Scripture
and supported the method of Biblical criticism. In

response to a question raised during his oral defense
of the thesis, he did not hesitate to declare that
"the redactor [editor] of the first chapter of Genesis
had not had the remotest suspicion of the doctrine of
evolution, and had no more condemned it than he had
approved it."[13]

In Loisy's view the roles of historical critic and
dogmatic theologian should be kept separate and distinct. The task of the historical critic was that of
impartially investigating church tradition and the
Bible. Such investigation would analyze critically
the relativities and changes which emerged in church
tradition, and it would use both lower and higher criticism in analyzing the Biblical writings. Thus, in his
critical studies of the Bible, Loisy affirmed, for
example, that the Pentateuch was written by several
authors instead of by Moses, that the New Testament
Gospels as written documents were not based on firsthand, eyewitness accounts of Jesus' career and teachings, that Mark was the earliest Gospel and was used
by the writers of Matthew and Luke, and that the Gospel
of John was later than the others and contains more of
the author's own theological reflections than narra-,
tives about Jesus' career and teachings.[14]

As a Biblical critic, Loisy came to the conclusion
that the Bible is not a kind of divine information service, dictated by God. It had not fallen from heaven,
but had been written by human beings subject to common
human limitations and the perspectives and thought
forms of ancient pre-scientific times. However, as a
theologian Loisy held that even though the message of
the Bible was expressed in the thought-forms of ancient times, it was a record of God's progressive revelation providing general religious and moral guidance.
The _forms_ are temporary since man changes through the
ages, but that which persists in spite of all changes
is the impulse given by Christ, the inspiration of his
spirit. To be kept alive and vital for modern man,
the Christian gospel must be accommodated to the
changes brought about by modern culture.

According to Loisy, not only the Bible but also
the church and its traditions had not fallen from heav-
en. The hierarchy, dogma, and sacraments of the church
had not been instituted directly by Christ but had
evolved in history. They are not unalterably fixed and
are not absolute. They are the expressions of human
experience and thus subject to its inescapable

348

relativities. The theological language of tradition and dogma inevitably contains symbols and metaphors, the utility of which varies with their dependence on man's intellectual and moral progress. Traditional theology by its undue attachment to the forms of the symbols obscures the very moral and religious insights for which the symbols stand. Thus dogmas need constant revision in order that they may give effective expression to the Christian spirit in the corporate life of the church and in the modern world. The expression of the Christian spirit is not simply an individual matter, for Christianity is a communal religion. The institutional church is as necessary to the gospel as the gospel is to the church, but the church should not be tied to the past. While past developments in the church were useful in their times, Catholicism cannot be justified by dubious claims concerning the Bible and past traditions. It can be justified by providing the conditions which make possible the deepest religious experience of the believers who give allegiance to this great historic institution and by meeting, insofar as it can, the recurring needs of all human beings.[15]

Another outstanding Modernist was George Tyrrell (1861-1909). He was reared in an Irish Protestant family, but at the age of eighteen he moved to London and converted to Catholicism. He then entered the Jesuit order, studied the writings of Thomas Aquinas, and was ordained a priest. For a while he taught philosophy at the Jesuit College at Stonyhurst. It was during this period that the Modernist approach began to play a role in his thinking. While influenced by Loisy, he was not as pre-eminent a historical scholar and Biblical critic as Loisy. Rather he was more of a religious thinker or theologian. Bernard Reardon has characterized him as "modernism's prophet, apostle, and most conspicuous martyr."[16] Personally deeply religious, he never ceased to regard himself as a devout Catholic, even after his excommunication.

Like Loisy, Tyrrell insisted that the doctrines of the inerrancy of the Bible and of the church were no longer tenable in light of the results of Biblical and historical criticism. Revelation was not an infallible body of doctrines given once for all in Apostolic times. It was the spirit or "idea" of Christianity which had been realized continuously in the experience of Christians. To be sure, the ultimate object of revelation was eternal but, similar to Loisy, Tyrrell claimed that

349

the historical _forms_ and _symbolic_ statements in which
revelation was received by human beings were not
eternal truths. They needed to be modified and improved continuously so that the spirit of Christianity
might be a vital reality in the life of the modern
world.

In Tyrrell's view Modernism was not a movement
away from _authentic_ Catholicism which he held to be
the only valid form of Christianity. Rather it was
simply the attempt to harmonize the essential truth of
the Catholic faith with the essential truth of modernity. This did not mean that the deposit of faith would
be ignored, but that it would be reinterpreted in light
of two criteria. Wherever it involved purported historical facts, the historico-critical method should be
used to determine the probable truth value of the
historical claims. The more important criterion for
judging matters of faith, however, is the religious
criterion, that is, the prayer-value of the belief.
Does the belief disclose the love of God for his creatures and increase human love for God and others?
Tyrrell, in a way similar to the perspective expressed
later by the French Catholic mathematician and theologian, Edouard LeRoy (1870-1950), emphasized a kind
of pragmatism in his theology. Dogmas are not to be
judged in terms of their truth-value but in terms of
their practical and experiential results. In a sense
dogmas are neither true nor false, but rather are prescriptions for action. Thus Tyrrell believed that
Catholic Christians can have confidence in their
creeds because of their value as practical guides for
the religious life. He expressed this point quite
clearly when he said:

> Assurance is found in the universally
> proved value of the Creed as a practical
> guide to the eternal life of the soul--
> a proof which is based on the experience
> not of this man or that, however wise or
> holy, but of the whole Christian people
> and of the Church of the Saints in all
> ages and nations.[17]

For Tyrrell, then, true Catholicism was a way of
life, a power of the spirit rather than of the letter.
The Church was a spiritual "organism" uniting its
members in the Christian way of life, the creed was
a practical guide for the Christian way of life, and
theology was an attempt to understand this way of life.

Since theology always represents contingent human formulations, and since culture is constantly evolving and changing, theological formulations are subject to constant change and improvement.

As we have seen, Modernism, even though it had a very small following, aroused strong opposition and was rejected adamantly by several popes. Loisy and Tyrrell were excommunicated. Less radical Modernists were not excommunicated, but some of them were removed from teaching positions and had their writings placed on the Index of Prohibited Books. In the papacy's perspective, Modernism was to remain a "dangerous" subject for Catholics until the Second Vatican Council (1962-1965), and yet it did have a measure of influence on the thinking of some Catholic scholars in the generation after Loisy and Tyrrell. It was not so much that these "younger" scholars agreed with the particular answers given by the earlier Modernists to the issues of modernity, but that given the upheavals of two world wars, the depression, and the threat of the atomic bomb, they thought it was crucial to find viable answers to the questions which had been of concern to the Modernists. Even though not as radical as the extreme Modernists, these scholars may be classified as leftwing or "liberal." A few have been disciplined to some extent by the Vatican, but none of them have been excommunicated. In general, they have had a much greater influence on subsequent Catholic thought and perspectives than did their Modernists predecessors. This influence is evident at a number of places in the Constitution, Decrees, and Declarations of the Second Vatican Council (to be discussed below).

As with the earlier Modernists, there is much variety of thought among these "liberals," most of whom were born during the period of World War I. They are similar to the Modernists in respect to the fact that they too have not established any organized movement. Yet they have held or do hold important positions, primarily in the academic realm. A few of the most prominent among these scholars and priests are the Europeans Pierre Teilhard de Chardin, Yves M. J. Congar, Karl Rahner, Edward Schillebeeckx, and Hans Küng, and the Americans Gustave Weigel, John L. McKenzie, and John Courtney Murray.[18] It is impossible to discuss in detail the thought of each one of these scholars. Instead a brief summary of certain points on which they agree in general, if not in detail, will be presented.

351

Like the earlier Modernists, these liberal Catholic scholars acknowledge the value of the historico-critical method of Biblical exegesis. Some of them have specialized in Biblical studies, learning linguistics, history, and methods in universities which have no ties with any particular religious institutions. Often, along with scholars of different religious affiliations, they have participated in scholarly societies concerned with Biblical studies, and in some cases they have been elected to positions of leadership in these societies. For example, in 1965 the members of The Society of Biblical Literature elected as its president the Catholic Biblical scholar, John L. McKenzie. This society publishes the distinguished journal, The Journal of Biblical Literature, and is the major society for Biblical studies in the United States and Canada.

The Biblical studies of the Catholic liberals have not led them, however, to the same radical conclusions of the extreme Modernists such as the denial of Jesus' divinity, his resurrection, and the legitimacy of the Apostle Paul's version of Christianity.[19] For the most part, they have been able to correlate scientific Biblical exegesis with the basic doctrines of Catholic Christianity. According to Gustave Weigel in the 1960 Taylor Lectures at Yale Divinity School:

> The presence of tradition does not hamper the action of the theological exegete any more than gravity hampers the racer. It only keeps him on the ground. . . . Nor is such exegesis static. It grows, and it grows precisely by the new insights of individuals which trigger the awareness of the total Church. . . . In fact, the cry of the Church to all its members is to deepen the awareness of all in the growing explanation of the word of God.[20]

The liberals also are similar to the Modernists in their acceptance of some form of evolutionist perspective. On this point, undoubtedly the most famous of those listed above was Pierre Teilhard de Chardin, a paleontologist of distinction and a priest in the Jesuit order. He attempted to relate the Christian understanding of God and the world to the scheme of evolutionary process. In his view, the fundamental ingredient of the universe is a kind of energy which is in the process of development. This process is

352

continuous but reveals three stages in which there are profound changes. The first stage is the emergence of inorganic matter; the second is the emergence of life; and the third is the appearance of thought or mind. In this stage is the emergence of man in which the cosmos becomes "personalitic." Yet the evolutionary process does not stop here, for it will continue in the future toward a higher consciousness, namely communion and socialization on a planetary scale. However, the process is not without an end, for Teilhard's thought contained an eschatological element. The end of the process is a point of convergence which Teilhard called the "Omega-point." In it all things will have reached a suprapersonal unity in God in which Agape (self-giving love) will reign supreme. But the Omega is not just the end point of the evolutionary process, it is also the logos or Word of God which directs the process toward this goal. The nature of this goal can be comprehended in the present since a foretaste of it has been given already in Christ, the Word of God incarnate. As Teilhard said, "In place of the vague focus of convergence demanded as a terminus for evolution, we now have the well-defined personal reality of the Incarnate Word in whom all things hold together."[21] Thus it was Teilhard's conviction that in Jesus Christ, God had taken the initiative and disclosed his ultimate purpose for all creation. Through this disclosure and the power of persuasion he seeks to lure human beings along the pathway leading toward the goal of a universal agapeistic fellowship in unity with himself and all reality.[22]

Generally supported by the Catholic liberals in recent times is the trend among some groups within modern Christendom to seek for a greater degree of interconfessional cooperation among the Christian churches. The technical term used to designate the theologies, policies, and actions which are directed toward the ultimate goal of world-wide Christian unity is "ecumenism." In a variety of ways the liberals have indicated a general commitment to the ecumenical ideal and have given some attention to the very grave practical and theological problems confronting the Ecumenical Movement. As a necessary preliminary to greater ecumenical relations with non-Catholic Christians, unlike Pius IX, they do not dismiss Protestantism as being something other than simply another form of the Christian religion, and they regard all non-Catholic Christians, Protestant and Eastern Orthodox, as Christian brothers. Further, they have advocated the

establishment of, and actively engaged in, dialogue
sessions between Catholic and non-Catholic Christians.
In a lecture on "Ecumenism and the Roman Catholic
Church" given in 1960 at the Lancaster Theological
Seminary (supported by the Protestant United Church of
Christ), Gustave Weigel concluded by saying:

> Catholic and Protestant ecumenists
> must develop the virtue of patience.
> Centuries of hostility have colored our
> attitudes towards each other and we cannot
> see simply what is simply there. Each mem-
> ber of the dialogue must keep on learning,
> keep on revising his concept and image of
> his partner in high talk. Misunderstandings
> cannot be avoided for some time to come
> but we must not harden the misunderstandings
> which the past has forced on us. . . . The
> ecumenical obligation is to promote col-
> loquy. To promote it we need to do more
> than merely be ready for it. We must with
> patience and forbearance overcome the
> difficulties which stand in the way of
> meeting.[23]

Given their support of ecumenism, it is not surprising that Catholic liberals have been strong advocates of religious freedom. For example, John Courtney
Murray has written extensively on this subject, claiming that religious freedom is a natural right of all
persons, that political unity does not require unity
in religion, that the state is not the secular arm of
the church nor the church the religious arm of the
state, and that Catholicism itself flourishes better
in a religiously pluralistic society where freedom of
religion is guaranteed. According to Murray, every
church should have the "freedom to define itself,
and . . . the consequent right to reject definition
at the hands of any secular authority. To resign this
freedom or to abdicate this right would be at once the
betrayal of religion and the corruption of politics."[24]

In addition to their general support for historico-
critical Biblical exegesis, evolutionist perspective,
ecumenism, and religious freedom, the liberals' perspective generally includes three other elements. First,
they tend to disapprove of a narrow juridical conception of the Church and the papacy and to advocate that
emphasis be placed on the role of service to mankind.
Secondly, they tend to be critical of Thomism (Thomas

Aquinas' theology, especially as taught by later advocates) and of the Greek substance philosophy in scholastic thought. Thirdly, they tend to advocate a theological and religious renewal rooted in the Bible, the Church Fathers, and a deepened understanding of the liturgy.

C. The Moderate Response of Pope John XXIII
and the Second Vatican Council

As we have seen, the reaction of the papacy to the challenge of modern culture was largely that of a right-wing response. From Pius IX through Pius XII the popes generally had demonstrated negative attitudes toward modern culture and had developed a tradition of protest against it. Thus in his first encyclical, Summi Pontificatus, Pope Pius XII denounced modern culture as full of evil and disorder, and affirmed that the ultimate source of this condition was the separation of large groups from the Roman Catholic Church which began at the Reformation. This act of infidelity was the basic causal condition for the rise in modern culture of liberalism, secularism, and atheistic socialism. Thus the Pope found the modern world worthy only of condemnation and unleashed a scathing attack on it. For example, among other things, he said the following:

> The beginning of all the troubles
> which are driving this age of ours by a
> headlong course into spiritual bankruptcy
> and impotence for virtue, is the impious
> attempt to dethrone Christ. . . . They
> [modern men] did not reflect that it would
> mean handing themselves over to a capri-
> cious ruler, the feeble and grovelling
> wisdom of men. They boasted of progress,
> when they were in fact relapsing into
> decadence; they conceived that they were
> reaching heights of achievement when they
> were miserably forfeiting their human
> dignity; they claimed that this century of
> ours was bringing maturity and completion
> with it, when they were being reduced
> to a pitiable form of slavery.[25]

The successor of Pius XII, Pope John XXIII (1958-1963), displayed a quite different attitude. Unlike his predecessors, he accepted and welcomed the modern world. It was not that he approved of all modern beliefs or that he was a liberal in all of his

theological understanding. He was rather conservative
as far as discipline and devotion were concerned. He
even admired Pius XII for his scholarly erudition and
quoted him frequently. Yet his innate good humor,
kindliness, optimism, and the simplicity and goodness
which he had acquired through years of rigorous devotional discipline predisposed him to emphasize the
goodness which he found in people and in the world.
While fully aware of the evils in the world, especially
of poverty, disease, disunity among nations and religious people, the threat of war and the atomic bomb,
he nevertheless disagreed with the prophets of doom.
He was reluctant to criticize and condemn and instead
emphasized the improvements, opportunities, and causes
for encouragement in the modern world. The Church,
he felt, needed to come into a closer relationship
with the world in order to serve it more effectively.

E. E. Y. Hales has contrasted the pontificate of
John XXIII with that of his predecessors as follows:

> There is this difference between Pope
> John's approach and that of his predeces-
> sors. Whereas they, in their major
> writings, couched their thoughts in terms
> of the need for a return to the fold, for
> recognition of the authority of the See
> of Peter, for an end to the great apostasy,
> Pope John did not. He may have longed, he
> may have prayed, he may have laboured as
> much as any of them for unity; and he knew
> quite as well as they that in that great
> structure of unity the Holy See must provide
> the corner-stone, that the special character
> of the papal authority must in the end be
> accepted. But he chose to say little about
> it. Where his predecessors lamented,
> appealed, or rebuked, he was silent. He
> was not directly trying to get the world
> 'back in'. He was going out into the
> world, to help the world, in whatever way
> the world was willing to be helped. And
> he did so because he was thinking of his
> role in different terms, he was thinking
> of all men as sons of God and therefore
> of himself as their spiritual father on
> earth, whether they chose to recognize
> him or no.[26]

Thus, even though Pope John did not advocate changes in

the substance of sacred doctrine or define any new dogmas,[27] he did advocate a change of emphasis in the Catholic Church from isolation, preoccupation with itself, and self-defense to what has been called an "open Catholicism."[28] That is, he advocated that the Church seek to move into closer contact with the modern world and to become more responsive to the needs of all human beings.

An incident related to Norman Cousins, editor of Saturday Review, by Monsignor Igino Cardinalle, Chief of Protocol in the Vatican, graphically illustrates Pope John's concern for an open Catholicism. In an audience with the Pope a Canadian dignitary asked him to explain the main objectives of his papacy in general and the Second Vatican Council in particular. Pope John arose, walked over to a window, opened it and said, "What do we intend to do? We intend to let in a little fresh air."[29]

It is surely the case that Pope John's family background, personal experiences, and variety of positions held in different countries during his long career before becoming Pope helped to prepare him with the insights and abilities needed for a pontificate which would support an open Catholicism. Angelo Guiseppe Roncalli was born in 1881 in a mountain village near Bergamo in northern Italy. His parents were rather humble farm workers, and he was the third of their thirteen children. Early in his life Angelo decided to become a priest, and with the financial assistance of a priest friend, he studied in the seminary at Bergamo. Later he earned a doctorate in theology at Rome, became secretary to the Bishop of Bergamo, accompanied the Bishop on frequent trips to France, and became fluent in French. During World War I he was a military chaplain and observed all the horrors and suffering caused by the war. In 1921 Pope Benedict XI appointed him a member of the Council of the Congregation for the Propogation of the Faith, one of the agencies of the Curia ("Curia" designates the administrative offices or agencies in the Vatican, somewhat analogous to the executive branch of government in Washington). Since the responsibility of this Congregation is foreign missions, Father Roncalli's work on the Council brought him a knowledge of churches, nations, and international issues around the world and thus broadened his vision. In 1925 Pope Pius XI, having consecrated Father Roncalli as a bishop and promoted him to the position of archbishop, sent him as Apostolic Delegate (papal ambassador)

to Bulgaria. Ten years later he was sent on the same
mission to Turkey. In both places he managed to win
the acceptance and good will of the civil and religious
authorities who were predominantly Eastern Orthodox and
Moslem.

Archbishop Roncalli's tenure as Apostolic Delegate
in Turkey included the years of World War II. He was
deeply disturbed by the brutalities of the war and the
sufferings of its victims, including the Jews. Several
of his biographies give accounts of his tireless efforts on behalf of refugees. For example, on one
occasion he was directly involved in saving the lives
of hundreds of Jewish children. A boatload of Jewish
children who had been smuggled out of Germany docked
in Istanbul. But because of its neutrality, the
Turkish government ordered that the children be returned to Germany. When he heard of this order, Archbishop Roncalli was horrified, knowing that a return
to Germany meant their death. Thus he immediately made
personal pleas on behalf of the children to the proper
governmental officials, and by the power of his considerable and unceasing diplomacy was able to persuade
the Turkish government to rescind the order and to
transfer the children to another neutral country. Concerning Archbishop Roncalli's efforts on behalf of
Jewish refugees, Dr. Isaac Herzog, chief rabbi of
Jerusalem, later wrote, "Cardinal Roncalli is a man
who really loves the People of the Book and through him
thousands of Jews were rescued."[30]

In 1944 Pope Pius XII appointed Archbishop Roncalli
Papal Nuncio to France, one of the Vatican's highest
diplomatic posts, and Permanent Observer for the Vatican to the United Nation's Educational, Scientific, and
Cultural Organization which had its headquarters in
Paris.[31] Early in January of 1953, at the age of
seventy-two, he was made a Cardinal by the Pope, and
it was reported that upon being informed of this pro-
motion he said to his secretary: "After this difficult
post [in France] I had hoped to become a pastor some
place or perhaps a bishop in Bergamo. But now I will
probably go to the Curia. I'll suffocate in dusty
documents and drown in bureaucratic mire."[32] However,
he was appointed Patriarch (responsible for several
bishoprics) of Venice where he soon won the hearts of
the people. When asked what his policy would be, he
replied, "I stand for that which unites, and I hold
at a distance that which divides."[33] For almost five
years, from age seventy-two into his seventy-sixth year

358

Cardinal Roncalli served as Patriarch of Venice. At a time of life when most people have retired from their careers, he did an enormous amount of work, founding thirty new parishes and a new seminary. In order to secure money for the seminary he sold a beautiful villa which the former Patriarchs had used as a country residence, and responded to those critics who pointed out that the villa provided a good place to rest by saying, "I sleep perfectly well in Venice."[34]

When Cardinal Roncalli went to Rome for the conclave of Cardinals after the death of Pope Pius XII on October 9, 1958, he most certainly had no expectation of being selected Pope. Who would have thought that his fellow Cardinals would come finally to select a man of his advanced age for the most exalted and demanding position in the Church? Yet on the third day of the conclave, October 28, 1958, his name appeared on more than the required two thirds of the Cardinals' ballots. His first act after accepting his election broke with precedent and was a portent of the new directions which his pontificate would take. Upon being asked, "By what name shall you be called," he replied, "I will be called John."[35] In this act he departed from the custom of popes in modern times of selecting names like Pius, Benedict, or Leo and turned all the way back to Pope John XXII in the fourteenth century. For five hundred years no pope had selected the name John because the last person to select it had been the anti-pope, John XXIII, whose election had been declared invalid. But the new Pope declared to the Cardinals that the name John was dear to him because it was the name of his father, of the parish church in which he was baptized, of John the Baptist and John the Evangelist. Thus he would bear the name of John XXIII and restore it to a legitimate place in the valid succession of popes.

In light of his background, it is not surprising that during his brief pontificate (October 28, 1958 - June 3, 1963) Pope John XXIII sought to be the "parish priest of the world"[36] and "to open the windows of the Vatican" to the world. This was evident not only in his encyclicals, especially _Mater et Magistra_ and _Pacem in Terris_, but also in numerous unique actions which demonstrated his deep sensitivity to the feelings and needs of all sorts of people.[37] He refused to become a "prisoner" of the Vatican, making unannounced personal visits to hospitals, orphanages, and prisons in Rome and receiving an enormous number of persons of all faiths for audiences. His concern for all human beings and his desire for an open Catholicism found expression also in his greatest accomplishment, namely the calling into being of the Second Vatican Council, the major purpose of which in his vision was to serve the goals of Christian unity and world peace. That a pope of the advanced age of seventy-six, whom many thought of as simply a transition or interim pope, would take such action was unexpected. But Pope John simply did not fit into the stereotyped images of an old person and a pope. In a certain sense he never became "old." The following description of an elderly friend by the philosopher, Martin Buber, aptly characterizes Pope John XXIII: "To be old is a glorious thing when one has not unlearned what it means to begin. . . . He was not at all young, but he was old in a young way, knowing how to begin."[38]

Preparation for the Council involved Pope John in an extraordinary amount of work and required the better part of three years, from the announcement early in 1959 that he would convoke the Council, to its first session in the Fall of 1962. There was the appointment of a pre-preparatory commission whose task was that of securing suggestions for the Council's agenda from the bishops, the Curia, the universities, and the seminaries. There was the selection of the members of the preparatory commissions, each one of which was to prepare a "schema" or report on a specific issue on the agenda which would be considered for adoption in the formal sessions of the Council. While the chairmen of the commissions were from the Curia, the members were drawn from all over the world and included some "liberal" names. In the announcement concerning his appointments to the preparatory commissions Pope John said, "The government of the Church, which is the occupation of the Roman Curia is one thing, and the Council is another."[39] Thus he made it clear that the Council was not to be under the control of the Curia. Indeed, he insisted that it was to be a genuinely free council.

In addition to the other commissions, Pope John appointed a central commission presided over by himself with the assistance of the newly created Secretariat For Christian Unity. The task of this commission was that of coordinating the work of the several commissions dealing with the issues on the Council's agenda. In the first meeting of these commissions in November of 1960 Pope John told the members that their task was not so much to concern themselves with this or that

point of doctrine as "to show in its true light and
restore to its true value the quality of human and
Christian life, of which the Church is the custodian
and mistress throughout the centuries."[40] Several
months before the Council opened, Pope John sent invita-
tions to non-Catholic Christian churches and communities
to send delegate-observers to the Council. While these
delegate-observers were without voice or vote in the
formal sessions of the Council, there was considerable
informal dialogue between them and the Council Fathers.

The first session of the Council was held from
October 11 through December 8, 1962 with 2500 Council
Fathers (Cardinals, Archbishops, bishops, apostolic
prefects, ecclesiastical deans, etc.) in attendance.
In his address to the Council on the opening day Pope
John emphasized again his desire that the Council make
a lasting contribution to the cause of concord, just
peace, and the brotherly unity of all. He indicated
his disagreement with the "prophets of gloom" who
could see nothing but error, degeneration, and ruin in
modern times. He insisted that the Church was not
simply against things but passionately for things, that
"she meets the needs of the present day by demonstrating the validity of her teaching rather than by condem-
nations."[41] Among the important statements in this
address which indicated Pope John's concern that the
deliberations of the Council would move the Church
in the direction of an open Catholicism are the following:

> Illuminated by the light of this
> Council, the Church--we confidently
> trust--will become greater in spiritual
> riches and, gaining the strength of new
> energies therefrom, she will look to the
> future without fear. In fact, by bringing
> herself up to date where required, and by
> the wise organization of mutual cooperation,
> the Church will make men, families, and
> peoples really turn their minds to heavenly
> things. . . .

> In order . . . that this doctrine [the
> Church's deposit of faith] may influence
> the numerous fields of human activity,
> with reference to individuals, to families,
> and to social life, it is necessary first
> of all that the Church should never depart
> from the sacred patrimony of truth received

from the Fathers. But at the same time
we must ever look to the present, to the
new conditions and new forms of life introduced into the modern world which have
opened new avenues to the Catholic apostolate. . . .

Authentic doctrine . . . should be
studied and expounded through the methods
of research and through the literary forms
of modern thought. The substance of the
ancient doctrine of the deposit of faith
is one thing, and the way in which it is
presented is another. And it is the latter
that must be taken into great consideration
with patience if necessary, everything being measured in forms and proportions of
a magisterium [the Church's teaching
authority] which is predominantly pastoral
in character.[42]

Pope John was not to witness the conclusion of the
Council. A few months after the first session, on
June 3, 1963, he died and was succeeded by Pope Paul VI.
Pope Paul continued the Council which met in formal
session three more times in the fall of each year from
1963 through 1965. From these sessions there emerged
sixteen documents which were approved by the Council
and the Pope and which in the Latin text, exclusive of
footnotes, run to approximately 103,000 words. In
terms of their impact on the life of the Church, of the
changes brought about in thought and practice, the
most important of the sixteen documents are the seven
which are summarized briefly in the following discussion.[43]

1. The Dogmatic Constitution on the Church

Although called a Dogmatic Constitution, the most
solemn form of conciliar utterance, this first of the
documents does not define any new dogmas. Like many
of the other documents it is primarily pastoral in
tone and ecumenical in spirit. In many ways it
reflects a shift in emphasis and provides certain
important theological bases for the other documents.
The shift in emphasis is evident in the first chapter
on "The Mystery of the Church," at the beginning of
which it is affirmed that "by her relationship to
Christ, the Church is a kind of sacrament or sign
of intimate union with God, and of the unity of all

362

mankind. She is also an instrument for the achievement of such union and unity" (Documents, P. 15).[44]
Emphasis is not on the Church triumphant but on the
Church's responsibility to be like Christ, a servant
of all.

Furthermore, in a discussion of the Church as the
mystical Body of Christ, there appears near the end of
Chapter One the following significant statement:

> This Church, constituted and organized
> in the world as a society, subsists in
> the Catholic Church, which is governed
> by the successor of Peter and by the
> bishops in union with that successor,
> although many elements of sanctification
> and truth can be found outside of her
> visible structure (Documents, P. 23;
> the italics are mine).

It should be noted that the term "subsists" means "to
continue to exist or inhere in." But the fact that
one thing inheres in another does not necessarily entail that it cannot inhere in other things as well.
To say that the Church as the mystical body of Christ
subsists in the Catholic Church leaves open the possibility that it may be present also in non-Catholic
churches. Clearly this is the meaning intended by the
Council since it is indicated explicitly that many
elements of sanctification and truth can be found
outside the visible structures of the Catholic Church.
Thus there is a definite shift away from the traditional
perspective that only the Catholic Church is "the ark
of salvation," a view held by previous popes (such as
Pius IX and Pius XII) who claimed that the Church as
the mystical body of Christ and the Catholic Church
are identical, and thus only the Catholic Church is
the true Church. The departure from this position in
the first chapter of the Constitution on the Church
expresses an ecumenical spirit, an expression which is
more fully developed in the Decree on Ecumenism.

A shift of emphasis is evident in the very order
of succession for the chapters in this constitution.
In the final draft, the chapter on the Church as "The
People of God" (Chapter II) precedes the chapter on
"The Hierarchical Structure of the Church With Special
Reference to the Episcopate" (Chapter III). Richard P.
McBrien has pointed out that "at the beginning [i.e.,
the first draft by the commission responsible for

writing this constitution] emphasis was on the institutional, hierarchical, and juridical aspects of the
Church," that the chapter on the hierarchy preceded
the chapter on the people of God, and that "to speak
of the Church's hierarchy before speaking of the
Church as People of God would simply carry forward
the . . . tradition that the Church is, first and
foremost, a hierarchical institution to which people
belong for the sake of certain spiritual benefits."[45]
However, as a result of vigorous debate within the
sessions of the Council, the positions of these two
chapters were reversed in the final draft. This order
of succession and the designation of the Church as the
People of God have several important implications.
First, it recalls the Biblical theme of the Covenant
people of God. Secondly, it replaces the static view
of the Church as triumphant, as already the kingdom
of God, with a dynamic view of the Church as a pilgrim
people journeying on the way toward the eschatological
goal of the kingdom of God. Thirdly, the expression
"People of God" has ecumenical implications since the
scope of its meaning is inclusive of all Christians
(see Documents, pp. 24-36). Fourthly, the order of
succession implies that the proper function of the
hierarchy is that of helping the People of God to fulfill their mission in history. The function of the
hierarchy and of the entire Church is not to dominate
but to serve.

     The Council's shift of emphasis is evident also
in the content of Chapter III on the hierarchical
structure of the Church. Although the Council affirmed
that the Pope and bishops have supreme authority over
the Church, it insisted that this authority is to be
exercised always in terms of service and in a collegial
manner. Bishops are not just vicars of the Roman Pontiff but are shepherds of the flock and should be like
the Good Shepherd who came not to be served but to
serve. In so doing, they should listen to and collab-
orate with the priests and laity of their dioceses so
that all might work together for the good of the whole.
With the Pope, bishops share in the entire leadership
of the Catholic Church. While the Council spoke of
papal infallibility with respect to defining doctrines
based on the deposit of revelation, it also spoke of
collegial cooperation between Pope and bishops in the
process of arriving at such definitions. According to
the Council, "the Roman Pontiff as the successor of
Peter and the bishops as the successors of the apostles
are joined together. . . . Together with its head, the

Roman Pontiff, and never without this head, the episcopal order is the subject of supreme and full power
over the universal Church" (Documents, pp. 42-43).
This collegial union is expressed not only in ecumenical councils but also "in the mutual relations of the
individual bishops with particular churches and with
the universal Church" (Documents, p. 44).

The implications of this theology concerning the
episcopacy in the Constitution on the Church were
developed further and made explicit in the "Decree on
the Bishops' Pastoral Office in the Church" (Documents,
pp. 396-429). In this decree the Council made two
important recommendations. First, it recommended that
the departments of the Roman Curia "be reorganized and
better adapted to the needs of the times, and of
various regions and rites" (Documents, p. 402). Secondly, it recommended the establishment of a "council
to be known by the proper name of Synod of Bishops.
Since it will be acting in the name of the entire
Catholic episcopate, it will at the same time demonstrate that all the bishops in hierarchical communion
share in the responsibility for the universal Church"
(Documents, pp. 399-400). Pope Paul VI established
such a Synod which has held five sessions since the
end of Vatican Council II. The central committee or
secretariat of the Synod is composed of fifteen members with only three appointed by the Pope and twelve
elected by and from the Synod's membership. Unlike
the executives of the Curia who live at the Vatican,
the members of the Synod's secretariat habitually live
at home in their own dioceses where they are more likely to be in touch with the real problems of the Church
and the world.

In the Constitution on the Church the Council made
it clear that its vision of the Church as the People of
God was not limited simply to the hierarchy in collegial
union. The whole People of God is inclusive of the
laity, the religious (members of monastic orders), and
the clergy (the priests). All have an essential and
proper role in the life of the Church. The role of
the laity is not simply that of participating in the
mission of the hierarchy. In Chapter IV of this constitution the Council declared that "the lay apostolate
. . . is a participation in the saving mission of the
Church itself" (Documents, p. 59). The laity are
encouraged to be the servants of Christ in the world
by means of their actions in their secular occupations.
The clergy (hierarchy and priests) are exhorted to be

the servants of Christ in the world. All are called
to holiness (Documents, pp. 65-72) so that the Church
may be a more effective servant of the world and fulfill its mission in history. The traditional distinction between higher and lower levels of Christian
faithfulness (see Chapter VII above, "The Medieval
Period") is abandoned. The Council understood holiness
as the sincere love of God and neighbor, and affirmed
that it is both a possibility and an imperative for all
Christians.

2. The Dogmatic Constitution on Revelation

The first chapter of this constitution reflects
the fact that the Council advocated a view of revelation which transcends the traditional view that the
nature of revelation is primarily a set of propositions,
and supported a view of faith which transcends the traditional view that faith is primarily intellectual
assent to a set of propositions. This is clearly evident in the following statements:

> In his goodness and wisdom, God chose
> to reveal Himself and to make known to us
> the hidden purpose of his will (cf. Eph. 1:9).
> . . . Through his revelation . . . the invi-
> sible God (cf. Col. 1:15, I Tim. 1:17) out
> of the abundance of His love speaks to men
> as friends (cf. Ex. 33:11; Jn. 15:14-15)
> and lives among them (cf. Bar. 3:38), so
> that He may invite and take them into
> fellowship with Himself. This plan of
> revelation is realized by deeds and words
> having an inner unity; the deeds wrought by
> God in the history of salvation manifest
> and confirm the teaching and realities
> signified by the words, while the words
> proclaim the deeds and clarify the mystery
> contained in them. By this revelation then,
> the deepest truth about God and the salva-
> tion of man is made clear to us in Christ,
> who is the Mediator and at the same time
> the fulness of all revelation. . . .

> The obedience of faith (Rom. 16:26;
> cf. 1:5, 2 Cor. 10:5-6) must be given to
> God who reveals, an obedience by which man
> entrusts his whole self freely to God,
> offering the full submission of intellect
> and will to God who reveals, and freely

assenting to the truth revealed by Him (Documents, pp. 112-113; the italics are mine).

In light of the view that God reveals his will through deeds in history, it follows that revelation is public. Yet it has to be made known to others by the testimonies of the recipients. The oral transmission of revelation becomes sacred tradition; put into writing it becomes sacred Scripture. Thus in Chapter II of this constitution the Council declared that "sacred tradition and sacred Scripture form one sacred deposit of the Word of God, which is committed to the Church" (Documents, p. 117), and that "the task of authentically interpreting the Word of God, whether written or handed on, has been entrusted exclusively to the living teaching office [Pope and bishops collectively] of the Church" (Documents, pp. 117-118). However, the Council insisted that the teaching office is not superior to the Word of God but its servant, and with the help of the Holy Spirit interprets it faithfully.

Four of this constitution's six chapters (3-6) deal explicitly with the Bible, and at certain points reflect a shift away from traditional perspectives. Among these points are the following: First, there is a departure from the traditional view that the Bible is inerrant or infallible in all respects. In the main the traditional view had held that Biblical passages express both a literal and an allegorical (spiritual) meaning, and that both meanings are infallible. The Council, however, declared that "the books of Scripture must be acknowledged as teaching firmly, faithfully, and without error that truth which God wanted put into sacred writings for the sake of our salvation" (Documents, p. 119). This statement appears to mean that in its affirmations about revelation and salvation the Bible is infallible, but that it need not be infallible in what it affirms about such things as political history and the natural world. If this is the case, the statement does not entail a quantitative distinction, namely that some passages deal with salvation and are infallible, and others deal with natural matters and are not infallible. Rather it is a formal distinction. That is, even those passages which speak of natural matters also have an allegorical or spiritual meaning. The spiritual meaning is infallible but the natural meaning need not be.

Secondly, the claim made above that the Council

did not hold that the Bible is infallible in all respects seems to be supported by the statement in which
the Council "encourages the sons of the Church who
are Biblical scholars to continue energetically with
the work they have so well begun" (Documents, p. 126).
This represents a definite shift from the perspective
of Pope Pius X who condemned scientific and critical
Biblical scholarship. Furthermore, the Council recommended that Catholic Biblical scholars cooperate with
Biblical scholars from non-Catholic churches in producing new translations of the Bible so that "all
Christians will be able to use them" (Documents, p.
126).

Thirdly, the Council recommended that "easy access
to sacred Scripture should be provided for all the
Christian faithful" (Documents, p. 125), and that all
the clergy and the laity should engage in careful study
of the Bible. Since the Bible is "the support and
energy of the Church" (Documents, p. 125), all the
"sons of the Church" need to become more familiar with
it. This recommendation departs from the traditional
reluctance of the Catholic Church to make the Bible
available to laity for fear that heretical views might
develop out of its misinterpretation.

3. The Constitution on the Sacred Liturgy

It is by means of corporate worship that the faith
in any religion is kept alive and vital. It is not
surprising, then, that the Council gave attention to
the sacred liturgy (public worship and its forms and
ritual). In the first chapter of this constitution
the Council declared that while "the sacred liturgy
does not exhaust the entire activity of the Church
[it] is the summit toward which the activity of the
Church is directed [and] the fountain from which all
her power flows." There was the reaffirmation of the
traditional view that "from the liturgy . . . and
especially from the Eucharist [the Mass or Holy Com-
munion], as from a fountain, grace is channeled into
us" (Documents, p. 142). However, even though the
Council retained certain basic theological and ritual
elements in the liturgy, it recommended many changes
with respect to its structure and language. In light
of its view of the Church as the People of God, the
Council affirmed that all the faithful must be encouraged to participate actively in the Church's worship
and celebrations of the sacraments. But active participation is impossible if the liturgy is unintelligible

to most people. Since the liturgy contains a wealth of signs and symbols, these signs and symbols must be understood in order that the liturgy be intelligible to participants. It was the principle of intelligibility which guided the Council in making recommendations for changes. These recommended changes included the replacing of Latin with the vernacular (the common language of people), the simplification of rites, more Scripture reading in sacred celebrations, the giving of a preferred place to the sermon in the liturgical service, more instruction for the laity in the liturgy, the revision of the liturgical year, and the establishment of liturgical commissions by bishops in their dioceses.

In a rather remarkable paragraph, the Council indicated a desire to accommodate the liturgy, as far as possible, with the perspectives and customs of different cultures. This paragraph is of such importance that it deserves quoting in full:

> Even in the liturgy, the Church has no wish to impose a rigid uniformity in matters which do not involve the faith or the good of the whole community. Rather she respects and fosters the spiritual adornments and gifts of the various races and peoples. Anything in their way of life that is not indissolubly bound up with superstition and error she studies with sympathy and, if possible, preserves intact. Sometimes in fact she admits such things into the liturgy itself, as long as they harmonize with its true and authentic spirit (Documents, p. 151).

4. The Decree on Ecumenism

In contrast to the constitutions which are primarily theological or doctrinal in character, those documents which are designated as decrees deal primarily with matters of discipline and practice. As we have seen, in "The Dogmatic Constitution on the Church" the Council approved a theological view of the Church which contained some significant ecumenical perspectives. The implications of these perspectives for the Church's discipline and practice were made explicit in "The Decree on Ecumenism." Reflecting to some extent the influence of "liberal" theologians, this document is remarkable for several reasons. First,

there is the complete absence of any suggestion that
Christian unity requires the return of non-Catholics to
the Catholic Church (the traditional position proclaimed
by many popes, including Pius XII). Instead, in the
introduction of this decree, it is said that a chief
concern of the Council is "promoting the restoration of
unity among all Christians" (Documents, p. 341, italics
are mine). There is the recognition and approval of
the ecumenical movement among non-Catholic churches,
concerning which it is said:

> Among our separated brethren also there
> increases from day to day a movement,
> fostered by the grace of the Holy Spirit,
> for the restoration of unity among all
> Christians. Taking part in this movement,
> which is called ecumenical, are those who
> invoke the Triune God and confess Jesus
> as Lord and Saviour (Documents, p. 342).

This is an obvious reference to the World Council of
Churches which was established in 1948 and which represents more than two hundred non-Catholic denominations.

Secondly, in this decree the ecclesiastical reality
of non-Catholic churches is acknowledged, and a share
in the blame for the divisions which sundered the
Church at the time of the Reformation is accepted.
These two points are expressed in the following significant paragraph:

> In subsequent centuries . . . quite large
> communities became separated from full
> communion with the Catholic Church--develop-
> ments for which, at times, men of both
> sides were to blame. However, one cannot
> impute the sin of separation to those who
> at present are born into these communities
> and are instilled therein with Christ's
> faith. The Catholic Church accepts them
> with respect and affection as brothers.
> Undoubtedly, the differences that exist in
> varying degrees between them and the Cath-
> olic Church--whether in doctrine and some-
> times in discipline, or concerning the
> structure of the Church--do indeed create
> many and sometimes serious obstacles to
> full ecclesiastical communion. These the
> ecumenical movement is striving to overcome.

370

Nevertheless, all those justified by faith
through baptism are incorporated into
Christ. They therefore have a right to
be honored by the title of Christian, and
are properly regarded as brothers in the
Lord by the sons of the Catholic Church
(Documents, p. 345).

Thirdly, according to the decree, the first step
on the pathway leading to the goal of Christian unity
is renewal and change of heart within the Church.
Other steps include joining with the "separated brethren" in study and dialogue groups, common worship and
intercommunion in special appropriate circumstances,
theological collaboration at the "professional" level,
and cooperative endeavors with respect to social action.

It is obvious that in this decree the Council
abandoned the Catholic Church's traditional stance of
isolation from other Christian churches. This is one
among the many indications that the Council took seriously Pope John's desire for an open Catholicism.

5. Declaration on the Relationship of the
Church to Non-Christian Religions

Whereas the decree on ecumenism reflects an open
stance toward non-Catholic Christian churches, this
declaration reflects an open stance toward the world's
non-Christian religions. While it does affirm that in
Christ men find the fullness of religious life, it
also declares:

The Catholic Church rejects nothing
which is true and holy in these religions.
She looks with sincere respect upon those
ways of conduct and of life, those rules
and teachings which, though differing in
many particulars from what she holds and
sets forth, nevertheless often reflect a
ray of that Truth which enlightens all
men (Documents, p. 662).

Furthermore, the declaration recommends that Catholics
"prudently and lovingly, through dialogue and collaboration with the followers of other religions, and in
witness of Christian faith and life, acknowledge, preserve, and promote the spiritual and moral goods found
among these men, as well as the values in their society
and culture" (Documents, pp. 662-663).

Finally, in the concluding section of the declaration the Council spoke of the many basic elements which Christians have in common with Jews. It rejected the historically false claim that all Jews at the time of Christ and subsequent to his time can be blamed for Christ's death, insisted that Jews are not to be regarded as repudiated by God, and condemned as foreign to the mind of Christ every form of persecution against any man and any kind of discrimination because of race, color, condition of life, or religion. It declared its desire "to foster and recommend that mutual understanding and respect which is the fruit above all of biblical and theological studies, and brotherly dialogue" (Documents, p. 665).

6. Declaration on Religious Freedom

The position expressed in the decree on ecumenism and the declaration on non-Christian religions certainly presupposes every person's right to religious freedom, and this presupposition is made explicit in "The Declaration on Religious Freedom." In it the Council definitely departed from the position of Pôpe Pius IX who, in his Syllabus of Errors, condemned the toleration of religions. Richard P. McBrien has written the following succinct appraisal and summary of this document:

> This declaration ends the so-called double standard by which the Church demands freedom for itself when in a minority position but refuses to grant freedom to other religions when they are in the minority. The council declares as a matter of principle that the dignity of the human person and the freedom of the act of faith demand that everyone should be immune from coercion of every kind, private or public, in matters pertaining to the profession of a particular religious faith (N. 2). No one can be compelled to accept the Christian faith, nor can anyone be penalized in any way for not being a Christian (N. 9). The supreme model is Jesus himself and, after him, the example of the early Church (N. 11).[46]

7. Pastoral Constitution on the Church in
the Modern World

As we have seen, the Council took an open stance
toward non-Catholic Christians and non-Christian religions. In this constitution it took an open stance
toward the modern world and its culture. According to
Richard P. McBrien:

> The impetus for this unprecedented 'pas-
> toral' constitution came from Pope John
> XXIII and Cardinal Leo-Jozef Suevens of
> Belgium. With the prior knowledge and
> approval of the Pope, Cardinal Suevens
> arose at the end of the first session
> (December 4, 1962) and urged the council
> to do more than examine the mystery of
> the Church in itself (ad intra). The
> council must also attend to the Church's
> relationship with the world at large (ad
> extra).[47]

The longest of all the documents (107 pages in the
English translation), this constitution is difficult
to summarize briefly. The sketch presented here will
give attention to some important elements which illustrate a more positive outlook on modern culture, a
greater desire to be involved with it, and a deeper
concern to work with all persons of good will toward
the solution of its problems. These elements reflect
a perspective which is quite different from that expressed by Pope Pius IX in his Syllabus of Errors when
he condemned the claim that the Pope can and ought to
agree with progress, liberalism, and civilization as
lately introduced (see first section of this chapter).

In this constitution the Council affirmed that in
order for the Church to perform its mission in the
world it has to be aware of "the signs of the times,"
to understand the changes which have occurred in
modern mores and intellectual formulations. Among the
signs of the times is the fact that "the human race
has passed from a rather static concept of reality to
a more dynamic, evolutionary one" (Documents, p. 204).
Therefore, "the institutions, laws, and modes of thinking and feeling as handed down from previous generations do not always seem to be well adapted to the
contemporary state of affairs" (Documents, p. 205).
On the one hand, these changed conditions have led growing numbers of people to abandon religion, since to them

it seems that religion is tied to ways of thinking and feeling which are alien to the contemporary state of affairs. But on the other hand, due to these same changed conditions, there has emerged a greater critical ability to distinguish religion from magic, to purify religion of superstition, and thus to gain a more viable faith and vivid sense of God. The modern world, then, can be of help to the Church.

However, in spite of the scientific and technological progress and the advantages in the modern world, it is still plagued with evils such as social, economic and political injustices, international conflicts, and the threat of an atomic holocaust. In large part, this is due to the fact that man's moral and spiritual knowledge has not kept pace with his scientific and technological knowledge. It is with respect to this condition, and in other ways, that the Church can be of help to the modern world. Thus in many very important ways, the Church and the world are mutually related.

With respect to the help which the Church receives from the world, the Council indicated that the growth of natural, human, and social sciences, the advances in technology, and the development of modern means of communication have opened "fresh avenues . . . for the refinement and wider diffusion of culture" (Documents, p. 260), and it affirmed that the Church "can and ought to be enriched by the development of human social life" (Documents, p. 260). It deplored those habits of mind, sometimes found among Christians, which would deny the independence of science (Documents, p. 234), and it exhorted the faithful to "blend modern science and its theories and the understanding of the most recent discoveries with Christian morality and doctrine . . . [in order that] their religious practice and morality can keep pace with their scientific knowledge and with an ever-advancing technology" (Documents, p. 269). It recommended that those who teach in theological seminaries keep in close contact with men versed in the other sciences so that the understanding of revelation may be kept in close contact with the times. If such collaboration is to be effective, the Church must recognize "that all the faithful, clerical and lay, possess a lawful freedom of inquiry and thought, and the freedom to express their minds humbly and courageously about those matters in which they enjoy competence" (Documents, p. 270).

374

Among the important affirmations of the Council
with respect to the help which the Church gives to
the world are the following: First, the Church in its
emphasis on the dignity of human persons serves as a
kind of leaven for human society. Human beings are
created in the "image of God" which, according to the
Council, is the human capacity for interpersonal communion. That is, the human person is innately social
and can find fulfillment of life only in community or
socialization. The Church serves the world through its
efforts to get persons, groups, and nations to acknowledge the dignity of persons and the need for socialization. Secondly, while it acknowledged that the basic
purpose of the Church's mission is its concern with
religious or "spiritual" matters, the Council insisted
that it is just as integral a part of her mission in
the world to work for the elimination of social evils
and the establishment of social structures and patterns
based on equity and justice. Those among the faithful
who think that the Church should be concerned only
with an individualistic morality and with individuals
attaining ultimate beatitude are mistaken (Documents,
pp. 228, 243). The Christian faith has relevance
for social issues, and thus the Church in fulfilling
her mission must seek to serve the world in order that
the world may become more humane. In this task, the
laity, through their knowledge and skill in secular
occupations and professions, have a special opportunity
(Documents, pp. 243-245). They are called to be the
servants of Christ in the world, and the clergy are
called to be the servants of the servants of Christ in
the world.

On the basis of these perspectives, the Council
gave attention to several social problems. Among them
was a consideration of marriage and the family. The
Council placed emphasis upon the sanctity of marriage
and the family as established by the Creator for the
fulfillment of persons in a community of love. Con-
jugal love was viewed not as simply a concession to
concupiscence and valid only for procreation but as
an integral aspect of the total expression of love
between husband and wife. On the question of birth
control, the Council appeared to have been deliberately
ambiguous (Documents, pp. 249-258). Other problems
considered were those involved in the economic, social,
political, and international realms. The Council
called for the elimination of racism and poverty,
recommended democratic forms of government which preserve the rights and freedoms of citizens, and urged

nations to cooperate in a "family of nations" so as to settle their differences peacefully instead of by war (Documents, pp. 248-305).

In our brief discussion of Vatican Council II, it has been indicated several times that the Council produced a shift in Catholic thought and practice toward a more open Catholicism. In the years since the conclusion of the Council, many Catholics, both clergy and laity, have sought and are seeking to extend this openness even further, especially with respect to such issues as ecumenism, liturgy, papal authority, priestly celibacy, birth control, women priests, and priests' involvement in political positions. Others feel that Vatican II went too far, that there have been too many changes in the Church since the Council, and that there should be a return to pre-conciliar perspectives and practices. According to a recent survey, sixty-seven percent of the Catholics in America approve the changes in the Catholic Church since Vatican II, but a sizable minority of twenty-three percent disapprove.[48]   Richard P. McBrien claims that the major reason why some Catholics disapprove is that all too often changes were instituted without adequate instruction of the laity with respect to the Council's theological basis and justification for such changes. Thus traditional Catholics grudgingly tolerated conciliar reforms while still holding to pre-conciliar theological perspectives. As the post-conciliar changes increased, their spirit of practical accommodation was pushed beyond its limits, and the traditionalists began to advocate a return to the pre-conciliar situation in the Church. This included not only a return to the Latin Mass and to pre-conciliar catechetical textbooks but also, according to McBrien, "ban on intercommunion of any kind and under any circumstance; the shepherding of religious women back into convents, distinctive garb, traditional apostolates, and monarchically administered discipline; a complete pullback from social and political involvement; . . . [and] the restoration of the cult of the Pope."[49]

With respect to the Roman Pontiff, it appears that the Popes (Paul VI and John Paul II, 1978-)[50] have chartered a course which lies somewhere between the positions of the traditionalists and the liberals. They have supported liturgical reforms (Pope John Paul II has opposed a return to the Latin Mass), instituted mild reforms in the Curia, established and held meetings of the Synod of Bishops, eliminated some

376

traditional ostentatious features in papal ceremonies, worked for closer harmony with the Eastern Orthodox Church, sent observers to meetings of the World Council of Churches, and in travels outside the Vatican have sought to ease world tensions. On the other hand, however, these Popes have not accepted full collegiality with the bishops since the Synod of Bishops has only an advisory function, and decision-making authority still remains only with the Pope and his Curia. They have opposed any modification in the doctrines of apostolic succession and papal infallibility and any democratizing of the monarchical episcopate. In spite of the fact that in the United States, at least, seventy-three percent of Catholics think that Catholics should be allowed to use artificial means of birth control and sixty-nine percent think that divorced Catholics should be permitted to remarry in the Church,[51] the Popes have insisted on the traditional position that the practice of artificial birth control and the remarriage of divorced Catholics are sinful. They have forbidden the abandonment of priestly celibacy and the ordination of women as priests, and Pope John Paul has forbidden priests to hold political positions.[52]

In the forefront of those who find in the theological presuppositions of Vatican Council II the basis for what they view as a completion of the reforms begun by the Council are many "younger" priests and theologians. In the Spring of 1977 a colloquium was held at the University of Notre Dame, the title of which was "Toward Vatican Council III: The Work that Needs to Be Done."[53] Some seventy-one Catholic theologians and social scientists from Europe and America participated. This colloquium, of course, was not an official Church meeting, and the title "Vatican III" was simply symbolic. Yet it did provide these theologians and social scientists with the opportunity of expressing their genuine concern for the Catholic Church in this period of her history. As the title of the colloquium indicates, the underlying concern which united the participants was that the direction for the Church begun at Vatican II be carried through to its conclusion. In the various papers presented, there was an attempt to clarify what this would entail in terms of the Church's theology, structure, discipline, and practices.

On the basis of the theology of Vatican II, especially the view of the Church as the "People of

377

God," not only those who met at Notre Dame but also other Catholic theologians and scholars view an agenda for further reform[54] as including the limitation of the Curia's power simply to administrative matters, the location of decision-making power in the Synod of Bishops in union with the Pope, the election of the Pope by the Synod of Bishops, the election of bishops by representative diocesan councils composed of priests and laity, the establishment of procedures whereby bishops will make important policy decisions with the advice and consent of priests and laity, and the elimination of the cult of the Pope. On this last point, some Catholic theologians (for example, Professor Hans Küng of Tubingen University in Germany) have raised serious questions about the historical and theological legitimacy of papal infallibility and monarchical authority. Professor Küng has argued that papal infallibility and monarchical authority prevent genuine ecumenism, that the Pope's legitimate authority is one of pastoral service, and that the Pope should seek to be the agent and symbol of Christian unity.[55] His public support for such a position resulted in Professor Küng being censured in December of 1979 by the Curia's Congregation For the Doctrine of the Faith with the approval of Pope John Paul II and his being deprived of the title, "Catholic theologian."[56]

Other points often made by the "younger" theologians are that the Catholic Church should join the World Council of Churches, that priestly celibacy has no Biblical, historical, or theological foundation, that the use of artificial means of birth control and the remarriage of divorced Catholics are not sinful, and that there is some historical precedent and much theological justification for ordaining women as priests. In general, what these theologians claim is that the laws, discipline, regulations, customs, and administrative procedures of the Church arose at a time when there was a vision of the Church different from that of Vatican Council II. Thus the need for the Church now is to permit the new vision of the Council to permeate and transform its institutional laws, discipline, regulations, customs, and administrative procedures so as to bring current practice and discipline into harmony with the Council's theology. Only then will the Church be fully renewed and brought up to date.

In light of the current situation in the Catholic Church, it is probably the case that in the near future

neither the traditionalists nor the "younger" theologians will gain a dominant position in the Church.
Even though the influence of the traditionalists may
impede some further progress, it is not strong enough
to turn the clock back to pre-conciliar times. While,
over a long period of time, the influence of the
"younger" theologians may produce some further changes
in the Church's thought and practice, it is not of
sufficient strength to bring about such changes in the
near future. Any institution with a long heritage
generally does not change rapidly or drastically. That
there was a Vatican Council II which produced such
notable changes in the Catholic Church is in itself
rather remarkable. It is probably the case that a
considerable period of time will be needed for adjustment to and assimilation of these changes so that they
will become an integral part of the Catholic tradition.
While it is by no means certain, it does seem likely
that the changes in the Church are over for some time
to come, and that the "younger" theologians' vision
of "Vatican III" is not likely to be actualized in the
near future. This is simply to say that at least for
the next several years the probable course which will
be followed by the Catholic Church is one which is
between the position of the traditionalists on the
one hand and that of the "younger" theologians on the
other.

[1] See Clyde L. Manschreck (ed.), A History of Christianity: Readings in the History of the Church From the Reformation to the Present (Prentice-Hall, 1964; reprinted by Baker Book House, 1981), pp. 371-372 or Henry Bettenson (ed.), Documents of the Christian Church, Second Edition (Oxford University Press, 1963), p. 271.

[2] Manschreck, ibid., p. 374 or Bettenson, ibid., p. 273. The italics are mine.

[3] Manschreck, ibid., p. 375.

[4] Ibid., pp. 374-375.

[5] For a more detailed discussion of the pontificate of Pius IX see Kenneth Scott Latourett, Christianity In a Revolutionary Age, Vol. I (Harper and Brothers Publishers, 1958), pp. 266-293; Justo L. Gonzalez, A History of Christian Thought, Vol. III (Abingdon Press, 1975), Chapter XIV, pp. 351-373.

[6] See Latourette, ibid., pp. 293-313; Williston Walker, A History of the Christian Church, Third Edition (Charles Scribner's Sons, 1970), pp. 525-526.

[7] See Manschreck, op. cit., pp. 392-395.

[8] Ibid., pp. 395-397.

[9] Bettenson, op. cit., p. 281.

[10] See Kenneth Scott Latourette, Christianity In a Revolutionary Age, Vol. IV (Harper and Brothers Publishers, 1961), pp. 45-63.

[11] Quoted from Bernard M. G. Reardon, Roman Catholics Modernism (Stanford University Press, 1970), p. 10.

[12] Quoted from Alec R. Vidler, The Modernist Movement in the Roman Church (Cambridge University Press, 1934), p. 3.

[13] My Duel With the Vatican (E. P. Dutton and Company, 1924), p. 121.

[14] See The Origins of The New Testament (George Allen and Unwin, L. F. D., 1950).

[15] See Alfred Loisy, The Gospel and the Church, translated by Christopher Home, New Edition (Charles Scribner's Sons, 1909). Also see Reardon, op. cit., pp. 16-39, 69-109; Vidler, op. cit., pp. 68-139.

[16] Ibid., p. 37.

[17] Quoted from James C. Livingston, Modern Christian Thought (The Macmillan Company, 1971), p. 287.

[18] With the exception of Teilhard and Weigel most of these scholars are still alive and active.

[19] See Gustave Weigel, S. J., Catholic Theology in Dialogue (Harper and Brothers, Publishers, 1961), pp. 29-48.

[20] Ibid., p. 48. Italics are mine.

[21] The Future of Man (Harper and Row, Publishers, 1964), p. 34; cited by Livingston, op. cit., pp. 490-491.

[22] See The Future of Man; also The Phenomenon of Man (Harper and Brothers, Publishers, 1959) and Doran McCarty, Teilhard De Chardin (Word Books, Publishers, 1976).

[23] Weigel, op. cit., p. 82.

[24] We Hold These Truths (Sheld and Ward, Inc., 1960), p. XI.

[25] Cited by E. E. Y. Hales, Pope John And His Revolution (Doubleday and Company, Inc., 1965), pp. 33-34.

[26] Ibid., p. 83.

[27] In an address to The American Academy of Religion, November 8, 1980, Hans Küng quoted Pope John as having said, "I never intend to speak ex cathedra."

[28] See G. C. Berkower, The Second Vatican Council and The New Catholicism (Wm. B. Eerdman's Publishing Co., 1965), p. 34.

[29] Norman Cousins, "The Improbable Triumvirate," Saturday Review, October 30, 1971, p. 33.

[30] The story concerning the children is told in Albert J. Nevins, M. M., The Story of Pope John XXIII (Gossett and Dunlop, Publishers, 1966), pp. 20-21. The quotation from Rabbi Herzog is cited in this book and in Lawrence Elliott, I Will Be Called John (Reader's Digest Press, 1973), p. 164.

[31] For the story of Archbishop Roncalli's skill at diplomacy in these two positions see Elliott, *ibid.*, pp. 171-205.

[32] Cited by Nevins, *op. cit.*, p. 25.

[33] *Ibid.*, p. 26.

[34] *Ibid.*, p. 28.

[35] *Ibid.*, p. 8.

[36] See Hales, *op. cit.*, p. 121.

[37] See Nevins and Elliott, *op. cit.*

[38] *The Eclipse of God* (Harper Torchbook, 1957), p. 6.

[39] Hales, *op. cit.*, p. 103.

[40] *Ibid.*, p. 104.

[41] Walter M. Abbott, S. J. (ed.), *The Documents of Vatican II* (The America Press, 1966), p. 716.

[42] *Ibid.*, pp. 712, 714, 715. Italics are mine.

[43] For a brief but excellent summary of the documents of Vatican Council II see Richard P. McBrien, *Catholicism*, Vol. II (Winston Press, Inc., 1980), Chapter XIX, pp. 657-690.

[44] Since there are so many references to *The Documents of Vatican II*, they will be noted in the body of the text instead of in these footnotes. In all cases these notations refer to pages in Walter M. Abbott, S. J. (ed.), *The Documents of Vatican II* (The America Press, 1966).

[45] McBrien, *op. cit.*, pp. 671-672.

[46] *Ibid.*, p. 678. Also see *The Documents of Vatican II*, pp. 675-696.

[47] *Ibid.*, p. 673.

[48] *Religion in America*, 1979-80 (Published by the Princeton Religion Research Center, 1980), p. 76.

[49] *The Remaking of the Church* (Harper and Row, Publishers, 1973), p. 21.

[50] Pope John Paul I died in 1978 after only one month in

office. The election of a cardinal from outside Italy as Pope
(John Paul II is from Poland) was certainly a significant departure from the tradition of several centuries.

[51] Religion in America, 1979-80, p. 76.

[52] Father Robert F. Drinan had to resign from his seat in
the House of Representatives in the U. S. Congress.

[53] The papers presented at this colloquium have been published in the book, Toward Vatican III, edited by David Tracy
with Hans Küng and Johan B. Metz (The Seabury Press, 1978).

[54] See Richard P. McBrien, The Remaking of the Church,
Chapter III, pp. 71-136.

[55] See "Vatican III: Problems and Opportunities For The
Future," Toward Vatican III, pp. 67-90; Infallible? An Inquiry
(Doubleday and Company, Inc., 1971). Professor Küng has written
a large number of books dealing with current issues confronting
the Church and some large theological works such as On Being
A Christian (Doubleday, 1976).

[56] See Leonard Swidler (ed.), Consensus In Theology (The
Westminster Press, 1980), pp. III-VIII and 159-165. The
latter pages contain an article by Professor Küng entitled,
"Why I Remain a Catholic."

SUGGESTIONS FOR FURTHER READING

Abbott, Walter M., (ed.), The Documents of Vatican II, The
America Press, 1966.

Bainton, Roland H., Christendom, V. II, Harper Torchbook, 1966,
Chapters XII - XIII.

Berkouwer, G. C., The Second Vatican Council and The New Catholicism, Wm. B. Eerdmans Publishing Co., 1965.

Berthold, Fred, Jr., et al., Basic Sources of the Judeo-Christian
Tradition, Prentice-Hall, 1962, Part Four.

Bettenson, Henry, Documents of the Christian Church, Oxford
University Press, 1963, Section XI.

Boney, Wm. J. and L. E. Molumby, (eds.), The New Day: Catholic
Theologians of the Renewal, John Knox Press, 1968.

Burkill, T. A., The Evolution of Christian Thought, Cornell
University Press, 1971, Chapters 34-35, 39-41.

Congar, Yves, Ecumenism and the Future of the Church, Priory
Press, 1967.

Cullmann, Oscar, Vatican Council II: The New Direction, Harper
and Row, 1968.

Elliott, Lawrence, I Will Be Called John, Readers Digest Press,
1973.

Gonzalez, Justo L., A History of Christian Thought, V. III,
Abingdon Press, 1975, Chapter XIV.

Hales, E. E. Y., Pope John and His Revolution, Doubleday and
Company, Inc., 1965.

Küng, Hans, The Church - Maintained in Truth, The Seabury Press,
1980.

_____, The Council, Reform and Reunion, Sheld and Ward Ltd.,
1961.

_____, Infallible? An Inquiry, Doubleday and Company, Inc.,
1971.

Küng, Hans, _Signposts For the Future_, Doubleday and Company, Inc., 1978.

Latourette, Kenneth Scott, _Christianity In a Revolutionary Age_, Vols. I and IV, Harper and Brothers, Publishers, 1958 and 1961.

Livingston, James C., _Modern Christian Thought_, The Macmillan Company, 1971, Chapters Ten, Thirteen and Sixteen.

Lohse, Bernhard, _A Short History of Christian Doctrine_, Fortress Press, 1966, Chapter Seven.

Loisy, Alfred, _My Duel With The Vatican_, E. P. Dutton and Company, 1924.

Manschreck, Clyde L., (ed.), _A History of Christianity_, Prentice-Hall, 1964, Chapters VII - VIII.

McAvoy, Thomas T., _A History of the Catholic Church in the United States_, University of Notre Dame Press, 1969.

McBrien, Richard P., _Catholicism_, Vols. I and II, Winston Press, 1980.

_____, _The Remaking of the Church_, Harper and Row, Publishers, 1973.

McCarty, Doran, _Teilhard De Chardin_, Word Books, Publishers, 1976.

Murray, John Courtney, _We Hold These Truths_, Sheld and Ward, Inc., 1960.

Nevins, Albert J., _The Story of Pope John XXIII_, Gossett and Dunlap, Publishers, 1966.

Reardon, Bernard M. G., _Roman Catholic Modernism_, Stanford University Press, 1970.

Schillebeeckx, Edward, _The Mission of the Church_, Sheld and Ward, Inc., 1973.

Swidler, Leonard, (ed.), _Consensus in Theology_, The Westminster Press, 1980.

Tracy, David, _et al._ (eds.), _Toward Vatican III_, The Seabury Press, 1978.

Vidler, Alec R., _The Modernist Movement in the Roman Church_, Cambridge University Press, 1934.

Weigel, Gustave, *Catholic Theology in Dialogue*, Harper and
    Brothers, Publishers, 1960.

CHAPTER XI

PROTESTANTISM IN THE MODERN WORLD

As we have seen in Chapter VIII, the Protestant
Reformation did not result in simply one Protestant
Church. Unlike Catholicism which found primary and
dominant expression in the one Roman Catholic Church,
from its very beginnings Protestantism splintered into
several churches. Today there are so many denominations
and sects which are included in the denotation of the
term "Protestant" that even the meaning of the term has
become rather vague in common usage. In the attempt to
define "Protestant" in such a way that the denotation
of the term would be sufficiently inclusive, Webster's
New World Dictionary defines "Protestant" as "any
Christian not belonging to the Roman Catholic or Orthodox Eastern Church." This minimum and vague definition
explicitly indicates very little. Yet it implicitly
entails that Protestant Christians are agreed in rejecting the authority of Popes and Patriarchs and the
reverence for saints, monasticism, and priestly celibacy. It implies also that they are agreed in accepting only the two sacraments of baptism and the Lord's
supper (often called "ordinances" rather than "sacraments"). Beyond this, Protestants generally, though
not always, regard the authority of Scripture as superior to that of the Church and ecclesiastical authorities, emphasize individual judgment in matters of
faith and Scripture interpretation, and proclaim the
reformers' doctrine of justification by faith even
though it may not be fully understood. Apart from
these common elements and beliefs generally held, there
is a wide variety of beliefs and practices among the
numerous denominations and sects labelled "Protestant."
This situation makes it difficult to formulate an adequate and brief general characterization of Protestantism in the modern world.

In spite of this difficulty, however, an attempt
will be made here to present a general characterization
of modern Protestantism in terms of the same schema
employed in the previous chapters on Judaism and Catholicism. That is, attention will be focused on the
Protestant right-wing, left-wing, and moderate responses
to the challenge of the modern scientific movement and
the bourgeois spirit (see Introduction to Part V). It

should be noted that these three responses are not channeled exclusively along denominational lines. While it is the case that some denominations tend to be more right-wing in their response and others more left-wing or moderate, these three responses generally cut across denominational lines. Unlike the situation in modern Judaism where rabbis generally identify with Orthodox (right-wing), Reform (left-wing), or Conservative (moderate) congregations, the right-wing, left-wing, and moderate groups of Protestant theologians and ministers include persons representing a variety of denominational affiliations. In some cases these groups have established inter-denominational organizations (recently several have appeared among those of the right-wing response), but for the most part, like the Catholic Modernists (see Chapter X), they have not established formal societies and associations.

In each of the previous chapters on Judaism and Catholicism, the discussion began with a description of the right-wing response to the challenge of modern culture. The reason for this was that the right-wing response in Judaism and Catholicism represented an attempt to preserve intact ancient traditions and perspectives. That is, it sought to continue the thought and practices of pre-modern eras and to either ignore or reject modern culture. To be sure, often there were vigorous attacks on the left-wingers who attempted to harmonize their theologies with the basic aspects of modern culture, but it was modern culture itself which was viewed as the main culprit.

The situation in modern Protestantism has been somewhat different. This is the case for the following reasons: First, most right-wing Protestants, at least in the United States, belong to groups which have come to be called "fundamentalists." "Fundamentalism," according to Webster's Third New International Dictionary, is "a militantly conservative movement in American Protestantism originating around the beginning of the 20th Century in opposition to modernist tendencies." Thus as a movement, Fundamentalism is of relatively recent origin. Furthermore, it is not simply an exact reduplication of the whole of "orthodox" or classical Protestantism (i.e., the thought of the reformers). While there are some points of similarity, there are also points of difference. For example, even though Martin Luther insisted on sola Scriptura, he was far from holding that the Bible is infallible as do the fundamentalists (see Chapter VIII above). Secondly,

as Webster's definition indicates, Fundamentalism arose
"in opposition to modernist tendencies." That is, for
fundamentalists generally the main culprit is Liberalism or Modernism (left-wing response), and it is against
this that the major focus of their attack is directed.
For example, J. Gresham Machen, a leading exponent of
Fundamentalism, proclaimed that Protestant Liberalism
was not simply a different type of Christianity, but
that Liberalism and Christianity had developed from
distinctly different bases and were different religions.
He viewed the "different religion" of Liberalism as the
chief opponent of Christianity.[1]

In modern Protestantism, since the right-wing
response (Fundamentalism) originated largely as a result of opposition to the left-wing response (Liberalism), it seems appropriate to reverse the sequence of
these topics as presented in the chapters on Judaism
and Catholicism and to discuss Liberalism prior to
Fundamentalism. The reason for organizing our discussion according to the chronological origins of these
movements is that such a procedure may be of help in
our task of acquiring clarity of understanding with
respect to the perspectives of both movements.

A. The Left-Wing Response of Protestant
   Liberalism

It was noted in the chapter on "Judaism in the
Modern World" that the ways of thinking which finally
emerged into Reform Judaism had their beginnings among
Jews in Germany. Similarly, it was among Protestants
in Germany, the original homeland of Protestantism,
that there developed ways of thinking which finally
emerged into Protestant Liberalism. An early thinker
who provided some important bases for Liberalism was
not a theologian but one of the greatest of modern
philosophers, Immanuel Kant (1724-1804). Kant's philosophy has had a definite influence on subsequent modern
Western thought in general. It is not surprising then
that liberal Protestant theologians concerned with
reconciling the Christian perspective with modern culture have been influenced in varying degrees by Kant-
ianism. Kant's philosophy was such a vast intellectual
construction that it is impossible to present here
even the barest outline of it as a whole. Instead attention will be centered on those aspects which have
been of influence in Liberalism, sometimes in very
obvious and direct ways.

Kant was one of the first thinkers to recognize that the methods and results of science (Newtonian physics) could be understood in such a way that they would lead to a naturalistic and/or mechanistic outlook on the world in which religion and morality were not basically possible (see Introduction to Part V above). He found this deeply disturbing since he had grown up in a devout Christian home, and thus one important concern in his philosophy was to show that science and religion can be reconciled. In his view both were important, and both were to be upheld fully. He believed that the cause of religion did not require and was harmed by attempts to demonstrate gaps in scientific knowledge and by attacks on the assured results of science. According to W. T. Stace, "He was as anxious to defend science against the attacks of religious men as he was to defend religion against the destructive ideas introduced into the world by scientific men."[2] But how was it possible to defend both science and religion as true when they contradict each other? It is an elementary rule of logic that two propositions which contradict each other cannot both be true of the same thing at the same time. For example, the claim that a particular ball is both entirely red and entirely green at the same time is an obvious contradition and cannot be the case. However, no contradiction is involved in the claim that there are two balls, one of which is entirely red and the other entirely green. These two are contraries, not contradictories. Basically it was along this line that Kant argued that science and religion do not contradict each other because they deal with two different realms. Thus the reasonable person may give full allegiance to both.

The meaning and implication of this important theme was explicated by Kant in many of his writings, especially in The Critique of Pure Reason, The Critique of Practical Reason, and Religion Within the Limits of Reason Alone.[3] These works are representative of Kant's attempt to provide answers to what he regarded as three fundamental human questions, namely, "What can I know?", "What ought I to do?", and "What can I hope for?" In The Critique of Pure Reason he seeks to answer the first question, and in the other two works he seeks to answer questions two and three. With respect to the different realms of science and religion, Kant locates science in the realm of what can be "known" and religion in the realm of what ought to be done or of morality, and this is inclusive of what can be hoped for.

At the risk of oversimplification we will attempt briefly to indicate Kant's perspective on epistemology (a theory of knowledge in terms of how and what we know) and why he located science in this realm. Then we will consider briefly his ethical theory and why he located religion in the realm of morality.

Prior to Kant there had been some philosophers (the Empiricists, John Locke and David Hume) who had insisted that all of our knowledge arises out of experience. John Locke had claimed that at birth the mind is like a blank sheet of paper upon which experience then writes. That is, by means of the sensory organs the mind receives impressions or sense data from the external world. Any idea or concept which may be classified under the rubric of "knowledge" is either a direct representation of a sense impression or constructed from several such impressions. If it is impossible to demonstrate that a concept has some connection either directly or indirectly with sense experiences, then it cannot be classified as an item of knowledge. Of itself, the mind brings little to the process of knowing other than the capacity of storing up impressions or sense data, remembering them, and utilizing them appropriately in successive situations. While Kant was influenced by this Empiricism, he modified it in a very significant way.

In the first sentence of the Introduction in The Critique of Pure Reason, Kant says, "There can be no doubt that all our knowledge begins with experience."[4] That is, experience "awakens" our faculty of knowledge and "in the order of time, therefore, we have no knowledge antecedent to experience."[5] Yet Kant hastens to add, "But though all our knowledge begins with experience, it does not follow that it all arises out of experience. For it may well be that even our empirical knowledge is made up of what we receive through impressions and of what our own faculty of knowing (sensible impressions serving merely as the occasion) supplies from itself."[6]

What "our own faculty of knowing supplies from itself" are two types of forms, structures, or categories. One of these two types of forms is the categories of perception (Kant called them "intuitions"), namely space and time. By means of rather complicated arguments, Kant sought to demonstrate that space and time cannot be "objective" realities, but instead must be categories which the mind brings to experience. For

391

example, he demonstrated that equally valid arguments can be provided for the claim that space and time are infinite and for the claim that space and time are finite.[7] But these two conclusions of equally valid arguments contradict each other. Thus space and time cannot be "objectively" real any more than a round square, the thought of which is contradictory, can be objectively real. Therefore space and time are the categories of perception which the mind brings to experience and in light of which the mind always perceives sensible data from the external world.

The second type of forms is the categories of the mind's conceiving or thinking faculty, the function of which is to organize the manifold data of sense experience into an intelligible world. These categories of thought or understanding include three of quantity (unity, plurality, totality), three of quality (reality, negation, limitation), three of relation (substantiality, causality, reciprocity), and three of modality (possibility, existence, necessity).[8] Just as the categories of space and time are the necessary forms of the mind's perceiving faculty, so the categories of thought are the necessary forms of the mind's conceiving faculty. As Kant himself said, "Without sensibility no object would be given to us, without understanding no object would be thought. Thoughts without content are empty, intuitions [perceptions] without concepts are blind."[9] Thus, while knowledge requires data from the external world, these data always are mediated to us through the categories of perception and conception, both types of which are inherent structures in the mind and not something in the external world. To use a rough analogy, it is as though a person had been fitted with a pair of green tinted contact lenses which could never be removed. Obviously, that person always would see everything as green. So for Kant human knowledge always is "colored" by the "lenses" of the mind's perceiving and conceiving categories, and it operates only in what he called the realm of "phenomena" or "phenomenal appearances."

It is in this realm that science is one hundred percent true, but in which religion and morality cannot be located. For example, science deals with matters in space and time, but religion deals with matters (such as God) which transcend space and time. Science operates strictly in accordance with the law of cause and effect, but religion and morality operate in terms of the principle of freedom. Furthermore, on the basis of his analysis of knowledge, Kant considers the classical arguments for the existence of God (such as those of Thomas Aquinas, see Chapter VII) and concludes that these arguments are not sound, do not prove the existence of God. With respect to the causal and design arguments, for example, Kant points out that from the features of causality and order in the sensible world, it cannot be concluded that there is a God in the sense of a necessary and perfect being. To draw such a conclusion from such premises is to be guilty of what Kant calls "a transcendental leap." That is, one has jumped far beyond what is warranted from our knowledge of the sensible world. From contingent effects one can infer only contingent causes. From the order and disorder in the sensible world one can infer only an architect who is limited by the material with which he works, not the Creator of the world to whose design everything is subject. Thus in terms of "knowledge" the existence of God cannot be proved, but neither can it be disproved.

In addition to the world of "phenomena," the realm of knowledge, there is, Kant claimed, the world of the "noumena," the realm of the objects of the external world as they are in themselves. While he held that the existence of external objects is a causally necessary condition for the occurrence of perception and thought, what these external objects are in themselves could not be known. What they were in not could be known, but what they were could not be known. That is, the way in which Kant viewed things-in-themselves is somewhat analogous to the high-pitched dog whistle that the human ear cannot hear. But from the fact that there could not be knowledge of the noumenal realm, it did not follow, Kant argued, that it was impossible to formulate reasonable postulates (assumptions required for a well-formed argument) about this realm, such as, for example, freedom, immortality, and God. Thus it might be said that what Kant took away with one hand on the basis of his analysis of knowledge in The Critique of Pure Reason, he gave back with the other hand in The Critique of Practical Reason.

It is in The Critique of Practical Reason that Kant seeks to answer the questions of what one ought to do and what one can hope for. The answers are based on reason alone, unmixed with prudential motives such as the avoidance of punishment or the lust for pleasures and success. That is, the answers arise out of pure practical reason. If one thinks clearly about human life, Kant claims, it is obvious that the basic human desire is the desire for happiness, the _summum bonum_ (supreme good). But in light of pure practical reason, it is evident that genuine happiness is not to be confused with fleeting pleasures, and that it is possible only if one is worthy or deserving of it. Happiness entails morality, and pure practical reason leads one to conclude that the fundamental principle of morality is that one ought always to act not simply in accord with duty but for the sake of duty. An action which is simply in accord with duty is not a genuine or pure moral action. It arises out of motives which are not moral but prudential or selfish, the desire to avoid something or to gain something. It entails the _hypothetical_ imperative that if you wish to attain or avoid something, then you ought to act in a certain way. By contrast, the genuinely moral act is one which is done solely for the sake of duty, and this means, according to Kant, that it is done in obedience to the _categorical_ imperative. Although there is one categorical imperative, Kant states it in two ways, namely, one ought always to act such that the principle of his action could be a universal maxim, or one ought always to act so as to treat others as ends, never as means.

In Kant's view, a rational justification of this fundamental moral principle requires three postulates. As we have seen, a postulate is not a proof but a reasonable assumption required for a well-formed argument. The three postulates which are required for the rational justification of duty (the categorical imperative) as the supreme moral principle are freedom, immortality, and God. Freedom is required because "ought" necessarily entails "can." Surely, it makes no sense to say to someone, "You ought to do thus and so," if the person cannot do what is commanded. Furthermore, it is evident in light of common human experience, that no one in this life even reaches perfection in fulfilling the categorical imperative. Therefore it is reasonable to postulate immortal life in which achievement of this goal may be reached. If no one could ever achieve the goal, the "ought" of the categorical imperative would not entail "can" and thus would be unreasonable and nonsensical. Finally, there needs to be the assurance that achieving the goal of virtue will result in happiness, the _summum bonum_. Thus it is reasonable to postulate the existence of a loving God who guarantees that the perfection of morality will result in happiness.[10]

Since Kant located science in the realm of "knowledge" (the phenomenal realm) and religion in the realm of morality (the noumenal realm), it follows that for him science and religion did not contradict each other. Neither could interfere with the other. Since scientific discoveries had relevance only for the realm of phenomena, it follows that no conceivable scientific discoveries could ever clash with religion. Similarly, since religion had relevance only for the realm of morality (the noumenal), it follows that no religious truth could ever conflict with the principles and conclusions of science.

Even though Kant located religion in the moral realm, he did not think of religion as the source of morality or of our understanding of moral responsibility. The source of our understanding of the categorical imperative, he insisted, was reason, not religion. Any person who exercised his capacity for pure practical reason could come to an understanding of the categorical imperative. The function of religion was that of inspiring us to fulfill the categorical imperative. While Kant believed that the tenets of true religion could not be proved as objects of knowledge, he did regard them as rational postulates. Thus he believed that true religion was universal, natural, and rational. He did acknowledge that Christianity as a historical religion possessed some unique characteristics which are largely associated with ecclesiastical matters, but he insisted that Christianity is fundamentally an expression of natural religion. Jesus did not found a new religion but taught about this natural, universal, rational, and true religion.[11] While his life and teachings provided the assurance that God forgives us for past moral deficiencies, their major function was that of providing us with the motivation to strive for moral perfection in light of the model of moral perfection in the life of Jesus. Unlike the Protestant Reformers who had insisted that the Christian is a sinner saved by the grace of God alone (see Chapter VIII above), Kant believed that salvation was achieved by that moral effort which finally makes one worthy of the summum bonum. As Kant himself said, "It must be inculcated painstakingly and repeatedly that true religion is to consist not in the knowing or considering of what God does or has done for our salvation but in what we must do to become worthy of it."[12]

In the century following Kant (d. 1804), his philosophy was to have great influence on the thought

of the educated classes in Western Europe, especially
on the thought of the philosophers and theologians.
Contrary to his own intention, there were some who
regarded Kant's thought as destructive of religion.
Some philosophers centered their attention on The
Critique of Pure Reason in which he had argued that
the tenets of religion could not be matters of "knowledge," and ignored his rehabilitation of religion in
The Critique of Practical Reason. Many theologians
also agreed with Kant that the tenets of religion
could not be proved in the phenomenal realm and thus
were not matters of knowledge. Unlike the philosophers, however, they did not regard this as destructive
of religion, but like Kant they shifted the ground of
religion to some area of human life other than knowledge. In their view religion was to be defended as a
natural endowment of this area. Among the several
outstanding German Protestant theologians who took
this general approach were Friedrick Schleiermacher
(1768-1834), Albrecht Ritschl (1822-1889), and Adolf
Von Harnack (1851-1930). In spite of differences between them, they agreed with Kant in shifting the
ground and justification of religion to an area other
than knowledge. In addition to this agreement, these
three and other liberal Protestant theologians, like
the Catholic modernists, were agreed in accepting some
form of evolutionist perspective, the historical critical method of studying the Bible and church history,
and the priority of the experiential in religion over
all external facts, dogmas, and authorities.

Friedrick Schleiermacher often has been called the
"father" of Protestant Liberalism. Like Kant he explicitly rejects the view that religion is a body of
knowledge similar to that of the sciences. Arguments
such as those which seek to prove God, miracles,
creedal statements as factually and literally true,
and the Bible as infallible not only are worthless but
also obscure the genuine essence of religion. For
that matter, any series of theological doctrines, no
matter how carefully and rationally they are formulated,
are always on the outside fringe of religion and thus
not of its essence. Unlike Kant, however, Schleiermacher does not locate religion in morality or a system
of morality. The heart of religion is neither a set
of theological dogmas nor an ethical system. There is,
of course, a relationship between religion on the one
hand and reason and morality on the other hand in that
the latter follow from the former. But Schleiermacher
insists that religion does not arise from something

else but is absolutely unique or <u>sui generis</u> (forming its own kind). It is the feeling of absolute dependence.[13]

For Schleiermacher the uniqueness of religion is that it is located in human "feeling" or "intuition." This is not "feeling" in the sense of a psychological category or of passing emotions, but it is "feeling" in the sense of a basic, universal, and profound awareness of <u>absolute dependence</u>. In every moment of experience, Schleiermacher claims, we are aware of both freedom and constraint, of relative independence and relative dependence. But these feelings are neither ultimate nor independent, for when we penetrate more deeply into our consciousness there is disclosed a region in which we encounter an awareness of being absolutely or unqualifiedly dependent. Then our freedom and self-activity no longer appear as our own but as originating from and constantly dependent upon something beyond us. This is the case because the awareness of <u>absolute</u> dependence could not arise from the relativities of our ordinary experiences and feelings. As Schleiermacher clearly states, "The common element in all howsoever diverse expression of piety, by which these are conjointly <u>distinguished</u> <u>from</u> <u>all</u> <u>other</u> <u>feelings</u>, or in other words, the self-identical essence of piety is this: the consciousness of being absolutely dependent, or, which is the same thing, of being in relation with God."[14] That is, even though absolute dependence can be discovered only through our subjective experience, through looking within, <u>what</u> is discovered is an objective relation with God. A rough analogy for this relation is the relation between our feeling and the mighty ocean whose awesome beauty we may enjoy. Surely that is an objective relation even though it can be discovered only in our subjective experience.

The sense of absolute dependence or God-consciousness may be discovered by anyone who reflects carefully on himself and his feelings. As Schleiermacher says, "If the feeling of absolute dependence, expressing itself as consciousness of God, is the highest grade of immediate self-consciousness, <u>it is also an essential element of human nature</u>."[15] This claim is not falsified by the fact that in infants and undeveloped peoples this consciousness has not yet awakened, for this is a period in which life is incomplete, in which other functions also are being developed only gradually. Neither is it falsified by the fact that in more highly developed religious communities there may be no <u>explicit</u>

mention of the "feeling" of absolute dependence. In spite of their variety of language and forms of expression, implicit in them is this fundamental reality. The sense of absolute dependence is a natural element or capacity of human life as such, and it is "to be reckoned as part of a complete human nature for everybody."[16] The fact that different individuals express the God-consciousness in different intellectual and ethical modes or forms accounts for the great diversity of religions. Since the God-consciousness is the ultimate source of all religions and is expressed to some degree in all of them, religions should not be divided into two mutually exclusive classes, the true and the false. Instead they should be ranked according to the adequacy of their forms for expressing the God-consciousness. On this basis, monotheistic religions rank higher than polytheistic religions, for the God-consciousness is the sense of absolute dependence, and the absolute is necessarily a unity. Of the monotheistic religions, Christianity, Schleiermacher claims, is to be ranked as the highest precisely because in its founder, Jesus Christ, there was the God-consciousness to a supreme degree such that he became the mediator between the divine and the human.

Schleiermacher advocated not only that religions should be evaluated in terms of the adequacy of their forms for expressing the awareness of absolute dependence or God-consciousness but also that Christian doctrines should be evaluated by this same criterion. He held that doctrines should be transcripts or reports of the Christian God-consciousness. As he said, "Christian doctrines are accounts of the Christian religious affections set forth in speech."[17] Past doctrinal formulations sometimes had failed to do this because they had become infected with abstract philosophical or metaphysical speculations. The modern theologian's task was both to reformulate Christian doctrines so that they would be accurate accounts of "Christian religious affections" and to present a systematic interpretation of this experienced relation. In his major theological work, The Christian Faith, Schleiermacher proceeded to undertake such a task.[18]

Among the results which Schleiermacher obtained through this process of a systematic interpretation of "Christian religious affections" are the following: First, the doctrine of creation does not deal with the chronological origin of the world for that cannot be a part of our present religious experience. Instead it

398

symbolically preserves the sense that God is the source of all that is and that our dependence on him is absolute. The Genesis Garden of Eden story is not historically true but is a valuable symbolic expression of the doctrine of original perfection, the meaning of which is simply that the world has been and still is a sufficient environment for the emergence of God-consciousness. Secondly, the ancient conception of sin as having originated with Adam's disobedience which then has been literally transmitted to succeeding generations is unacceptable. It is inconceivable that human nature could be so different before and after Adam's fall and that a single individual could so completely change the human race. The doctrine of original sin has value only if it is understood to symbolize the universal human experience of the innate God-consciousness as being hindered by the conflict between our fleshly, sensuous nature and our higher spiritual nature. Also it symbolizes the fact that since human beings are social beings, sins always occur in a social matrix as we are influenced by and in turn have an influence on others. Thirdly, as we have seen, Schleiermacher affirmed that the God-consciousness, which is at least latently present in all human beings, was supremely expressed in Jesus Christ. There was no qualitative difference between Jesus and other men, but there was a quantitative difference in that in Jesus the God-consciousness was supremely present. This did not require one to believe in the ancient doctrines of the pre-existence of Christ, the Trinity, the Virgin Birth, the resurrection of Christ, or the miracles. Instead it was in the life and teachings of Jesus that one encountered the supreme manifestation of God-consciousness, the absolute dependence on a God of love. Fourthly, in the teachings, life, and suffering of Christ one encounters a God who suffered not in our stead (the substitutionary-satisfaction view of atonement) but on our behalf. In this encounter with a God of self-giving love one finds forgiveness of sins and reconciliation so that his own more feeble God-consciousness is stimulated and made stronger by the entrance of the living influence of Christ into his own life. Fifthly, it is in the church that the spirit of Christ lives on, and one who is drawn into that fellowship experiences the forgiveness of sins and the motivation to grow in Christ-likeness.

Finally, in light of even this brief sketch of Schleiermacher's theology, it should be evident that for him the work of historical Biblical criticism was

not destructive of Christianity. The ultimate authority
is not the Bible but the "feeling" of God-consciousness.
The Bible, especially the New Testament, witnesses in
many ways to the Christian God-consciousness, and Biblical criticism helps us to understand that witness
more clearly. This is especially the case with respect
to acquiring a more complete and accurate picture of
Jesus, his life and teachings. Furthermore, since God
is known in man's _feeling_ of absolute dependence, no
distinction need be drawn between the natural and the
supernatural. God is not "outside" the natural world,
does not transcend it in a spatial sense, but is within
it in a special way which requires no miraculous inter-
ventions on his part. Thus there need be no conflict
between religion and science, since religion deals with
the "inward," and science (at least in Schleiermacher's
time which was prior to the advent of modern psychology)
deals with the external world.

The positions of the two other outstanding representatives of Protestant Liberalism in Germany, Ritschl
and Harnack, were similar to that of Schleiermacher
in insisting that religion is a unique and irreducible
factor of human existence. But unlike Schleiermacher,
they followed Kant more closely in locating this irreducible factor in the realm of morality, the human
capacity for making value-judgments. Ritschl rejected
Schleiermacher's definition of religion as "the feeling
of absolute dependence" for the following reasons:
First, Ritschl thought that Schleiermacher's emphasis
on the Christian consciousness of the individual came
dangerously close to subjectivism. As a historian as
well as a theologian, Ritschl insisted that Christian
doctrine should be formulated in light of an objective
norm, namely, the historical Jesus. Secondly, Schleiermacher's emphasis on feeling did not properly locate
the essence of religious experience. For Ritschl the
heart of religion was neither metaphysical knowledge
nor mystical feeling but the very practical and concrete
matter of human valuing activity. That is, God was
known neither intellectually nor intuitively but prac-
tically in the valuing activity of the moral and spiritual life. As Ritschl said, "Apart from this value-
judgment of faith, there exists no knowledge worthy of
this content."[19] Obviously, Ritschl, and his theological disciple Harnack, who was also a great historian,
understood the essence of religion in the same way in
which Kant had understood it. Unlike Kant, however,
they placed greater emphasis on the corporate character
of religion. The supreme form of human valuing activity

400

(the revelation of God) which was manifested in the historical Jesus had been mediated through the fellowship of disciples who together had formed the nucleus of the primitive church.

In spite of their disagreement with Schleiermacher concerning the nature of religion's essence, certain aspects in the theologies of Ritschl and Harnack were similar to aspects in Schleicrmacher's theology. Religions are not to be divided into two mutually exclusive classes, the true and the false. Rather they are to be evaluated in terms of the adequacy of their forms for expressing the essence of religion. This is the case also with respect to Christian doctrines. Ancient Christian doctrines, with their mixture of metaphysical and speculative concepts, have tended to obscure rather than to clarify the essence of religion. The task of the modern theologian is to formulate doctrinal statements in such a way that they give full and understandable expression to the supreme manifestation of the essence of religion. But unlike Schleiermacher the essence of religion for Ritschl and Harnack was not the feeling of absolute dependence but human valuing activity which was supremely manifested in the historical Jesus.

Both Ritschl and Harnack viewed ancient doctrines such as original sin, the trinitarian and christological creeds, and the substitutionary-satisfaction atonement as dependent on the ancient philosophical concept of substance and thus as obstacles to understanding and faith in modern times. These doctrines fail to provide one with a realistic appraisal of human nature, a clear understanding of the historical Jesus in whom moral valuing activity was supreme, and the experience with God which strengthens one's own activity of moral valuing. Similarly, some of the Bible's content such as miracle stories, the virgin birth, and the resurrection of Jesus simply serve to alienate the modern reader. But these are the "husks" and not the "moral and spiritual kernel." The husks must be eliminated so that the "pure grain" may be discerned. This "pure grain" is the life and teaching of a superb master in the art of living, namely the historical Jesus. According to Harnack attention should be focused on the gospel of Jesus rather than on the gospel about Jesus. The three principle motifs which he found in the life and teachings of Jesus were: the kingdom of God and its coming, or the rule of God in the soul; the fatherhood of God and the infinite worth of each human being;

401

the higher righteousness and the commandment of love.[20]

Ritschl and Harnack viewed reconciliation with God, or salvation, as awakening in one the experience both of the forgiveness of sins and the inspiration to live according to the model provided by Jesus. This salvation, however, is not simply an individualistic matter. It is corporate in that it originates in the church, the value-creating community which originated due to the influence of Jesus and in which his influence continues to be experienced. Reconciliation is corporate also in that it is directed toward the goal of the kingdom of God. The church is not an end in itself but the value-creating community whose task is to work for the realization of the kingdom of God on earth. That is, the kingdom of God is not simply a supernatural order but a new order of life on earth. It was begun by Jesus and will be actualized fully whenever there is loving and free mutual service among all human beings in all of human society.

The Protestant liberal theology in Germany soon spread to America and among its most outstanding advocates in this country were William Adams Brown (1865-1943), Harry Emerson Fosdick (1878-1969), and Walter Rauschenbush (1861-1918). While there were many other liberal theologians in the United States, some of whom were more radical and others less radical than these three, they were perhaps most representative of Protestant Liberalism in the United States. According to Kenneth Cauthen, "Brown was liberalism's most eminent teacher, . . . Fosdick its foremost preacher . . . [and] Rauschenbush . . . [its] greatest prophet."[21] After completing graduate study of theology in the United States, both Brown and Rauschenbush continued their studies with liberal theologians in Germany (Adolf Van Harnack, for example) and then returned to the United States to pursue teaching careers. Fosdick studied at Union Theological Seminary in New York City where Brown was one of his teachers. Of the three, Fosdick became the most widely known due to the fact that for many years he was pastor of the famous Riverside Drive Church in New York and the regular preacher for the Sunday afternoon Vesper programs on the National Broadcasting Company's radio network.

Although there were some differences in emphases, the theologies of Brown, Fosdick, and Rauschenbush were basically similar. Like the German liberal theologians, they sought to base their theologies on the essence of

402

historical Christianity, and thus regarded themselves as standing squarely within the Christian tradition. They were convinced that the Christian faith could not be of any real influence in the modern world unless its essential elements were explicated in a theology which could be understood and believed by "intelligent moderns." Fosdick expressed the fundamental principle of liberal theology when he spoke of "Abiding Experiences and Changing Categories"[22] in the history of Christianity. That is, while the Christian _experience_ has remained constant throughout the ages, changes in cultural and intellectual outlooks have resulted in changed categories for understanding and communicating this experience. So in the modern world the categories of past ages are inadequate, and the "abiding experiences" need to be translated into the modern idiom. The discussion which follows will sketch briefly the basic elements in the "translation" of the three American liberal theologians, and this will constitute a brief summary of Protestant Liberalism in general.

1. As we have seen, liberals, whether Protestant or Catholic, accepted biological evolution as a fact and some theory of evolutionary progress in history. They denied that the acceptance of evolution and the conviction that God was responsible for the beginning of the Universe and continuously at work in it in creative ways was contradictory. Instead they insisted that these two beliefs were complimentary. Thus in his book, _God at Work_, William Adams Brown wrote:

> Wherever we look, in the universe as a whole, on our planet with its compara-
> tively brief astronomical history, or in
> the life of man who inhabits it, we
> find new phenomena appearing which, how-
> ever dependent they may be upon their
> antecedents, cannot be wholly accounted
> for by them. There is evolution, and
> there are laws of evolution: but it is
> emergent, and in its most significant
> and outstanding phenomena appears to us
> creative. It is creative not only in the
> sense that it cannot be wholly accounted
> for by its antecedents but in the sense
> that now that it is here it lends itself
> to uses, takes its place as part of a
> larger pattern, and gives birth to ele-
> ments which without its presence could
> not have been. How shall we account for

> this amazing phenomenon? What better
> answer can we give than was given by the
> Psalmist three thousand years ago? It
> is because God has been at work. The
> universe is his handiwork, serves his
> purpose and reveals his will.[23]

In light of this view, it is not surprising that
the liberals rejected the doctrine of original sin
(the fall of Adam) as being literally true. This doctrine was viewed as an outmoded, prescientific attempt
to account for the origin of sin. In its place was
substituted the evolutionary view of man's long development upward from the level of the beast toward the
attainment of moral personality. Sin was understood
as the fossilized remainder of man's animal beginnings,
his fleshly impulses, which impedes his moral and
spiritual growth. It was transmitted socially due to
the sinful influences of one generation on another
and of the social environment on the individual. If
the doctrine of original sin was to be retained at all
(and most liberals thought it better to eliminate it
altogether from Christian theology), it should be
understood as simply symbolizing the social matrix of
sin.

2. While liberals generally held that the Bible
was inspired, they did not understand inspiration in
terms of a literal, verbal inspiration or "whisper"
theory which holds that God imparted or "whispered"
the words in the Bible directly to its authors. Instead, the liberals claimed, the Bible contains some
narratives such as those dealing with miracles, demons,
a three layer universe, etc., which cannot be taken as
literally true. On the basis of the historical critical method of study, however, it is possible to discern
the essential message of the Bible. This message witnesses to the progressive human discovery of God's
developing revelation in the historical experiences
of Israel which finally culminated in the supreme
disclosure of God in the historical Jesus. Thus in
the introduction of his book, A Guide to the Understanding of the Bible, Harry Emerson Fosdick said:

> Any idea of inspiration which implies
> equal value in the teachings of Scrip-
> ture, or inerrancy in its statements,
> or conclusive infallibility in its ideas,
> is irreconcilable with such facts as this
> book presents. The inspirations of God

404

fortunately have not been thus stereotyped and mechanical. There is, however,
nothing in the process of development
itself, whether in the organic world
in general or in the realm of mind and
morals, to call in question the creative
and directive activity of God. . . . The
supreme contribution of the Bible is not
that it finished anything but that it
started something. Its thinking is not
so much a product as a process.[24]

3. Since the high point of God's revelation is
to be found in the life, teachings, and personality of
the historical Jesus, the liberals regarded him as
the source and norm of the Christian's experience of
God. The disclosure of God in Jesus is not something
alien to human reason and experience, but is continuous
with the best in human reason and experience. Since
revelation itself possesses inherent reasonableness
and practical value, it could be validated in actual
experience. In his book, A Theology For the Social
Gospel, Walter Rauschenbush said that, while past
Christian theologies had tended to make the divinity
of Christ a matter of his nature rather than his
character,

The social gospel is not primarily interested in metaphysical questions; its
christological interest is all for a real
personality who could set a great historical process in motion; it wants his work
interpreted by the purposes which ruled
and directed his active life; it would
have more interest in basing the divine
quality of his personality on free and
ethical acts of his will than in dwelling
on the passive inheritance of a divine
essence. . . . His personality was an
achievement, not an effortless inheritance. . . . So we have in Jesus a perfect
religious personality, a spiritual life
completely filled by the realization of
a God who is love. All his mind was set
on God and one with him. Consequently
it was also absorbed in the fundamental
purpose of God, the Kingdom of God.[25]

4. Liberals definitely rejected the notions of
predestination and of the substitutionary-satisfaction

405

atonement as demeaning of God and destructive of human
responsibility. Christ's saving work was not a matter
of his taking upon himself the punishment which sinful
human beings merited and thus satisfying God's justice.
Since God is always loving and forgiving, his attitude
toward his creatures does not need to be changed. Instead it is the attitudes and lives of human beings
which need to be changed so that they will be reconciled to God and pattern their lives, individually and
socially, after the model presented in the life and
teachings of Jesus. In Christian Theology In Outline
William Adams Brown claimed that salvation is both an
individual experience and an historical process. In
each of these modes salvation has a twofold aspect.
One aspect of salvation in the mode of individual
experience is that it is a religious experience which
"involves the consciousness of reconciliation between
God and man, manifesting itself on God's part in forgiveness and acceptance, and on man's part in repentance
and trust."[26] The other aspect of this first mode is
a moral experience in which "salvation involves a
change of character, manifesting itself in the adoption
of Christ's principle of self-sacrificing love as the
guide of life."[27] But salvation is not simply an
individualistic matter, for there is also its mode as
an historical process. Thus Brown claimed,

> From the point of view of history,
> salvation is the process by which the
> divine ideal is realized in society through
> the establishment of the Kingdom of God
> among men. This process has two main
> aspects. On the one hand, it consists in
> the progressive revelation of the divine
> will; on the other hand, it involves the
> progressive realization of that will in
> society.[28]

5. The liberals' view of salvation had important
implications with respect to their views of the church,
ecumenism, and the kingdom of God. Since for them
salvation is primarily a matter of the experience of
that reconciliation with God which is oriented largely
toward the goal of a change in moral character rather
than the giving of mental assent to a set of dogma and
traditions, it is not surprising that the liberals
tended to view the church as a fellowship or community
founded on Christian experience. As we have seen,
they held that the norm of authentic Christian experience is the life, teachings, and personality of Jesus.

406

Given the unity of this norm, there should be a unity among all Christians. Sectarian divisions which had arisen because of unessential doctrinal and traditional differences between denominations constitute a great scandal of modern Christendom, seriously weakening its effectiveness in the world. Sacramental, ritualistic, institutional, and doctrinal aspects of the churches should be subordinated to a common loyalty to Jesus. This would pave the way for the churches to modify those divisive aspects in such ways that there could be a reunion of Christendom for the sake of greater ethical effectiveness. It was due to this perspective that liberal theologians were active in the Protestant ecumenical movement which resulted in some church unions across denominational lines (such as the formation of the United Church of Christ which brought together four different denominations), and in the establishment of the National Council of Churches in the United States and The World Council of Churches.

The liberals insisted that the church does not exist for itself but for the sake of the kingdom of God. No one emphasized this point more strongly than did Walter Rauschenbush, Liberalism's "prophet" of the "social gospel." He insisted that if the churches proclaim a message which deals only with the salvation of individuals, they are not proclaiming the _full_ Christian gospel, for "the establishment of a community of righteousness in mankind is just as much a saving act of God as the salvation of any individual from his natural selfishness and moral inability."[29] The churches, Rauschenbush believed, are fellowships of worshipping Christians. To be fully Christian, however, they must accept the kingdom of God ideal of a just and righteous social order as the criterion in light of which their influence in the world is tested and corrected, and as the goal toward which they should strive to lead human society.

6. While the liberals placed major emphasis on living as a Christian in this life, which included personal moral growth and the working for the realization of the kingdom of God on earth, they did not ignore the Christian conviction that there is life after death. They did not think of this in physical terms, in the categories of a literal last judgment and of a literal heaven and hell. They rejected all attempts, as someone has said, to describe the furniture of heaven and the temperature of hell. Instead they talked of life after death in terms of _immortality_

407

instead of _resurrection_. For example, in his lecture "Abiding Experiences and Changing Categories," Harry Emerson Fosdick explicitly rejected the belief in the resurrection of the flesh and any claim of knowledge concerning the details of the future life. However, he did affirm "I believe in the persistence of personality through death."[30]

B. The Right Wing Response of Protestant Fundamentalism

As we have seen, Fundamentalism arose as a movement around the beginning of the twentieth century. While many fundamentalist beliefs had been present in the evangelical revivalism and Calvinism of the preceding century, the fundamentalist movement crystallized, augmented, and developed these beliefs into an arsenal of doctrines with which to defend "true" Christianity against the attacks of its foe, Protestant Liberalism.[31] It is not so much science and culture (properly understood), but Liberalism which threatens Christianity.

J. Gresham Machen (1881-1937) claimed that even conservative Christians (he preferred this term rather than fundamentalist) need to recognize that modern culture is here to stay. He did express respect for those conservatives who took the simple position that the Bible is inerrant and infallible in all of its parts, and on this basis held that if science conflicts with the Bible, then so much the worse for science. These "simple" conservatives were correct in their main point, but Machen thought that it was the responsibility of intellectual conservatives to show that "true" Christianity, the Christianity of the New Testament, was not in conflict with science, but rather that it was the spurious Christianity of the liberals which was in conflict with science. The liberals thought they were defending Christianity by locating science and religion in the two different realms of fact and value, but instead they actually had made their understanding of natural science's method and results into the ultimate standard in light of which they deleted or abandoned the Biblical doctrines which are the foundations of Christianity.[32] Biblical doctrines contain both factual and religious meaning. Deleting their factual aspects results in an un-Christian perspective. When properly understood, science supports rather than contradicts these doctrines.

In a scholarly book, _The Virgin Birth of Christ_,

Machen gives expression to this thesis. The theological significance of the virgin birth, he believes, depends on it having been a supernatural event which occurred as an actual fact of history. He argues at length that there is considerable historical evidence to support this claim. Thus the virgin birth is not in conflict with science. In this connection Machen says a great deal about the relation of the natural and the supernatural, of science and Christian doctrines. Since much of what he says on this issue is rather representative of the position held by intellectual fundamentalists, it merits quoting at some length:

> We are often told, indeed, that if the virgin birth is accepted, it can only be accepted as a matter of 'faith,' and that the decision about it is beyond the range of historical science. But such a distinction between faith and history is, we think, very unfortunate. . . . It is certainly true that in order to believe in the virgin birth of Christ one needs to do more than merely examine the immediate documentary evidence; for one needs to take the documentary evidence in connection with a sound view of the world and with certain convictions as to the facts of the human soul. But the sharp separation between documentary evidence on the one hand and these presuppositions about God and the soul on the other is far from being truly scientific. A science of history that shall exist by itself, independent of presuppositions, is an abstraction to which no reality corresponds. As a matter of fact, scientific history as well as other branches of science rests upon presuppositions; only, the important thing is that the presuppositions shall be true instead of false.

> So it is an unwarranted narrowing of the sphere of history when history is made to deal only with those events which stand within the order of nature, as distinguished from events that proceed from an exercise of the immediate, or creative, power of God. The true sphere of history is the establishment of all

facts, whatever they are, that concern
human life--the establishment of these
facts and the exhibition of the relations
between them. . . . If we are to be truly
scientific, there must be a real synthesis
of truth; there can scarcely be a greater
error than that of keeping different kinds
of truth in separate water-tight compart-
ments in the mind; there can scarcely be
a greater error than that of regarding
'religious truth,' for example, as in some
way distinct in kind from 'scientific
truth.' On the contrary, . . . all truth,
ultimately, is one. As we must continue
to insist, even in the face of widespread
opposition, that if the virgin birth is a
fact at all, it belongs truly to the realm
of history.[33]

Machen, of course, insisted that the virgin birth
was indeed a fact of history. Since generally the
liberals viewed the virgin birth and miracle stories
either as obstacles to faith which should be eliminated
or as simply symbolic of religious truths rather than
facts of history, it is not surprising that for the
most part Machen and fundamentalists generally have
regarded Liberalism as un-Christian.

It was due primarily to the reaction of conservatives against Liberalism that Fundamentalism became
a movement. Liberalism had gained adherents in a few
of the leading theological seminaries and was spreading
to some extent among the churches. In opposition to
this trend, the fundamentalists sought to consolidate
their own ranks and to gain support for their theology
in a number of ways such as Bible conferences, religious literature, Bible schools or institutes, and
various associations of like-minded fundamentalists.
According to C. Allyn Russell, "the mother of the
conferences was the Niagara Conference (named after
Niagara-on-the-Lake, Ontario, its most frequent place
of meeting) which convened for annual summer assemblies
from 1875 to 1901."[34] Among the important publications
were the Scofield Reference Bible and The Fundamentals:
A Testimony to the Truth. Edited by two teachers at
the Moody Bible Institute, Ruben H. Torrey and A. C.
Dixon, The Fundamentals was a group of twelve booklets
(published between 1909-1912) which set forth in a
brief and simple style the "fundamentals" of the Christian faith. Two wealthy California businessmen

provided sufficient financial support so that copies
of these booklets were distributed free of charge all
over America to millions of pastors and church members
of virtually every denomination. Some scholars of
American religious history regard this event as mark-
ing the beginning of Fundamentalism as a movement.[35]

It is often the case that a scholarly discussion
of a particular subject will begin with a definition
of the term designating that subject. As we have seen,
dictionaries do contain definitions of the term "Fundamentalism," but since it is difficult to formulate
brief, simple, and adequate definitions of complex
religious movements, the definitions alone do not provide us with an adequate understanding of this movement. In his study of Fundamentalism, James Barr
argues that an adequate understanding can be provided
only by means of an extended description. However, he
admits that an investigation of something requires
as a starting point at least a vague recognition of
this something. With respect to "Fundamentalism" this
recognition is of a group of characteristics which most
Christians perceive as being shared by those they
classify as fundamentalists. According to Barr, the
most prominent of these characteristics are:

(a)   a very strong emphasis on the inerrancy of
the Bible, the absence from it of any sort of
error;

(b)   a strong hostility to modern theology
and to the methods, results and implications
of modern critical study of the Bible;

(c)   an assurance that those who do not share
their religious viewpoint are not really
'true Christians' at all.[36]

These are not all the characteristics of Fundamentalism,
Barr affirms, but they do serve as a recognition starting point. That is, they serve to identify the fundamentalist, to distinguish the fundamentalist from other
types of Christians.

In addition to these three characteristics, fundamentalists have given expression to several others.
The Presbyterian General Assembly of 1910, for example,
endorsed certain "fundamentals" which must be believed
if one is to be a "true" Christian.[37] In his book,

411

<u>Orthodox Christianity Versus Modernism</u>, William Jennings
Bryan reaffirmed these "fundamentals."[38] They included
not only the inerrancy and infallibility of all of the
Bible, but also the virgin birth and deity of Jesus
Christ, the substitutionary-satisfaction view of salvation, the physical resurrection of Christ and his
bodily return to earth in a second coming. Implicit
in these "fundamentals" are three others, namely the
rejection of evolution and the insistence on the doctrines of creationism and original sin, the bodily
resurrection of the dead which is to be followed by a
literal last judgment and an eternal heaven and eternal
hell, and the church as a fellowship of "true" believers. There have been, of course, some differences in
emphases among fundamentalists. C. Allyn Russell, in
his <u>Voices In American Fundamentalism</u>, indicates such
differences when, for example, he designates J. Gresham
Machen as a scholarly fundamentalist, William Jennings
Bryan as a statesman-fundamentalist, and Clarence E.
Macartney as a preacher-fundamentalist.[39] Yet, just
as was the case with the liberals, in spite of some
differences in emphases, generally the fundamentalists
have been in agreement on the basic issues, the "fundamentals." Thus the remainder of our discussion will
describe briefly the basic elements in the fundamentalist's position on each of the "fundamentals."

1. As we have seen, a characteristic which provides a recognition starting point for a description of
Fundamentalism is the strong insistence on the inerrancy
and infallibility of the Bible and thus the rejection of
the historical critical method (higher criticism, see
Chapter II) of Biblical study. The doctrine of the
inerrancy and infallibility of the Bible might be called
<u>the</u> fundamental of the "fundamentals" since, in the
fundamentalists' view, all the others are dependent
upon and guaranteed by this one.

In an article on "Revelation and Inspiration" in
<u>The New Bible Commentary: Revised</u>, J. I. Packer claims
that the divine inspiration of the Biblical authors is
not to be confused with the "inspiration" of the creative artist. Instead it was due to the supernatural
influence of God's spirit on the writers. This divine
inspiration did not imply always some abnormal state
of mind in the Biblical writer or require the destruction of his personality. In most cases, he believes,
God directed the writers to perform their tasks through
the normal use of the abilities which he had given them.
But since God directed them, what the Biblical authors

412

wrote <u>was</u> inerrant and infallible, and thus Packer
says:

> Since truth is communicated through
> words, and verbal inaccuracy misrepresents
> meaning, inspiration must be verbal in
> the nature of the case. And if the words
> of Scripture are 'God-breathed,' it is
> almost blasphemy to deny that it is free
> from error in that which it is intended
> to teach and infallible in the guidance it
> gives. Inerrancy and infallibility cannot
> be proved (nor, let us note, disproved) by
> argument. Both are articles of faith;
> corollaries of the confession, which Christ's
> teaching demands and the Spirit's testimony
> evokes, that canonical Scripture was breathed
> out by the God who cannot lie. He who de-
> nies them thereby shows that he rejects the
> witness of Christ, the apostles and the
> historic Christian church concerning the
> nature of 'God's Word written,' and either
> does not possess or has not understood the
> <u>testimonium Spiritus Sancti internum</u> [the
> internal witness of the Holy Spirit].[40]

While in what might be called "popular" Fundamentalism
there are some who claim that the inerrancy of the
Bible can be proved, Packer claims that this is an
article of faith. Yet in his view the only <u>right</u> way
to approach the Bible is with a faith in its inerrancy
and infallibility. Furthermore, this approach requires
the rejection of any historical, critical method of
studying the Bible which stands in contradiction with
this faith.[41]

In popular Fundamentalism the English of the
Authorized Version (King James Version) of 1611 usually
is regarded as the inspired text, and there is little
awareness of or concern with the fact that the ancient
texts were written by hand in the Hebrew and Greek
languages. However, fundamentalist Biblical scholars
generally are familiar with these ancient texts and of
the variations among them due not least to the fact
that for centuries they were copied by hand. Recently
there has emerged a group of so-called "new" fundamentalist scholars who engage in "lower" or textual
criticism (see Chapter II), and they justify this
endeavor on the ground that it ensures the substantial
<u>purity</u> of the text. For example, in his <u>An Introduction</u>

413

to <u>Christian Apologetics</u>, the scholarly fundamentalist theologian,[42] Edward J. Carnell (1919-1967) says:

> Contrary to what the untutored may think, neither the King James Version nor the Vulgate is plenarily inspired, for plenary inspiration is an attribute which is reserved solely for the <u>original</u> <u>writings</u>, those autographs of Moses, the prophets, and the apostles which are now all lost. . . . In the hundreds of years which have elapsed since the Bible was written, a few transcriptional errors have crept into the text. The original text is wholly inspired; the present text is in a state of substantial purity. . . .
>
> Conservatives [fundamentalists] have historically led the research in lower criticism, being stimulated to restore the original text by a consideration of the doctrines of original inspiration.[43]

Thus in Carnell's view fundamentalists may engage in lower criticism without endangering the doctrine that the original text of the Bible was totally inerrant and infallible. He claims, however, that higher criticism must be rejected because it is inconsistent with this doctrine.

In conclusion, it may be said that there are two ways in which the Bible is of primary importance for fundamentalists. First, it is important as the infallible source or textbook for all of their other doctrines. Secondly, the doctrine about the Bible, that it is inerrant and infallible, is a primary and basic doctrine. It is as important as the doctrine which affirms that Christ, the Son of God, is personal Lord and Savior. The inerrancy and infallibility of Scripture and Christ as Lord and Savior are two doctrines which fundamentalists hold together in a kind of reciprocal relation. Thus, as James Barr points out, even those fundamentalists who seldom read the Bible and have little knowledge of it, regard it as "the supreme <u>tangible</u> <u>sacred</u> <u>reality</u>."[44]

2. Given this doctrine concerning the Bible, it follows that fundamentalists believe the Genesis account of creation to be factually true and evolution to be false. One of the most famous opponents of

414

evolution was William Jennings Bryan. He argued that evolution was an unproven hypothesis which was inconsistent with and destructive of the Word of God, and if permitted to spread unchecked, it would annihilate revelation, paralyze religion, and undermine faith.[45]

In popular Fundamentalism today there are those who strongly hold to the Biblical account of creation and who reject evolution in all of its forms. By various means they seek to compel school administrators to require science teachers to present "creationism" along with their teaching of evolution. At the same time, however, there are at least some among the "new" fundamentalist Biblical scholars and theologians who have yielded to some degree on this issue. While all of the "new" fundamentalists hold to the essential truth of the first chapter of Genesis, there are some who interpret the six days of creation as six geological ages.[46] Others go a bit further as, for example, Edward J. Carnell who argues that while the Biblical account is not compatible with "total" evolution, it is compatible with what he calls "threshold evolution." Unlike the total view which claims that the gaps between kinds of plants and animals are due to our ignorance and that in time we will discover the "missing links," the "threshold" view insists that the gaps are real and were decreed by God in the original creation so as "to mark off the original kinds." According to Carnell, "We expect organic evolution within the 'kinds,' for God has only promised the 'fixity' of the broad 'kinds,' not of the infinite 'species' that can develop out of them."[47]

3. On the basis of their doctrine of the Bible, fundamentalists not only accept the Genesis account of creation as factually true but also insist that the Genesis narrative concerning the fall of Adam and Eve is descriptive of historical fact. By disobeying God, Adam and Eve fell into guilt and condemnation.[48] This sin and guilt was transmitted in a very realistic way from Adam and Eve to all succeeding human beings. Thus sin is understood in a semi-metaphysical sense. Carnell claims that "man is, by nature, a sinner."[49] It follows, then, that sin is a universal feature of human life. It not only brings disruption and misery into the human realm but also spoils the universe which God had created originally as perfect. Similar to Augustine (see Chapter VI), Carnell claims that the sin of man is responsible for all of the evil in the world, both natural and moral.[50]

According to James Barr, fundamentalists "formalize" the doctrine of sin in two ways. One of these ways is that sin is "constantly emphasized." The other way is that sin plays a dominant role in the fundamentalists' presuppositions. Concerning this point, Barr says:

> It provides the reason why certain things are said and believed. If you ask what is the reason why one should be a conservative evangelical [an expression which Barr uses as a synonym for fundamentalist] rather than some other sort of Christian, the answer will very likely be: because of sin. Sin is so powerful and bad that conservative evangelicalism is the only faith that faces up to its awfulness. Sin is the reason why we have a Jesus Christ, why we have a substitutionary atonement, why we have a Holy Spirit, why we need a second advent. It is, in short, the reason why we have got to be conservative evangelicals. Sin is a valuable intellectual resource to this form of religion: without it, it could not get anywhere.[51]

4. We have seen that in Fundamentalism the doctrine of Jesus Christ as Lord and Savior plays a complimentary role with the doctrine of the Bible's inerrancy and infallibility. All fundamentalists hold to a very high Christology. In popular Fundamentalism this sometimes takes the form of claiming that Jesus is God. It is admitted, of course, that Jesus had a body, but it is emphasized that it was God walking around and teaching in a man's body. William Jennings Bryan, for example, claimed that Jesus Christ should be taken out of the man class and put into the God class.[52] Thus the Christology sometimes expressed in popular Fundamentalism is similar in some respects to ancient Gnosticism (see Chapter VI). The ordinary fundamentalist believer is likely to be uninformed concerning the history of Christianity,[53] the ancient Christological controversies, and the reasons why the Council of Chalcedon insisted on the full deity and the full humanity of Jesus Christ. He tends to emphasize the deity and to ignore the humanity.

Scholarly fundamentalists, however, reaffirm the Christology of traditional orthodoxy. For example, Edward J. Carnell claims that Jesus Christ "was very

416

God of very God and, in virtue of His incarnation, true man."[54] In one sentence Carnell provides a succinct summary of both his Christology and his doctrine of salvation when he says, "Happiness is secured for man by Jesus Christ, who being true God, consubstantial with the Father and the Holy Spirit, having left heaven, took on the form of a servant, fulfilling the covenant of grace by obeying the law of God perfectly, died an expiatory death on the cross as a full atonement for the sins of many, and now lives eternally as the God-Man making intercession for the righteous."[55] Most scholarly fundamentalists agree with the Christology of the Chalcedon creed (see Chapter VI) and view Christ "as both God and man in two distinct natures and one person forever."[56] Yet even they tend to place greater emphasis on the deity of Christ than on his humanity. Undoubtedly, the major reason for this is their opposition to the liberals whose Christology tends to emphasize Christ's continuity with all men (see section A above).

Since fundamentalists place great emphasis on the deity of Christ, it is not surprising that they insist on the factual truth of the virgin birth of Jesus Christ. This must be believed for two reasons. First, the nativity narratives are found in the inerrant and infallible Bible (the Gospels of Matthew and Luke). Secondly, the virgin birth serves the function of guaranteeing and protecting the doctrine of Christ's deity. It is not that the birth narratives are the sole source of the doctrine of Christ's deity, for the entire New Testament witnesses to that. Conceivably, one who did not know the birth narratives but was familiar with the rest of the New Testament would believe in the deity of Christ. Yet his knowledge of Christ, according to Machen, would be seriously impoverished. The virgin birth is important, Machen claims, because it establishes the time of the incarnation and guarantees that the Son of God lived a completely human life on earth, for it could not have been complete unless it began in the mother's womb. Machen concludes his argument with the following question: "How, except by virgin birth, could our Saviour have lived a complete human life from the mother's womb, and yet have been from the very beginning no product of what had gone before, but a supernatural Person come into the world from the outside to redeem the sinful race?"[57]

5. As we have seen, in the fundamentalists' view man is by nature a sinner. All persons have inherited

the sin and guilt of Adam and thus stand under the
curse of punishment and eternal damnation by a righteous
and just God. No one can be freed from that curse by
his own moral efforts, even if that involves following
the example of Christ. He can be saved from that curse
only if he believes that for the sake of mankind who
was condemned to death because of sin, Christ, the Son
of God, came to earth, took man's place, suffered the
penalty of death in perfect obedience, and by this
vicarious sacrifice (analogous to the sacrificial lamb
of the Old Testament) satisfied divine justice and thus
overcame sin and death. In principle and objectively
Christ has made atonement for all, but for it to be
actual in the life of a person it must be appropriated
by the response of faith. When one responds in faith
(which means believing all fundamentalist doctrines
as well as trust), then God forgives one's sins, grants
the "new birth" and sends the gift of the Holy Spirit,
the Sanctifier, into one's heart.[58]

It has been indicated already in the discussion of
his Christology that Edward J. Carnell understood salvation in terms of the substitutionary-satisfaction doctrine. This is evident also when Carnell claimed that
"the first Adam brought sin and death on the human race"
but that Jesus Christ, "the last Adam," through his
obedience and righteousness "propitiated the offended
judicial sentiment in God." Indeed, Carnell claimed,
the doctrine that "Christ satisfied divine justice . . .
[is] the very essence of the gospel."[59] All fundamentalists would agree that this is the case.

6. Fundamentalists generally, including the scholarly theologians, have not explicated a fully developed
doctrine of the church. Thus there tends to be considerable vagueness in Fundamentalism concerning the issue
of the relation of the universal church of true believers with the actual organized churches in the world.[60]
Perhaps one reason for this is that, with few exceptions, fundamentalists belong to several kinds of
churches or denominations rather than to one which is
exclusively fundamentalist. When fundamentalists do
express views about the church, they are likely to
utter one or more of the following three statements.
First, the churches or denominations (even the ones
of which they are members) often fall short of totally
and faithfully witnessing to sound doctrine (those
specified above) and thus are corrupting the true
Christian faith. Secondly, since the Bible is inerrant
and infallible, it is the final and absolute authority

in all matters concerning the churches' faith, doctrine, and polity. Thirdly, the true church is the fellowship of all _true_ believers. Thus Carnell, affirming that "God made a covenant with Abraham, and Jesus Christ is the blessing of this covenant," claims that "the church is a fellowship of all who share in the blessings of the Abrahamic covenant."[61] He does say that the church also is an organization, but he is rather vague about the relationship between the church as an organization and the church as the "seed of Abraham."

In spite of the fact that fundamentalists of different denominational affiliations cooperate in Bible conferences and "Moral Majority" associations, they generally reject ecumenism. They tend to be suspicious of and hostile to ecumenical movements. Undoubtedly, this is due to a number of reasons. Among them, as Barr indicates, is the fact that ecumenism requires adknowledging the essential Christianity of those who hold to different doctrinal and ecclesiastical traditions, the tendency of fundamentalists to resist change, the fact that non-fundamentalists often have provided the leadership in Protestant ecumenical movements, and the fact that some fundamentalists tend to view any universal organization which seeks to overcome the divisions of mankind into nations and churches as a force for evil, claiming such divisions were ordained by God.[62]

7. As we have seen, the fundamentalists' doctrine of salvation places great emphasis on life after death. Eschatology (a view of the end-time) plays a major role in fundamentalists' views of history. Yet there are some disagreements among them concerning particular eschatological issues. In general these disagreements cluster around the doctrine of Christ's second coming and involve the following three issues. First, some strongly emphasize an apocalyptic view of the second coming in which there are vivid pictures of the cataclysmic destruction of the prevailing powers of the world, the destruction or binding of Satan, and the establishment of God's kingdom. While this view has some influence on all fundamentalists, at least in the negative sense of minimizing concern for the social application of the gospel, not all fundamentalists are so dominated by such graphic apocalyptic pictures of the end of history.[63]

"Moderate" fundamentalists believe that "kingdom of God" refers to that state of things after the

judgment, to God's eschatological annihilation of
everything hostile to his sovereignty, including
Satan, but they refrain from expressing this in vivid
apocalyptic terminology.[64] Secondly, some fundamentalists are convinced that the precise date of the end-
time can be determined, and/or that it is very near.
Others deny that it can be dated. It may be near, but
God alone knows when it will occur (Mark 13:32).
Thirdly, some fundamentalists hold to premillennialism
("millennium" means a thousand) while others hold to
postmillennialism. The former believe that the return
of Christ to earth will precede the thousand years
during which time, Satan having been bound, Christ with
the saints will rule on earth. They believe also that
at the end of the millennium Satan will be unbound and
will deceive many nations, but very soon will be consigned to hell. The dead will be raised and judged,
with the wicked consigned to hell with Satan, and the
righteous to heaven. The postmillennialists believe
that the millennium will be ushered in by the work of
the Holy Spirit through the church, and that the second
advent of Christ will occur at the end of the millennium.[65] In spite of these disagreements, however, fundamentalists are agreed in insisting on Christ's bodily resurrection from the dead as a basic supporting
pillar of the doctrine of salvation, the second coming
of Christ in personal and bodily form, the bodily
resurrection of all the dead, a literal last judgment,
the eternal bliss of the faithful in heaven, and the
eternal damnation of the faithless and wicked in hell.[66]

C. Neo-Orthodox or Neo-Reformation Theology

The theologians to be considered in this section
generally are labelled as Neo-Orthodox. This catchword
is far from adequate, since in some respects their theologies are different from that of traditional orthodoxy. Yet Biblical perspectives play an important role,
and they are loyal to the original spirit of Reformation theology. For this reason they are sometimes
called Neo-Reformation theologians. This does not mean
that they are conservative in either the traditional
or fundamentalist sense, for the roots of their thought
are as much in the modern world as in the remote past.
Neither are they theological liberals, for even though
their formal theological education was received from
exponents of Liberalism, their mature theological
thought differs from Liberalism on many important issues. In the following discussion an attempt will be
made to describe briefly the basic features in the

420

theologies of two of the most famous exponents of so-called Neo-Orthodox theology, Karl Barth and Reinhold Niebuhr,[67] and to indicate their major differences with both Liberalism and Fundamentalism.

The "theological revolution" of Neo-Orthodoxy began with Karl Barth (1886-1968). The son of a minister, and Professor of New Testament at Bern, Switzerland, Barth began his study of theology at the University of Bern and then, following the European custom, continued to study at other distinguished universities such as the Universities of Berlin and Marburg. At these latter two universities he studied with leading exponents of Protestant Liberalism (for example, Adolf Von Harnack). Upon receiving his degree, he was ordained, and for about a decade served as pastor of a Reformed church in a Swiss village. Due in part to this experience, he became dissatisfied with liberal theology. Later he was to say about this experience that the people came on Sunday with a need to hear the Word of God, to be confronted with a message which came from beyond man, but that he was unable to speak to this need with a liberal theology. Liberal theology concentrated on an analysis of man's religion, suggesting that man should simply heighten his religious responses instead of abandoning human activity and listening to the Word of God. Having found that liberal theology was not well adapted to preaching, Barth began to re-study the Bible intensively, seeking to find a central message which he could identify as God's Word to man. One result of this study was the publication of his first book, The Epistle to the Romans, which brought him to the attention of theological scholars and resulted in his appointment as Professor of Theology at the University of Gottingen. For almost fifteen years he taught theology at several distinguished German universities. In 1935, as a result of his opposition to Hitler and his involvement in the establishment of the free Confessing Church which opposed the Nazis,[68] Barth was dismissed from his teaching position at the University of Bonn (he refused to begin his classes with the customary "Heil Hitler") and expelled from Germany. Almost immediately he was called to be Professor of Theology at the University of Basel in Switzerland where he worked for the remainder of his long career, teaching and writing his numerous books including the famous multivolumned Church Dogmatics (six million words on seven thousand pages). Many regard him as a modern "church father," and claim that his name belongs in the list of the greatest Christian theologians such as Augustine, Aquinas, Luther, and Calvin.[69]

Reinhold Niebuhr (1892-1971), whom many regard as the greatest native-born American theologian, had a career which in some respects parallelled that of Karl Barth. The son of a minister in the Evangelical Synod of North America, a denomination which combined both the Lutheran and Reformed traditions,[70] Niebuhr studied at Elmhurst College and Eden Theological Seminary, both of which were supported by his denomination. He completed his graduate theological education at Yale University Divinity School where one of his teachers was the distinguished liberal theologian, Douglas Clyde Macintosh. From 1915 to 1928 he served as pastor of the Bethel Evangelical Church in Detroit, Michigan, and, similar to Barth, this experience led him to question the adequacy of liberal theology. Concerning this period in his life, he later wrote, "I underwent a fairly complete conversion of thought which involved rejection of almost all the liberal ideals with which I ventured forth in 1915."[71] Although a busy and effective pastor, during this twelve years Niebuhr wrote some forty articles which were published in journals such as The Christian Century, The Atlantic Monthly, and The World Tomorrow, and his first book, Does Civilization Need Religion?, which was published in 1927. These publications, along with his numerous addresses on college campuses, brought him to the attention of the scholarly theological world, and in 1928 he was appointed Professor of Applied Christianity at Union Theological Seminary in New York City. He remained at Union throughout the rest of his long career. Although he was continuously involved not only in lecturing and preaching at Union, on other campuses and in churches but also in many social and political causes, Niebuhr wrote some thousand articles and twenty books, the most famous of which was his two-volumned The Nature and Destiny of Man.[72]

Even though the theologies of Barth and Niebuhr are being considered in this section on Neo-Orthodoxy, it would be a mistake to think of them as carbon copies of one another. There were significant differences between them. In spite of Niebuhr's statement that he had rejected almost all of the "liberal ideals," certain aspects of liberal theology continued to play a larger role in his thought than in Barth's theology. Some have claimed that, while Niebuhr's theology is somewhat comparable to Barth's Neo-Orthodoxy, it is

actually a new liberal theology formulated on a more
realistic basis, and thus should be designated as
"Christian Realism."[73] However, both Barth and Niebuhr
regarded the basic features of both Liberalism and Fundamentalism as inadequate, and there was a greater
degree of similarity between their theologies than
between that of either one and the theology of Liberalism or of Fundamentalism. There is some justification,
then, for classifying both as representatives of Neo-
Orthodoxy. In the following sketch, some of the differences between Barth and Niebuhr will be noted, but
attention will be centered primarily on the basic features of Neo-Orthodoxy which stand in contrast with
Liberalism and Fundamentalism.

1. Similar to the Protestant Reformers, the Neo-
Orthodox theologians insisted that it was only in light
of the knowledge of God that man genuinely understands
himself. Thus Niebuhr said that for man "to understand
himself truly means to begin with a faith that he is
understood from beyond himself, that he is known and
loved of God and must find himself in obedience to the
divine will."[74] That is, the proper place for the
beginning of true wisdom concerning the self is in the
knowledge of God, for only in this knowledge is there
the answer to the problem and mystery of human existence.

Just as had the Reformers so also the Neo-Orthodox
theologians placed emphasis on revelation as the source
of our knowledge of God. Unlike the liberals who had
located the knowledge of God in a natural human capacity
such as God-consciousness or moral valuation, Neo-
Orthodoxy insisted that knowledge of God comes from
beyond man in God's revelation. Barth was quite clear
about this when he said:

> What man can know by his own power accord-
> ing to the measure of his natural powers,
> his understanding, his feeling, will be
> at most something like a supreme being.
> . . . Man is able to think this being; but
> he has not thereby thought God. God is
> thought and known when in His own freedom
> God makes himself apprehensible. . . .
> God is always the One who has made Himself
> known to man in His own revelation, and
> not the one man thinks out for himself
> and describes as God.[75]

Given this view, it is not surprising that Barth rejected the notion that man has a general natural knowledge of God, that there is a "point of contact" which enables him to accept special revelation. It was his belief that revelation comes entirely as a gift of God with God himself creating the receptivity for hearing his Word. While Niebuhr was equally insistent that the full knowledge of God must be God's gift, he had a larger place in his thought for general revelation in the created order, for the general experience of being confronted from beyond ourselves. Thus he claimed that there is a "point of contact" in the natural man which enables him to receive the full or special revelation of God.[76] Yet, while man has the capacity to receive it, he cannot initiate the revelation. The initiative must be that of the revealor. In any experience, if that which is experienced is more than a mere object and instead is a subject, then his character cannot be known by us unless he takes the initiative. In such cases, Niebuhr claimed, "the principle of interpretation must be something more than merely the general principles of knowledge which illumine a particular experience. The principle of interpretation must be a 'revelation.'"[77] For example, we cannot know the "thou" of another person until that person takes the initiative and speaks to us. Thus Niebuhr said, "In the same way, the God whom we meet as 'the other' at the final limit of our own consciousness, is not fully known to us except as specific revelations of His character augment this general experience of being confronted from beyond ourselves."[78] For both Barth and Niebuhr the revelation of God occurs in actual historical events, in the historical experiences of Israel, and supremely in that historical event at the center of which was Jesus Christ, the Word of God. Without such a revelation it is neither possible to have an adequate knowledge of God nor to arrive at an understanding of the meaning of life and history.[79]

2. As we have seen, fundamentalists equate the revelation of God with the Bible, and thus regard the Bible as "a tangible sacred reality." On the other hand, liberals view the Bible as containing the progressive human discovery of God's progressive revelation. The ultimate norm for liberals is the Christian experience of God-consciousness or moral valuation as demonstrated in the historical Jesus. Whatever Biblical content reinforces this experience is to be taken seriously. In contrast to both fundamentalists and liberals, the Neo-Orthodox view of the Bible is much more

424

akin to that of the Reformers. The Bible witnesses to the Word of God and as such is the authority for the church. Thus, according to Barth:

> Holy Scripture is the document of the basis of the innermost life of the Church, the document of the manifestation of the Word of God in the person of Jesus Christ. We have no other document for this living basis of the Church; and where the Church is alive, it will always be having to re-assess itself by this standard.[80]

However, in Barth's view, only the Word of God (God's self-disclosure in Jesus Christ) is absolute. Since it was written by fallible human beings, the Bible as a book is as relative and problematical as anything else produced by human beings. Its authority is not of the legal kind, and it is not a "paper pope."[81] The verbal inspiration view is not only false to the intention of the Biblical writers but also obscures the doctrine of revelation. The Word of God cannot be embalmed between the covers of a book.[82] To insist on the infallibility of the Bible is to resist the "miracle" of revelation, namely, "that here fallible men speak the Word of God in fallible human words." It is to "resist the sovereignty of grace in which God Himself became man in Christ, to glorify Himself in His humanity."[83]

For Niebuhr also the doctrine of Biblical inerrancy and infallibility obscures the doctrine of revelation. The Bible is not itself the revelation of God but a witness to this revelation. Since revelation occurred in historical events, the use of the historical, critical method of Biblical study is an aid in obtaining a clearer understanding of what they were as objective events. While in Barth's view the use of this method is not an impious activity and makes a limited contribution to greater knowledge of the Bible, it does not provide much assistance with respect to "hearing the Word of God" or to greater theological understanding. On this point Niebuhr's view differs from that of Barth. According to Niebuhr, there should be a continual interchange between historical study and theological construction so that the former might enrich the latter. To be sure, only faith can decide concerning the significance of the revelatory event in Jesus Christ, but historical criticism can render a service to faith in making vivid the concreteness, wholeness, and historical character of the revelatory event. The application of

the scientific, historical method to the study of the
Bible is a contribution of Liberalism which should not
be sacrificed. With respect to theology, the primary
contribution of this method, according to Niebuhr,
is that it has "emancipated Christianity from the
necessity of regarding any moral attitude, fortuitously
enshrined in its own canon, as final and authoritative.
It permitted the Christian law of love to stand out
in Christian ethics as the only final norm."[84]

Since neither Barth nor Niebuhr accepted the Bible
as inerrant or infallible, they did not accept the
Genesis accounts of creation as literally or factually
true. In this sense they were not "creationists." For
them, the Genesis account was a "myth" (Niebuhr) or a
"saga" (Barth) which preserved the truth of God's freedom and transcendence, the inherent goodness of the
created order, and the graciousness of the divine nature. Its central meaning was that God does not exist
simply in and for himself but in relation to a reality
distinct from himself. Its great truth was _that_ God
created, not _how_ he created. Both accepted biological
evolution as a fact,[85] but on the basis of their view
of human sin, they rejected the liberals' view of a
natural and inevitable evolutionary development or
progress in the spiritual and moral arena of human
history.

3. As we have seen, liberals tend to view sin as
a kind of fossilized remainder of man's animal beginnings, a lingering residue of fleshly impulses at war
with the spirit. Fundamentalists, on the other hand,
hold that the Genesis account of Adam's fall is literally true, and that all human beings inherit Adam's
sin and guilt so that man by nature is a sinner. Neo-
Orthodox theologians reject both the evolutionist or
semi-Pelagian view of the liberals and the literalistic
or ontological view of the fundamentalists. They view
sin as a universal human state or condition of being
which is characterized by pride, rebellion, and estrangement, but it is neither an inherited tendency
nor an ontological fate.[86] It is in his freedom that
man absurdly seeks to establish his own essence by
denying both God and himself, and thus sins at the very
center of his being. Furthermore, with the Protestant
Reformers, Neo-Orthodox theologians maintain that only
in light of the answer to his problem does man have the
courage to see himself as he is, a sinner in estrangement from God, others, and himself. In Church Dogmatics
Barth explicitly states that he develops a doctrine of

426

sin in light of the doctrine of grace. It is by means
of the Word of God disclosed in Jesus Christ and his
suffering at the hands of men that both the grace of
God and man's sin or constant rebellion against God
become fully known.[87] Niebuhr makes a similar claim
when he says, "the content of revelation is an act
of reconciliation in which the judgment of God upon
the pride of man is not abrogated, in which the sin
of man becomes more sharply revealed and defined by
the knowledge that God is Himself the victim of man's
sin and pride. Nevertheless the final word is not one
of judgment but of mercy and forgiveness."[88]

Since Niebuhr was concerned always with integrating
the insights of Christian revelation with an analysis
of the human situation, he sought to show that the
Christian understanding of man was supported by a realistic appraisal of the human condition. Man, Niebuhr
claimed, is that creature who exists at the juncture
of nature and spirit. Like other natural creatures,
he is subject to the laws and limitations of nature,
but unlike them, he can transcend all of this through
his consciousness. As spirit, he can transcend both
his world and himself. Thus he is suspended between
finitude and freedom, and this gives rise to a deep
seated anxiety which, although not itself sin, is the
precondition of sin. That is, man seeks to escape the
discomfort of anxiety by abolishing either one or the
other of the dual aspects of his nature. He seeks to
become either a god or a beast. If he seeks to abolish
his freedom, his self-transcendence, he falls into
sensuality. If he seeks to abolish his finitude, to
evade nature, he falls into pride. Niebuhr placed
greater emphasis on pride because he viewed it as more
basic than sensuality and because in part the latter
is derived from the former. He viewed sin as being
much more a matter of the will than of the flesh, and
claimed that its most insidious form is pride. While
pride has many faces, it manifests itself primarily
in pride of power, the pride of knowledge, and the
pride of virtue. It is at the higher and more established levels of human life, Niebuhr insisted, that
the sin of pride is the most dangerous, precisely because it is a mixture of self-sufficiency and insecur-
ity. Thus he said:

> The more man establishes himself in
> power and glory, the greater is the fear
> of tumbling from his eminence, or losing
> his treasure, or being discovered in his

> pretension. . . . Thus man seeks to make
> himself God because he is betrayed by both
> his greatness and his weakness; and there
> is no level of greatness and power in which
> the lash of fear is not at least one strand
> in the whip of ambition.[89]

The sin of pride finds its most horrible manifestations
in the "collective egotism" of groups such as nations
and churches,[90] for in groups such as these the pride
of power is strongly reinforced by the pride of virtue.
Both individuals and groups too easily ignore the mixture of good and evil in themselves, and imagine themselves to be sinless saints. Throughout history fierce
idealists all too often have "derived a cruel fanati-
cism from their fierce idealism."[91]

Both Barth and Niebuhr viewed sin as a universal
fact in human life. While sin does not follow from
the natural condition of human life as such, no human
life is completely free of it. Thus while Niebuhr
denied that sin was an ontological necessity, a defect
of essential human nature, he spoke of it as an inevitable self-contradition made possible by the fact of human
freedom.[92] It was in this sense that Barth and Niebuhr
used the term "original sin." Niebuhr explicitly defined it this way when he said, "the universal inclination of the self to be more concerned with itself than
to be embarrassed by its undue claims may be defined
as 'original sin.'"[93] For him, the doctrine of original
sin was not to be understood as a theological abstrac-
tion, but as a poetic myth which refers to the life we
actually live and which can be verified in our experience of our actual condition. While it was not to be
taken literally, it was to be taken seriously.[94]

4. Given their view of the depth and universality
of sin in human life, it follows that Barth and Niebuhr,
very much like the Reformers, insisted that reconciliation with God was God's gift through Jesus Christ.
Since, for them, both the full knowledge of God and
reconciliation with him come by means of Christ, it is
not surprising that Christology was the central and
fundamental basis for their theologies.[95] Like the
Reformers, they tended to emphasize the "benefits" or
saving work of Christ in their Christologies, but since
atonement presupposes incarnation, they also said a
great deal about the person of Christ. Unlike the
liberals who centered their attention primarily on
the "Jesus of history" rather than the "Christ of

faith," and the fundamentalists who emphasized the deity of Christ to the virtual exclusion of his humanity, Barth and Niebuhr spoke of Christ as the God-man. They differed, however, in their views concerning the precise meaning of this term. Barth understood it in terms of the traditional definitions of Nicea and Chalcedon, while Niebuhr interpreted it symbolically and functionally.

According to Barth, the Nicene and Chalcedonian creeds formulated the meaning of the New Testament assertions concerning Jesus Christ. He was of _like_ nature with the Father and not just of _similar_ nature. As Barth said:

> Jesus Christ is indeed man, true man, but He is not just a man, nor just an extra-ordinarily gifted or specially guided man, let alone a super-man; but, while being a man, He is God Himself. God is one with Him. His existence begins with God's special action; as a man He is founded in God, He is true God. . . . Jesus Christ is not 'only' true God, that would not be real incarnation--but neither is He an intermediate being; He is a man like us all, a man without reservation. He not only resembles us men; He is the same as us. As God is the Subject in the life of Jesus Christ, so man is the object to be acted upon, but of a man who is in action. Man does not turn into a marionette in this meeting with God, but if there is genuine humanity, here it is where God Himself makes Himself a man.[96]

In Niebuhr's view the metaphysical or speculative Christological definitions of Nicea and Chalcedon were both contradictory and deadeningly abstract. Thus he claimed:

> All definitions of Christ which affirm both his divinity and humanity in the sense that they ascribe both finite and historically conditioned and eternal and unconditioned qualities to his nature must verge on logical nonsense. It is possible for a character, event or fact of history to point symbolically beyond history and to become a source of

429

disclosure of an eternal meaning, purpose and power which bears history.
But it is not possible for any person
to be historical and unconditioned at
the same time. But the logical nonsense
is not as serious a defect as the fact
that the statement tends to reduce Christian faith to metaphysical truths which
need not be apprehended inwardly by
faith.[97]

That which faith inwardly apprehends is that "God was
in Christ reconciling the world unto Himself" (II Corinthians 5:19). The truth of this Christology, Niebuhr claimed, becomes meaningful with reference to the
Cross. The Cross is the central symbol of Christianity
precisely because it symbolizes the perfection of love
(agape). Such love can be symbolized only by one who
consistently refused to engage in the power rivalries
of one ego interest against another. Thus Niebuhr said,
"the final majesty, the ultimate freedom, and the perfect disinterestedness of the divine love can have a
counterpart in history only in a life which ends tragically, because it refuses to participate in the claims
and counterclaims of historical existence."[98] While
the Cross transcends history, it is relevant to history,
because "it is the final norm of a human nature which
has no final norm in history because it is not completely contained in history."[99]

The fact that Niebuhr presented a mythical or
symbolic analysis of Christological doctrine did not
mean, anymore than with the analysis of "original sin,"
that he found no truth in this doctrine or failed to
take it seriously. In order to understand Niebuhr's
position on this point, it is necessary to consider
briefly his threefold classification of myth or symbol.
First, there are pre-scientific myths which "disregard
what may have always been known, or have now become
known about the ordered course of events in the world."
Secondly, there are the symbols of modern science
which "are verifiable by strict measurement and observation." Thirdly, there are "permanent myths or symbols"
which describe some meaning or reality, which is not
subject to exact analysis but can nevertheless be
verified in experience."[100] Niebuhr provided an example of what he meant by this claim when he said:

That 'God was in Christ reconciling the
World unto Himself' is verifiable in the

430

experience of everyone who experiences the mercy and new life which flows from true repentance in the encounter with God. It is also verifiable by the proofs that alternative methods of explaining or dissolving the mystery and the meaning which governs and surrounds us lead to observable miscalculations in regard to the nature of man and of history. Thus there is a significant distinction between the 'myths' with which a pre-scientific world describes natural phenomena and the symbol which is central to the structure of Christian faith, namely, the assertion that a Jesus of Nazareth was the 'Son of the living God.'[101]

5. We have seen that the liberals understood salvation primarily as a matter of patterning individual and social life after the model presented in the life and teachings of Jesus, and that the fundamentalists understood it in terms of the juridical substitutionary-satisfaction doctrine. Neo-Orthodox theologians re-emphasized the Reformers' doctrine of justification by faith.[102] That is, on the basis of our trust in God's grace disclosed in Jesus Christ, God accepts us in spite of the fact that we are unacceptable.

In speaking of God's gracious forgiveness revealed in Jesus Christ, the Neo-Orthodox theologians did affirm that in Christ God takes the sinfulness of man into himself. Barth claimed that God's "free affirmation of man, His free concern for him, His free substitution for him"[103] is found in Christ. However, the use of this language did not mean that the Neo-Orthodox theologians accepted the fundamentalists' penal, juridical view of the Atonement which claims that Christ by his sacrifice satisfied the divine justice operative in the old dispensation of law, and thus enabled God to inaugurate a new dispensation of grace in which he is now merciful to sinful man. Instead they insisted that God's sovereignty is a sovereignty of love (agape), that God's nature always has been that of love. In Barth's words, "God is God by virtue of the fact that in His eternal Son, and therefore from all eternity, He was, is and will be the God of men, who loved, loves and will love men."[104] That God's eternal nature is to love was nowhere expressed with greater clarity and sensitivity by Barth than in several sermons he preached to the inmates of the Basel prison. The following

quotations from two of those sermons illustrate this
theme:

> For unlike sin [the wages of sin is death],
> God is no paymaster or employer or cashier
> ready to settle accounts. God does not
> settle accounts. God is a very distinguished
> gentleman whose privilege and enjoyment it
> is to give freely and to be merciful. . . .

> God has mercy on us. He says 'yes' to us,
> he wills to be on our side, to be our God
> against all odds. . . .

> This he proved in Jesus Christ not only by
> words, but by the mightiest of his deeds.
> He gave himself for us in his dear Son
> and became man, our brother. This is the
> mighty deed and through it the word of
> God's mercy on all has been spoken.[105]

Both Barth and Niebuhr viewed the relation between
God's love and justice in a dialectical manner. For
them God's justice both arises out of and is in the
service of his love. The "no" of God is the form which
the divine love assumes against that which contradicts
love. Thus the "no" of God's judgment is simply the
other side of God's eternal "yes."[106] It is precisely
because of his love that God not only stands in judgment against sin but also voluntarily takes the consequences of his judgment upon and into Himself. Niebuhr
explicitly claimed that "commercial and juridical
theories of God's justice" tended to obscure "the
mystery of the Atonement,"[107] the fact that the suffering of Christ discloses God's suffering because of
man's sin and rebellion. This revelation, so to speak,
is the divine "shock treatment" which awakens us from
our indifference and callousness, makes us aware of
the seriousness of sin, and brings us to that despair
about ourselves which makes possible the contrition
necessary for our acceptance of divine forgiveness and
mercy. As Niebuhr said, "It is in this contrition and
in this appropriation of divine mercy and forgiveness
that the human situation is fully understood and overcome."[108]

With the Reformers, Barth and Niebuhr affirmed
that one is not justified by works but by grace through
faith. Faith which is trust, reliance on the faithfulness of God, is itself a gift of God. Barth insisted

that men do not have a disposition for faith and thus lack the capacity for receiving it. It is "not prepared for by anything on our side," but is God's free gift, "making possible what is impossible on our side."[109] As we have seen, Barth rejected the notion of a "point of contact" in sinful man which enables him to accept the Word of God. Faith is entirely God's gift. In this context, Barth developed a doctrine of double predestination, but one which was quite unlike that of John Calvin (see Chapter VIII). Barth claimed that in Jesus Christ, God had <u>elected</u> himself for rejection and suffering, but also had <u>predestined</u> <u>sinful</u> <u>man</u> for election and eternal life. The person of faith gratefully acknowledges his election as a gift of God's grace and neither arrogantly glories in his election nor regards others as damned. Indeed, Barth regarded the final deliverance of all men as a real possibility.[110]

While Niebuhr was convinced that, given the fact of sin, man cannot will himself into faith, that faith is a gift of grace, he claimed that Barth was wrong both in his denial of a "point of contact" and in his doctrine of predestination. With respect to the former, Niebuhr insisted that in spite of his sinfulness there remains always in man a "residual element of <u>justitia</u> <u>originalis</u> in his being,"[111] namely, his essential structure of freedom and self-transcendence. Thus even one without faith cannot escape an "uneasy conscience" concerning his "sinful egotism," and "this is the 'point of contact' between grace and the natural endowments of the soul. . . . As long as there is such a point of contact there is something in man to which appeal can be made."[112] While man cannot create his faith, in his freedom he can stubbornly reject or gratefully accept God's gift of grace, and the acceptance of the gift is grounded in repentance. Precisely for this reason Niebuhr rejected the doctrine of predestination, claiming that "a doctrine of divine determinism would seem to imperil every sense of human responsibility."[113]

With the Reformers, Barth and Niebuhr were convinced that while the experience of justification by faith brought a change in the lives of persons, it did not make them into sinless saints. Indeed, the experience of the undeserved grace of God produces genuine humility and saves "the Christian life from the intolerable pretension of saints who have forgotten that they are sinners."[114] The Christian is aware that even his best works stand under the judgment of God, and that he is justified not by works but by faith. Such faith can save one both from self-righteousness and from despair. Niebuhr expressed this eloquently when he said:

> Nothing that is worth doing can be achieved in our lifetime; therefore we must be saved by hope. Nothing which is true or beautiful or good makes complete sense in any immediate context of history; therefore we must be saved by faith. Nothing we do, however virtuous, can be accomplished alone; therefore we are saved by love. No virtuous act is quite as virtuous from the standpoint of our friend or foe as it is from our standpoint. Therefore we must be saved by the final form of love which is forgiveness.[115]

6. Given their view of salvation as justification by faith, it is not surprising that Barth and Niebuhr held to a doctrine of the church similar to that of the Reformers. They viewed the church as a fellowship of those who have been gathered by Christ, a community of contrite and hopeful believers who both listen and witness to God's word of judgment and mercy. Barth expressed this view when he said:

> The essence of the Church is the event in which men are placed together before the fact of the reconciliation of the world, which has taken place in Jesus Christ and thus under the condemning grace and the gracious judgment of God, that thereby they may be summoned to give thanks together and to love their neighbor to His praise. In that this peculiar togetherness takes place in the midst of the general history of the world, with its combinations and contradictions, the congregation of Jesus Christ comes into being and endures, the church exists.[116]

Even though Barth and Niebuhr viewed the church as the living community of believers in Christ, they did not think of it as an end in itself, as the church victorious or the Kingdom of God. Indeed, the most serious temptation encountered by those within the fellowship of believers is the temptation to think of themselves as "sinless saints" instead of "forgiven sinners." According to Niebuhr the church is always "in danger of becoming a community of the righteous who ask God to vindicate them against the unrighteous; or, even worse, who claim to vindicate God by the fruits of their own righteousness. In that case the church loses the true love of Christ, which is the fruit of a contrite heart."[117] The true community of Christ is sent into the world and exists for the world. It "is not the Kingdom of God. The church is the place in human society where the Kingdom of God impinges upon all human enterprises through the divine word, and where the grace of God is made available to those who have accepted his judgment."[118]

Given this view of the church as the community of forgiven sinners called together by the living Christ to hear and to witness to God's word of judgment and mercy, it is not surprising that Barth and Niebuhr emphasized the unity of the church and gave active support to the ecumenical movement. Barth expressed an ecumenical outlook rather well when he said:

> Christians are simply summoned to believe in God as the common origin, the common goal of the Church to which they are called. We are not placed upon a tower, from which we can survey all varieties of Churches; we simply stand on the earth at a definite place and <u>there</u> is the Church, the one Church. We believe in the unity of the Church, in the unity of the congregations, if we believe in the existence of our concrete Church. If we believe in the Holy Spirit in <u>this</u> Church, then even in the worst case we are not absolutely separated from the other congregations. The truly ecumenical Christians are not those who trivialise the differences and flutter over them; they are those who in their respective Churches are quite concretely the Church. 'Where two or three are gathered together in my name, there am I in their midst'--that is the Church. In Him, despite all varieties in the individual congregations, we shall somehow be bound up with one another.[119]

Since in their view the church is sent into the world to serve the world, Barth and Niebuhr insisted

that it must give attention to the social problems which
plague mankind. If it fails to do this, it is not witnessing to the full gospel. While they were critical
of the "naive idealism" and "utopianism" of Liberalism,
they were just as active as the liberals in working for
the elimination of social evils and just as emphatic in
proclaiming that neither the individual Christian nor
the church can be neutral concerning the evils which
infect society. Barth expressed this rather vividly
when he said that the ministry and the church "became
dumb dogs and their service a serving of the ruling
powers, if they are afraid to tackle at their social
roots the evils by which they are confronted in detail."[120] Thus he insisted that if the church is to
genuinely witness to God's love as disclosed in Jesus
Christ, it must be as concerned with social issues as
with the salvation of individuals.

Concerning the question of the precise nature of
Christian ethics, there was some disagreement between
Barth and Niebuhr. Both held that the one absolute is
the love (agape) of God as revealed in Jesus Christ.
But Barth, since he denied any "point of contact" between grace and the natural endowments of man, insisted
that Christian ethics should be neither correlated with
any kind of philosophical ethics nor consist in the
development of principles, rules, and programs. Instead, in his view Christian ethics is entirely a matter of making clear the meaning of the revealed word of
God for the concrete situations in human life. Since
the word or grace of God is revealed in those events
of history such as the Covenant and the life of Jesus
Christ, concerning which the Bible gives testimony,
the Ten Commandments and the Sermon on the Mount do
have a role to play in Christian ethics. Yet Barth
insisted that the Bible is not some sort of lawbook
for Christian ethics. Rather its central message is
the grace of God, supremely disclosed in Jesus Christ.
Thus Barth declared that the meaning of "evil" in
the Christian sense is that any deed is evil "in which
man, openly or in secret, because of anxiety or pride,
is unthankful." Conversely, in the Christian sense
of "good," any deed is good "in which man is thankful
for God's grace."[122] Faithful discipleship, for Barth,
means that the Christian will become informed concerning the various personal, social, economic, and political situations in the world, and given the realities
of those situations, seek to act in such ways as to
support the realization of the closest possible approxi-
mations of love (agape) in those situations. Thus

Barth's Christian ethics is sometimes called "situationalism."

In Niebuhr's view, Barth had correctly emphasized the ultimate peak of the Christian faith, the grace of God disclosed in Christ, but he was wrong in ignoring the foothills where people have to make practical and concrete moral decisions. Since Niebuhr held that there was a "point of contact" between grace and man's natural endowments, he argued that it was important to recognize the validity of the essentially universal principles of justice which men have rationally conceived and in light of which they have formulated specific rules and systems of justice. Thus he claimed that "Karl Barth's belief that the moral life of man would possess no valid principles of guidance, if the Ten Commandments had not introduced such principles by revelation, is as absurd as it is unscriptural."[123] It was not that Niebuhr thought that the principles of justice are ultimate or absolute, for he was convinced that only God's _agape_ (love) as revealed in Christ is the absolute and transcendent norm for Christian ethics. But in a world in which the prideful self-interest of individuals and groups prevails, he felt it was not possible to fully actualize this norm, and thus justice was required as an instrument of _agape_.[124] The principles of justice could provide guidance for the Christian in his effort to make concrete moral decisions in the actual situations of life. This does not mean that Niebuhr regarded _agape_ as relevant only for the salvation of the individual and thus as irrelevant with respect to man's personal and social relationships. He insisted that _agape_ is relevant to man's actual historical and communal existence in two ways. First, it is relevant in that it stands in judgment on both our moral pretensions and our achievements, personal and social. Secondly, it is relevant in that it is the motive for seeking for the greatest degree of justice possible in any given situation and thus for the closest possible approximation of _agape_ under the conditions of sin. Since Niebuhr's view of Christian ethics included _agape_, the actual and concrete situations of man's personal and communal existence, and the middle or proximate principles of justice, it is sometimes called "contextualism."[125]

In spite of their differences concerning the nature of Christian ethics, Barth and Niebuhr affirmed that both the individual Christian and the church should be aware always of their responsibility to work

for the realization of the closest possible approximation to _agape_ in human society. It was not that, like
the liberals, they thought the church could **build** the
kingdom of God on earth. Given the sin of man, the
kingdom remains always beyond the church and history,
and yet it is always relevant to the church and history
as both norm and goal. Aware that it stands under the
judgment of this norm and motivated by the love of God,
the church with humility will seek to undertake those
actions which will contribute to producing the closest
possible approximation to the kingdom of God in actual
human society.

    7. Unlike the liberals who tended to minimize
eschatology and the fundamentalists who tended to
emphasize a literalistic and apocalyptic eschatology,
the central theme of Neo-Orthodox eschatology emphasized the ultimate triumph of God's grace and purposes
beyond nature-history in an ultimate fellowship in
which there is perfect freedom and faithfulness. Niebuhr claimed that such Biblical symbols as the second
coming of Christ, the last judgment, and the resurrection cannot be taken literally, but neither can they
be dismissed as unimportant. The symbol of the second
coming of Christ expresses "faith in the final supremacy of love over all forms of self-love."[126] The
last judgment symbolizes "the moral ambiguity of
history to the end."[127] And the doctrine of resurrection expresses the faith that "the ultimate consummation is not an absorption into the divine but [a] loving fellowship with God,"[128] a fellowship which ultimately will become all inclusive.[129]

    As we have seen, Barth insisted that the Chris-
tian's faith is a free gift of God. Similarly, he
insisted that eternal life is a free gift of God
through Christ. In an Easter sermon to the inmates
of the Basel prison, Barth expressed this eloquently
in a passage which provides a fitting conclusion
for our discussion of Neo-Orthodox eschatology.

        With Christ's resurrection from the
dead, God's free gift, eternal life,
entered the world. He, the dear son, he,
the faithful and obedient servant, he who
was willing to make our sin his own and
to die our death in replacement of us,
he, Jesus Christ, was raised from the dead
and recalled from the tomb by the Father.
He was robed in eternal life. But now

438

remember also, dear brothers and sisters,
that God so acted in Jesus Christ in
order that we, truly all of us, without
exception, may share in this free gift of
life eternal. . . . Eternal life is a
strong and no longer weak life; joyous and
no longer sad; true and no longer deceit-
ful. Eternal life is man's indestructible
life because it comes from God and is
sustained by him. It is life everlasting,
extending beyond any natural end which now
can no longer be death.[130]

In the discussion of Protestantism in the modern
world in this chapter we have sought to sketch briefly
the basic features in the three major types of theology,
namely, Liberalism, Fundamentalism, and Neo-Orthodoxy.
Except in those cases where the beliefs of popular
Fundamentalism were described, the discussions of these
positions were based on the thought of scholarly theologians. Due in part to the lack of unity, the variety
of denominations, and the rampant pluralism in Protestantism, these positions, with the exception of popular
Fundamentalism, have not gained an identifiable and
committed following among large numbers of Protestant
laity. Whatever influence Liberalism and Neo-Orthodoxy
have had on Protestant laity has been largely very indirect, diffused, and unrecognized as such. Unlike
the situation in modern Judaism and Catholicism where
the "moderate" position (Conservative Judaism and the
Catholicism of Vatican Council II) has gained a large
identifiable following, Protestant laity, generally
uninformed with respect to the options in modern
Protestant theology, have not identified consciously
with Neo-Orthodoxy in any large numbers. During the
time of Neo-Orthodoxy's greatest popularity (ca. 1920-
1960), especially among seminary students, professors,
and clergymen, most laymen gained little knowledge of
this theology. Even though it dominated the theological perspectives proclaimed at the establishment of
the World Council of Churches in 1948,[131] the average
layman had little knowledge concerning this meeting
and even less of the theology proclaimed. Thus there
has been nothing in Protestantism analogous to Vatican
Council II, the documents of which were widely dissem-
inated among Catholics and others.

In recent years there has arisen a new generation
of "professional" Protestant theologians, many of
whom have abandoned not only Neo-Orthodox theology but

also the other great theologies of the past. According to Lonnie D. Kliever:

> For these new theologies, there are no established traditions or acknowledged masters to whom homage, whether conservative or liberal, is due. . . . The revered traditions and towering giants of the theological past have been supplanted by a bewildering variety of theological programs and pundits. Theologies of secularity, process, liberation, hope, play, and story have emerged like the overlapping bursts of a fireworks display.[132]

There are, of course, some Protestant theologians who still defend some version of Neo-Orthodoxy, claiming that most if not all of the new theologies are simply fads which like all fads will soon vanish. Whether this is true or not (and only the future will tell), it is the case that current Protestant theology, especially in the United States, is characterized by a rampant pluralism. Unlike the situation twenty-five years ago, Neo-Orthodox theology is no longer the dominant theology taught in most leading Protestant theological seminaries. It is overshadowed by a plethora of new theologies. Thus it is rather unlikely that 'Neo-Orthodoxy will gain a sizeable, identifiable following among Protestant clergy and laity similar to the sizeable following of Conservative Judaism among Jewish rabbis and laity, or the sizeable following of Vatican II Catholicism among Catholic clergy and laity.

In terms of a definite and strongly held belief system, fundamentalists undoubtedly constitute the most easily identifiable group among Protestant clergy and laity. Due in large part to its very definite and authoritarian belief system and to its continuing emphasis on evangelism (revivalism), in recent years Fundamentalism has grown more numerically in the United States than any other Protestant group. A relatively large portion of this growth has been among teenagers, many of whom seek personal security through unquestioning commitment to some tangible authority.[133] In spite of this growth of Fundamentalism, nevertheless it seems to be the case that the average member of any one of the major Protestant denominations (Baptist, Methodist, Presbyterian, Episcopal, etc.) feels uncomfortable with the militancy of Fundamentalism on the

440

one hand and the extreme positions of Liberalism on the other. Inundated with the practical concerns of life and the pressures of a secular society, the average lay person tends to be impatient with theological disputes and rather moderate or conservative in religious perspectives and practices. Were he or she informed concerning the options in modern Protestant theology, probably it would be the case that Neo-Orthodoxy would be viewed as coming closer than Liberalism, Fundamentalism, or recent theologies to preserving the essential nature of the Christian faith while rendering it intelligible in the modern world, and thus would be preferred to the other options.

NOTES

[1] See Christianity and Liberalism (William B. Eerdmans, 1923); discussed in C. Allyn Russell, Voices of American Fundamentalism (The Westminster Press, 1976), pp. 144-146; also see W. A. Criswell, Look up, Brother (The Broadman Press, 1970), pp. 7, 98, 103.

[2] Religion and The Modern Mind (J. B. Lippincott Company, 1952), p. 212.

[3] These works are contained in The Philosophy of Kant, Carl J. Friedrich (ed.), (The Modern Library, 1949).

[4] Immanuel Kant's Critique of Pure Reason, unabridged edition, Norman Kemp Smith, translator (St. Martin's Press, 1921), p. 41; italics are mine.

[5] Ibid.

[6] Ibid., pp. 41-42; italics are mine.

[7] Ibid., p. 396.

[8] Ibid., p. 113.

[9] Ibid., p. 93.

[10] See The Critique of Practical Reason, L. W. Beck, translator (Bobbs-Merrill Company, Inc., 1956), especially Book II, Chapter II.

[11] See Religion Within the Limits of Reason Alone, T. M. Greene and H. H. Hudson, translators (Harper and Brothers, 1960).

[12] Ibid., p. 123; cited by Justo L. Gonzalez, A History of Christian Thought, V. III (Abingdon Press, 1975), p. 313.

[13] See On Religion: Speeches to Its Cultures Despisers, J. Oman, translator (Harper and Brothers, 1958).

[14] The Christian Faith, Vol. I, edited by H. R. Mackintosh and J. S. Stewart (Harper Torchbooks, 1963), p. 12; italics are mine.

[15] Ibid., p. 26; italics are mine.

[16] Ibid., p. 27.

[17] Ibid., p. 76.

[18] See The Christian Faith, Vols. I and II (Harper Torch-books, 1963).

[19] The Christian Doctrine of Justification and Reconciliation, edited by H. R. Mackintosh and A. B. Macaulay (Reference Book Publishers, Inc., 1966), p. 212.

[20] See What is Christianity, second edition, Thomas Bailey Saunders, translator (G. P. Putnam's Sons, 1902), pp. 21-80.

[21] The Impact of American Religious Liberalism (Harper and Row, 1962), p. 102. In the Notes for Chapters 3, 4, and 5 on Brown, Fosdick and Rauschenbusch, Cauthen provides bibliographic references to the major writings of these three.

[22] See The Modern Use of the Bible (The Macmillan Company, 1925), pp. 97-130.

[23] God at Work (Charles Scribner's Sons, 1933), p. 189.

[24] A Guide to the Understanding of the Bible (Harper and Brothers, 1938), pp. XIV-XV.

[25] A Theology For the Social Gospel (The Macmillan Company, 1918), pp. 150-151, 154-155.

[26] Christian Theology in Outline (Charles Scribner's Sons, 1906), p. 312.

[27] Ibid., p. 314.

[28] Ibid., pp. 315-316.

[29] Rauschenbusch, A Theology For the Social Gospel, pp. 139-140.

[30] The Modern Use of the Bible, p. 98.

[31] See James Barr, Fundamentalism (The Westminster Press, 1978), pp. 1-39, 160-165. Barr's book is both a descriptive and critical study of Fundamentalism. The reader should consult the helpful bibliography on pages 363-367. Another recent study of Fundamentalism is C. Allyn Russell, Voices of American Fundamentalism (The Westminster Press, 1976).

[32] See *Christianity and Liberalism*, op. cit., pp. 2-12.

[33] *The Virgin Birth of Christ* (Harper and Brothers, 1930), pp. 218-219.

[34] *Voices of American Fundamentalism*, op. cit., p. 17.

[35] *Ibid.*, p. 18.

[36] Barr, op. cit., p. 1.

[37] See George C. Bedell, Leo Sandon, Jr., and Charles T. Wellborn, *Religion in America* (Macmillan Publishing Co., Inc., 1975), pp. 232-233.

[38] (Fleming H. Revell Company, 1923), pp. 7-13.

[39] Russell, op. cit.; see the Chapter titles.

[40] *The New Bible Commentary: Revised*, Third Edition (William B. Eerdmans Publishing Co., 1970), p. 17.

[41] See *Fundamentalism and the Word of God* (William B. Eerdmans Publishing Co., 1958), especially pp. 7, 47, 74, 94-101.

[42] Even though throughout *An Introduction to Christian Apologetics* Carnell generally uses the term Conservative Christian, in the "Preface to the First Edition" he spoke of "our defense of Fundamentalism." In a later book, *The Case For Orthodox Theology* (Westminster, 1959), he claimed that at the turn of the twentieth century Fundamentalism was a *movement* which preserved the faith. With the collapse of modernism, however, it shifted from being a movement to being a *mentality*. As a mentality, "Fundamentalism is orthodoxy gone cultic," and is "orthodoxy's gravest peril" (see pages 113-124). This does not mean that Carnell had converted to liberal or Neo-Orthodox theology, but that he had rejected the militancy, bigotry, obscurantism, narrowness and occultism expressed among some fundamentalists. He still argued for the basic fundamentalist doctrine.

[43] *An Introduction to Christian Apologetics* (William B. Eerdmans Publishing Co., 1948), pp. 192-193; italics are mine.

[44] Barr, op. cit., p. 36; italics are mine. See also pages 40-89, 279-302.

[45] Bryan, op. cit., p. 23; see also C. Allyn Russell, op. cit., pp. 183-185.

444

[46] See Barr, op. cit., p. 92.

[47] Carnell, op. cit., pp. 239-240.

[48] See Carnell, ibid., p. 165.

[49] Ibid., p. 116; italics are mine.

[50] Ibid., p. 294.

[51] Barr, op. cit., p. 177.

[52] Bryan, op. cit., pp. 16-21.

[53] Barr claims, op. cit., p. 15, that the ordinary fundamentalist is characterized both by his concentration on doctrinal conformity and by his non-historical understanding of Christianity.

[54] Carnell, op. cit., p. 354.

[55] Ibid., p. 90.

[56] J. Gresham Machen, The Virgin Birth of Christ, op. cit., p. 394.

[57] Ibid., p. 395; see also pp. 380-397.

[58] See Barr, op. cit., pp. 27-29.

[59] See The Case For Orthodox Theology, op. cit., pp. 68-73.

[60] See Barr, op. cit., pp. 29-30.

[61] Carnell, op. cit., p. 21.

[62] Barr, op. cit., pp. 328-331.

[63] See Barr, ibid., p. 115.

[64] See George F. Ladd, Jesus and His Kingdom (Harper and Row Publishers, 1964), pp. 116, 329.

[65] See C. Norman Kraus, Dispensationalism in America (John Knox Press, 1958). Also see Barr, op. cit., pp. 190-207.

[66] See Carnell, An Introduction to Christian Apologetics, pp. 336-339.

[67] During the time of Barth and Niebuhr there were several other distinguished theologians who in some ways were more

sympathetic with Neo-Orthodoxy than with Liberalism. Among them were Emil Brunner (1889-1966), Rudolf Bultmann (1884-1976), H. Richard Niebuhr (1894-1962), Dietrich Bonhoeffer (1906-1945), and Paul Tillich (1886-1965). There were many significant and important differences among these theologians, and it would be a mistake to label them simply as Neo-Orthodox. The major characteristic of modern theologians generally has been a liveliness, openness, and determination to follow where the facts and truth lead. Thus no simple classification can adequately characterize their theologies. The reader who is interested in the entire range of modern theology should consult studies such as: William Nicholls, Systematic and Philosophical Theology (Penguin Books, Inc., 1969); James C. Livingston, Modern Christian Thought (The Macmillan Company, 1971), and Bob E. Patterson (ed.), Makers of the Modern Theologian Mind (Word Books, 1972-   ). There are seventeen volumes in this series.

[68] See Karl Barth, The German Church Conflict (John Knox Press, 1965); Bernhard Lohse, A Short History of Christian Doctrine (Fortress Press, 1978), pp. 230-236; Clyde L. Manschreck (ed.), A History of Christianity (Prentice-Hall, Inc., 1964), pp. 528-532.

[69] For a brief biography of Barth see David L. Mueller, Karl Barth (Word Books, 1972), pp. 13-48. This book also provides a helpful introduction to Barth's theology and a useful bibliography of his writings, pp. 169-172.

[70] As such this denomination no longer exists. In 1934 it joined with the German Reformed Church to form the Evangelical and Reform Church. Then in 1957 this denomination joined with the Congregational-Christian Church to form the United Church of Christ.

[71] "Ten Years That Shook My World," The Christian Century, Vol. 56 (April 26, 1939), p. 542.

[72] For a brief biography of Niebuhr see Bob E. Patterson, Reinhold Niebuhr (Word Books, 1977), pp. 13-62. Patterson's book is an introduction to Neibuhr's thought and contains a useful selected bibliography of Niebuhr's writings, pp. 161-163. Also see Charles W. Kegley and Robert W. Bretall (eds.), Reinhold Niebuhr: His Religious, Social and Political Thought (The Macmillan Company, 1956). This book contains an intellectual autobiography by Neibuhr (pp. 3-23), articles about his thought by other scholars and Niebuhr's response. It contains an extensive bibliography of Niebuhr's writings up to 1956 (pp. 455-478).

[73] See Livingston, op. cit., p. 446. Bob E. Patterson entitles the first chapter of his book, op. cit., "The Making

of a Christian Realist."

[74] *The Nature and Destiny of Man*, Vol. I (Charles Scribner's Sons, 1943), p. 15; italics are mine.

[75] *Dogmatics in Outline* (Harper Torchbooks, 1959), p. 23; italics are mine. See also *Against The Stream* (Philosophical Library, Inc., 1954), pp. 205-240, and *Church Dogmatics*, Vol. I, Part 1 (T. and T. Clarke, 1936), pp. 141-283, Vol. II, Part 1 (T. and T. Clark, 1957), pp. 168-169.

[76] Niebuhr, *op. cit.*, pp. 265-280.

[77] *Ibid.*, p. 129-130.

[78] *Ibid.*, p. 130.

[79] See Niebuhr, *Beyond Tragedy* (Charles Scribner's Sons, 1955), pp. 13-14.

[80] *Dogmatics in Outline*, p. 13.

[81] *God Here and Now* (Harper and Row, Publishers, 1964), p. 56; see also pp. 45-60.

[82] See *Against The Stream* (Philosophical Library, Inc., 1954), pp. 217-225.

[83] *Church Dogmatics*, Vol. I, Part 2 (T. and T. Clark, 1956), p. 529; also see pp. 457-537 and Vol. I, Part 1, pp. 122-135.

[84] "Ten Years That Shook My World," *The Christian Century*, Vol. 56, (April 26, 1939), p. 544.

[85] See Barth, *Dogmatics in Outline*, p. 51; Niebuhr, *The Self and The Dramas of History* (Charles Scribner's Sons, 1955), pp. 109-110, *The Nature and Destiny of Man*, Vol. I, pp. 132-135.

[86] See Niebuhr, *The Self and The Dramas of History*, p. 18 and Barth, *Church Dogmatics*, Vol. II, Part 1 (T. and T. Clark, 1957), pp. 503-504.

[87] *Church Dogmatics*, Vol. I, Part 2, p. 882.

[88] *The Nature and Destiny of Man*, Vol. I, pp. 147-148.

[89] *Ibid.*, pp. 193-194.

[90] *Ibid.*, pp. 186-219.

[91] "The Son of Man Must Suffer," a sermon delivered at the Memorial Church, Harvard University, April 15, 1962; contained in _Justice and Mercy_, edited by Ursula M. Niebuhr (Harper and Row Publishers, 1974), p. 93; also see pages 38-69 and 94-95.

[92] Niebuhr, _The Nature and Destiny of Man_, Vol. I, p. 17.

[93] _The Self and The Dramas of History_, p. 18.

[94] _The Nature and Destiny of Man_, Vol. II (Charles Scribner's Sons, 1943), p. 50.

[95] See Barth, _Church Dogmatics_, Vol. I, Part 2, p. 347; _The Humanity of God_ (John Knox Press, 1960), p. 47; and Kegley and Bretall, _Reinhold Niebuhr_, pp. 252-280, 438-439.

[96] _Dogmatics in Outline_, pp. 96-97.

[97] _The Nature and Destiny of Man_, Vol. II, p. 61.

[98] _Ibid._, p. 72.

[99] _Ibid._, p. 75.

[100] _The Self and The Dramas of History_, pp. 97-98.

[101] _Ibid._, p. 98.

[102] See Barth, _Church Dogmatics_, Vol. IV, Part 1 (T. and T. Clark, 1961), pp. 514-562; Niebuhr, _The Nature and Destiny of Man_, Vol. II, pp. 103-104, 120-125, 148-149.

[103] _The Humanity of God_, p. 51; italics are mine.

[104] _God Here and Now_, p. 29.

[105] _Deliverance to the Captives_ (Harper and Brothers, 1961), pp. 148, 87, 86; italics are mine.

[106] See Barth, _Church Dogmatics_, Vol. IV, Part 1, p. 489.

[107] _The Nature and Destiny of Man_, Vol. II, p. 56.

[108] _Ibid._, p. 57.

[109] _Dogmatics in Outline_, p. 18.

[110] See _Church Dogmatics_, Vol. II, Part 2 (T. and T. Clark, 1957), pp. 94-506; Vol. IV, Part 3 (T. and T. Clark, 1961-62), pp. 270-274.

[111] Niebuhr, _Nature_ and _Destiny_, Vol. II, p. 64.

[112] Ibid., p. 117.

[113] Ibid., p. 116. See also _Faith_ and _History_ (Charles Scribner's Sons, 1959), pp. 151, 179.

[114] Ibid., pp. 125-126.

[115] The _Irony_ of _American_ _History_ (Charles Scribner's Sons, 1952), p. 63.

[116] God _Here_ and _Now_, pp. 62-63. Also see pages 61-85; Church _Dogmatics_, Vol. IV, Part 1, pp. 643-739; Vol. IV, Part 3, pp. 681-901; and Niebuhr, _Faith_ and _History_, p. 238.

[117] Ibid.

[118] Beyond _Tragedy_, p. 62. Also see Barth, _Dogmatics_ _in_ _Outline_, pp. 146-148.

[119] _Dogmatics_ _in_ _Outline_, p. 143.

[120] Church _Dogmatics_, Vol. IV, Part 3, p. 893. It should be remembered that Barth strongly opposed the Hitler movement as early as 1934 and was expelled from Germany.

[121] God _Here_ and _Now_, p. 89; italics are mine.

[122] Ibid., p. 88; see pages 86-93 on "Christian Ethics."

[123] The _Nature_ and _Destiny_ of _Man_, Vol. II, p. 254.

[124] See _An_ _Interpretation_ of _Christian_ _Ethics_, "Preface For the 1956 Edition" (Meridiam Books, 1956), p. 9.

[125] See The _Nature_ and _Destiny_ of _Man_, Vol. II, pp. 244-286; The _Children_ of _Light_ and _the_ _Children_ of _Darkness_ (Charles Scribner's Sons, 1944); _Christian_ _Realism_ and _Political_ _Problems_ (Charles Scribner's Sons, 1953); "Christian Faith and Social Action" in _Christian_ _Faith_ and _Social_ _Action_, John A. Hutchison (ed.), (Charles Scribner's Sons, 1953), pp. 225 ff.

[126] The _Nature_ and _Destiny_ of _Man_, Vol. II, p. 290.

[127] _Faith_ and _History_, p. 237.

[128] Niebuhr, _op._ _cit._, p. 297.

[129] See The Self and The Dramas of History, p. 238.

[130] Deliverance to the Captives, pp. 149, 148.

[131] See Clyde L. Manschreck, A History of Christianity (Prentice-Hall, Inc., 1964), pp. 495-501.

[132] The Shattered Spectrum (John Knox Press, 1981), pp. 2, 1.

[133] See Religion in America 1979-80 (The Princeton Religion Research Center), pp. 63-66.

SUGGESTIONS FOR FURTHER READING

Barbour, Ian G., _Issues in Science and Religion_, Prentice-Hall, Inc., 1966.

Barr, James, _Fundamentalism_, The Westminster Press, 1978.

Barth, Karl, _Deliverance to the Captives_, Harper & Brothers, 1961.

_____, _Dogmatics in Outline_, Harper Torchbook, 1959.

_____, _God Here and Now_, Harper and Row Publishers, 1964.

Bedell, George C., _et al._, _Religion In America_, Macmillan Publishing Co., Inc., 1975.

Brown, William Adams, _God at Work_, Charles Scribner's Sons, 1933.

Carnell, Edward J., _An Introduction to Christian Apologetics_, William B. Eerdmans Publishing Company, 1948.

Cauthen, Kenneth, _The Impact of American Religious Liberalism_, Harper and Row Publishers, 1962.

Dillenberger, John and Claude Welch, _Protestant Christianity_, Charles Scribner's Sons, 1954, Chapters VIII–XIV.

Fosdick, Harry Emerson, _Adventurous Religion_, Blue Ribbon Books, 1931.

Hordern, William, _A Layman's Guide to Protestant Theology_, The Macmillan Company, 1956.

Kegley, Charles W. and Robert W. Bretall (eds.), _Reinhold Niebuhr: His Religious, Social, and Political Thought_, The Macmillan Company, 1956.

Kliever, Lonnie D., _The Shattered Spectrum_, John Knox Press, 1981.

Kraus, C. Norman, _Dispensationalism in America_, John Knox Press, 1958.

Livingston, James C., _Modern Christian Thought_, The Macmillan Company, 1971.

Mackintosh, Hugh R., _Types of Modern Theology_, Nisbet and Co., Ltd., 1937.

451

Marty, Martin E. and Dean G. Peerman, A Handbook of Christian Theologians, Meridian Books, 1965.

Nicholls, William, Systematic and Philosophical Theology, Penguin Books, Inc., 1969.

Niebuhr, H. Richard, Christ and Culture, Harper Torchlight Edition, 1956.

Niebuhr, Reinhold, Beyond Tragedy, Charles Scribner's Sons, 1955.

_____, Justice and Mercy, edited by Ursula M. Niebuhr, Harper and Row Publishers, 1974.

_____, The Self and The Dramas of History, Charles Scribner's Sons, 1955.

Packer, J. I., 'Fundamentalism' and the Word of God, William B. Eerdmans Publishing Co., 1958.

Patterson, Bob E. (ed.), Makers of the Modern Theological Mind, Word Books, 1972.

Rauschenbush, Walter, A Theology For the Social Gospel, The Macmillan Company, 1918.

Russell, C. Allyn, Voices of American Fundamentalism, The Westminster Press, 1976.

EPILOGUE

In light of the developmental study of Judaism
and Christianity presented in the previous pages of
this book, an obvious major conclusion is that in their
long historical odysseys both religions have demonstrated a remarkable resilience and creativity. Not
only have they managed to survive in different epochs
and cultures but also to create new thought forms and
concepts with which to communicate the essences of the
ancient faiths in meaningful ways to the people of
these succeeding epochs and cultures. In spite of the
variety of perspectives and practices which have
emerged, and in spite on some differences in interpretation, the essential meanings of certain basic views
generally have remained constant. Prominent among
these basic views (see Chapter I) are: 1) ethical
monotheism; 2) the desacralization of nature's elements
and forces but with an accompanying emphasis on the
worth of nature as God's creation; 3) the relative
freedom of human beings; 4) sin and/or sins as fundamentally rebellion against God; 5) the revelation of
God as occurring in actual historical events, pre-
eminently those witnessed to in sacred Scripture; and
6) some kind of eschatology, that is, a hope for the
future based on what God has done in the past.

For Christians, in contrast to Jews, there is
another basic view, namely, that in some fashion or
other God revealed himself conclusively in Jesus
Christ and in the circle of events at the center of
which Jesus lived and worked. In spite of differences
in the various interpretations of the person and work
of Christ, of the Trinity and Christology, an emphasis
on the significance and uniqueness of Jesus Christ
has remained constant. To be sure, there are some modern Christian theologians, both Catholic and Protestant,
who interpret the Trinity and Christology in functional
and/or symbolic concepts rather than in terms of the
metaphysical concepts of the ancient creeds.[1] Yet
still they attribute to Jesus Christ a unique role in
the revelation of God and the salvation of man. With
the growth of ecumenism in our times, the earlier differences between Protestants and Catholics concerning
the precise nature of salvation have been reconciled
to a large extent. There are some post-Vatican Council
II Catholic theologians who are emphasizing the primacy

453

of faith while not neglecting the importance of the Christian community, the church and its traditions. Similarly there are some Protestant theologians who are reemphasizing the importance of the Christian community, the church, as universal or catholic in time and space while not minimizing the primacy of faith. That is, there are contemporary Catholic theologians who are evangelically oriented and contemporary evangelical or Protestant theologians who are Catholic oriented in the sense of an emphasis on the essential role of the church in the life of the Christian.[2]

We have seen in Part V of our study that the challenge of modern Western culture with its scientific movement and bourgeois spirit resulted in a threefold response within Judaism, Catholicism, and Protestantism, namely, right-wing, left-wing, and moderate. In contemporary Judaism the Conservative movement (moderate response) has experienced the largest numerical growth, at least in the United States. In Catholicism many of the reforms suggested by Vatican Council II have become rather firmly established in the Church in spite of the sizeable minority who advocate a return to preconciliar perspectives and practices. Yet in the view of many "younger" Catholic theologians the movement toward an "open" Catholicism begun at Vatican Council II has not been brought to completion. While it is probably the case that the fully "open" Catholicism envisioned by these theologians will not become actual in the very near future, it may become so in the long run. In contemporary Protestantism the right-wing or fundamentalist movement appears to have experienced the largest numerical growth among the laity. The majority of theologians, however, have responded more to the challenge of contemporary culture and developed more open theologies, whether of a neo-orthodox type or of one of the more recent and somewhat more radical theologies of secularity, process, liberation, play, and story. In all of this there is the attempt, whether successful or not, whether simply a passing fancy or the wave of the future, to interpret the Christian faith in ways which are meaningful in light of the creative uncertainties of our time.

In spite of the wide variety of theologies and the significant differences between them, a major motivation held in common by theologians of the left-wing and moderate responses has been to provide cultural relevance for the Jewish and Christian faiths. Beyond this, they are in general agreement, as we

454

have seen, in the acceptance of some kind of evolutionary perspective (biological and/or historical),
of the historical critical study of sacred Scriptures,[3]
of ecumenism (interconfessional and interreligious cooperation), of the relevance of religion for social
issues and problems, and of a hope for an ultimate
kingdom of God either within history or beyond history
or both. Whether all of these perspectives will win
the allegiance of the majority of lay believers or not,
it is most unlikely that any of them will be abandoned
in the future by the majority of theologians. This
is the case because they are not simply the result of
arbitrary decisions or whims on the part of a few
theologians, an intellectual elite, but the result of
a sincere attempt to relate faith in a meaningful way
to both universal truth and contemporary culture.
Whatever differences there may be between them, these
theologians are in general agreement with respect to
the conviction that, since God is the source of all
that is, the author of all truth, the truth from whatever area of life and experience it may come cannot
be denied without denying the spirit of God. That is,
if religion is to remain alive and vital, it must be
able to incorporate in a meaningful way all human
strivings for truth, all human aspirations for peace
and love in individual and community relations, and
all legitimate human desires for the good life. In
short, the kingdom of God ideal must be inclusive with
respect to all truth, beauty, goodness, and love.

Near the end of the nineteenth century Matthew
Arnold wrote: "At the present moment two things about
the Christian religion must surely be clear to anybody
with eyes in his head. One is that men cannot do without it; the other, that they cannot do with it as it
is."[4] This observation about the status of Christianity in late Victorian England may appropriately be
extended to characterize the situations encountered
by both Judaism and Christianity as in their long
historical odysseys they moved through different conceptualizations of even their most abiding experiences.
It appears that this challenge is even greater in
Western culture today, the most dynamic and rapidly
changing culture in history. Indeed, it is often
claimed that contemporary Western culture, characterized by a pluralistic and relativistic consciousness,
is rapidly moving into a post-modern and perhaps even
a post-Judeo-Christian era. While there are many who
in some fashion or other still hold to the Jewish or
the Christian faiths even though they are unable to

deal with them as traditionally or even recently con-
ceptualized, in contrast to Arnold's era, there are
large and growing numbers of people who find it possible to do without them altogether. Neither the older
metaphysical formulations and traditional practices
nor the more recent conceptualizations strike them
with a sense of authenticity or relevance. The questions and proposed solutions with which theologians
dealt until quite recently seem to impress the post-
modern mind as unreal questions with unreal answers.
It is precisely this situation which has led many
theologians to engage in an attempt to provide radical
new reconceptions of the forms and symbols of the
Jewish and Christian faiths and visions. The result
has been a radical pluralism in theology today. Whether and how long this situation may continue, no one
can predict. Which of the current new theological
programs, the theologies of secularity, process, liberation, play, and story, simply represent passing fads
or provide viable reconceptualizations which will
preserve the essence of the Jewish and Christian faiths
cannot now be determined with any degree of certainty.
It may be that some other type of reconceptualized
theology not now envisioned will appear in the future
to provide cultural relevance and a sense of authenticity.

It must be acknowledged that such a conclusion
is unsatisfying, but then any historical study is
necessarily unsatisfactory because as the last sentence
is written history marches on with the appearance of
new and unique events and embodiments of meaning.
While the future shape of theology cannot now be pre-
dicted with any degree of certainty, it does not follow
that one need be reduced to silence or despair. Surely
our study has demonstrated, among other things, that
neither Judaism nor Christianity has been inextricably
tied to any world-view or cultural pattern. Basically
both are communities of faith and ways of life based
on the conviction that ultimately God is the Lord of
history. Thus both have less reason to fear the flux
of history than any other communities. Whatever particular conceptual shapes Jewish and Christian theologies
may take in the future in the search for coherent
understanding and cultural relevance, these communities
of faith undoubtedly will be sustained by the old but
ever new experiential conviction that the God who in
the past has disclosed himself as a forgiving and accepting God of love will not abandon his creation.
Rather he will continue to love mankind and all of

456

creation no matter what contingencies the future will present. In this faith the Jew and the Christian will not fear the flux of history but will look to the uncertain future with confidence viewing it as a sign of promise and hope.

NOTES

[1] For example, the Christology of the Catholic theologians Edward Schillebeeckx and Hans Küng is somewhat similar to that of the Protestant theologian Reinhold Neibuhr. See Schillebeeckx, _Jesus_ (Vintage Books, 1981), Küng, _On Being a Christian_ (Doubleday and Co., 1976), and Niebuhr, _The Nature and Destiny of Man_, Vol. II (Charles Scribner's Sons, 1943).

[2] See Hans Küng, "Why I Remain A Catholic," _Consensus in Theology?_, Leonard Swidler (ed.) (Westminster, 1980), pp. 162-165; Hans Küng, _Does God Exist?_ (Doubleday and Co., Inc., 1980); Eric G. Jay, _The Church_ (John Knox Press, 1978), Part 6; Paul Tillich, _The Religious Situation_ (Meridian Books, 1956), Part Three.

[3] The application of the historical critical method to the study of sacred scriptures originated in the West, and its use by Jewish and Christian scholars in studying their own scriptures is unique in the history of world religions. Only recently, due largely to contacts with Western scholarship, have adherents of other world religions begun to use this method in studying their own scriptures.

[4] Quoted from James C. Livingston, _Modern Christian Thought_ (The Macmillan Company, 1971), p. 501.

461

About the Author

Robert H. Ayers (B.D., Yale, Ph.D., Vanderbilt) is
Professor of Religion at the University of Georgia. While
his publications are primarily in the areas of historical
and philosophical theology, he teaches courses in other
areas such as Biblical Studies and Philosophy of Religion.
His teaching responsibility involves not only the teaching
of courses at the graduate and advanced undergraduate levels
but also for many years the teaching of the undergraduate
"service" course entitled Introduction to Western Religious
Traditions. He was among seven professors in the College
of Arts and Sciences to be selected for the first four-
year term (1978-1982) as Sandy Beaver Teaching Professors,
an award for excellence in teaching.

466